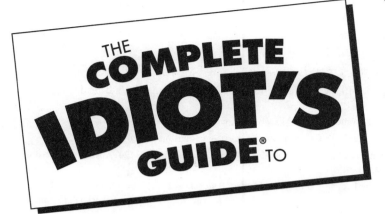

THE COMPLETE IDIOT'S GUIDE® TO

Bridge

Second Edition

by H. Anthony Medley with Michael Lawrence

ALPHA

A member of Penguin Group (USA) Inc.

ALPHA BOOKS

Published by the Penguin Group

Penguin Group (USA) Inc., 375 Hudson Street, New York, New York 10014, U.S.A.

Penguin Group (Canada), 10 Alcorn Avenue, Toronto, Ontario, Canada M4V 3B2 (a division of Pearson Penguin Canada Inc.)

Penguin Books Ltd, 80 Strand, London WC2R 0RL, England

Penguin Ireland, 25 St Stephen's Green, Dublin 2, Ireland (a division of Penguin Books Ltd)

Penguin Group (Australia), 250 Camberwell Road, Camberwell, Victoria 3124, Australia (a division of Pearson Australia Group Pty Ltd)

Penguin Books India Pvt Ltd, 11 Community Centre, Panchsheel Park, New Delhi - 110 017, India

Penguin Group (NZ), Cnr Airborne and Rosedale Roads, Albany, Auckland, New Zealand (a division of Pearson New Zealand Ltd)

Penguin Books (South Africa) (Pty) Ltd, 24 Sturdee Avenue, Rosebank, Johannesburg 2196, South Africa

Penguin Books Ltd, Registered Offices: 80 Strand, London WC2R 0RL, England

Publisher: *Marie Butler-Knight*
Product Manager: *Phil Kitchel*
Senior Managing Editor: *Jennifer Chisholm*
Senior Acquisitions Editor: *Mike Sanders*
Development Editor: *Michael Koch*
Production Editor: *Megan Douglass*

Copy Editor: *Keith Cline*
Illustrator: *Chris Eliopoulos*
Cover/Book Designer: *Trina Wurst*
Indexer: *Julie Bess*
Layout: *Ayanna Lacey*
Proofreading: *Mary Hunt*

For my father,
A caring provider,
A loving, sympathetic, and interested parent,
An honest businessman,
Smart, considerate, and funny,
The best example a son could have,
A pal I miss every day of my life.

Contents at a Glance

Contents

Appendixes

Foreword

It seems only fair to warn the reader at the outset that learning to play Bridge will absolutely ruin your life. It's sad, but true. Ask any of the millions of players who are already hopelessly addicted to this infuriatingly fascinating game and they'll tell you firsthand how Bridge has warped their very existence.

And now we have H. Anthony Medley—abetted by Bridge superstar Mike Lawrence—luring more unsuspecting victims into the clutches of the greatest game ever devised with this new edition of *The Complete Idiot's Guide to Bridge*. Don't be fooled by Medley's enjoyable and easy-to-follow descriptions of how to play Bridge: like an addict jonesing for his next fix, you'll find it impossible to stop thinking about the last hand you played or when the next game will be.

If you're worried that this book is only for people who already know something about cards, don't be. The author starts by assuming that some readers have never even seen a deck of cards before and explains the game from the ground up. Experienced card players will also benefit from the early chapters, however, as Medley explains not only the basics of playing cards, but also important bridge terms and tips on successful play.

If you're someone who learned the game decades ago but haven't played much recently, this book is for you as well. Whether as a refresher course to remind you of the basics or as a way to find out about the latest bidding theory (much has changed since Bridge greats like Charles Goren walked the earth!), you'll find it all here.

You'll learn how to evaluate your hands properly, how to communicate effectively with your partner (that fellow-addict sitting across the table from you) and how to make life difficult for the opponents.

Medley also makes a good presentation of two major variations of the game: Rubber Bridge, the kind you're most likely to encounter in informal settings, and Duplicate Bridge, played by the hardcore addicts at clubs and tournaments. Whatever your preference, you'll learn something about both forms of Bridge.

In addition to a careful discussion of the mechanics of bidding and play, Medley and many-time World Champion Lawrence repeatedly emphasize the core principle of Bridge: trusting and respecting your partner. In Bridge, as in life, this is accomplished through honest communication and sticking to agreements.

So go ahead, give it a try. True, you'll spend (and thoroughly enjoy) hours and hours playing the game, and you'll spend a few more hours laughing and arguing about past deals. No doubt you'll regret ever learning about Bridge, but at least you've been warned.

This book is a great teaching tool as well as a first-rate reference guide that you'll want to keep for years. After reading *The Complete Idiot's Guide to Bridge, Second Edition*, you'll experience the thrill of bidding and making a grand slam, the fun of executing a strip-and-endplay, the exhilaration of perfect defense, the *schadenfreude* of nailing the opponents with a juicy penalty double, the indescribable feeling of … oh, sorry. Did I mention I'm a Bridge player?

Paul Linxwiler
Managing Editor of *The Bridge Bulletin*
American Contract Bridge League

Introduction

My mother taught me how to play Bridge when I was in high school, and I taught my fraternity brothers how to play at UCLA. But after graduating I played basketball, baseball, football, tennis, golf, Poker, Gin Rummy—everything but Bridge.

Years later, after I had given up basketball and taken up tennis as my primary recreational activity, a friend of mine, Earl Cohen, called me and asked if I'd join him in a game of Rubber Bridge at the Marina City Club, where I lived. Because I had been away from the game for so long, I was afraid I'd make a fool of myself. "No way," I said. "Come on," he said. "No way," I said.

Earl is a psychiatrist, so three hours later I had spent a wonderful afternoon playing Bridge by the pool. Despite my lengthy sabbatical, I remembered the game easily. Bridge is so logical. After you learn the fundamentals, you don't forget them.

After our game by the pool, Earl invited me to enter a Bridge tournament with him. "Why not?" I said. We won, and I was hooked.

I played Rubber Bridge for several years before being introduced to Duplicate Bridge, a more competitive form of the game. Duplicate is different in form only. The fundamentals are identical to Rubber Bridge.

It was during this period that I was preoccupied with what I thought were things that were worrisome. I found that while playing Bridge my problems receded like the tide pulling back from Mont-Saint-Michel. While you're playing Bridge, you think about nothing but the cards. And it's so much fun!

The trepidation I felt when Earl asked me to join him for a poolside game isn't unusual. Unfortunately, this feeling of anxiety is more normal than unique. I want to soothe the apprehension that people seem to feel at the mere mention of Bridge. The wonder of Bridge is that the more you play, the more you want to play.

That's the germination of this book. Bridge is such a wonderful game, and it's easy to learn and play. Although I was taught the game in my teens, because I was away from it for an extended period, I stand as a prime example of someone who took up Bridge much later than many, yet became an accomplished player in a short period of time. I feel a missionary-like zeal to spread the word of what a great game Bridge is and how easy it is to learn. That's what you're going to learn in this book.

I've tried all the games. Nothing compares to Bridge.

Why This Book Is Different from the Others

What makes this book unique is that it is written in an easy-to-understand way by a professional writer who also happens to be a dedicated Bridge player. Most Bridge books are written by Bridge players who only write because they are Bridge players. That's not to deprecate them. I admire people like Freddy Sheinwold, Charles Goren, and others who have contributed so much to the game.

But because I'm a writer first and a Bridge player second, I have the unique opportunity to produce a first-class book that is both educational and entertaining. It also allows me to give something back to a game that has given me so much joy and pleasure.

This book has a unique perspective. It's aimed at the person who wants to learn how to play Bridge, but doesn't want to take lessons or read a lot of complicated books on bidding and play. I've put everything here in one easy reference. Here, at last, you'll learn everything you need to know to play the wonderful game of Bridge without jumping from book to book.

Extras

In this book, I've added bonuses for you in the form of boxes scattered throughout the book to call your attention to special information.

> **Tricks of the Trade**
>
> These are tips—nonessential extra information that will give you an edge.

> **Alert**
>
> These boxes are cautions, reminders of things for which you should always be watchful.

> **Lingo**
>
> These boxes define specialized Bridge terms to teach you the language of Bridge.

> **Bridgebit**
>
> These boxes tell you things you might never know about Bridge, its history and humor.

Acknowledgments

Many people have contributed to my development as a Bridge player, and, thus, to this work. I've learned from all my partners, but want to single out three for special mention. My golden partner, Luanne Leonard, was with me for 80 percent of my gold points and generously introduced me to some of the greats of the game. Millie Garrison was not only my partner for my first big tournament win, a huge victory in Palm Springs where we beat some of the best players in the world, but she also suggested Alpha Books as a likely publisher. Finally, E'Anne Conaway has provided constant encouragement, help, and advice.

I especially want to thank Marie Butler-Knight, publisher of Alpha Books, for recognizing the need for this revised edition; my acquisitions editor, Mike Sanders, for his unfailing help; my production editor, Megan Douglass, who has been a dream to work with; and my development editor, Michael Koch, who has been cooperative, prompt, and accurate. In sum, it's been wonderful to be associated with such consummate professionals.

This is an update to the book I wrote in 1997 to teach people the best game in the world. The book has been successful beyond my wildest imagination, going through printing after printing. But there were two reasons I wanted to add to it. First was that I wanted to add some advanced bidding techniques, like the Two-over-One system that is used by most tournament players, which I've done with the new Chapter 25. Second, and more important, was the opportunity to work closely with Michael Lawrence in updating the book. When I was growing up in the 1950s, I wanted to be a baseball player and Mickey Mantle was my idol. Michael Lawrence is the bridge equivalent to how I pictured Mickey Mantle. When Mike said he wanted to work with me in updating the book, I would have done it for nothing (but don't tell my publisher!). I think you'll enjoy this updated version of my book as much as I enjoyed updating it with Mike.

Special Thanks to the Technical Reviewer

The Complete Idiot's Guide to Bridge was reviewed by two experts who double-checked the accuracy of what you'll learn here, to help us ensure that this book gives you everything you need to know about Bridge.

Alan LeBendig reviewed the original manuscript while it was being written. He checked for technical accuracy and made helpful suggestions in the process. Alan is a Grand Life Master, has won sectional and regional titles, and is Chairman of the Board of Governors of the American Contract Bridge League (ACBL). He is co-owner, with E'Anne Conaway, of the Barrington Bridge Club and runs some of the most popular club games in Los Angeles. He writes a regular column on ethics for the *Bridge Bulletin*, published monthly by the ACBL.

Michael Shuman reviewed the finished original manuscript. He not only ensured the accuracy of the information, he provided valuable suggestions for additions. Mike is a Grand Life Master, is twenty-first on the all-time master point list, and has won national, sectional, and regional titles.

Trademarks

All terms mentioned in this book that are known to be or are suspected of being trademarks or service marks have been appropriately capitalized. Alpha Books and Penguin Group (USA) Inc. cannot attest to the accuracy of this information. Use of a term in this book should not be regarded as affecting the validity of any trademark or service mark.

Part 1

Introduction to Bridge

Be forewarned. When you read this book, you're learning an addiction. This part will whet your appetite as you learn the basics of the game. It covers how Bridge developed over the years and introduces some terminology. Bridge is a game with its own language. You'll also learn the bidding process and how to play a hand. After you finish reading these four short, easy-to-read and easy-to-understand chapters, Bridge will no longer be a mystery, and you'll be firmly on the road to becoming a Bridge player.

Welcome to Bridge!

In This Chapter

- Playing cards
- The ranking of the cards and the suits
- How players sit at the table
- Shuffling and dealing the cards

Can you add to 40? Can you count to 13? If you can do these two things, you can play Bridge.

Card games have been around for at least a millennium. Bridge is a fast-paced four-player card game played with a standard 52-card deck. Its reliance on concentration and skill has made it popular with all ages for more than 75 years. This chapter gives you a brief history of how Contract Bridge came to be, and what you need to play the game.

What's Past Is Prologue

Tracing the origin of Bridge is not unlike tracing the origin of baseball. Despite many historical references to games with a ball and bat in earlier centuries, legend says baseball was invented in Cooperstown, New York, in 1839, by Abner Doubleday (even though nobody can prove Doubleday was anywhere near Cooperstown in 1839). A card game similar to Bridge was around for a long, long time before the wonderful game of Contract Bridge, played today by millions, was invented.

Bridgebit

It is said that Bridge got its name from the Galata Bridge, which spanned the Golden Horn in Istanbul. According to this theory, approximately 14,000 British troops were stationed in Istanbul in 1854, and the officers who crossed the Galata Bridge every day to play a card game in a coffeehouse referred to the game as Bridge in honor of the bridge they crossed to get there.

Bishop Latimer referred to a Bridge-like card game in a sermon in 1529, when Henry VIII was courting Anne Boleyn and trying to figure out how to dump his longtime spouse, Catherine of Aragon. Bridge is probably of Turkish or Russian derivation. An early rendition was originally called *Khedive* when first played in the nineteenth century on the French Riviera, and that was the title of the Turkish viceroy.

A game called *Whist*, the forerunner of Bridge, was played in England starting in the late nineteenth century. It was replaced by Bridge Whist and then by Auction Bridge around the turn of the century.

In Whist, there was no bidding. The last card dealt was turned up and that suit was trump. (You'll learn about trump in Chapter 3.) Bridge Whist allowed the dealer or her partner to name trump, and added the concepts of doubling, redoubling, and exposing the dummy hand. Auction Bridge added the concept of having the opposing pairs bid to get the privilege of naming trump.

Contract Bridge as we know it today was born as a result of a game on October 31, 1925, on board a ship called the *Finland*. While waiting to pass through the Panama Canal, Harold S. Vanderbilt (the author of a revision of Yachting right-of-way rules, which are still known as the Vanderbilt Rules) and two friends needed a fourth person to play a Bridge-like game called *Plafond*. They allowed a lady who was a fellow passenger to join their game. She, however, attempted to suggest one exotic change after another based on a game she said she had learned in China. This irritated Vanderbilt so much that the next day, during the canal crossing, he worked out the scoring table for Contract Bridge, which remains remarkably the same today, more than three quarters of a century later. On that night, November 1, 1925, the first game of Contract Bridge was played, scored under Vanderbilt's new rules. Today, the most prestigious American team trophy in Bridge is the *Vanderbilt Cup*, named after—guess who.

Vanderbilt recalled later that "We enjoyed playing my new game on board the *Finland* so much that, on my return to New York, I gave typed copies of my scoring table to several of my Auction Bridge playing friends. I made no other effort to popularize or publicize Contract Bridge. Thanks apparently to its excellence, it popularized itself and spread like wildfire."

And grow it did! Today, Contract Bridge is played in every country in the world by more than 100 million people, 17 million in the United States alone. There are 3,700 individual Duplicate Bridge clubs in the North American Contract Bridge League, and 80 sovereign countries are officially represented in the World Bridge Federation. Contract Bridge is the game that most people who don't play cards want to learn.

> **Bridgebit**
>
> Ely Culbertson published *Contract Bridge Blue Book* in 1930, only five years after Vanderbilt's creation, and became the recognized authority on the game. When Charles Goren popularized the methods of point-count valuation, he supplanted Culbertson as the game's premier authority. Goren's mathematical approach to bidding simplified the game and its popularity exploded.

Bridge Is Easy!

When the U.S. Playing Card Company, which manufactures 75 percent of the cards sold in America, asked respondents what card game they wished they knew how to play, 47 percent said Bridge, by far the most popular response. But when asked what card games they *intended* to learn in the near future, Bridge was not in the top five. The reason? They had the feeling that Bridge was too complicated and they didn't have the time to learn it. Balderdash! As mentioned at the start, if you can add to 40 and count to 13, you can play Bridge, and play it well. This book will show you that learning how to play Bridge is easy. All you need to do is read on, learn a few principles, and then go and play. You don't believe me? In my Bridge infancy, I played with a kindergarten teacher named Nancy Kelly. Nancy was a lively grandmother who played a very old-fashioned, simple game of Bridge. That was right in line with me, because that's what I played at the time. But we competed against very good players who played all the fancy systems. We had no systems. Zero. Nada. Guess what? We generally beat the socks off of everyone. Why? Because our game was very simple and we communicated with each other very well. That's all you need to do. Know the basics, which you'll learn in the first part of this book, and be able to communicate with your partner.

Believe it or not, after the first two chapters, you'll be able to play hands. The rest of the book will help you play the game better. Remember when you first learned to ride a bike? The only way you could learn was by actually getting on a bike (and, of course, falling off a few times). Well, the same goes for Bridge. The only way you'll be able to master the game is to pull out a deck of cards and play!

Bridge Basics

Bridge is played by four people, comprised of two pairs. You and your partner play against two other people. At the table you are positioned opposite your partner while your opponents sit on either side of you.

By the way, in the examples throughout this book, your partner will be female and your opponents will be male, so references to your partner will be to "she" and "her" and references to your opponents will be "he" and "him." I've adopted this convention to keep from getting twisted up in the pronouns, but of course you can play Bridge with any combination of either sex!

Lingo

In Bridge terminology, you are sitting in directions named after points on the compass. So if you and your partner are sitting **North-South**, your opponents are sitting **East-West**, and vice versa. These are just terms and have no relevance to true magnetic north.

The Cards

Bridge is played with regular playing card decks, consisting of 52 cards. It is standard practice to have two decks on a table; while the dealer is dealing, his or her partner shuffles the other deck to prepare it for play in the next hand.

Suits and Card Ranks

Playing cards were known in China as long ago as 979 C.E. Decks were divided into 4 suits of 14 cards each. Today's decks have only 13 cards per suit.

The four playing card suits, as you probably already know, are Spades (♠), Hearts (♥), Diamonds (♦), and Clubs (♣).

Each suit has 13 cards, but they aren't numbered 1 through 13. The numbers 2 through 10 are indeed numbered 2 through 10. The Jack, Queen, and King, in that order, are 11, 12, and 13. The Ace is 1, and it's the highest-ranking card, even higher than the King! That's an important point to keep in mind: *The Ace is the strongest card in the suit, not the weakest.*

So here's how the cards rank in Bridge in descending order of importance:

Number	Name	Number	Name
1	Ace	7	7
13	King	6	6
12	Queen	5	5
11	Jack	4	4
10	10	3	3 or Trey
9	9	2	2 or Deuce
8	8		

Rank of the Suits

In Bridge all suits are not equal. In fact, they are, by definition, unequal. Following are the suits, ranked in descending order of importance:

> Spades
> Hearts
> Diamonds
> Clubs

An easy way to remember which suits rank where is simply to think of them in alphabetical order: C-D-H-S. Clubs is the weakest suit, whereas Spades is the strongest.

The Shuffle

Before you deal the cards, you must mix, or shuffle, them so they are in random order. You shuffle the cards by dividing them into two approximately equal piles and mixing them together. Do this several times, at least three, after each hand. It is said that shuffling the cards seven times will result in the most random deal, but that many shuffles is not necessary.

Choosing Partners and the Dealer

If you don't have established partners, spread the cards out on the table, face down. Each player picks a card and turns it over. The players with the two highest-ranking cards become a partnership, and the players with the two lowest-ranking cards become a partnership for the first *rubber*. The player with the highest-ranking card is the dealer for the first hand. After the rubber ends, you can choose partners again in the same way.

Lingo

A **rubber** is a unit of measurement. When one pair has won two games, the rubber is ended. The winner of the rubber is the pair with the most points when the rubber ends. Rubber and game are explained in more detail in Chapter 4.

The Deal

After you've shuffled the cards, one person distributes them to each player, delivering one card to each player face down in turn, clockwise, until they have all been distributed. This is called the *deal* or dealing the cards. The person who deals is called the dealer. The deal rotates in a clockwise manner. If you deal first, the person on your left deals next, then your partner, the person on her left, and so on.

You generally play with two decks of cards. You should use decks with different colors or markings so it's easy to differentiate one deck from the other. When you are dealing, your partner is *making* the other deck. This means that she is shuffling the cards for the next dealer. When the deck is made, it is placed to the maker's right.

The Cut

When the hand is over, the next dealer, the person on the previous dealer's left, picks up the cards on his left, where the maker has left them, and offers them to the player on his right to *cut*. Note that it is card-playing etiquette, not just Bridge etiquette, to place the cut *toward* the dealer. This allows the dealer to always place the correct cards on top without having to ask, "Which way did you cut?"

Tricks of the Trade

If the bottom card has been exposed during the making, your cut puts the bottom card somewhere in the middle of the deck. If the cards aren't cut and someone saw the bottom card, that player would know at least one card in the dealer's hand, because the dealer always gets the last card. That may not seem too important now, but as you get more proficient at the game, knowing where any card is can be very valuable.

To cut the cards, you pick up approximately half of them and place them toward the new dealer. He then picks up the rest of the deck and places it on top of the part that you took off, or cut. You don't have to cut the deck exactly in half. You can cut it to any depth you wish.

He then deals the cards while his partner makes the deck with which you just played. This speeds up the game and gets rid of the dead space that can occur while the old cards are being shuffled and dealt. The dealer's partner always makes the cards while his partner is dealing.

The Least You Need to Know

- The Ace is the highest-ranking card; the Two (Deuce) is the lowest-ranking card.

- Spades is the highest-ranking suit followed by Hearts, Diamonds, and Clubs. An easy way to remember ranking is to think of alphabetical order, low to high: C-D-H-S.

- The dealer picks up the preshuffled cards on his left and offers them to the player on his right to cut.

- The cards are dealt clockwise starting on the dealer's left, with the dealer receiving the last card.

- The partner of the dealer makes (shuffles) the other deck while the dealer is dealing.

Basic Bridge Skills

In This Chapter

- ◆ What a trick is and how it is played
- ◆ Who keeps track of the tricks, and how
- ◆ What the lead is, and who leads
- ◆ Following suit, reneging, and revoking
- ◆ An introduction to Bridge terminology

Every card game is different. In Poker for example, the game is based on nerve. Each player bets that he has the best or worst hand at the table. The game is grounded on winning and losing money. In Gin Rummy, each player tries to accumulate groups of three or more cards of the same rank or a sequence of three or more cards in the same suit and be the first to meld all his cards. These games are both extremely simple to learn and understand. You can play either with virtually no introduction, and just a short explanation. You might not be good at them, but you can play them.

Bridge, however, has a reputation for being difficult to learn. Although it is not as simple as Poker or Gin Rummy, its basic principles are extremely easy to comprehend. However, Bridge is like Poker and Gin Rummy in that knowing how to *play* and knowing how to *play well* are two entirely different things.

I'm going to teach you the rules of Bridge, so that you will know how to play. Getting to the point of playing *well* will be entirely up to you. Be warned, however—I am teaching you an addiction. When you know how to play Bridge, you will be hooked. It's more fun than you can possibly imagine.

The basics of Bridge are very simple. This chapter explains what these basics are. When you're finished with this chapter and the next two, which are fairly short, you will be able to play the game. As you read subsequent chapters, you will get even better. By the time you finish this book, you should be able to sit down with your Bridge-playing friends without trepidation.

Tricks

When you deal the cards and start to play, the entire concept of the game is predicting how many *tricks* you or your opponents can take. What's a trick? Well, it's not a prank. A trick is of the very essence of Bridge. If you play a card, everyone else plays a card, too, starting with the person on your left and going clockwise. Each of you has played a card. That's a trick. Each person can play only one card to a trick. Each person must play in order, clockwise from the person who *led*.

Each hand consists of 13 tricks. Why? Because each person starts with 13 cards. The hand is over when each person is out of cards, which should happen simultaneously. If it doesn't, something is dreadfully wrong. There may have been a misdeal, or perhaps two cards stuck together and were played as one. If a determination of what happened can be made, appropriate Bridge laws apply. Otherwise, the hand is voided and redealt, which is what normally happens in Rubber Bridge.

Lingo

The term **lead** means to play the first card played to a trick. So when someone asks, "Is it my lead?" he is asking if he is supposed to start the trick. If you tell someone, "It's your *play*," it means that someone has led the first card of the trick and it is his turn to play a card to it.

Lingo

In Bridge the person sitting on your left is referred to as your **left-hand opponent** (LHO). The person sitting on your right is referred to as your **right-hand opponent** (RHO).

Playing Tricks

The highest card played of the suit led wins the trick. So let's say, for example, that you lead and you play the Two of Hearts. Let's say your *LHO* plays the Three of Hearts. Now it's your partner's turn. So let's say your partner plays the Eight of Hearts. That leaves your *RHO*, who is sitting to your partner's left, to play. And let's say he plays the Five of Hearts.

Because your pair has played the highest card in the suit on this trick (your partner's Eight of Hearts), your pair wins the trick. But you no longer have the lead. Why?

One of the rules of Bridge is that the person who plays the highest card in the suit (and who, thus, wins the trick) also wins the lead. So your partner, who won the trick with the Eight of Hearts, now gets to lead.

And she can lead anything she wants. She can lead another Heart, or any other suit. If she leads the King of Spades and your RHO plays the Ace of Spades and you play the Seven of Spades and your LHO plays the Six of Spades, then your RHO has won the trick because the Ace is the strongest card in the suit. Because your RHO has won the trick, it is his lead.

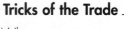 **Tricks of the Trade**

When you win one trick, place all the cards sideways. Then when you win another trick, place that trick on top of the last trick you won, but slightly to the right of it, and at right angles to it. That way it's easy to differentiate one trick from another and to keep count of how many tricks your side has won. Keep doing this with each subsequent trick.

Keeping Track of Tricks

The person who wins the trick takes all the cards played on that trick and places them in front of her, all four cards in a unit, so that they look like one card. One player from each team keeps all the tricks for that team. It doesn't matter which one does it.

That's the gist of the game. It occurs 13 times each hand, because there are 13 tricks. When the last card has been played, you count the tricks you've taken, and the tricks your opponents have taken, and that's the result of the hand. If you've played correctly, the total should add up to 13.

Two Rules on Tricks

There are a couple of rules you should know. First, you must follow suit. That means that if someone leads a Heart, for instance, and you have a Heart, you must play it. You can't play a Spade or any other card from any other suit if you have a Heart when a Heart is led. This is called *following suit.* If you have a Heart but play a card from another suit instead of a Heart, you are said to have *reneged* or *revoked*, and there are penalties for that.

A revoke is established when someone on the offending pair has led or played to the next trick. Here are the penalties for a revoke:

1. If the revoking pair took the trick on which the revoke occurred and no other tricks, the penalty is one trick.

2. If the revoking pair took the trick on which the revoke occurred and another trick, the penalty is two tricks.

3. If the revoking pair did not take the trick on which the revoke occurred, but did take a trick afterward, the penalty is one trick.

4. If the revoking pair did not take the trick on which the revoke occurred, but did take a trick afterward, and then took another trick with a card that it could legally have been played to the revoke trick, the penalty is two tricks.

For example, if the revoking team took eight tricks during the play of the hand, when the hand is completed it only gets credit for taking six or seven tricks, depending on the circumstances above.

If you revoke and you realize what you have done before your pair leads to the next trick, you can bring your revoke to everyone's attention and withdraw it by playing a card from the suit led. The players who played to the trick after you are then given the right to withdraw the card they played to that trick and substitute a different card.

Second, if you don't have a card from the suit led, you can play any card from any suit you like. This is called a *discard*. But that card is worthless as far as taking the trick is concerned. If your opponent leads the Two of Hearts and you don't have any Hearts, you can play the Ace of Spades if you like. But the Ace of Spades can't take the current trick. When a Heart is led, the Two of Hearts is more powerful than the Ace of Spades.

Tricks of the Trade

Because an Ace may very well take a later trick, it would be better strategy to discard a low-ranking card in a suit other than the one led if you are unable to follow suit. In choosing discards you want to pick your least important card unless you are using a discard as a signal to your partner. But I'll cover that in Chapter 22.

Now you know how tricks are played, so stop and play some. Deal out some hands and play the tricks. It's better if you have three companions, so each of you can have a hand. But if you don't, you can do it open-handed. Just deal out four hands and play the tricks looking at each hand in turn. Do this until you're comfortable with the concept of tricks and how they're played.

The Least You Need to Know

- ◆ A trick consists of one card from each player played face up on the table. Play proceeds in a clockwise rotation.

- ◆ Each trick is won by the highest card played of the suit that was led.

- ◆ The player winning the current trick leads a card to start the next trick.

- ◆ A player must follow suit if possible. If not, he or she may discard any card.

- ◆ Completed tricks are kept by one member of the pair winning the trick.

- ◆ You and your partner as a team want to win as many tricks as possible in each hand.

Chapter 3

The Language of Bridge

In This Chapter

- ◆ The auction and the contract
- ◆ How the trump suit is established
- ◆ More about following suit
- ◆ Declarer, defenders, and the dummy
- ◆ What is No Trump?

Now that you know how the hands are played, you need to discover how you actually get into playing the tricks. This is the essence of Bridge. The communication between the partners really sets Bridge apart from other card games.

It's such a wonderful feeling to look at the 13 cards in your hand and communicate with your partner through bidding and playing. You tell her what you have in your hand without saying, "Partner, I have the Ace of Spades and the Two of Hearts." Based on her response, you can infer that she has the King of Clubs, without her saying, "Partner, I have the King of Clubs."

By polishing your bidding (communication) with your partner, you'll learn to assess the number of tricks your side can win. This is your first major step toward becoming a Bridge player. In this chapter, you start learning how you communicate with your partner.

Bidding

When you're comfortable with tricks, try to predict how many tricks you're going to take before you play. Start with you leading first, and predict the number of tricks you think you can take just by looking at your hand. Then play the hand out and see how you did. Then let your LHO predict how many he and his partner will take, and play that hand out.

After you do this a few times, try this: Let the dealer make a verbal prediction of the number of tricks she and her partner will take. After she makes a prediction, the dealer's LHO will make a prediction, then the dealer's partner, and then the dealer's RHO. Then play the hand, with the dealer leading first, and see how you did. These predictions by each player are called *bids*.

Lingo _____

If you don't take the number of tricks you predicted, you are **set** or **down**. That means that your opponents get a score based on the number of tricks you took under what you predicted. So if you predicted you'd make eight tricks and only made seven, you are said to be *set 1* or *down 1*, and your opponents get points for each trick under your prediction, or **bid**.

Eventually, you will see that your prediction can help your partner make her prediction! If you predicted that you can take three tricks, she can look at her hand, add what you predicted to what she can take in her own hand, and increase your team's bid. Similarly, the second of your opponents to bid will have the benefit of his partner's prediction in estimating how many tricks they will take. As you continue to do this, you'll get more accurate in your predictions.

Winning the Auction

Congratulations. As you do this predicting, or bidding, you've started to play Contract Bridge! Your prediction of how many tricks you think you can take is called an *auction*. You win the auction by predicting that you can take more tricks than your opponents predict they can take. If you finally say that you can take 10 tricks and your opponents don't think they can take more, they *pass*, in effect saying, "Okay, go ahead and try." You win the auction.

Winning the auction doesn't mean necessarily you *won* the hand. All it means is that you get to name the *trump* suit (explained shortly) and play the hand as *declarer*. (The opponents play the hand as *defenders*.) If you and your partner win the auction, you must take at least the number of tricks you predicted in order to win the hand. Otherwise you will be *set*, and that's not good—the opponents will receive a numerical score in their favor.

Think of the auction as a conversation using a different language. You are communicating to your partner what you have in your hand by the way you bid. Instead of saying, "Partner, I have five Spades in my hand," your bid communicates this by simply mentioning a number (not five, ironically enough) and the word *Spades*. Similarly, you can communicate to your partner how strong your hand is through this language of Bridge.

Six Tricks Makes Declarer's Book

During the auction, however, you have to know something else. Scoring in Bridge is not just saying, "I can take seven tricks." When you score in Bridge, as *declarer*, the person who won the auction, you don't get credit for any tricks until you've taken six tricks. After you've taken six tricks, you then start to count. Every trick over six is credited to you. So if you think you can take seven tricks, you don't say, "I think I can take seven tricks." Instead, you say, "I think I can take one trick."

You're probably thinking, "That doesn't make any sense." Well, it does. Because for the declarer, Bridge only scores the tricks over the first six. The first six tricks taken by the declarer is called book. So if you say you can take one trick, you mean you can take six (book) plus one additional.

In the previous example, when you thought you could take 10 tricks, you don't say, "I can take 10 tricks." Instead, you say, "I can take four tricks (book, six, plus an additional four). If you don't think you and your partner can take more than six tricks, then you don't have any business making an estimate. (See the following section).

Pass

If you don't have the qualities to bid (more about this in Part 2) you must say, "Pass." This means, "I don't have a suit I want to bid at this time, so I'm passing the bid to my LHO." You may, however, change your mind and make a bid later when it's your turn again. It communicates a lot to your partner. After you've passed, you can't bid again until all three other players have bid or passed.

The Trump Suit

Now that you're familiar with tricks and how they are played, let me introduce you to a new concept, *trump*. The trump suit, for the duration of the hand, outranks all other suits. A Deuce (Two) of trump will win a trick over the Ace of a nontrump suit.

What's trump? Simply, it's the suit in which you want to play the hand, which is generally the suit you and your partner think you have the most of between you. Because you have more cards in this suit than any other, it's to your great advantage to promote it to be the highest ranking.

Getting to name trump is what the auction is all about. That's what you're bidding for. Your pair might have a lot of Hearts, and your opponents might have a lot of Spades, so you're dueling to see who thinks they can make the most tricks if they name trump.

During the auction, if you want to make Hearts trump, you don't just say, "I think I can take seven tricks." Instead, you say, "I think I can take seven tricks if Hearts is trump." The way you say this is very simple. When it's your turn to bid, you just say, "1 Heart." This means, "I can take seven tricks, book (six) plus one additional, if Hearts is trump."

Lingo

A **contract** is the final bid, the undertaking by the pair that wins the auction that they will take the specified number of tricks they bid at their final bid.

When estimating how many tricks you can take, keep in mind that you can't just play a trump card whenever you please. You can't play trump when another suit is led unless you don't have any of that suit. If Clubs is trump and someone leads the Ace of Hearts, for example, you can't play the Two of Clubs to win the trick unless you are out of Hearts (also called being void in Hearts). So if your opponents lead the Ace of Hearts and you have a Heart, you must play it to follow suit.

Now that you know about trump and bidding, let's try it. For the following *contracts*, convert them into Bridge lingo by saying how you would bid:

1. 11 tricks in Spades

2. 7 tricks in Hearts

3. 9 tricks in Diamonds

4. 5 tricks in Clubs

Number 1 is bid by saying, "5 Spades" (book plus 5).

Number 2 is bid by saying, "1 Heart" (book plus 1).

Number 3 is bid by saying, "3 Diamonds" (book plus 3).

Number 4? Were you tricked? You don't have a bid. If you don't think you can at least make book plus one, you shouldn't bid. Each bid means "I can take six tricks *plus* the number I bid." Making the first six tricks is a condition of your making your bid. So your bid for Number 4 is "Pass."

The Auction Revisited

In the prior auction, when your partner *opens* 1 Heart, your LHO might think he can take seven tricks if Spades are trump. So he would bid 1 Spade.

What, however, if your LHO thinks he can take seven tricks if Clubs is trump? Remember the rank of the suits we learned in Chapter 1? Hearts outranks Clubs. That means that he can't bid 1 Club if you have already bid 1 Heart. If you bid 1 Heart before him, he must bid 2 Clubs if he wants Clubs to be trump.

You can't bid an inferior suit over a superior suit at the same numerical level. You can bid 1 Heart over a 1 Club bid, but you can't bid 1 Club over 1 Heart. So, if he thinks he can do better than you if Clubs is trump, and if he thinks he can take eight tricks, he says, "2 Clubs" after you've said, "1 Heart."

Your partner has been sitting there listening to the two of you. She looks at her hand and sees that she has four Hearts! If you think that the two of you can make 1 Heart without knowing what's in her hand, and she has almost a third of the Hearts in the whole

Lingo

Open means the first person to bid in the auction. It doesn't have to be the dealer necessarily, although the dealer gets the first chance at it. Let's say you are in third position from the dealer and both the dealer and your RHO pass. If you bid 1 Spade, you have opened.

Alert

After the bidding has been opened, all bidding ends after three consecutive passes. So if you open and it is followed by three passes, you don't get another chance to bid.

deck, there's a good chance that her hand can help you make one or two more tricks. She looks at her Clubs and they're weak. If Clubs is trump, the opponents might be able to make their 2 Clubs bid. But if Hearts is trump, she thinks you can make 2 Hearts, so she bids "2 Hearts," saying to you, basically, "Partner, if you think you can take seven tricks, I have at least one additional trick in my hand, so together we should be able to take eight tricks."

Your RHO has been listening to this, too. He looks at his hand and sees he has four Clubs. He says to himself, "If my partner thinks he can make 2 Clubs all by himself, I bet he can make at least one more with my four Clubs to contribute." Based on this reasoning, he bids "3 Clubs."

You listen to all this and say to yourself, "Wait a minute. I thought I could take 1 Heart all by myself, but my partner has at least one trick in her hand. And I thought I could *probably* make 2 Hearts before I heard her bid. So, if she has enough to tell me she thinks we can make 2 Hearts, I think we can make 3 Hearts," so you bid "3 Hearts."

Well, the bidding has gotten a little high, and your LHO looks at his hand and says, "I don't think my partner and I can make 4 Clubs," so he passes. Your partner is satisfied, so she passes, too. Your RHO is also a little doubtful about making 4 Clubs, so he passes.

There it is! An auction! And a contract! The bid has been auctioned. You've won the right to name trump. You and your partner have entered into a contract in which you are going to try to make 3 Hearts. This is what Contract Bridge is all about.

The Dummy and the Declarer

No, no, this is not a newly discovered novel by Dostoyevsky. The *dummy* is the hand held by the partner of the player who won the auction. Because it was a team effort, how do you decide which of you actually won it? Well, the person who wins the auction is the person who first bid the suit that ended up as trump. In the preceding example, the trump suit was Hearts because 3 Hearts was the winning bid. The first person to bid Hearts was you, so you would play the hand as declarer.

After the auction is over, it's time to play. Declarer's LHO always has the opening lead. After that opening lead, dummy puts her cards face up on the table, with trumps placed on the dummy's right, declarer's

> **Lingo**
>
> The **declarer** is the first person of the partnership to bid the suit in which the final bid is made that won the auction. The **dummy** is the partner of the declarer. So you are declarer and your partner is dummy for this hand only.

left. The cards are placed with the highest ranking on the top as declarer is looking at them, and in descending order. Most people, when they are dummy, place the cards in alternating order of color—red, black, red, black—but this is not a rule. You can place them in any order, as long as trump is on declarer's left as declarer looks at the cards.

Trump, which in this instance is Hearts, is on declarer's left as she looks at dummy, or on dummy's right. The rest of the cards are laid out so everyone at the table can see each card, its suit, and denomination. While the hand is being played, dummy cannot collaborate with declarer on the correct play of the hand.

Play of the Hand

There are two options to play the hand. The first, and better way, is during the play of the hand, declarer calls the card she wants played from dummy and dummy follows her instructions and plays the card. So in playing the hand you see spread in the following illustration, if declarer led a low Heart from her hand and her LHO played the Nine of Hearts, declarer would call out the card she wanted played, without touching it, like, "Queen of Hearts." Dummy would then play the Queen of Hearts.

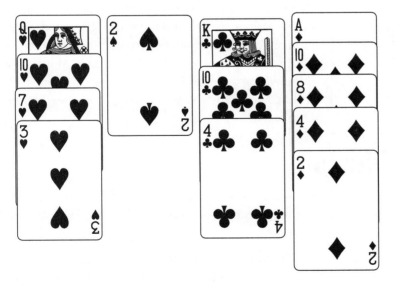

This is the way a dummy's hand looks to the declarer.

The previous figure is a graphical representation of a typical bridge hand. The following is the notation for that same hand:

   ♠ 2
   ♥ QT73
   ♦ AT842
   ♣ KT4

For the purposes of displaying hands in this book, the hands will always be arranged in descending order of the rank of the suits, Spades first, followed by Hearts, Diamonds, and Clubs, in that order. Although this notation may take some getting used to, it's a common and fairly intuitive method for displaying card hands and one that I'll be using throughout the book.

The second way, and the way most *Rubber Bridge* players play, is for declarer to actually play the card from dummy. In this example, dummy just sits there and watches, while declarer does all the work. I suggest that you learn the first way, with dummy playing the card under declarer's direction. There are several advantages to this. The first is that it involves dummy in the play of the hand. If she's playing the cards, she has a chore to do and feels that she's still a part of the game.

Lingo

In **Rubber Bridge,** the object is to win the rubber and the bonus points awarded. It's been called the most popular form of Contract Bridge. In **Duplicate Bridge,** each hand is separate and stands on its own. At the end of a duplicate game, the pair that has the best overall score on all the hands is the winner.

The second advantage to dummy playing the cards under declarer's direction is that this is the way cards are played in *Duplicate Bridge*. Although I'm teaching you Rubber Bridge in this book, it is inevitable that many of you will become so enamored of the game that you will want to progress into Duplicate, which is competitive, social, and more fun than a barrel of monkeys. It's better practice to learn good habits now, when you are a novice. If you learn to play dummy's cards yourself when you are declarer, it will be harder for you to unlearn if you advance into Duplicate.

No Trump: The Fifth Suit

Thought you had it all, didn't you? Well, I sort of tricked you. You thought the only suits you had to remember were Spades, Hearts, Diamonds, and Clubs. Well, it's not quite that simple.

Sometimes people who have what they think are balanced hands want to play a hand without any trump. When this first started, it took years before players could figure out what to call it. Finally, they took the problem to the top of a mountain and asked the Bridge guru. Since then it has been called *No Trump.* Was that genius or what?

The point is that you don't always have to play the hand with a trump suit. If you play it in No Trump, you get more points for your tricks than if you played it with a suit as trump. This fifth suit makes the rankings of the suits as follows, with the strongest on top:

No Trump
Spades
Hearts
Diamonds
Clubs

So, as you've learned, you can bid 1 Heart over 1 Club, but if 1 Heart has already been bid, you can't bid 1 Club over 1 Heart. If you want Clubs as trump in this scenario, you have to bid at least 2 Clubs.

But what if you want to play the hand without anything being trump? Then you bid 1 No Trump. And you can bid 1 No Trump over any suit bid at the 1 level. So if your opponents have bid 1 Spade, heretofore the most powerful bid at the 1 level, you can still stay at the 1 level by bidding 1 No Trump.

If you win the auction with a No Trump bid, you will be playing the hand without any suit being trump, kind of like you did when you learned about tricks and were just playing the cards to see how it went.

Let's go over the bidding again. Deal some hands and bid them, allowing the dealer to bid first, then proceeding clockwise around the table. Bid, enter into the contract or let your opponents take the contract, lay down the dummy hand, and play the cards.

If you can do this, you're playing Bridge! The rest of the book will tell you how to improve. But as you read you should continue to play. Each time you read, try to play in addition to reading. Each time you play you will improve and learn. Playing is as important as reading.

This chapter has just set forth the basics of the game. If you're comfortable with the concepts of shuffling, dealing, bidding, and playing, you're ready to go on to the next chapter, which will teach you how to communicate with your partner through the bidding process. This communication helps you make informed decisions about what suit should be trump (if any), at what level you should be playing the contract, and whether you should let your opponents play the contract with you defending.

The Least You Need to Know

◆ Bidding is the act of predicting how many tricks you and your partner may win. Dealer is the first player to bid, and it proceeds clockwise, each player in turn.

◆ The highest bid wins the contract and determines if there is a trump suit and which suit it will be.

- The first player of the partnership that wins the contract in bidding is declarer.

- Declarer's LHO makes the opening lead, after which declarer's partner places her hand face up on the table, becoming dummy for that hand only.

- Each player must follow suit if possible. If he can't, he can play a trump if he has one, or play a card from another suit.

- No Trump is designated as the fifth suit and ranks above Spades. When the contract is No Trump, the highest card of the suit led wins the trick.

Chapter 4

What Do I Have and What Does It Mean?

In This Chapter

- How to sort your cards
- Counting high card points, distribution points, and quick tricks
- Major and minor suits
- What's a rubber, what's a "game," and how to score
- How to get vulnerable and why it matters

Now that you have started to communicate with your partner, you need to know how to evaluate your hand so you can tell your partner what you have. If one of you has the Ace of Spades, what does that mean to you? Does that mean anything more than that you might be able to take one Spade trick?

You bet your sweet bippy it does. This is where it begins to get fun. In this chapter, you're going to learn if you have anything in your hand that you want to tell your partner.

You're also going to learn something about how to score the game, because if you don't know how the game is scored, you won't have any idea what your evaluation of your hand really means. So I'm going to tell you a little bit about what your goals are when you play Bridge.

Bridgebit

When people learn that I'm a tournament Bridge player, they almost always ask me how much money I can win in a tournament. It's hard for people to understand that most Bridge players don't play for money. I play for fun, relaxation, entertainment, and social interaction. What do tournament players *get?* We get fun, relaxation, entertainment, social interaction, and the respect of our fellow players. Believe me, for a Bridge player, that's a lot more valuable than a monetary prize.

Sorting by Suit

When you pick up your cards, they are mixed or shuffled, and in no particular order. The first thing you do is arrange your hand by suit. Most people alternate the colors—red, black, red, black. This helps distinguish one suit from another and avoids confusing similar cards, such as the Two of Clubs and the Two of Spades.

Sorting by Rank

Most players also arrange the cards by rank, with the highest card in a suit on the left, and then in descending order. Again, this is done mainly so you are less apt to play the wrong card. If you want to play the Queen of Clubs, for example, and you have the suit sorted as follows, AQ943, you know exactly where the Queen is. But if you have them arranged randomly, you are more liable to pick out the wrong card and play it.

There's a disadvantage to sorting by suit and rank, however. A very astute player can watch you play and may be able to make judgments about how many cards you have in a suit and what their ranks are. I have seen players just pick up their cards, bid, and play them as they were dealt. For me, this makes it too confusing and inordinately difficult to play. I remember watching a guy who played like this; I asked him why. He replied that he did it so no one could determine what was in his hand. The problem was that *he* was included in that group. I watched him make some mistakes, and I thought they were because he didn't arrange his cards. I strongly advise against randomly arranged hands and encourage you to always sort your hand immediately by suit and rank.

Counting High Card Points

After you've picked up your cards and sorted them, it's time to evaluate your hand. Are you going to bid or pass? What are you going to tell your partner about your hand?

In Bridge each card in each suit has a *high-card point* (HCP) value. These points have no bearing on scoring, which you will soon learn, but are used solely to evaluate your hand. The values, or points, are as follows:

Card	Points	Card	Points
Ace	4	Jack	1
King	3	Everything else	
Queen	2	(2–10)	0

The Ten, Jack, Queen, King, and Ace are called **honors.** When someone asks you how many honors you have in a suit, you count each of these cards as one honor. For example, if you have AQT74 in a suit, you have three honors: the Ace, the Queen, and the Ten.

Even though Tens and Nines aren't assigned numerical values, they are far better than lower spot cards. For example, AQT98 is a better suit than AQ432. So, Tens and Nines sprinkled around the hand are at least worth a plus value, if for no other reason than they may eventually take tricks ahead of lower spot cards.

Lingo

Whenever I give you a hand in this book, the suits are listed in order of rank, as they are above. The first suit is always Spades, the second suit Hearts, the third listed is Diamonds, and the last listed suit is Clubs. This is standard in the world of Bridge.

Let's take a little test. Count the HCP in the following hands. Cover up the answers that follow the hands.

1. ♠ 742
   ♥ AK52
   ♦ QJ9
   ♣ 432

2. ♠ 743
   ♥ J53
   ♦ AJ52
   ♣ QT7

3. ♠ AKQ7
   ♥ KQJ
   ♦ QJT
   ♣ KJ9

4. ♠ T987
   ♥ 864
   ♦ 974
   ♣ T75

Hand 1: 10 points. 4 for the Ace of Hearts, 3 for the King of Hearts, 2 for the Queen of Diamonds, and 1 for the Jack of Diamonds.

Hand 2: 8 points. 1 for the Jack of Hearts, 4 for the Ace of Diamonds, 1 for the Jack of Diamonds, and 2 for the Queen of Clubs. (Remember, Tens, although they are honors, still are worth 0 points in HCP.)

Hand 3: 22 points (a powerful hand). 9 for the Ace, King, and Queen of Spades (4 plus 3 plus 2); 6 for the King, Queen, and Jack of Hearts (3 plus 2 plus 1); 3 for the Queen and Jack of Diamonds (2 plus 1); and 4 for the King and Jack of Clubs (3 plus 1).

Hand 4: 0.

Counting Distribution Points

Lingo

Shortage points or **shortness** are sometimes referred to as **distribution points** throughout this book.

A **fit** is said to occur between you and your partner if you have at least eight cards between you in the trump suit.

Now you know how to count HCP. But hands can also have *distribution* points. Distribution points are determined two ways, either by adding points for length in suits, or adding points for shortage in suits. Advanced players generally use length points to determine whether to open a hand and then shortage points later in the auction after a trump *fit* has been established. For your benefit, I'm going to teach you the way I learned, by using *only shortage points* (also referred to as shortness or as distribution points). So for now, forget that length points even exist.

Shortage points are as follows:

Number of Cards in Suit	Points	Number of Cards in Suit	Points
3 to 13	0	1 (singleton)	2
2 (doubleton)	1	0 (void)	3

If you open up a hand and see 13 cards in the same suit, after you bid it and play it, stop the game, take a picture, and save the hand. Thirteen cards in a suit in one hand is rarer than hen's teeth.

Now, count the shortage points in the following hands.

1. ♠ A
   ♥ J9875
   ♦ Q9432
   ♣ 87

2. ♠ 782
   ♥ AKQ
   ♦ AKQ
   ♣ 8642

3. ♠ J97
   ♥ void
   ♦ 98743
   ♣ AKQJ9

4. ♠ T9873
   ♥ 853
   ♦ 3
   ♣ J987

Hand 1: 3 shortage points, 2 for the singleton Spade (it doesn't matter that it's an Ace), and 1 for the doubleton Club.

Hand 2: 0 shortage points. This is called a 4-3-3-3 distribution.

Hand 3: 3 shortage points for the void in Hearts.

Hand 4: 2 shortage points for the singleton Diamond.

You give yourself distribution points because long and short suits have definite value as you play a hand. As you will learn when I discuss trump, if you have a singleton Heart and your opponents have the Ace, King, and Queen of Hearts and Clubs is trump, you can trump two of their apparent winners, the King of Hearts and the Queen of Hearts. So your singleton has a value, even if it's only a Deuce. Counting distribution points in this way gives you a way to evaluate the worth of the shortness as you communicate with your partner.

Combine your knowledge that you just gained and count the last four hands for both distribution and HCP.

Hand 1: 10 total points. 7 HCP (4 for the Ace of Spades, 1 for the Jack of Hearts, and 2 for the Queen of Diamonds) and 3 distribution points.

Hand 2: 18 total points. 18 HCP (2 Ace, King, Queen combinations) and 0 distribution points because of its 4–3–3–3 distribution.

Hand 3: 14 total points. 11 HCP (10 for the Ace, King, Queen, and Jack of Clubs and 1 for the Jack of Spades) and 3 distribution points for the Heart void.

Hand 4: 3 total points. 1 HCP (the Jack of Clubs) and 2 distribution points for the Diamond singleton.

Lingo

When reading Bridge hands, it's common usage to list any card below honor rank as *x* when the actual rank of the card is unimportant to the discussion. Sometimes you will see a hand that looks like this—AKxxx— meaning a five-card suit headed by the Ace and King with three cards under the rank of Ten.

Quick Tricks

Another concept to consider when evaluating your hand is called quick tricks. A *quick trick* is a card or combination of cards that will probably win a trick. An Ace is a quick trick. A King and a Queen in the same suit are a single quick trick. Why? Because the Ace can only take one of them. After the Ace is played, the other, either the King or the Queen, whichever was not played when the Ace was played, will win the trick for certain because it's the highest card left in the suit. The following table shows a list of quick tricks. The card(s) listed are always in the same suit.

Card(s)	Quick Tricks	Card(s)	Quick Tricks
Ace	1	AQ	1½
K (singleton)	0	AK	2
KQ	1	Kx	½

A general rule of thumb is to consider opening a hand if it contains three quick tricks, even though it might not meet the other requirements for opening (discussed in Chapter 6).

Making Game

You're probably thinking, "So now I know how many points my hand has, so what?" You're asking this question because you don't know *why* you're trying to take tricks. Let me explain.

What you're trying to do is make game. *Game* is when one team has made a certain number of scoring points (not HCP). You get scoring points by the number of tricks you take as declarer, and whether or not you have successfully contracted to take that number of tricks.

Scoring is heavily weighted toward accurately predicting how many tricks you'll make. If you take all the tricks available (13), you've made seven (book, plus seven). But if you only contracted to make three, the four additional tricks you actually made are much less valuable than if you had contracted to make seven.

Scoring per Trick

The value of each trick varies depending on the contract. If you're playing in Hearts or Spades, called *major* suits, the tricks are more valuable than if you're playing in Clubs or Diamonds, the *minor* suits. If you're playing in No Trump, the first trick is more valuable than if you are playing in a *major* suit.

The following table lists the values of tricks in each suit.

Suit	Points
Spades and Hearts	30 per trick
Clubs and Diamonds	20 per trick
No Trump	40 for first trick, 30 per trick thereafter

Game is when you've made 100 points *below the line* (explained in the "Scoring" section later in this chapter). But you have to convert that into a number of tricks.

Making Game in a Major Suit

If you are playing with Spades or Hearts as trump, you must make four tricks over book to exceed 100 (at 30 points per trick), so you have to take 10 tricks. If you make exactly four Hearts or Spades and bid it, your score is 120. You don't get anything for the six tricks you took to make book; you start scoring after you've made book. Then, if you're playing in a major suit, you get 30 points per trick; so four tricks over book would be 120—what you need for game.

Making Game in a Minor Suit

If you're playing in a minor suit, Clubs or Diamonds, you must take an extra trick to reach 100. You must take five tricks over book or 11 tricks total, because minor suit tricks are only worth 20 points each, not the 30 you get if you're playing in a major.

Trump determines how much each trick is worth. If you're playing a contract of 5 Diamonds, and you lead a Spade and everyone follows suit and you win the trick, you only get 20 points for that trick, even though it's a Spade trick. When the contract is reached, if it's in Clubs or Diamonds, declarer only gets 20 points per trick, regardless of the suit led. If the contract is in a major suit, Hearts or Spades, each trick is worth 30 points, even if it's a minor suit trick. You only get these points for each trick over book.

Making Game in No Trump

If you're playing in No Trump, you only need to take three tricks over book to reach 100, a total of nine tricks. Why? Because the first trick you take over book in No Trump is worth 40, then each succeeding trick is worth 30. So if you make three No Trump, you get 40 for the first trick over book and 30 for the other two, for a total of 100. This is one of the advantages of playing in No Trump: You need one less trick to make game.

Scoring

But it's not quite that easy. You get different types of points: points *above the line* and points *below the line*. What's the line?

The *line* is what separates above the line from below the line. A Rubber Bridge scoresheet looks like this:

We	They

You write the score for the tricks you *contracted* to take below the line and the score for the tricks you took *over and above* what you contracted for above the line. Only scores below the line are counted in determining whether or not you make game.

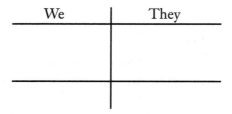

Lingo

If you don't bid game, but make a **partial**, you are said to have a **partscore**. This is referred to as having so many points *on*. So if you bid 2 Spades and make 3 Spades, you get 60 points below the line and 30 points above the line. You are said to be *60 on*.

So if your contract was 2 Spades, and you made 3 Spades, your score would be 60 points below the line (for the 2 Spades you contracted and made) and 30 points above the line for the extra trick you made over and above what you contracted. This extra trick is called an *overtrick*. The score below the line, if it's less than 100 is called a *partial*. You keep scoring until one team has 100 total points below the line. It doesn't matter how many points you have above the line when determining game.

After one pair has won a game, another line is drawn under all the points each pair scored below the line and the new game is scored below that line.

Defensive Scoring

If you don't make your contract, your opponents get points instead of you. Generally, the defenders get 50 points for each trick you fail to take under your contract. So if you bid 4 Spades and only made 2 Spades, the defenders would get 100 points: 50 points per trick. All defenders' points are *above the line*. If declarer is *vulnerable* (see later in this chapter), defenders get 100 points per trick for every trick you fail to make under your contract.

The Rubber

When one pair wins two games, that constitutes a *rubber*. One pair must score 100 points below the line twice in order for them to win the rubber. Winning the rubber entitles a pair to bonus points. If one pair wins a rubber without the other pair making a game, it gets 700 points bonus. If a pair wins a rubber after their opponents have made one game, the winning pair only gets 500 bonus points. Bonus points are above the line.

At the end of the rubber you add up all the points, above and below the line, and whoever has the most is the overall winner. It's possible to win the rubber but not be the overall winner.

Rubber Bridge Score Sheet

A Rubber Bridge score sheet might look like this:

PLAYERS	YOU	PARTNER	YOUR RHO	YOUR LHO
FIRST RUBBER	870	870	250	250
SECOND RUBBER				
THIRD RUBBER				
TOTALS				

WE	THEY	WE	THEY	WE	THEY
500					
60	20				
30	50				
60	80				
40					
60	100				
120					
870	250				

Explanation:

(1) This is the *line* that separates above the line from below the line.

(2) This means that you ("we") were in a major suit contract at the 2 level and made 3. For that you got 60 points below the line for the 2 you bid and made, and 30 points above the line for the overtrick.

(3) Apparently you also bid a contract and went down 1; that is represented by the 50 your opponents have above the line.

(4) Your opponents then bid 4 Clubs or 4 Diamonds and made 5. They got 80 points below the line for the 4 that they bid and 20 points above the line for the overtrick they made.

(5) On the next hand, you either bid and made 1 No Trump for 40 or 2 in a minor suit, which would also be 40. You did not make an overtrick because you got nothing further above the line.

(6) Because you made game, 100 points below the line (60 on the first hand plus 40 on the third hand), you drew a line under those hands and started another game

(7) You then bid 2 of a major suit and made 4. For this you got 60 points below the line for the 2 you bid and made, and 60 points above the line for the two over-tricks.

(8) Your opponents then made game, either bidding and making 3 No Trump or 5 of a minor, because both of those contracts get the bidders 100 points. They did not make an overtrick, so they got nothing above the line.

(9) You then drew another line, like you did in number 6 above, and started another game. Remember, a rubber continues until one pair makes two games.

(10) Then, you bid game in a major suit, either 4 Hearts or 4 Spades, and made it exactly, so you got 120 below the line for bidding and making your 4. You did not make an overtrick, so you got nothing further above the line.

(11) Because you won two games in the rubber, you won the rubber, so you got a 500-point bonus. Had you won the rubber without your opponents making a game you would have received a 700-point bonus.

You then add up your points. You and your partner were the overall winners because you had the most points. You move the points up to keep the running score of each player at the top. You can then change partners, if you want, and play another rubber and put those scores next to the boxes for the second rubber. Then if you want to change partners again, you do it all over for the third rubber. Then, if you want to quit, you add up everyone's points and find out who was the overall winner for the entire match.

If declarer was *doubled* (see Chapter 18 for details), the points received by defenders are substantially increased if they defeat the contract. If defenders don't defeat the contract, declarer's score is increased.

What It Means to Be Vulnerable

If you have won a game (you have more than 100 points below the line), you are said to be *vulnerable*. This means that if you go set (don't make your contract), your penalty is twice as severe. If you go set nonvulnerable, your penalty is 50 points for each trick you are short of your contract. So if your contract is 2 Spades and you only make 1 Spade, you are one trick short and your penalty is 50 points. These points go to your opponents above the line.

Bridgebit
Guess where the term **vulnerable** came from. Give up? The lady you met in Chapter 1, who was invited to join Harold Vanderbilt's game of Plafond on October 31, 1925, coined the term when Vanderbilt and his three compatriots were out of ideas. As you can see, she had an enormous influence on the game. Not only did her attitude so infuriate Vanderbilt that he invented a new game, but she also came up with one of Bridge's most famous terms!

However, if you go set when you are vulnerable, your penalty is doubled. So if your contract is 2 Spades and you only make 1 Spade, you are said to be down 1 and that penalty, instead of being 50 points, is doubled to 100. Again, those points go to your opponents above the line.

Stop reading now and, using what you've learned in Chapters 1 through 4, play some hands before moving on to the next chapter.

The Least You Need to Know

- ◆ After receiving a Bridge hand, sort the cards by suit and rank in descending order.

- ◆ Count high card points (HCP) and distribution points. Adding HCP to distribution points gives you the bidding value of the hand.

◆ Your goal is to bid game if possible. Game in a major suit is 4 Hearts or 4 Spades, 10 total tricks. Game in a minor suit is 5 Clubs or 5 Diamonds, 11 total tricks. Game in No Trump is 3 No Trump, nine total tricks.

◆ You get points below the line if you make the number of tricks you contracted. You get points above the line for the tricks you make over what you contracted. Only points below the line count toward game.

◆ You get points above the line when you are on defense for every trick your opponents fail to make under what they contracted.

Part 2

Opening Bids

In Bridge, you want to avoid the famous admonition to *Cool Hand Luke*, "What we have here is a failure to communicate!" Bridge is based on effective communication between partners. In this section, you'll learn how to evaluate your hand for the purposes of making an opening bid. Then you'll learn different types of bids that will describe your hand to your partner. You'll also learn how to determine whether you or your partner is the captain of your pair. This section will teach you strategy and how to make bids that will not only communicate what you have to your partner, but will also interfere with your opponents' ability to communicate with one another.

Surrendering Command: Opening No Trump Bids

In This Chapter

- How to communicate with your partner through the bidding process
- High card points and distribution points required for game
- Requirements for game in No Trump
- Stoppers
- Point count and distribution requirements for 2 No Trump and 3 No Trump openings

By now, you should be getting the feeling for what we're doing. Now you know how to count your hand. But this is just knowledge that you have. You have to communicate this to your partner in a way that allows her to make some determination of what the two of you can accomplish in this hand.

In this chapter, you're going to learn how to tell your partner what you have in your hand. She can convert what you tell her into a mathematical formula that will enable her to make a fairly accurate estimate of the number of tricks you can take.

You're also going to learn how to start bidding a hand that is a very good hand, indeed—a No Trump opening. When you finish this chapter, you'll be well on your way to being a Bridge player.

Relating Points to Goals

There are 40 total HCP in each hand, distributed among the four players. When you bid, you are basically telling your partner how many of those points you have. She listens to your bid, looks at her hand, adds her points to yours, and tries to determine how many tricks the two of you can take. How does she do this? The gods of Bridge have realized over the years that if a pair has a certain number of points, it will probably take a certain number of tricks. The following table presents a generalized list showing how many total points it takes to make game.

Contract Suit	Points Required
Hearts and Spades	26 (HCP plus distribution points)
Clubs and Diamonds	28 (HCP plus distribution points)
No Trump	25 (HCP only)

Bridgebit
Milton Work, a Philadelphia lawyer who took a leave of absence in 1917 to concentrate on Bridge, devised the HCP count method of evaluating the hand. From 1917 to 1931, he was the recognized authority. By 1928, he was paid $7,000 a week for brief lectures on the game. Interestingly, as a player he was not highly rated by his contemporaries. He died in 1934 at the age of 69.

Why the difference? Simple. You can make game in No Trump by only taking nine total tricks, so you only need 25 of the total 40 points available. If you're playing with Hearts or Spades as trump, you need to take one additional trick over what you would need to take in No Trump, so you need a more powerful hand, more points. You need at least 26 points. As you'll soon see, however, having this many points doesn't *guarantee* you can make game; it's just a very good indication.

If you're playing in a minor suit, Diamonds or Clubs, you need yet another trick to make game, 5 above book or 11 total. This means that you need to take all the tricks but two. For this you need 28 points or more.

Your Opening Bid

Your opening bid is the first communication you have with your partner. You want to communicate as much to her as you can when you state your bid. After you have arranged your cards and counted your points, you should know what your opening bid is going to be.

Opening bids of one of a suit may have as little as 13 HCP and meet suit distribution requirements. (You'll learn about these in Chapter 6.) But what if you have more than 14 points? If you just opened every hand with more than 13 points, 1 of a suit, your partner wouldn't know if you had 13 points or 25. Opening bidding has been refined so there are many bids you can make that describe the strength of your hand.

Bridgebit

Work's disciple, Charles Goren, added distribution points in 1944, and became the primary advocate for what came to be known as the *Goren System*. In the Goren System, 13-point hands are optional, 14-point hands must be opened, and 11-point hands can be opened in third seat. Under this system, Goren determined that 26 points would produce game in a major suit, whereas 29 points were required for game in a minor suit.

Opening 1 No Trump

If you have a fairly balanced hand, no voids or singletons, and more than 14 points, you want to communicate this to your partner in your first bid. With a hand containing 15 to 17 HCP, no singletons or voids, and no more than two doubletons, you can open 1 No Trump. This says, "Partner, I have 15 to 17 HCP in my hand, no singletons or voids, and no more than two doubletons."

This is enormously helpful information to your partner because it limits your hand. You have at least 37 percent of the total HCP available; in addition, you have at least two cards in each suit! Further, you have limited your hand by telling your partner that you have less than 42 percent of the total HCP

Alert

Many Rubber Bridge players play that an opening of 1 No Trump promises 16 to 18 HCP. Although the modern trend is for a 15 to 17 HCP No Trump range, many of the people with whom you play Rubber Bridge will be playing 16 to 18. Discuss this with your partner before you play to make sure you're on the same wavelength.

available. So she knows you have 37 to 42 percent of the total HCP available. And you've told her all this in just one bid!

Because she knows that you need 25 to 26 points to make game, if she has just 10 points in her hand, she knows that you should probably be playing this hand in game somewhere.

When you open 1 No Trump, you designate your partner as the captain of the team for the hand. Why? Because she knows an incredible amount about your hand, whereas you know virtually nothing about hers. She may want to determine if the two of you have enough cards in any suit to qualify it as trump. On many hands she will merely choose to play the hand in No Trump. You can just sit back, answer her questions, and let her place the contract for the partnership.

Specific Description of High Card Points

When you open 1 No Trump, you are giving your partner a specific description of how many HCP you have in your hand. You have between 15 to 17 HCP—no more, no less. If you have 14, you will probably open 1 of a suit. If you have 18, you will treat the hand differently. If you open an 18-point hand 1 No Trump, you are giving misinformation to your partner, and that's a cardinal sin in Bridge. I remember the last time I opened an 18-point hand 1 No Trump. It turned into a disaster, and it was all my fault. I was dealt an 18-point hand with perfect No Trump distribution, 4–3–3–3. I thought, "Well, there's only 1-point difference, and I do have perfect distribution, so I'll lie a little," and opened 1 No Trump.

To my dismay, the hand was passed out, meaning everyone else passed, leaving me to play the hand in 1 No Trump. My partner came down with 7 HCP. My 18 plus her 7 equaled 25, which is enough to make game, and I did make game, 3. But because we only bid 1, we got a very poor score because the other two tricks were above the line—we missed an easy game.

Had I opened 1 Club, which is what I should have done, my partner would have been forced to *respond* with her longest suit, showing me at least 6 points (more on this in Chapter 10). I would then have jumped to 2 No Trump, showing at least 18 points, and my partner would have added her 7 to my 18, gotten 25, and bid game, 3 No Trump.

So you must be extremely disciplined. It's very important that you don't lie to your partner. If you open 1 No Trump, saying you have 15 to 17 HCP, then that's what you had better have, or you will be in trouble!

The Distribution

An opening of 1 No Trump not only describes the HCP in your hand, but it also promises your partner that you have a very specific distribution in your hand. It promises, basically, that you have at least two cards in each suit. You cannot open 1 No Trump if you have a void in a suit, a singleton in a suit, or more than two doubletons.

If you have 15 to 17 HCP, but have a hand with a singleton or void, then you have to find another bid to make other than 1 No Trump. We'll discuss this situation in Chapter 6.

What is called perfect No Trump distribution is a hand that contains four cards in one suit and three cards in every other suit, which is what 4–3–3–3 refers to. This doesn't mean that you *must* have 4–3–3–3 distribution to open 1 No Trump, however. You may open any 15 to 17 point hand without voids, singletons, or more than two doubletons 1 No Trump, with one or two exceptions. This means that you might have a hand with 5–4–2–2 distribution and open it 1 No Trump.

The reason for this is that it communicates the strength of your hand to your partner in one bid. Just because you open 1 No Trump doesn't mean that you are going to end up playing in No Trump! Remember that when you open 1 No Trump, you designate your partner as the captain of the hand. It's up to her to determine whether it's better to play the hand in No Trump or a suit, or to defend if your opponents enter the bidding.

Stoppers

A *stopper* is a card or distribution of cards that enables you to take a trick in the suit. An Ace is a definite stopper. A King and a Queen comprise a stopper because even though the opponents may lead an Ace, it will only take the Queen, and you'll still have the King to take a trick. Kx and Qxx are full stoppers, in spite of what might happen. Partial stoppers are Jxx or Qx.

A King and one card in a suit is a stopper. It's true that if your RHO gets the lead and he leads that suit, and your LHO has the Ace and the Queen, your King will be dead as a doornail. Why? Well, what are you going to play when your RHO leads the suit in which you have Kx? If you play the King, your LHO will play the Ace and then you won't have a stopper. If you play low, your LHO will play the Queen and then the Ace will take your King. Only if your LHO leads the suit will your King be a stopper. But Kx and Qxx are considered full stoppers for bidding purposes.

Lingo

To **duck** means to refuse to win a trick or play a higher card when you have the capability to play low. Ducking is covered in detail in Chapters 19 through 22, on play of the hand.

Have you figured out why the King is a stopper only if your LHO leads the suit? Think about it. If the LHO leads the suit, he's leading into your hand, because your hand will be the last one to play to the trick. So if the LHO leads, no matter what he leads, and no matter what your RHO plays on the trick, your King will be a definite winner at some point. If the RHO plays the Ace, your King is the high card out. If the RHO *ducks*, you can win the trick with the King. You'll be in trouble if they get the lead again and attack the suit, because your stopper will be gone. But that's why Bridge is such a challenge.

The same is true of a Queen and two in a suit. Your opponents, if the Ace and the King are in alternate hands, can lead through your Queen and you can lose it. How? Well, let's say your LHO has the lead and he leads low. Your RHO has the Ace and plays it and returns the same suit, through your Queen. If you play the Queen, your LHO will take it with his King. If you play low, your LHO may take it with a lower card, then lead the King and your Queen will fall. But it's still considered a full stopper.

The term *partial stopper* is defined in Bridge language as Qx or Jxx or T9xx (rare). Think in terms of the lead coming from declarer's left: Kx is a stopper; Qx or Jxx requires help from your partner. (True that the lead may be a side suit to RHO's Ace, then back through our Kx, but this isn't a consideration when determining stoppers for No Trump purposes.)

The Kx is a better stopper than the Qxx, because the Kx is a definite stopper if your LHO is on lead and leads the suit. Then, no matter what your RHO does, your King will take a trick. With the Qxx, however, even if your LHO is on lead, you can be left without a stopper if your opponents defend correctly.

Exceptions to Opening 1 No Trump with 15 to 17 HCP

There are two basic exceptions where you should consider not opening a balanced 15 to 17 HCP hand 1 No Trump.

1. Don't open a hand 1 No Trump if you have two suits without stoppers. Especially, if you're opening a hand with two doubletons, you should have stoppers in the two doubletons. Sometimes you'll have to open a hand 1 No Trump with one suit unstopped.

2. Don't open a hand 1 No Trump if you're 5–4 or 4–5 in the majors. If you have five cards in one major and four cards in the other, it's better to open the bidding by bidding your five-card major. If your partner doesn't support you, you can then rebid your four-card major. More on opening in your major suits in Chapter 6.

> **Bridgebit**
>
> Bridge is not a game for the faint of heart. One of my best teachers used to say, "If you're scared, go play tiddlywinks!"

Opening 2 No Trump

You aren't limited to opening the bidding at the 1 level. You can open a hand at any level you like. But each opening transmits specific information to your partner. If opening 1 No Trump shows a balanced hand with 15 to 17 points, what would a 2 No Trump open show?

It doesn't show the next level up, 18 to 20, which is what you probably thought. (Another series of bids describes hands that have 18 to 19 points.) When you open 2 No Trump you're telling your partner that your distribution is the same as if you opened 1 No Trump, no voids or singletons, and no more than two doubletons. But your HCP are much higher. A 2 No Trump opening tells your partner that you have 20 to 21 HCP. Following are some typical 2 No Trump openings:

1. ♠ AKQ	2. ♠ JT9	3. ♠ 83	4. ♠ QJT72
♥ KJ95	♥ KQ2	♥ Q64	♥ AQ
♦ A75	♦ KQ5	♦ AKJT	♦ KJ
♣ K84	♣ AKQ3	♣ AKQJ	♣ AQJ6

The first two hands are no-brainers. You have 20 HCP and perfect 4–3–3–3 No Trump distribution. The third hand gives pause because you have a doubleton— Spades—unstopped. But you have 20 HCP, all but 2 in the minors. By opening 2 No Trump, you describe your strength to your partner and you take away your opponents' bidding room and limit their flexibility to see if they have a major suit fit.

In the fourth hand, you have a five-card major (Spades); some players don't like to open No Trump with a five-card major. But the problem with not opening this hand

2 No Trump is that you mislead your partner in your opening bid, by either initially describing a hand that is weaker than you have, or one that is stronger. This five-card major is far too weak to even think about opening anything other than 2 No Trump. If the Spades were AKQJx instead of QJTxx, then it might give you some pause. But with a weak five-card major, 20 points, and no voids or singletons and no more than two doubletons, you should always open 2 No Trump.

Opening 3 No Trump

By now you've probably gotten the drift of this. Logic would say that a 3 No Trump open would be 22 to 24 HCP. Wrong! There's another bid for that hand, regardless of its distribution. It's called a Strong Two bid, and I cover it in Chapter 7.

> **Lingo**
>
> A **slam** is when you bid and make six or seven, which means that you bid and take all tricks but one in the case of a six bid (a **small slam**) and when you bid and take all the tricks in the case of a seven bid (a **grand slam**). That's the best thing that can happen offensively in Bridge.

If you have 25 to 26 points and no voids or singletons, and no more than two doubletons and stoppers in all suits, you can open 3 No Trump. This tells your partner that you really don't need her, you have everything you need to make game in your own hand. It invites her to explore for *slam*, about which you will learn in Chapter 15, or place the contract in a major suit if she has a long one. The hand is the same as the 2 No Trump open, except it has more HCP.

Now deal out some hands and bid and play them in accord with what you've learned in Chapters 1 through 5.

The Least You Need to Know

- Requirements for game are generally 25 HCP in No Trump, 26 points (HCP plus distribution points) in a major suit, and 28 points in a minor suit.

- An opening bid of 1 No Trump describes a hand of *exactly* 15 to 17 HCP with no singletons, no voids, and no more than two doubletons.

- An opening bid of 2 No Trump describes a hand of *exactly* 20 to 21 HCP with the same distribution as a 1 No Trump opening.

- An opening bid of 3 No Trump describes a hand of *exactly* 25 to 26 HCP with the same distribution as a 1 No Trump opening.

- You must be disciplined and not lie to your partner.

Chapter 6

Clothed in Information: Opening 1 of a Suit

In This Chapter

- HCP requirements to open 1 of a suit and counting shortness
- The five-card major rule and how to determine which suit to open
- Opening in first and second position versus third and fourth position
- Evaluating hands with unusual distribution
- Ruffing

So now you know how to open a very good hand, one with between 37 percent and 42 percent of the HCP in it. But what if you don't have that type of hand? In this chapter, you learn the requirements for opening 1 of a suit. As you will see, you can open 1 of a suit with a weaker hand than required for opening 1 No Trump.

You also learn that it matters where you are sitting in relationship to the dealer. Your evaluation of your hand changes depending on whether you are the first or second player to make a *call*, or the third or fourth. A *call* is any bid, double, redouble, or pass made by a player. You will learn about doubles and redoubles in Chapter 18.

Ah, the wonders of Bridge. It's so varied.

Point Requirements for Suit Bids

To open 1 of a suit, you must meet specific point count and suit length requirements. You should have a minimum of 13 points, combining HCP and distribution points, to open 1 of a suit. Generally speaking, an opening of 1 of a suit indicates a hand of 13 to 14 points. There are exceptions to this rule, however, depending on distribution. As we've seen in 1 No Trump openings, you can't open 1 No Trump if you have more than 17 HCP, and you can't open 2 No Trump if you have less than 20 HCP, so what do you do with 18 to 19–point hands? We'll cover that in Chapter 13.

Tricks of the Trade _____

You can open 1 of a suit with a hand that's too strong or too distributional to open 1 No Trump. For example, you could have 15 to 17 HCP but a singleton or void. You can't open that 1 No Trump, but you must open it. I'll cover that in Chapter 13. For now, just remember that an opening of 1 in a suit does not *limit* the hand to 14 points. It could have more.

Many experts suggest that you add or deduct if you have all or no Aces in your hand. You deduct a point if you have no Aces and you add a point if you have all four Aces. So it would be unwise to open in the following hand:

  ♠ J64
  ♥ J84
  ♦ KQ7
  ♣ KQJ3

There are 13 HCP. But if you deduct a point for no Aces you're down to 12 HCP. That's not attractive enough to take a chance.

Adding a point for all four Aces is a good technique because Aces tend to be slightly undervalued. But subtracting a point for no Aces should be limited to hands with 4–3–3–3 distribution. So, passing the example hand above is correct. But the following hand should be opened 1 Diamond because, although it is Ace-less, it is not 4–3–3–3 distribution:

  ♠ JT4
  ♥ J8
  ♦ KQT7
  ♣ KQJ3

Hand evaluation is not a computer science. As you learn the game, you'll develop a feel for borderline openings. At this stage, to generalize, Ace-less hands and 4–3–3–3 distributed hands suggest underbidding your values, whereas hands with, for example, JT9, are more valuable than a holding of J32.

Suit Length Requirements for Suit Bids

You should have at least five cards in the suit if it is a major (Hearts or Spades). The modern trend is to open a major only if you have a minimum of five cards in it. The older style was to open any suit if it had four cards. I'm going to teach you the newer, *five-card major* style of bidding. This means, for example, that if you have 13 points, but you don't have a five-card major, then you must open a minor suit (Clubs or Diamonds), even though you may not have any honors in that suit.

Tricks of the Trade

Remember, when you play a bidding system, your bids promise your partner that your hand contains what you say it does. So if you open 1 Spade, you're promising your partner that you have at least five Spades in your hand. She'll make her bid based on that commitment. Accepting the concept of commitment is very important in the formation of a Bridge partnership. Nothing is more critical than trusting your partner.

If you have fewer than five Spades in your hand, it will mislead her and her reply could mislead you. You'll be progressing rapidly down the road to ruin on this hand. So when you agree to play a system, like the five-card major system I'm teaching here, stick with it and don't deviate. In other words, if you agree that your opening bid of 1 Spade promises at least five Spades, don't later decide that, for one hand, you can open 1 Spade with only four Spades. You must exert discipline in your bidding.

Bridgebit

There are innumerable bidding systems. The *Official Encyclopedia of Bridge* lists 54 different systems. In this book, you are learning **Standard American,** the most widely used system in America. If you sit down at a table, despite what system your opponents are actually using, it would be unusual if they hadn't learned Standard American first. Regardless of what system your opponents are using, you and your partner must use the same system in order to communicate.

Opening

But, you ask, what if I have 13 points, but no five-card major? Good question. If you have a five-card minor (Clubs or Diamonds), open that. But, often you have one or both four-card majors and no five-card minor. What then?

Because you can't open a four-card major, you are allowed to open a minor, even if it is only three cards in length.

For starters, here are the basic rules of opening 1 of a suit:

- ◆ You must have at least 13 points.

- ◆ An opening bid in a major suit, Hearts or Spades, promises at least five cards in the suit.

- ◆ If you have 13 points but no five-card major, open your longest minor.

- ◆ If both minors are four cards in length, open 1 Diamond.

- ◆ If both minors are three cards in length, open 1 Club.

That's it for opening 1 bids. Following are some hands. Determine whether or not you would open each, and if so, what your opening bid would be.

1. ♠ AK982	2. ♠ 763	3. ♠ JT42	4. ♠ 976
♥ QT54	♥ AK75	♥ AK642	♥ AKQJ
♦ K5	♦ 74	♦ 87	♦ A62
♣ J3	♣ 8754	♣ 64	♣ 632

Hand 1: A clear 1 Spade open. You have 13 HCP and a good five-card Spade suit.

Hand 2: Pass. Not enough points.

Hand 3: Pass, even though you have a nice five-card Heart suit. You only have 8 HCP, 10 total points with distribution, and that's not enough to open. If you open this hand you're telling your partner you have at least 13 points, and even though your Heart suit is very attractive, you would be lying to your partner.

Tricks of the Trade

One of the worst things you can do in bidding in Bridge is to make a *unilateral* bid, saying to yourself, "I like this hand and I'm going to bid it. The heck with what my partner thinks or has in her hand." When you do this—and a lot of players do—you're just begging for trouble.

Hand 4: Open 1 Club. Sure, your Hearts are terrific, but there are only four of them. If you open 1 Heart, you're telling your partner you have at least five

Hearts, and you don't. Whatever you do, you don't want to lie to your partner, because she's relying on you for accurate information in evaluating her hand and making her bid.

Opening 1 Club doesn't necessarily guide the partnership toward a final Club contract. You may easily end up in Hearts, your best suit, or even No Trump. Subsequent bidding will determine this (discussed in Chapters 10, 11, and 13).

Determining Which Suit to Open

Okay, so far it has been pretty easy. The sample hands have had fairly obvious answers. Alas, Bridge is not that cooperative. Generally your hands are thinkers, because they contain elements that vary from the rules. So let's start with some right now. What do you do if you have two five-card majors? Which suit do you open? Look at these hands:

1. ♠ AK964	2. ♠ JT865	3. ♠ 98642	4. ♠ 98632
♥ AK865	♥ AKQ53	♥ AJT76	♥ QT852
♦ 76	♦ 3	♦ AK	♦ A
♣ 7	♣ 96	♣ 4	♣ AK

How would you open each? I know that you don't know any of the rules yet, but just use your common sense and write down how you'd open each.

Now for the answers. 1 Spade.

What? Which hand are you talking about? What do you mean 1 Spade? Well, the answer to all four hands is 1 Spade. When you have two five-card suits in a hand, major or minor, you always open the higher-ranking suit. This is true when both five-card suits are majors. So if you have five Hearts and five Spades, you open 1 Spade, even if the Heart suit is much, much stronger than the Spade suit.

Why? The answer to this is a little complicated. Let's assume the bidding goes as follows.

You	LHO	Partner	RHO
1 Spade	2 Clubs	Pass	Pass
2 Hearts	Pass		

This tells your partner that you have at least five Spades and at least four Hearts. If your partner likes Spades more than Hearts, she can still remain at the 2 level by choosing the appropriate suit.

Think about what would happen if you had hand 2, 3, or 4 and opened Hearts first. The bidding would have gone as follows.

You	LHO	Partner	RHO
1 Heart	2 Clubs	Pass	Pass
2 Spades	Pass		

Now, what if your partner is void in Spades, but has three little Hearts and only 4 points? Obviously you should be playing in Hearts, but she has to go to the 3 level with her terrible hand. What to do? She's in a quandary.

Tricks of the Trade

Keep in mind that at all times during an auction each partner is called on to make decisions. When your partner shows two suits, she is asking you to choose which of her suits you prefer. Even though the choice is not always pleasant, you must make a choice. I will repeat this concept frequently.

If you open 1 Spade, even though your Spades are much weaker than your Hearts, and then rebid 2 Hearts, she could pass, showing her preference to play in Hearts, and you're at a much safer and lower 2 level instead of 3 level. If her holding is reversed, and she has three Spades and a Heart void, she could just simply bid 2 Spades over your 2 Hearts, telling you, "Partner, my hand stinks, but I'd rather you play this in Spades than Hearts."

Regardless of how strong your Hearts are, you're better off playing in a suit in which you and your partner have eight cards between you than a suit in which you only have five or six cards between you.

Open Your Longest Suit

When opening, you should open your longest suit, regardless of its high card strength. If you have a six-card minor and a five-card major, open the minor. Look at the following hands:

1. ♠ AKQJT
   ♥ 8
   ♦ QJT987
   ♣ 7

2. ♠ 987654
   ♥ AKQJT
   ♦ 7
   ♣ 8

Hand 1: 1 Diamond. Your Spades are nice and you should be able to show them at a subsequent bid. But, you have to tell your partner that your Diamonds are longer. If you open 1 Spade and then rebid Diamonds, you're telling your partner that your Spades are longer than your Diamonds or that they are of equal five-card length.

Hand 2: 1 Spade. Again, even though your Hearts have a lot of high-card strength, your Spades are longer. If your partner has two Hearts and two Spades, your Spades are your stronger suit and should be the trump suit. Note that even though this hand only has 10 HCP, it has 14 total points given two points for each of the two singletons, so it's a hand that must be opened.

Opening in Third Position

When you are in the first or the second bidding seat, your evaluation of your hand is different from when you are in the third or fourth seat. In the first and second seats, you have not heard from your partner yet. In the *first seat* you haven't heard from anyone. You will be the first to describe your hand to everyone else.

When you're in second seat, although you haven't heard from your partner, you have heard from your RHO. If your RHO has passed, you know that he probably has fewer than 13 points. This tells you something, but not too much, about what everyone else is holding.

Lingo

First seat is synonymous with first position. Both mean the first player to make a call. The dealer is always in first seat; dealer's LHO is in second seat; dealer's partner is in third seat; dealer's RHO is in fourth seat.

But when you're in second seat and your RHO has opened the bidding, you not only know something about his hand, you know a lot about the hands of everyone else. From the RHO's bid, you know the placement of a substantial number of the cards in the deck.

If your RHO has opened 1 of a suit, or 1 No Trump, you know approximately how many HCP are in his hand. Let's say he opens 1 No Trump, and that you have 12 points in your hand. You know you and your RHO hold between 27 and 29 of the total of 40 points in the hand. That means that your partner and your LHO have a total of 11 to 13 points between them.

But when you are in third seat and your partner and your RHO have passed, you can ease the stringent requirements to open your hand. Why? Because you know that neither your partner nor your RHO have an opening hand. So if you have a minimum opening hand, you and your partner probably don't have game, because her maximum holding should be 12 points. If you have 12 points, you may have a maximum total of 24 points between you, not enough for game. If you don't bid, you will be abandoning an opportunity to tell your partner something about your hand with very little risk involved.

Tricks of the Trade

Are you saying to yourself, "How can I bid with only 8 points?" Realize that if you have a six-card suit, headed by the AKJ, you must have a hand that contains at least 10 points, because a hand with a six-card suit must have at least either a singleton or two doubletons in its 13 total cards.

Bridgebit

Yarborough was named after an English lord who would give odds of 1,000 to 1 against someone coming up with such a hand, which was defined as a hand with no card higher than a Nine. The actual odds are 1,827 to 1, so, as with most bookies, he had a nice edge.

There is a further advantage to bidding in third seat with a less than opening hand. It is the only chance you will have to give your partner a suggestion of an opening lead in case you are defending. What if you're sitting there with the AKJxxx of Clubs, and nothing much else? If you open 1 Club and your LHO does have a powerhouse and ends up playing a contract, your partner will know that you want her to lead a Club. If you don't make your third seat opening bid, she'll be in the dark about your hand.

Of course, you're guessing whether your partner had a hand close to opening, like 10 to 12 points, or a *Yarborough* (a hand containing no points, a disaster). You are also in the dark about your RHO's hand. Does he have 12 points, or 0? This lack of knowledge about two hands at the table leaves you in the dark about your LHO's hand.

If both your partner and your RHO have Yarborough hands and you have a minimum opening, your LHO could be sitting there with a powerhouse. So if you want to get in a bid, now is the time to do it. Maybe you have a good Spade suit and little else, maybe 10 points. What to do? Answer: Make a tactical light opening in the third seat.

Rules for Light Third Seat Open

If you are opening in third seat, you should have the following at a minimum:

◆ At least 10 points

◆ A good suit, headed by the AK or KQJ, for lead directing purposes

Look at the following hands:

1. ♠ 975   2. ♠ QJ2
   ♥ 873   ♥ QJ3
   ♦ 7   ♦ 6
   ♣ AKJT75   ♣ QJ6432

Hand 1: 1 Club. You have 10 points, but a terrific Club suit. If your LHO gets the bid, you definitely want your partner to lead a Club. This is your only chance to tell her. If you get the contract in 1 Club, you won't be hurt too much. If your partner raises Clubs, or bids either of the majors, you have minimal support. If she bids Diamonds, you can rebid your Club suit.

Hand 2: Pass. This hand contains 11 points, but has no lead directing values. If your LHO gets the contract, do you want your partner to lead a Club? If your LHO bids a major and your partner bids 2 Diamonds, what are you going to do? You certainly don't want to be playing this in 3 Clubs if your partner doesn't have support for you.

Your partner should be aware that you might be opening light in third seat, so she should not jump to optimistic conclusions if she's holding a hand with just slightly less than opening values. If she has 12 points and she hears you open, she should proceed with caution, knowing that you might be opening a 10-point hand for lead-directing purposes.

Opening in Fourth Position

Things change again when you are sitting in fourth position. If all three players pass the bid around to you, you know that nobody has an opening hand. You may also assume that your RHO is not very close to an opening hand because he might have opened light in the third seat.

But when the bid is passed around to fourth seat, and you are sitting with a little less than an opening hand, the odds are against you opening, because your two opponents probably have 9 to 11 points in each of their hands. Your partner might be sitting there with 5 or 6 points.

Tricks of the Trade

You need a full opening hand in fourth seat. If you don't have a full opening hand, it is wiser to pass and deal again.

The danger of opening a marginal hand in fourth seat is that you might give your opponents the opportunity to get a plus score when they are ready to pass the hand out. You don't have game. What's the point of bidding in the blind hope that you have a fit with your partner or your partner is sitting there with some points to help you out?

The situation is completely different from what you faced in third seat. There, you don't know what your opponent in the fourth seat has in his hand. He could have a powerhouse. That could be your only chance to bid a suit that is headed by the Ace–King.

In fourth seat, however, you have no worry about someone bidding behind you with a powerhouse, leaving you without a bid. If you pass, the hand will be passed out. In Rubber Bridge that can never really hurt you, whereas bidding on a marginal hand and allowing your opponents to find a partial will definitely hurt you.

Opening Hands with Unusual Distribution

One of the wonders of Bridge is that you can set forth all these rules, but you will constantly get hands that tax your ingenuity in applying the rules. In fact, you will rarely get a hand that will not cause you to think, and that's why Bridge is so challenging and so much fun.

What we've said so far is pretty straightforward, and the hands we've given you as examples comply with the rules we've given you. But there are literally billions of combinations of cards that you can get in a Bridge hand.

So how would you open the following hands, applying the rules you just learned?

1. ♠ KQJT76	2. ♠ 97654	3. ♠ 6	4. ♠ 754
♥ 6	♥ QT985	♥ 8	♥ void
♦ KQT5	♦ A	♦ KQJ865	♦ QJT32
♣ 64	♣ A7	♣ KQT42	♣ AQJT7

Clearly, these hands do not follow the norm. And clearly, even without much help from your partner, you'll make book and then some if you play these hands.

Hand 3 only has 11 HCP, but conceivably you could lose only four tricks and make three with your partner sitting there with a Yarborough. If things are right—and they don't need to be unusually right—you lose all four Aces and that's it. If you get a favorable lead, like the Ace of Clubs, you might make more. And if your partner has something, you might make game. Clearly, you must open this hand.

All these hands have potential, but they illustrate the value of distributional hands. You'd feel very uncomfortable passing any of them, even if you're in first seat, despite their minimal HCP holdings.

Hand 1: 1 Spade. You have 11 HCP, a singleton, and a doubleton. That's 14 points.

Hand 2: 1 Spade. You have 10 HCP and a singleton and doubleton for 13 points, a minimal opening hand.

Hand 3: 1 Diamond. Again, you have 11 HCP and two singletons, still enough to open 1 Diamond with 15 total points.

Hand 4: You have 10 HCP and a void. That's 13 points. But let's take a look at this hand and see what happens if you open a two suited hand when the suits are relatively weak.

Let's say you open 1 Diamond, which this hand calls for (the higher ranking of two five-card suits, remember?). What's your partner going to bid? Right, almost definitely when you have a hand like this and you open your partner bids your void. So she bids 1 Heart. What now? Well, you mention your other five-card suit, and bid 2 Clubs.

What does she do? Because the gods of Bridge are perverse, she will almost definitely repeat her Hearts, showing six Hearts. (You'll learn about that in Chapter 14). Now your hand is extremely diminished in value. Not only is your void in Hearts not going to give you any *ruffing* power if Hearts is trump, but you don't have anywhere to go. She might be six Hearts, four Spades, and two and one in your suits. And you certainly don't want to play at the 3 level in a 5–1 fit. You're left having to pass her out at 2 Hearts with your void. Therefore, Hand 4 is a hand you may choose to pass, even though you have 13 total points.

> **Lingo**
>
> **Ruff** is another word for trump used as a verb. To trump or ruff simply means that you have taken a non-trump trick by playing a trump, which, as you remember, you can't do unless you're void in the suit led.

If Clubs or Diamonds is trump in Hand 4, you can ruff, or trump, any Heart that is led. Theoretically you can't lose a Heart trick. But if your partner's suit is Hearts, your ruffing power is greatly diminished because she probably won't have a lot of Heart losers anyway.

Opening a 15 to 17 HCP Hand with a Five-Card Major

Many players don't like to open a hand in No Trump with a five-card major. Some limit this to not opening No Trump with a *good* five-card major. How you open a hand and who plays the hand can have a major determination on your result.

For the purposes of your learning, you should adopt a consistent rule to play with your partner. If you have a 15 to 17 HCP, balanced hand with a five-card major:

♦ Open in 1 of your five-card major if you have an unstopped doubleton.

♦ Open 1 No Trump if you have all the suits stopped.

Look at the following hands:

1. ♠ KQJ85   2. ♠ QJT85
   ♥ AQ3   ♥ AT3
   ♦ K73   ♦ KQ3
   ♣ 75   ♣ K5

Hand 1: 1 Spade. You have a good five-card Spade suit and you have an unstopped doubleton Club.

Hand 2: 1 No Trump. Your Spade suit isn't that great and you have all the suits stopped.

The point of which you should be aware is that if you open up a 15 to 17 HCP hand with your five-card major and your partner doesn't have support, your pair will conceivably end up playing the contract in No Trump. However, your partner could easily be the one to bid the No Trump, so the strong hand will be displayed as dummy whereas the weak hand will be playing it. This is not a disaster, but it's better to have the strong hand concealed.

Alternatively, if you open up 1 No Trump, and your partner has a weak hand but three in your major, you're not going to find your eight-card major suit fit; so, you'll be playing the hand in the wrong contract. This is the beauty of Bridge. Sometimes what you do is correct. Another time with the same hand it might be incorrect.

Now, stop reading. Deal, bid, and play some hands, using what you have learned in Chapters 1 through 6.

Alert

Play with consistency. If you choose to open all hands with a five-card major with 1 of the major, then do so, but then you should always open a hand with five-card majors the same way. One of the worst things you can do is be inconsistent. As long as your partner knows what she can count on when you bid, you should be okay.

The Least You Need to Know

◆ Opening suit bids at the 1 level contain at least 13 total points.

◆ Open the longest suit if two suits are at least five cards in length; Open the higher-ranking suit if both are five or six cards in length.

◆ Open a major suit only if it contains at least five cards.

◆ With no five-card major, open the longer minor. If both minors are equal in length, open 1 Diamond if both minors have four cards, open 1 Club if both minors have three cards.

◆ Count HCP and distribution points to determine whether you should open a hand; Deduct a point if a hand contains no Aces and has a 4–3–3–3 shape.

Chapter 7

Thou Shalt Not Pass: Strong Twos

In This Chapter

- ◆ How to open a hand of more than 22 points
- ◆ How to respond when your partner opens a Strong Two
- ◆ How to rebid when you open a Strong Two

Now you know how to open hands that contain 15 to 17 HCP, 20 to 21 HCP, and hands that contain at least 13 points but fewer than 22 points. As Peggy Lee asked, "Is that all there is?"

No, Peggy, there's more. Sometimes you get hands that contain more than 21 points. Statistically you'll get a hand like this, with more than 21 points, about one hand out of every 200 you play. That sounds like a lot, but it really isn't. I play approximately 100 hands a week. You might not play as often as I do, but the game is going to grab you and you'll play hundreds, if not thousands, of hands a year. You're going to get hands like these occasionally, and you have to know how to handle them.

There are two basic ways to handle big hands: Weak Two and Strong Two. When Charles Goren wrote his last, huge volume on the game in

1985, he incorporated the five-card major bidding system you're learning here. He also incorporated the Weak Two bidding system.

Alert _____

Because there are so many different systems, whenever you play with a new partner or new opponents, it is wise to ask them what systems they play before the game starts. That way you will know in advance what their bids mean, or if they mean something different than what your bids mean.

In this chapter, you're going to learn the Strong Two system for showing big hands. Most modern players use Weak Twos, but in this book you're learning how to play Rubber Bridge, and most Rubber Bridge players play Strong Twos. In case you want to learn Weak Twos as well, I've included Chapter 23 on the Weak Two system. Because most of the players you will encounter in Rubber Bridge will be playing Strong Twos, it's better for you to learn Strong Twos now and Weak Twos later. If you only know Weak Twos, it will limit the number of partners with whom you can play.

Definition of a Strong Two

A Strong Two is a hand that is of one of two types. It is either …

◆ A hand containing at least 22 points; or

◆ A hand that guarantees $8^1/_2$ tricks if trump is a major suit or $9^1/_2$ tricks if trump is a minor suit. Put another way, if you have a hand with which you know you can make at least one trick less than game with no help from your partner, you should open it with a Strong Two, regardless of the number of points you hold.

When you open a Strong Two, your partner is required to keep bidding until one of you bids game, unless you rebid your opening suit. In that case, your partner may pass. This prevents your partner from passing the hand out short of game, thereby emasculating your big, 1-in-200 hand by playing it in a partscore.

Hands Containing 22 Points with a Five-Card Suit

If you open a Strong Two in Diamonds, Hearts, or Spades, you are guaranteeing that your suit contains at least five cards, and that your hand contains at least 22 points. Look at the following hand:

♠ AKQJT9
♥ AKQJ
♦ A8
♣ 7

This is a typical Strong Two Spade opening hand.

You might be looking at this hand, remembering what you've learned, and asking yourself, "This hand is *cold* for 4 Spades. Why not just open 4 Spades? Why open at a lower level?"

If you asked yourself this question, I like the way you're thinking. But there are reasons why you don't just open 4 Spades with this hand. One is that an opening of 4 Spades shows a different hand, as you will learn in the next chapter.

Lingo

Cold is a slang term meaning an easily makeable contract.

Another reason is something we've hinted at before—the possibility of *slam*. Sure, 4 Spades is cold. But you might be able to make more. If your partner has the Ace of Clubs or the King of Diamonds, 6 Spades is cold. If she has both, 7 Spades is cold. So why bid 4 Spades, a bid that your partner can pass? The opening bid of 2 Spades basically tells your partner, "Look, pard, I can make 4 Spades pretty easily with only a little help from you. I want you to tell me about your hand to see if we can make slam."

Another reason is something we'll discuss in detail in the next chapter. You don't want to constrain your ability to communicate with your partner by getting the bidding too high when you might be able to make slam with a little communication between you.

A more typical 2-level opening would be the following hand:

♠ AKQ42
♥ AKQ
♦ AT6
♣ 83

That's a 23-point hand, but if your partner has a Yarborough and is short in Spades, you only have seven cold tricks, although with a five-card Spade suit like this you can generally count on at least four Spades, which would elevate it to eight tricks. You have to open this 2 Spades. Game is not cold. You need information from your partner. But you don't want your partner to pass. Maybe your partner has five Clubs including the Queen-Jack along with four Diamonds. If that's all she has, you should make 3 No Trump if she doesn't have three Spades in her hand.

The point is this: You must tell her what you have so she can evaluate her hand and tell you whether or not she has a trick or two, or three Spades in her hand, or both. An opening at the 2 level allows your partner to reevaluate her hand. A hand that looked terrible when she first looked at it can suddenly look surprisingly powerful when her partner opens with a Strong Two. Look at the following hand in responder:

North

♠ AKQ42

♥ AKQ

♦ AT6

♣ 83

South (Responder)

♠ J32

♥ 985

♦ K652

♣ 542

Is that a stinkeroo, or what? But look at the first hand I described, the 27-point hand that opened 2 Spades. Your King of Diamonds and Jack of Spades make this hand cold for 6 Spades! Because you have three Spades to the Jack in your hand, it's almost certain your partner won't lose a Spade trick. She can't lose a Heart trick. Your King of Diamonds ensures she won't lose a Diamond trick. Her only loser is her singleton Club.

A 2 Spades opening allows you to say, "Hey, this stinkeroo is starting to smell like Joy perfume! I've got three of my partner's trump with an honor, and the King of Diamonds. We could be going someplace here!" Without the 2 Spades opening, just hope you get the contract in as low a Spade bid as you can.

Balanced Hands with 22 or More Points

If you open a Strong Two in Clubs, your hand either contains 22 points and five Clubs, or it contains 22 points and is balanced, without a five-card suit. If it contains five Clubs, it's no different from the Spade hands discussed earlier, and the bidding is made the same way.

Bridgebit
A hand with 24 HCP and 27 total points can't really be thought of as *typical*. A 24 HCP hand occurs approximately once out of every 2,000 hands.

But if it's balanced without a five-card suit, there's an entirely different way to bid this. Take the following hand as an example:

♠ AQJ

♥ AK53

♦ AQ87

♣ K6

You can't open this hand in any of the No Trump bids we've discussed. Do you remember why? *You can't lie to your partner*, that's why. You've agreed with your partner that an opening bid of 1 No Trump promises between 15 to 17 HCP, no more, no less. An opening bid of 2 No Trump promises between 20 to 21 HCP, no more, no less. An opening bid of 3 No Trump promises between 25 to 26 HCP. When you make a No Trump opening, you cannot be outside the range promised, either below *or* above.

This hand has 23 HCP, 24 total points with the doubleton Club. You cannot open it in No Trump. You cannot open it in any other suit bid because any opening in Diamonds, Hearts, or Spades at the 2 level promises a five-card suit.

Lingo

A **waiting bid** is one that says nothing about the suit bid, but is forced by your partner's opening bid. A response of 2 Diamonds to a Strong Two Club open just says to your partner, "I don't have a five-card suit headed by the King-Jack, so tell me more about your hand."

This is where the Strong Two Club bid comes into play. You open this hand 2 Clubs. Then, if your partner responds with a suit you can't support, you respond 2 No Trump. I'll cover responses to Strong Two openings in the next section of this chapter.

An opening bid of 2 Clubs, followed by a fairly standard response of 2 Diamonds, a *waiting bid* (explained below), and a rebid of 2 No Trump tells your partner that opener has a balanced, 22 to 24 point hand with no singletons or voids and no more than two doubletons.

Now bid the following hands:

	1.	2.	3.	4.	5.
♠	AKQJ874	J7	A	A	86
♥	A6	AKQJ	86	KQJT	KQT
♦	A5	AKQJ	AKQT9874	865	AKQ
♣	87	J76	A8	AKQJ8	KQJ98

Hand 1: 2 Spades. Even though this hand only contains 21 points, you can take nine tricks—seven Spade tricks and your two Aces—so it can be opened at 2 Spades.

Hand 2: 2 Clubs. You have 22 points, but no five-card suit. So open 2 Clubs and rebid 2 No Trump if your partner bids a suit you can't support.

Hand 3: 2 Diamonds. Like Hand 1, this contains only 21 points, but you can take 10 tricks—8 Diamonds and your 2 Aces.

Hand 4: 2 Clubs. You can open 2 Clubs with a five-card Club suit. You tell your partner that you are not opening up a balanced hand without a five-card suit at

2 Clubs by not bidding 2 No Trump at your next bid. Instead you will bid your other suit of four cards or better, 2 Hearts, promising your partner at least four Hearts and that your Club suit is longer than your Heart suit. You'll learn more about opener's rebids in Chapter 13.

Lingo

A **Strong Two** is sometimes referred to as a **demand bid**, meaning that opener is *demanding* that your partner keep the bidding open. Some people refer to it as a *two demand*.

Hand 5: 2 No Trump. This is a 21-point hand with 20 HCP. You can't make a two demand because you don't have enough points.

The difference between opening 2 of a suit and opening 2 No Trump is that 2 No Trump is not a *demand bid*. Your partner may pass an opening bid of 2 No Trump, but she may not pass an opening bid of 2 in a suit.

Responding to Strong Two Openings

First rule: You may not pass after your partner opens a 2 bid if your RHO has passed. If you value your life, you won't pass. I once opened 2 Spades. My LHO passed. My partner passed! My RHO passed. I almost fell off my chair. "You can't pass when I open 2 Spades," I said. "But I only had 1 point," my partner replied. "I had 25 points, you had 1. 25 plus 1 equals 26. 26 equals game." "I'm never going to bid a 1 point hand," she replied. We never played together again. Bridge players take this commitment seriously.

Think about it, gentle reader. If your partner has a huge hand, more than half the points in the deck, you probably won't have much. But that doesn't mean that you don't have much between you. As I told my ex-partner, 25 + 1 = game. *When your partner opens a 2-level bid, you don't need much to make game.*

So when are you off the hook? When may you pass? Answer:

♦ You may pass when the partnership has bid game; or

♦ When opener rebids her suit.

The corollary to this rule is this:

If opener bids a new suit, partner must bid again.

Opener is definitely in control of this hand. Responder must respect opener's bidding. No matter how terrible responder's hand, unless opener lets her off the hook by bidding game or by rebidding her suit, responder must keep the bidding open.

Responder may bid her own suit, but she must have a five-card suit with at least King-Jack. However, if she responds to an opening 2-level bid with a suit bid of her own (other than a 2 Diamonds response to a 2 Clubs open, which is a semiautomatic bid that both have agreed says nothing about Diamonds, which I'll explain later), she is making a 100 percent game-forcing bid. Whereas a Strong Two opener can stop short of game by rebidding her suit, if you, as responder, bid a new suit at your first bid, you and your partner have agreed you will not stop short of game.

Lingo

A **forcing bid** is a bid that requires your partner to make a bid other than Pass if there is no intervening bid. It *forces* your partner to keep the bidding open so you can make another bid when it comes back to you.

Weak Response to Opening 2 Bids in Diamonds, Hearts, and Spades

If you have absolutely nothing, you respond to your partner's Strong Two opening bid in Diamonds, Hearts, or Spades with a bid of 2 No Trump. This implies that it is a negative response, so your partner immediately suspects you are holding dreck. She doesn't know it for sure, but it's a strong suspicion.

Opener *cannot pass* a 2 No Trump response by you. This is important because a 2 No Trump response does not absolutely promise a terrible hand. You might have a balanced hand with some points but without trump support for your partner's opening bid. What then? You would have to respond 2 No Trump. So 2 No Trump is a bid that warns your partner you might not have much, but still holds out the hope that you do have something. This is why your partner must bid again. A response of 2 No Trump can be interpreted as asking your partner to bid her second suit if she has one. But it must be a four-card suit. Let's look at a hand held by responder:

♠ 53
♥ 9864
♦ 765
♣ 8742

Phew! But your partner opens 2 Spades—your worst fear. Not much to think about, right? You respond 2 No Trump, saying, "My hand smells to high heaven, but do you have another suit because a five-card Spade suit won't work?"

Your partner rebids 3 Hearts, telling you she has at least four Hearts (and probably denying that she has six Spades, because, as you will learn in the section on rebids by opening bidder later in this chapter, she can rebid a six-card suit). Hearts is a new suit, so you have to bid again. Since you do have Heart support, and you know you have at least eight Hearts between you, you can bid 4 Hearts.

Rules for Responding to Strong Two Opening Bids in Diamonds, Hearts, or Spades

There are at least seven things you should know about responding to a Strong Two opening bid in Diamonds, Hearts, or Spades.

◆ You cannot pass.

◆ If you have a five-card suit headed by the King and Jack, you should bid it.

◆ If you do not have a five-card suit but you do have at least one King, and if you also have three-card support for your partner's opening suit, you should raise immediately. It is worth noting here that when you have a fit, a singleton in an outside suit becomes as valuable as a King. You'll learn more about responding in Chapter 10.

◆ The only circumstance under which you may pass after your first response is if you respond 2 No Trump and your partner rebids her opening suit.

◆ If you bid your own suit in response to your partner's opening bid you must keep the bidding open to game, even if your partner rebids her suit.

◆ You cannot support opener's second suit unless you have at least four cards in it.

◆ If your RHO bids, you may pass.

Bid these hands with your partner opening 2 Diamonds:

1. ♠ KJ863	2. ♠ 86	3. ♠ KJ76	4. ♠ A4	5. ♠ 9865
♥ 863	♥ QT742	♥ 874	♥ T9632	♥ Q63
♦ J74	♦ 98	♦ JT9	♦ JT3	♦ 42
♣ T7	♣ QJT4	♣ 842	♣ 632	♣ 8542

Hand 1: 2 Spades. You have a five-card Spade suit headed by the King-Jack and 6 points. This is a perfect hand with which to make a positive response. Your partner is promising at least 22 points, and you have 6 points. You should have game somewhere, so your bid forces opener to keep the bidding open to game, and you promise the opener that you'll keep the bidding open to game.

Hand 2: 2 No Trump. Even though you have 7 points, you can't bid your five-card Heart suit because it is headed by less than the King-Jack. You have a very good hand and intend to tell your partner about it after her rebid. Remember, a 2 No Trump response does not promise a terrible hand; it only implies it. Opener cannot pass your bid of 2 No Trump.

Hand 3: 3 Diamonds. You can't bid your Spades because you don't have five. But you do have three-card support for opener's suit, so you should tell her this.

Hand 4: 3 Diamonds again. You can't bid your Hearts because they aren't strong enough, but you do have three Diamonds and an Ace.

Hand 5: 2 No Trump. This is a stinkeroo. The only thing that could save it would be for her to rebid her Diamonds, in which case you could pass, or for her to bid Spades at her second bid, in which case you could go to 4 Spades because you'd be assured of a 4–4 Spade fit.

Bidding Sequence

Let's look at a bidding sequence when responder has a Yarborough. This is your hand when you hear your partner open 2 Spades:

♠ 986
♥ 875
♦ 954
♣ 9832

Partner	You
2 Spades (1)	2 No Trump (2)
3 Diamonds (3)	3 Spades (4)
4 Clubs (5)	4 Spades (6)
Pass (7)	

(1) I've got a *great* hand with at least five Spades.

(2) I'm glad yours is good. Mine stinks.

(3) I've also got a Diamond suit. At least four of them. I don't care how bad your hand is, I *insist* you bid again.

(4) Okay. I do have some support for your Spade suit. I'm still not happy about this and would like to pass next time. Can I pass?

(5) I'm glad to hear about your Spade support. I've also got something in Clubs. No, you can't pass because we can definitely make at least game. Can you give me any help? We may have a slam!

(6) If I've said this once, I've said it a million times. I have absolutely no interest in slam. So far as I can tell we can't make anything. I have no help for you except three Spades. Please, can we pass?

(7) Pass. Okay, pard. I trust you.

This was your partner's hand:

♠ AKQJT
♥ A
♦ AKJ7
♣ AK8

She bid it well. She communicated with you as agreed. She could continue to bid with complete confidence that you would not pass her out in either of her secondary suits, Diamonds and Clubs, so long as she continued to bid new suits.

After you had established Spades as your agreed-upon trump, all of your partner's remaining bids were simply to tell you that she had strength in these suits. If you had anything at all in those suits, you would have supported them and she would have ended up in slam. All you needed was the Queen of Clubs or the Queen of Diamonds and the hand was cold for 6 Spades.

This is a classic example of how partners must trust one another. Your partner trusted you to continue to bid as long as she bid a new suit. She could bid a four-card suit, Diamonds, knowing that you'd bid again. She could bid a three-card suit, Clubs, knowing that you'd bid again. See what a disaster it would have been if you had four Clubs and passed her 4 Club bid because you thought your hand was terrible and wanted to "save" her?

You trusted her by continuing to bid. Your hand was awful, but you continued to bid in response to her forcing bids. That was your agreement. You cannot make unilateral decisions and nullify your agreements with your partner. If you've agreed upon a system, like continuing to bid when your partner opens a Strong Two whenever your partner bids a new suit, you must comply with that agreement, regardless of your interpretation of the strength of your hand.

Finally, she trusted your weak responses and closed out at 4 Spades. Many people with less trust in their partners would ignore all the negative information you had transmitted, and *unilaterally* gone on to slam by themselves, to their ultimate chagrin.

Response to Strong Two Club Opening

When your partner opens a Strong Two in Clubs, your responses change. You can still bid a decent five-card suit headed by at least the King–Jack. But your negative, or *waiting* response is now 2 Diamonds, not 2 No Trump.

The reason 2 Diamonds is used as a waiting bid is to keep the bidding low so opener can describe her hand at the lowest level possible. Because opener would have opened with a bid of her five-card suit, her response is almost always 2 No Trump when you bid 2 Diamonds. About the only time her response is not 2 No Trump is when she has opened a five-card or better Club suit.

Rules for Responding to Strong Two Club Opening Bid

The following list explains what you should know about responding to the Strong Two Club opening bid:

◆ You cannot pass an opening bid of 2 Clubs.

◆ If you have a five-card suit headed by the King–Jack or better, you should bid it.

◆ If you don't have a five-card suit headed by the King–Jack, you must bid 2 Diamonds as a waiting bid, regardless of the strength or length of your Diamond suit.

◆ If opener rebids 2 No Trump, she is telling you she has a balanced hand with 22 to 24 points. You may pass with less than 3 points.

◆ As long as opener bids a new suit, you must continue bidding if your RHO passes the bid to you.

◆ If RHO bids, you may pass.

◆ You cannot support opener's second suit unless you have at least four cards in it.

◆ If opener responds 2 No Trump to your 2 Diamonds waiting bid, the hand is treated as if opener opened a No Trump bid, and you respond in accordance with Chapter 9 on No Trump responses.

◆ Make a note here that No Trump response systems are *on* when opener rebids 2 No Trump after a Strong Two Clubs open. You don't know what this means yet. You will learn about this in Chapter 14, and at that time this will make sense to you.

If opener opens 2 Clubs and then bids a new suit after you make your 2 Diamonds waiting bid, what does that tell you about her hand? Think about it before you answer, because this is the type of question you should always be asking yourself in Bridge.

What does it tell you? It tells you that she opened up a Club suit with at least five cards in it, that she probably has at least four of the suit she bid at her second opportunity, and that she has more Clubs than she has of her second suit. She has not opened up a balanced 22+ point hand. That's quite a lot of information, don't you think?

Example Hands Responding to Strong Two Club Opening Bid

Your partner opens with a bid of 2 Clubs. How do you respond with the following hands?

1. ♠ KJ75	2. ♠ T974	3. ♠ KJ983	4. ♠ 3	5. ♠ 87
♥ QT864	♥ QJ97	♥ 986	♥ 9854	♥ 863
♦ KJ7	♦ 4	♦ 96	♦ 973	♦ T9865
♣ 9	♣ QJ98	♣ KT8	♣ KQ965	♣ 983

Hand 1: 2 Diamonds. You don't have a five-card suit headed by the King-Jack, so 2 Diamonds is your only bid. Your Heart suit, which has five cards headed by two honors (the Queen–Ten) isn't strong enough, and your Spade suit, headed by the King-Jack isn't long enough. So 2 Diamonds just says, "I'm here. Tell me more."

Hand 2: 2 Diamonds. This bid says nothing about your Diamond suit. It just says that you are complying with your agreement to keep the bidding open, but denies that you have a five-card suit headed by the King–Jack.

Hand 3: 2 Spades. You have a good five-card suit headed by the King–Jack and 8 points. That's plenty good enough to tell your partner what you have.

CAUTION

Alert

A 2 Diamond response to an opening bid of 2 Clubs is automatic if you don't have a five-card suit headed by the King–Jack. It can be negative or neutral. It just keeps the bidding open for your partner to further describe her hand.

Hand 4: 3 Clubs. Any five-card suit headed by two of the top three honors is worth an immediate bid even if it's Clubs. The reason: If you bid 2 Diamonds first, planning on showing 3 Clubs later, the Strong Two bidder won't realize your suit is this good! You may be bidding 3 Clubs for lack of anything better on QJTx4, or KT9xx.

Hand 5: 2 Diamonds. You're not bidding your five-card Diamond suit. You're just keeping the bidding open. If your RHO bids after your partner's 2 Clubs opening bid, you should pass because you have no obligation to make a free bid (discussed in Chapter 10) that would indicate a fairly good hand. The obligation to bid only arises in the situation where opener's bid could be passed around to her. Because opener will have another opportunity to bid over RHO's bid, you need not bid. Your pass after RHO's bid communicates your weakness to her.

Rebids by Strong Two Bidder in Diamonds, Hearts, or Spades

After you've opened a Strong Two bid, you must continue to describe your hand to your partner until the two of you have arrived at a decision as to what the best contract is. Because the bidding has started at a high level, however, there isn't a lot of bidding space for you to communicate.

So the first thing you do is evaluate your partner's response:

- ◆ Did she bid a new suit? If so, you know she has at least a five-card suit headed by at least the King–Jack.

- ◆ Did she raise your suit? If so, you know she's probably working on a minimum, which, at this level, isn't much, but she has at least three cards in your suit.

- ◆ Did she bid 2 No Trump? Then you know that she probably (but not definitely) has a hand without an Ace or a King and she has less than 4 points. With a Yarborough—no card higher than a Nine—but three-card support for your partner's suit, after a Strong Two opening, don't raise your partner's suit. Bid 2 No Trump first, then show your support for your partner's suit at your second response. Raising immediately to 3 Spades shows that you have a little something in addition to your three-card support. So you must evaluate what you know from your partner's response.

Some Rules for Rebids

Here are two rules for rebid by opener in 2 Diamonds, Hearts, or Spades:

1. If your partner has given you a positive response by bidding a new suit, it is forcing to game, so you can never pass until game is reached. Even rebidding your suit is forcing your partner to bid because she has made the bid that forces your pair to game.

2. If you bid a new suit, it is forcing on your partner for one round. The only time your partner may pass you is if you rebid No Trump or rebid your own suit.

Here are two rules for rebid by Strong Two Club opener:

1. If your partner has made a 2 Diamond waiting bid, any bid of a suit by you shows a second suit shorter than your Club suit. The second suit may be only four cards in length.

2. A response of 2 No Trump shows 22 to 24 HCP and a balanced hand, whereas a response of 3 No Trump shows 27 to 28 HCP and a balanced hand. Any No Trump rebid by a 2 Club opener usually implies that opener doesn't have a long Club suit.

With this in mind, look at the following hand:

♠ AKQJT4
♥ AKQ7
♦ A8
♣ 4

After your 2 Spades opening bid, your partner responds 2 No Trump. Now what? If you rebid your strong six-card Spade suit, your partner may pass. You don't want that to occur because you have a cold game in your hand.

You can bid 4 Spades, but you don't need to do that yet. Remember, *you are in control.* Your partner may not pass if you bid a new suit. And you have a four-card major you can bid, Hearts. So, you bid 3 Hearts. This bid is forcing, but it only promises a four-card suit.

Lingo

To **pull trump** or to **draw trump** means for declarer to lead trump until opponents have no more trump in their hands. It's a standard method of playing a hand, and you'll learn all about it in Chapter 20.

If your partner raises your Hearts, she is promising a four-card suit. *Responder cannot raise opener's second suit without at least four cards in it.* If she raises Hearts, then just play it in 4 Hearts and don't worry about your six Spades. They'll come in very handy after you *pull trump.*

If your partner responds 3 No Trump or 4 of a minor to your Heart bid, you can return to 4 Spades at that time. That puts you in game and is a bid that your partner may pass.

Playing 3 No Trump After Opening a Strong Two Bid in Diamonds, Hearts, or Spades

Sometimes when you have a long suit and an unbalanced hand, 3 No Trump is still your best contract. Look at the following:

♠ 9
♥ AKQ76
♦ AQJT
♣ AK6

You	Partner
2 Hearts (1)	2 Spades (2)
3 Diamonds (3)	3 Hearts (4)
3 No Trump (5)	Pass (6)

(1) I've got a *terrific* hand with at least five Hearts.

(2) I've got something. In fact, I've got at least five Spades and they are headed by not less than the King–Jack.

(3) I've got at least four Diamonds. Do we have a fit in either Hearts or Diamonds? Give me a preference.

(4) Okay, of the two suits, I prefer Hearts to Diamonds, but I'm not promising great Heart support, maybe only two.

(5) I've shown you everything I have. Your five-card Spade suit is interesting but I don't have more than two. I don't know how many Hearts you have. I'm satisfied to play this in 3 No Trump but if you have three Hearts, take the bid to 4 Hearts. Because you know my hand is exceptionally good, I am relying on you to take it to a higher level if you have more in your hand than the decent Spade suit you have already told me about.

(6) I've told you all I can. I only have two Hearts. Let's play it in 3 No Trump.

Your partner's hand?

♠ KQ986
♥ 75
♦ 97
♣ Q873

In 3 No Trump you have three Heart tricks, three Diamond tricks, three Club tricks, and Spades stopped twice. You should make at least 4 No Trump, but you will definitely make 3.

Stop reading. Deal, bid, and play some hands, using what you've learned in Chapters 1 through 7.

The Least You Need to Know

◆ A Strong Two bid is a hand containing at least 22 points or can take 8 tricks in a major or 9 tricks in a minor.

◆ An opening bid of 2 Clubs may either be a Club suit or a balanced hand with 22 to 24 HCP.

◆ Strong Two bids are forcing to game unless the suit opened is repeated at the 3 level. A rebid of 2 No Trump after a strong 2 Club opening is nonforcing.

◆ If responder's first bid to a Two Demand in Diamonds, Hearts, or Spades is a new suit it's game forcing.

Chapter 8

When Weakness Is a Weapon: Preemptive Openings

In This Chapter

◆ What a preempt is

◆ Making preemptive bids at levels higher than 2

◆ Rule of 2, 3, and 4

◆ Responses to preemptive opening bids

Now you know how to evaluate and open hands that contain at least 13 points. But sometimes you have a hand that doesn't have 13 points, but contains qualities that should be described to your partner. This chapter tells you what these hands are, how to evaluate them, and how to bid them.

We're talking preempts now! This is real down and dirty because a preempt is a defensive bid. Essentially you're trying to foul up your opponents. You basically don't have a very good hand, but your hand does possess the qualities that can allow you to throw a monkey wrench into your opponents' bidding. Ah, preempts are a lot of fun!

A Concise Description of a Nonopening Hand

From what you've just read, you should now be able to deduce what kind of hand *not* to open at the 1 level. You shouldn't open if you don't have at least 13 points. Basically, if you pick up your cards and count your points and they don't add up to at least 13, you are probably going to pass.

But what if you have a long suit, and not much else? Is there any value in communicating this to your partner? And, if so, how do you do it? "Pass" doesn't tell her much, except that you don't have 13 points.

But what happens if one of your opponents has 13 points and a five-card Club suit headed by the Ace–King, and you open 3 Diamonds in front of him? He had a hand that he would have clearly opened 1 Club. But you've bid 3 Diamonds! What's he to do? Is his hand worth bidding 4 Clubs when he has no idea what his partner has? It puts him in a terrible dilemma. You could steal a bid at 3 Diamonds when they could, conceivably, have a game. You've kept them from finding the game by starting the bidding at a level that makes it dangerous for them to bid.

What Is a Preempt?

A *preemptive bid* is one that is made at a high level. It is made with a hand with a long suit and not many HCP. Its purpose is to constrict opponents, who may have most of the HCP, and make it more difficult for them to find their contract. Plus, if your partner has the right cards, a preempt can let you play a game your way!

Point and Suit Quality Requirements

When you are in first or second seat, your preempts should be fairly disciplined. You should promise at least a good suit, headed by two of the top five honors in the suit, and some values, but not much.

You shouldn't preempt when you have more than 9 HCP. Why? What you've learned here is that you should open a hand at the 1 level if you have 13 points. If you have a seven-card suit and 10 HCP, you must have at least 13 points, which would require an opening at the 1 level instead of a preempt. Look at the following hand:

♠ AKQJ873
♥ 87
♦ 75
♣ 52

You have 10 HCP. You have three doubletons, each of which is worth a point. That's 13 points. Open 1 Spade. Even if the six non-Spade cards are changed around so you have a different combination of singletons and voids, your hand will always add up to 13 points. A hand with 10 HCP that includes a seven-card suit will *always* have 13 total points. Thus any hand with a seven-card suit and 10 HCP must be opened at the 1 level.

Look at your partner's possible hand:

♠ 973
♥ AK432
♦ 9
♣ 9876

That's only 9 points, so she passed originally. If you open 3 Spades, she'll probably pass again. If you open 1 Spade, however, she's going to support you because she has 9 points and three Spades. As you'll learn soon in Chapter 10 on responding to opening bids of 1 of a suit, she has to support you with her hand. And you're cold for 4 Spades. If you bid your 10-point hand preemptively, you're preempting yourselves out of a cold game. You must have all of the following in order to open a suit at the 3 level:

- A seven-card suit

- A suit headed by at least the Queen–Ten

- 4 to 9 HCP

- No *outside* Ace

- Not more than one outside King

- When opening in a minor suit, no four-card major

Lingo

Any honor in a suit other than your long suit is said to be **outside**. So if your long suit were Hearts and you had the Ace of Spades, it would be an *outside Ace*.

Preempts Are Effective—Making an Opponent's Life Miserable

Think how you feel when you look at a terrific, 15-point hand with five Hearts. You're in the second seat and you're just salivating to get into this hand, when you hear your RHO say, "3 Spades." Wow! What do you do? You know he's weak with seven Spades, but where are the HCP in this hand? Do you just bid 4 Hearts—

game—with 15 points? Maybe your LHO is sitting there with 15 points, too, and he's just waiting to pounce on you.

This is just an example of how preempting can really throw the next bidder (in this case, you) for a loop! Your RHO really caught you off guard; you're not sure what to do now. Here's another scenario that shows a preempt's effectiveness. The evening before I wrote this, I was playing against two very good players. The bidding went, pass, pass, and I opened up a 6-point hand with a seven-card Club suit headed by the Ace–Queen at 3 Clubs. My LHO made a bid called a *takeout double*.

He had 19 points and three Hearts. When my partner passed, his partner had to bid, so he bid 3 Hearts. At this point, because he had to start at such a high level, his partner's hand was pretty much undefined. He didn't know if he had 0 points or 9, four Hearts or five. He had the Ace–Queen–Jack of Hearts, so he went to 4 Hearts. They went down four tricks because his partner, who had been forced to bid, had only 4 points and four Hearts! Had I not opened up at the 3 level, they probably would have found a partscore in the right contract. Because of my preemptive bid, they got a terrible result.

Lingo

You will learn later that a **takeout double** is a forcing bid that requires the partner to bid, regardless of the strength of his hand.

That's the value of a 3-level preempt. It makes life miserable for the opponents because it raises the level of the bidding so high. Because you are opening on a seven-card suit, and some values, you might be set a couple of tricks if you get the contract. But you might find your partner with some values, and make three, stealing a game from your opponents.

First Position Opening

Any preemptive bid constrains subsequent bidders, including your partner. So when you are in first seat, you should be aware that nobody has bid yet. But in first seat, the numbers are still with you because while you are constraining three people, two of them are your opponents. As former UCLA and Los Angeles Rams coach, Tommy Prothro once said, "When you put the ball in the air, three things can happen, and two of them are *bad* for your side." So, when you are in first seat, the odds are at least 2–1 in your favor that a substantial portion of the rest of the points will be in your opponents' hands. Therefore, you have more to gain by making a preemptive bid when you're in first seat than when you're in second seat.

Second Position Opening

The numbers change, however, when you are in second seat and your RHO has passed. Now you are preempting only two people, one of whom is your partner. You know that your RHO doesn't have 13 points, and you have a weak hand, so there are probably at least 25 HCP distributed in the two remaining hands, one of whom, as I've said, is your loving partner. She might be waiting over there across the table from you, eager to open this hand 1 No Trump, or, maybe even a two demand, as you learned in Chapter 7. Can you imagine the look you're going to get when you preempt *her* and open 3 Diamonds? Because you already know that one of your opponents, your RHO, has less than an opening hand, a preempt in second seat is less effective than a preempt in first seat. You can do it, but be prepared for your partner's reaction if she's the one with the points.

Third Position Opening

Here's where you can really take a chance. Your partner has already passed, so you know she doesn't have an opening hand. She was in first position and didn't bid. So if your RHO has passed, and you have a seven-card suit and only 5 points, you can rest assured that your LHO has a very good hand indeed. While it's true that both your partner and RHO might have passed 12-point hands, it's not highly probable. So this is where your 3-level preempt is called for, no matter what the strength of your suit.

In third position, there's only one person you are constraining, and that's your opponent, your LHO. You need have no fear that your partner is sitting there with a good hand because she's already told you she doesn't have one. So, basically, the sky's the limit.

Let's say you're looking at a hand with 4 HCP and seven Spades headed by the Queen–Ten. How many points are in the other three hands? Did you say 36, subtracting your 4 HCP from the total of 40 HCP? Well, if you did, you were wrong. You forgot to distinguish between "points" and HCP.

Alert

The weaker your hand in the third seat, the more incentive you should have to make a preemptive bid.

Sure, there are 40 total HCP in a hand, but if you have seven Spades (or seven of any suit), then there are 3 extra points spread around the table. There are only six Spades spread among three hands. That's an average of two per hand. So how many points does that give each of the three other players? If they're evenly divided, 2 points per hand—each of the other players will have 1 distribution point to be added to their HCP. No matter how you divide the cards among the three other players, there must be 3 distribution points in this hand, in addition to the HCP, if you have seven cards in one suit.

So there are 39 points divided among the other three players. Because your partner and RHO have passed, they can't have more than 12 points each, a total of 24. So, your LHO must have at least 15 points in his hand (39–24). What a great time to preempt!

Fourth Position Opening

All the rules change in fourth position. There's no need to preempt because nobody has much of a hand. So why open up a weak hand at the 3 level when you might go set? Why open up at all? You might force your opponents into bidding if you open at the 1 level, and they might find a partscore. Better to pass the hand out. Remember this rule: *Don't open in the fourth seat unless you have a legitimate opening hand.*

Preemptive Openings at the 4 Level

If you need a seven-card suit to open a weak hand at the 3 level, how long must your suit be to open at the 4 level? Did you say eight cards? Right on!

You can open any eight-card suit at the 4 level if it meets all of the following requirements:

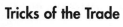

Tricks of the Trade

When you are in fourth seat and nobody has opened in front of you, you have total control of the hand. If you bid, bidding continues and your opponents will each have another opportunity to discover a contract with their subopening hands. If you pass, however, the hand is over; nobody will have another chance to bid.

- At least eight cards in length (is this redundant, or what?)
- At least two of the top four honors (at least King–Jack) in your long suit
- 4 to 9 HCP
- No outside Ace
- Only one outside King
- If opening a minor suit, no four-card major

Again, you must be sensitive to the seat in which you are sitting. In the first or second seat you'll be preempting your partner, as well as your opponents, so you must tell her what you have. There's no problem with preempting at the 4 level in first or second position—just be certain that you have what you say you have. If your partner has a big hand, she can then make a decision whether or not to explore higher bids.

Possible Double

One thing you should be sensitive to when opening at the 4 level in Hearts or Spades is that opponents are more liable to *double* you than if you open at the 3 level. When you open at the 3 level, they would be *doubling you into game*, which, if you made it, would give you a huge bonus.

There is no such fear, however, if you open up in a major at the 4 level because you are bidding game, so the penalty to the opponents for failure is much less. For example, if you are nonvulnerable and bid and make 3 Hearts, doubled, you would get 530 points above and below the line, whereas if you were undoubled you would only get 90 points below the line, a difference of 440 points!

However, if you bid and make 4 Hearts doubled you would only get 590 points above and below the line versus 420 above and below the line undoubled, only 170 points more. So the difference between *doubling into game* versus doubling a game bid is huge. So if you open up a preemptive hand at the 3 level, your opponents will be reluctant to double you because of the huge penalty they will suffer if you make your contract. But if you open up a preemptive hand at the 4 level in a major suit, your opponents will feel freer to double because the penalty for failure is much less. The risk of being doubled is something you should take far more seriously when you open up a preemptive hand in game than if you preempt below game.

Lingo

Double is a call that increases the scoring value of odd tricks or undertricks on an opponent's opening bid. You make it when you believe the opponents have bid too high and that you can set them.

Lingo

Doubling into game means your opponents have doubled what would only be a partial, like 2 Hearts. If you make it, you get the equivalent of 4 Hearts, game, because you have been doubled. Doubling into game is risky, and the penalties for failure are severe.

Preemptive Openings at the 5 Level

Okay, class, if you need a seven-card suit to open a weak hand at the 3 level, and an eight-card suit to open a weak hand at the 4 level, how long must your suit be to open at the 5 level? Can you say "nine cards"?

Well, if you did, you should have qualified it. You can open preemptively at the 5 level only in a minor suit. You should not open a major suit at the 5 level preemptively. Why? Because game in a major suit is only 4, so if you have a nine-card major suit and otherwise satisfy the requirements for a 5-level opening, just open at the 4 level. Why overbid if you don't have to?

Requirements to open a suit at the 5 level are as follows:

Bridgebit
Why the requirement that the hand be weak to open up at high levels, especially when you are opening at game, (4 level for majors and 5 level for minors)? The reason is because of the possibility of a slam. You don't want to preempt your partner because you don't want to preempt yourselves out of finding a slam. As promised, I'll discuss slam bidding in Chapter 15.

- Must be Clubs or Diamonds
- Nine-card suit
- Suit must be headed by at least two of the top four honors (at least King–Jack)
- 4 to 9 HCP
- No outside Ace
- Only one outside King

Rule of 2, 3, and 4

One simple way of determining whether or not to make a preemptive opening is to count your tricks. The *rule of 2, 3, and 4* may be used as a guide for you.

- If you are vulnerable and your opponents are not (this is called *unfavorable vulnerability*) you can overbid your hand by two tricks. That is, if your hand shows you can take seven tricks with your long suit as trump, you can make a preemptive 3-level opening.

- If you and your opponents both have the same vulnerability—either you are both vulnerable or you are both nonvulnerable (this is called *equal vulnerability*)—you can overbid your hand by three tricks. That is, if your hand shows you can take six tricks with your long suit as trump, you can make a preemptive 3-level opening.

◆ If you are not vulnerable and your opponents are (this is called *favorable vulnerability*), you can overbid your hand by four tricks. That is, if your hand shows you can take five tricks with your long suit as trump, you can make a preemptive 3-level opening.

Tricks of the Trade

As a general rule of thumb, you can figure that a good seven-card suit should take five tricks, and eight- and nine-card suits should have a maximum of two losers, regardless of their high card strength. So an eight-card suit should take six tricks, and a nine-card suit should take seven tricks. It doesn't always work out like that, but it will most of the time.

Example hands follow:

Unfavorable Vulnerability	Equal Vulnerability	Favorable Vulnerability
♠ 98	♠ QJT9874	♠ QJT9852
♥ 7	♥ KQ	♥ J85
♦ QJT9642	♦ 865	♦ 74
♣ KQJ	♣ 6	♣ 3

In the unfavorable vulnerability hand, you should have five Diamond tricks and two Club tricks. That's seven tricks, so you can open 3 Diamonds in any seat.

In the equal hand, you have five Spade tricks and a Heart trick for six tricks, so you can open 3 Spades.

In the favorable vulnerability hand, even though you only have 4 HCP, and only 7 total points, you should have five Spade tricks, so open this 3 Spades. There are 36 HCP spread among the other hands. If your partner has a substantial number, she knows that you have seven Spades and can go to 4 Spades if she has outside power and even as little as one Spade in her hand. If the points are in your opponents' hands, however, you have constrained their bidding substantially. The worst that can happen is that you are down 2, for 100 points above the line for them, undoubled.

How to Count Sure Tricks

You count sure tricks the same way you count quick tricks. But in this instance, for the purposes of evaluating your hand under the rule of 2, 3, and 4, you can also count any four-card suit as a trick. So look at the following hand:

♠ QT97653

♥ 7

♦ 8754

♣ Q

This has 4 HCP, but you can count your seven-card trump suit as capable of producing five tricks, and your four-card suit should produce an additional trick, so this should be a six-trick hand that could be opened 3 Spades with favorable or equal vulnerability. In fact, in third seat, you shouldn't hesitate to open this 3 Spades, because it could cause your RHO in fourth seat, who is undoubtedly salivating to open his huge hand with a demand bid, to go ballistic.

Opener's Subsequent Bidding

Under no circumstances should a preemptive opener bid again unless partner makes a forcing bid. You've described your hand to your partner. You have no idea what's in her hand. She knows your hand much better than you know hers. You've told your story. Leave it up to her. If she bids, fine. If she bids a new suit below game, you are forced to bid. Otherwise, stay out of it! It's up to her to place the contract. If she doubles opponents for penalty, trust her. If you haven't lied to her, she should know what to do.

Let's try bidding some hands:

1. ♠ 5	**2.** ♠ 75	**3.** ♠ 873	**4.** ♠ QJ98643	**5.** ♠ J876543
♥ 9832	♥ 84	♥ KJ985432	♥ 76	♥ KQ
♦ KQJ9832	♦ 6	♦ KJ	♦ void	♦ 97
♣ 7	♣ KJ986532	♣ void	♣ KQ87	♣ 87

Alert ____

Remember that whenever you make a preemptive bid, even if you are bidding game, as you are doing in Hand 3, you are showing a weak hand, a hand that does not have enough points to open at the 1 level.

Hand 1: Pass in the first or second seat because you have a four-card major. However, I'd open 3 Diamonds in third seat. You have four Hearts, but only 6 HCP. In third seat your LHO probably has a good hand. It's worth the risk that you and your partner might miss a Heart fit to preempt this hand in third seat only. There are 34 HCP and at least 3 distribution points in the other three hands, a total of 37. If your partner and RHO have the maximum of 12 each, that leaves 13 for LHO. But the odds are that both your partner and LHO don't have

12 each, so your LHO is sitting there with a big hand. Hit him now while you have a chance.

Hand 2: 4 Clubs. Again, count the points. There are 36 HCP and 4 distribution points in the other three hands (five Clubs distributed among three hands equals 4 distribution points no matter how you slice it). So that's 40 points in the other three hands. Because you know your partner and RHO can't have more than 12 each, that leaves a minimum of 16 points in your LHO's hand. Your LHO is undoubtedly sitting there with a big hand.

Tricks of the Trade

Vulnerability is an important factor in evaluating your hand for making a preemptive bid. You have to weigh the risk of constraining your opponents' ability to communicate against the possibility of being doubled and set for a big score above the line against you.

Hand 3: 4 Hearts. The difference between this hand and Hand 2 is that this hand has side strength. And you're opening up in game.

Hand 4: Open this 3 Spades at all levels of vulnerability and in all seats. This is a maximum preempt, because you have 8 HCP, 12 total points. You don't need much help from your partner for game. If your partner has only the Ace of Hearts and the Jack of Clubs, you have a very good shot at game. But if you open 1 Spade, you'd be lying to your partner because you don't have 13 points. A danger in opening Hand 4 with 1 Spade is, not that you don't have ample "playing tricks" to make some number of Spades, but that, when the opponents compete, which they surely will, your partner will "double" them, counting on you for more defensive values.

Hand 5: Pass in first and second seats. Open 3 Spades with equal or favorable vulnerability in third seat. Pass with unfavorable vulnerability. Your suit is very weak, but you can still count on five tricks from it, plus a Heart trick.

Everyone listens to the bidding. When you make a preemptive opening you tell *everybody*, not just your partner, that you have a weak hand. So what you have is no secret.

Responses to Preemptive Openings

How do you respond if your partner makes a preemptive opening? You're going to learn how to respond to opening bids that promise 13 or more points shortly. Because responses to preempts are completely different, I'm going to explain them here. After you finish the book, you'll be able to put it all together.

RONF—Raise Is the Only Nonforcing Bid

If your partner opens with a preemptive bid and you bid anything other than game or to support her suit, she must bid again. If you bid game in a major or 3 No Trump, your partner must pass. If you raise her suit, she can pass. That's all you need to know. Next subject.

Okay, okay, I'll show you some hands because you can get into real trouble when you have a good hand and your partner opens with a preempt, especially when it's short of game. In the following hands, your partner opens 3 Diamonds:

1. ♠ KQ73	2. ♠ K87	3. ♠ AKJ863	4. ♠ K84
♥ KQ73	♥ QJT	♥ AK984	♥ 83
♦ 7	♦ A73	♦ 8	♦ 983
♣ KQ83	♣ QJ83	♣ 7	♣ QJT94
5. ♠ KJ98653	6. ♠ 8		
♥ Q73	♥ KJ84		
♦ void	♦ J52		
♣ Q93	♣ QT942		

Hand 1: Pass. Surprised? Are you saying to yourself, "Wait a minute, I have 15 HCP. This is a terrific hand. I've got all the other suits stopped twice! We can make 3 No Trump." If this is what you're saying, then you have a lot of company. I have partners today who would want to bid 3 No Trump with this hand. But it would be a big, big mistake. Why? Because you have no source of tricks from your partner, that's why. Are you saying, "But she opened 3 Diamonds! She's got Diamond tricks!"? Wrong! She is telling you she has a *weak* hand! Because she opened in first or second seat (you would have opened if you were bidding before her!), she is only promising you a suit headed by the King–Jack and 4 points. That's her minimum. Would you want to play this in 3 No Trump and see the following hand come down from her?

♠ 652

♥ 8

♦ KJ86542

♣ 62

Can you make 3 No Trump with these two hands? If so, you are ready for the Bridge Hall of Fame. But this hand is all your partner is promising you when she opens 3 Diamonds in first seat. Never lose sight of the fact that the primary message your partner is sending you when she makes a preemptive opening is

"My hand is *weak!*" She might be at the top of her bid, 9 points, but you can't count on that. You have to count on her having a minimum when you respond, especially when you respond in game.

In addition to the fact that you will have a hard time making 3 No Trump, you've got a terrific defensive hand. If opponents compete and bid anything else at the 3 or 4 level, you have a great chance of setting them because you've got length and strength in all the other suits. So just sit back and reap the rewards! This is a hand where you pass and pray that your opponents bid. You want them playing this hand, even though they will know that you have the power.

Hand 2: 3 No Trump. Fooled you! Now you must really be confused. Why can't you bid 3 No Trump on the first hand, that has 15 HCP, but can bid 3 No Trump on this hand with only 14 HCP? The answer is because you have good Diamond support for partner's bid. She has promised *at least* KJxxxxx of Diamonds. You have Axx. You should be able to take at least six Diamond tricks, probably seven if the Diamonds don't split 3–0. And you have *transportation*, because, in addition to the Ace of Diamonds, you have two small Diamonds to lead to the dummy.

> **Lingo**
>
> **Transportation** is the ability to get the lead back and forth between declarer's hand and the dummy. In Hand 1 you have no transportation to dummy, because you only have one Diamond and no other way to get back to dummy, because dummy has no other *entries*. An **entry** is a card that enables you to get the lead into a specific hand.

Hand 3: 3 Spades. This is a hand where you want to be playing in game, either 4 Hearts or 4 Spades. So you bid 3 Spades. This forces your partner to bid again because if you bid a new suit it is *forcing*, remember? So, unless your partner bids 4 Spades, you're going to bid 4 Hearts at your next call. This tells your partner, "I want to play this in 4 Hearts or 4 Spades, so take your pick. If she has two in one suit and one in the other, she will pick the one in which she has two. If her best suit is Hearts, she passes 4 Hearts. If it's Spades, she bids 4 Spades. If she has relatively equivalent holdings in both, she should choose your first bid suit, Spades, because you should have an equal number or longer Spades. Under no circumstances can she take the contract to 5 Diamonds. She must trust you to know you have power in your two suits.

Hand 4: 4 Diamonds. Remember the title of this section: "RONF—Raise Is the Only Nonforcing Bid." You have a five-card Club suit that might be able to be developed as a source for tricks, shortness in Hearts, the King of Spades, and three trumps. So you should make a competitive bid to restrict your opponents' bidding space. And your partner has a fair chance of making it, depending on her hand.

Hand 5: Pass. Sure, you'd rather play this in 3 Spades than 3 Diamonds. But you can't make a preemptive bid over your partner's preemptive opening. If you bid 3 Spades, it's a forcing bid that tells your partner you have a big hand. You don't. That's the risk one takes when making a preemptive opening. Your partner may have a better preempt. If your partner makes a preemptive opening and you have this type of hand, you just have to ride it out and let her play it in a less favorable contract. Remember this rule: When your partner preempts, you cannot make a preemptive bid in another long suit. And this is true even if you're void in your partner's suit. Don't try to save her.

Hand 6: 4 Diamonds. There are two instances in which a raise of her suit is a good idea. The first was Hand 4, where you had a nice outside five-card suit you might be able to develop and three-card trump support. The second is if you have a singleton with at least three trump, which is what you have here in Hand 6. Shortness in an outside suit doesn't help you much if you are also short in trump. But if you have at least three trump, your partner should be able to get at least one, maybe two tricks by trumping your short suit in dummy.

Stop reading. Deal, bid, and play some hands, using what you've learned in Chapters 1 through 8.

The Least You Need to Know

- Use rule of 2, 3, and 4 to determine whether to make a preemptive open.

- A 3-level opening bid shows a seven-card suit headed by at least the Queen–Ten.

- An opening 3-level preempt contains no outside Ace and not more than one outside King.

- A 3-level preempt contains 4 to 9 HCP.

- Raise is the only nonforcing response.

- Preemptive opener may not bid again.

Part 3

Responses to Opening Bids

After your partner has made her initial description of her hand, it's up to you to respond. If her opening bid was a No Trump bid, your response will tell her that you have taken control of the hand. Instead of telling her what you have, you'll be asking her for a more specific description of her hand so you can place the final contract. This section will tell you how to evaluate your hand in light of her opening No Trump bid.

If her opening bid was in a suit, your response will tell her the most about your hand that you can with one bid. In this section, you'll learn how you must respond depending on the values in your hand and the opening bid she has made. You'll also learn about forcing bids, weak bids, bids that show support, and bids that deny support.

Taking Control: Responses to No Trump Openings

In This Chapter

- ◆ When to pass
- ◆ Invitational bids and forcing bids
- ◆ The captaincy principle
- ◆ Natural bids versus conventional bids
- ◆ How to deal with interference by your opponents

Enough about opening. Now we start the real interaction that takes place at the polite Bridge table, the actual communication with your partner. Up until now we've been talking about what you tell your partner with your first bid.

In this chapter, you learn about responses—how you, or your partner, take the information imparted by whomever opened, evaluate it, and then communicate back what you have in your hand. This chapter is limited to responding when your partner opens the bidding by telling you she has a pretty big hand, 15 to 17 HCP and with No Trump distribution. Chapter 10 will tell you how to respond to an opening bid of 1 in a suit.

Basic Arithmetic Prevails

You have two basic goals in bidding in Bridge:

◆ Bid game if you have it.

◆ Stop at as low a level as possible when you're certain you don't have game.

When bidding in a No Trump contract, arithmetic is more important than when bidding in a suit contract. In a suit contract, you can take an Ace with the Deuce of trump. In No Trump, you're stuck with the suit that was led. High cards are much more valuable, because the highest card in the suit led will always take the trick.

Tricks of the Trade

Remember when evaluating No Trump you don't count distribution points, only HCP.

So when you're bidding No Trump you always have 25 points in mind. When your partner opens 1 No Trump, do you remember what she's telling you? That she has between 15 and 17 HCP and no singletons or voids, and no more than two doubletons. So there are some simple rules to start. If you, as responder, add up your HCP, this is what you do with balanced hands.

HCP	Bid
0–7	Pass
8–9	2 No Trump
10+	3 No Trump

A Discussion of Yes, No, and Maybe

In evaluating your hand to respond to a No Trump opening, you may think in terms of three little words. No, they aren't *I love you*, they're *yes*, *no*, and *maybe*.

Yes

If you have 10 or more points, what should you do? Of course, you bid game by responding 3 No Trump. Why? Even if she's at the bottom of her bid with 15 points, when added to your 10 you should be able to make game. This tells your partner, "Great! You have at least 15 points, and I have at least 10 points; we should definitely be playing this hand in game."

No

When you have 0 to 7 points, you must pass. Why? Go back to your basic arithmetic. What's the maximum amount of HCP your partner can have when she opens 1 No Trump? Seventeen, right? How many points do you need for game? Twenty-five. If you have a maximum of 7, add that to her maximum possible of 17. What do you get? Twenty-four. That's not enough for game. So you don't want to bid further. You communicate to your partner by your pass that you have 7 or fewer points. You are telling your partner, "Well, it's nice that you have such a pretty hand, with at least 40 percent of the points in the deck, but my hand is too weak for us to make game, so let's stop bidding."

Maybe

If you have 8 to 9 points, you might be saying, why not bid 3 No Trump, because 17 plus 8 is 25? Because, when evaluating whether or not to bid with 0 to 7, you were looking to see what the best thing that could happen would be if you were both at the top of your bid. And the best thing that could happen was that you wouldn't make game with your total maximum points. So what's the purpose of bidding?

When you have 8 to 9 points, you look at it the other way. Your partner might have 17, but she might have 15 or 16. And if she has 15 or 16, your 8 points won't be enough for game. And if you have 9 and she only has 15, you still won't have enough for game. So, because her hand is undefined between 15 and 17, you must tell her what you have by making an *invitational* bid of 2 No Trump. This tells her that you have 8 to 9 points. And it says to her, "Partner, if you're at the top of your bid with 17 points, go on to game. But if you're in the middle or at the bottom, just pass and we should be able to make 2 No Trump."

Forget algebra, geometry and computer programming. When your partner opens 1 No Trump, all you need is simple arithmetic. You add your points to hers and decide whether it is *yes*, *no*, or *maybe*.

Understanding the Captaincy Principle

When your partner opens 1 No Trump, in addition to describing her hand to you, she's telling you, "That's it, partner. You now know what I have. You are the captain of this hand. Place the contract where you think we have the best chance."

One No Trump is one of the most descriptive bids in Bridge by an opener because it severely limits her hand. Most other bids in Bridge are slightly limiting, but have a varying range, and the differences are communicated by subsequent bidding. But 1 No Trump limits the hand to what we've discussed. Never could (or should) your partner open a hand 1 No Trump without having the precise qualities we've discussed: 15 to 17 points, no singletons or voids, and no more than two doubletons.

Because of this severe limitation, the opener designates responder as the "captain" of the hand. Because you know what she has in her hand, it's up to you to use your knowledge of Bridge and your own hand to place the contract. Your partner will be trusting you to either place it in a suit or to leave it in No Trump, but at the proper level. You might ask her more about her hand, but, in the end, it's up to you to determine where the contract will be played; there is no bid that responder can make that is as limiting as partner's 1 No Trump open.

Nonpolitical Conventions

A *convention* is a bid that means something different than what it appears to mean. A *natural* bid is one that means what it says. One No Trump, meaning 15 to 17 points and a balanced hand, is a *natural* bid. Two Clubs, on the other hand, when it means a huge hand as discussed in the preceding chapter, is a *conventional* bid because it doesn't say anything about Clubs.

Many conventional bids have been developed as responses to your partner's opening bid of 1 No Trump. You should only learn one of them at this stage. It has become so widespread that it is considered to be standard.

The Stayman Convention

Because your partner can open a hand 1 No Trump but still have one or two four-card major suits (Spades or Hearts), it's quite possible that you'll also have at least four cards in one of the major suits and that you should be playing this hand in the major suit and not in No Trump.

It's conventional Bridge wisdom that if you and your partner hold at least eight cards in a major suit combined, you should be playing the hand in that suit and not in No Trump. Because you control most of the trumps, you should get one more trick than if you were playing in No Trump.

But how do you find this? And how do you find what suit it is in which your partner holds four cards?

The answer is *Stayman*, which is a very simple conventional bid. It says, simply, that if your partner opens 1 No Trump and you have four cards in a major suit and at least

Chapter 9: Taking Control: Responses to No Trump Openings   **99**

8 points, you respond with a bid of 2 Clubs. This says absolutely nothing about the Clubs you are holding in your hand. When you respond 2 Clubs to your partner's opening bid of 1 No Trump, you are saying to your partner the following:

"Partner, I promise you I have the following:

- At least four cards in at least one major suit

- At least 8 HCP

Please further describe your hand to me."

That's all it says. You could be *void* in Clubs and still bid 2 Clubs if you have a four-card major and at least 8 HCP.

<table>
<tr><td>Bridgebit</td></tr>
<tr><td>The Stayman convention was invented by George Rapee. In 1945, Sam Stayman wrote an article on it and, like Amerigo Vespucci, the convention was named after him. Unfortunately, George Rapee hasn't been remembered as well as Christopher Columbus, who was the discoverer of Vespucci's namesake.</td></tr>
</table>

How to Respond to Stayman

If you're the opening bidder and your partner responds 2 Clubs to your 1 No Trump opening, you are required to answer her question. If you have a four-card major, you bid it. So if she responds 2 Clubs and your hand contains three Spades, four Hearts, three Diamonds, and three Clubs, your next bid must be 2 Hearts.

Now, under the captaincy principle, responder knows as much about your hand as she needs in order to place the contract. If she has four Hearts and 10 points, with her four Hearts and your four Hearts, she will bid game—4 Hearts. If she has 8 to 9 points, she'll bid 2 No Trump without four Hearts or bid 3 Hearts if she has four Hearts in her hand. Both of these bids say *maybe*. If you've opened with 17 points and she bids 3 Hearts, you should accept her invitation and bid game. If you're at the bottom of your bid and opened with 15 points, you would just pass her 3 Heart bid and play the hand in 3 Hearts.

But what if you, as opener, don't have a four-card major? Then you *must* bid 2 Diamonds. Again, this is a conventional bid. It says nothing about the Diamonds in your hand. The 2 Diamond response to a Stayman bid of 2 Clubs simply denies a four-card major. You have no choice in this matter. If you're playing the Stayman convention (and just about everybody does), you must respond 2 Diamonds if you do not have a four-card major.

Responder then places the contract. If responder has 10 points, she bids 3 No Trump (answering *yes*). If she has 8 to 9 points, she bids 2 No Trump, telling you *maybe*. And that's where the contract is played unless you have opened the bidding at the top of your bid with 17 points. In that event, you can close out the contract at 3 No Trump. Responder has promised at least 8 points and added to your 17, you should have game. Responder's bid of 2 No Trump is considered invitational, inviting you to go to game if you are at the top of your bid.

So the basics for responder to bid Stayman are the following:

◆ At least one four-card major

◆ At least 8 HCP

If you are responder and your partner opens 1 No Trump and your hand satisfies these two simple rules, you should bid 2 Clubs.

The last thing to discuss is what you do if you have at least 8 or 9 HCP but don't have a four-card major. Simple, regardless of where your points are, you bid 2 No Trump. A bid of 2 No Trump over opener's 1 No Trump says the following:

◆ I have exactly 8 to 9 HCP, but less than 10 HCP.

◆ I don't have a four-card major.

Your partner now knows your hand pretty well. If she opened a 17-point hand or an attractive 16-point hand she goes to 3 No Trump. Otherwise she passes and you play the hand at 2 No Trump.

That's all there is to it. And for now, that's all you need to know.

Now, bid these hands as responder after your partner has opened 1 No Trump:

1. ♠ 9765
   ♥ AQ73
   ♦ K763
   ♣ 6

2. ♠ 743
   ♥ Q65
   ♦ 62
   ♣ KQJ73

3. ♠ JT86
   ♥ 85
   ♦ AK864
   ♣ 86

4. ♠ J643
   ♥ J965
   ♦ K3
   ♣ 985

5. ♠ J84
   ♥ Q93
   ♦ K632
   ♣ Q52

6. ♠ J753
   ♥ J642
   ♦ J9732
   ♣ void

Hand 1: 2 Clubs. You have 9 HCP and two four-card majors. It doesn't matter that you only have a singleton Club. Your 2 Club bid describes a hand that has at least 8 HCP and at least one four-card major, which is what this hand has.

Hand 2: 2 No Trump. You have 8 HCP, but you don't have a four-card major, so you can't bid Stayman. Although you have a very nice Club suit, you can't bid Clubs, because that would be Stayman. Remember, bidding 2 Clubs in response to your partner's 1 No Trump opening doesn't say anything about Clubs! It's asking your partner to bid a four-card major. You'd much rather play a hand in No Trump because No Trump tricks are worth more than a minor suit trick.

Hand 3: 2 Clubs. You have a nice Diamond suit and your Clubs are terrible. But you have 8 HCP and four Spades. This is a hand that requires a 2 Club bid if you're playing Stayman.

Hand 4: Pass. Even though you have two four-card majors, you don't have enough points to bid. Better to let your partner play this in 1 No Trump. This is a hand where you must be disciplined. I know a lot of players who are tempted to bid 2 Clubs on this hand on the outside chance that they'll find their partner with a four-card major and they'll be able to play it in a 4–4 fit at the 2 level. The problem with this is, what if your partner responds 2 Diamonds, denying a four-card major? You can't pass when you only have 2 Diamonds. Your partner might have opened up the following hand:

♠ KQ7
♥ KQ3
♦ 98
♣ AK764

When you bid 2 Clubs, she must bid 2 Diamonds. Because she doesn't have a four-card major, she must comply with the rules of the Stayman convention you agreed to play. She can't respond anything else, so if you pass, she'll be playing in a 2–2 trump fit and you'll be looking around for a new partner because she's never going to want to see you again. So if she bids 2 Diamonds in response to your 2 Club bid, your only choice is to bid 2 No Trump and hope and pray that she wasn't opening up a 17-point hand. If she was, she's going to be in 3 No Trump with two chances—slim and none. So the result of your gamble will probably be that your partner will be playing a hand in 2 No Trump or 3 No Trump that she could have played in 1 No Trump. She might have made 1 No Trump but will have very little chance at the higher level. You must be disciplined when you bid. If you have two four-card majors, but not enough points to bid, pass.

Hand 5: Pass. This is the one hand with 8 HCP that you should pass, when distribution is 4–3–3–3.

Hand 6: 2 Clubs. When you bid 2 Clubs, you know that your partner must respond with a bid of either 2 Diamonds, 2 Hearts, or 2 Spades. This hand is terrible, but you want it played in your eight- or nine-card trump fit. So when you bid 2 Clubs, you're forcing your partner to bid one of your three suits. No matter which suit your partner bids, you pass and you're in a better contract for your pair than 1 No Trump would be, considering your horrible hand.

Weak Responses

If you have a lousy hand, less than 8 points, but a five-card major, it's probably better for the hand to be played in 2 of the major than to have declarer play it in 1 No Trump. Remember that your partner cannot open 1 No Trump without at least two cards in every suit. So if you have a five-card major, you should bid it at the 2 level.

Alert

Eight cards is the magic number when determining a trump fit.

This is a *drop dead* or *sign-off* bid and partner must pass.

So if your partner opens 1 No Trump and you bid 2 Diamonds, Hearts, or Spades, you are telling your partner that you have a weak hand with at least five cards in the suit you bid, so she should pass. This applies whether or not you're playing Stayman.

Invitational Five-Card Major Responses

If a direct bid of a major over your partner's 1 No Trump opening is weak, how do you show an invitational or game-going hand with a five-card major? If your partner has at least three cards in your suit, you should be playing it in your 5–3 major suit fit instead of No Trump.

Lingo

Strain refers to Spades, Hearts, Diamonds, Clubs, or No Trump.

The answer is that you must first bid 2 Clubs, and then if your partner responds in your major you're in good shape. If she responds with 2 Diamonds or 2 of the other major, showing four cards in that suit, you just bid your suit. That shows her you have at least five and at least an invitational hand. Then it's up to her whether to bid again and, if so, what level or *strain*.

Game-Forcing Five- or Six-Card Major Responses

If you have 10 points and a five-card major, you should bid 2 Clubs, then if your partner denies four cards in your suit, jump to 3 of your suit. That tells her that you have at least 10 points and five cards in your major. It's then up to her whether to play it in 3 No Trump, or 4 of your suit. If she has three-card support for your suit, she'll bid 3 No Trump. Finally, if you have at least 9 points and a six-card major, you should immediately jump to game in your six-card major.

Interference and Stayman

What if you have a four-card major and your RHO bids 2 Clubs. You can't say, "Wait a minute; that's what I was going to bid!" Too bad, too, because that would tell your partner what you wanted her to know. But, unfortunately, Bridge won't allow you to do that. So you must have some response. How do you let your partner know you have a four-card major if opponents interfere?

Just about everybody plays that in this situation, when you intended to bid 2 Clubs and your RHO took it away from you, that a double by you shows that your RHO took your bid. So a double of 2 Clubs says, "Partner, I was going to bid 2 Clubs but this jerk did it before I could."

That's pretty easy. But what if you intended to bid 2 Clubs and your RHO bids 2 Diamonds? Not too pretty. But, never fear, it has come up and the Bridge gods have figured something out. If you want to bid Stayman but your RHO bids a higher ranking suit than Clubs before you can bid, there is a way to handle it: You cue bid RHO's suit.

Lingo

A **cue bid** is a forcing bid in a suit in which bidder cannot wish to play. A bid of opponents' natural suit bid is a cue bid and forces your partner to bid again to further describe her hand. It's used to get more information from your partner, and at higher levels after suit agreement, to show control in the opponents' suit.

A bid of your opponents' naturally bid suit is a *cue bid*. Clearly, if you're of sound mind you probably don't want to play the contract in a suit that opponents felt so good about that they wanted to play the contract in that suit. So why would you bid your opponents' suit? The only reason would be to tell your partner something other than suggesting that it might be a good idea to play the hand in this suit yourself.

When using a cue bid after interference after your partner has opened the bidding 1 No Trump, you're telling your partner that you wanted to bid 2 Clubs as Stayman, but the intervening bid kept you from it.

You must have at least 10 HCP to make a cue bid as Stayman because it's a game-forcing bid. You shouldn't do it if you don't have a hand in which you are willing to have your partner play in 3 No Trump if she doesn't have a four-card major, or if her four-card major is not your four-card major. If it isn't, you'll have to bid 3 No Trump after she bids her four-card major.

If RHO bids a major suit at the 2 level, and you cue bid that suit at the 3 level, you are promising four cards in the other major. You should not do this unless you have at least 10 HCP and are willing to have your partner play the hand in either 3 No Trump or 4 of your major suit.

As you can see, interference by your RHO when you are responder causes severe problems. Because of this, it's a good idea, when trying to bid Stayman over interference, not to continue unless you have a game going hand. You're going to be forcing the bidding to the 3 level, and your prospects are not too good if you have a weak hand. If opponents interfere and you have a weak hand, don't try to find the 4–4 major card fit. Just pass and defend. You might find that your results are much better than if you try to play the hand.

So, over interference, you can bid Stayman two ways:

- If RHO has bid 2 Clubs, by doubling
- If RHO has bid a suit higher than 2 Clubs, by cue bidding RHO's suit at the 3 level

Requirements for bidding Stayman over interference follow:

- At least one four-card major
- At least 8 HCP if you are doubling 2 Clubs, or
- At least 10 HCP if you are cue bidding RHO's suit at the 3 level

Jump Bids

What if your partner opens 1 No Trump and you have an unusual hand? Maybe six cards in a minor suit, but not many points? The jump bid over your partner's opening of 1 No Trump can give you some solutions.

Invitational

What would you think a bid of 3 Clubs would mean over your 1 No Trump opening?

Well, it could mean whatever the partnership agrees that it means. But the way I play it, and the way a lot of the better players play it, is that it means your partner has a *broken* six-card suit. By broken, I mean that she has some honors, but there are some cards missing. Like maybe she has AQTxxx of Clubs, missing the King and the Jack. The jump is telling you, "Partner, I have a six-card Club suit and nothing else. But my suit contains several honors with holes. If you can fill in the holes, then you can probably take six tricks in Clubs; so if you have stoppers in the other suits we could make 3 No Trump." It's a great way to get to 3 No Trump with responder only having 6 points, but a suit that makes the contract cold.

Weak

If you bid Stayman, 2 Clubs, in response to your partner's 1 No Trump opening, and then rebid 3 Clubs or 3 Diamonds over whatever she bids, you are demanding that your partner pass. This bid shows a bad six-card or longer suit and a very weak hand. Remember that when your partner opens 1 No Trump she is promising at least two cards in every suit. So if you have a six-card suit, you are assured of at least an eight-card fit between you. If you have a truly terrible hand, maybe it's better to play it in your minor with the ruffing power it will have, instead of forcing your partner to play it in 1 No Trump, a contract in which you can give her no help at all.

Tricks of the Trade

If you have a very weak hand, you can bid Stayman *without* a four-card major. It's just a way of telling your partner that you have a weak hand with a six-card minor and it's better to play it in the minor. You might get lucky. Your long suit might be Diamonds and she might respond 2 Diamonds, denying a four-card major. Then you can pass and she'll be playing the hand in 2 Diamonds, your weak six-card suit, instead of the 3 Diamonds you thought you might be forced into if she bid 2 Hearts or 2 Spades, or 2 No Trump.

With that as a prelude, take a look at the following hands, which you will open 1 No Trump and decide what you'll do with your partner's jump bid:

1. ♠ T54	2. ♠ AK	3. ♠ KQ7	4. ♠ KQT7	5. ♠ A6
♥ AK7	♥ QT7	♥ 643	♥ K752	♥ 64
♦ K742	♦ 875	♦ KJ4	♦ A84	♦ QJ65
♣ AQ8	♣ KQJ65	♣ AQ42	♣ QJ	♣ AKJ83

What if your partner responds to your 1 No Trump open with a bid of 3 Diamonds and you're playing it as invitational as described above?

Hand 1: This is a tough call because if you get a Spade lead you could be down before you get the lead. I'd take the chance because there's a good chance Spades will split 4–3–3–3 and you may not even get a Spade lead. Remember, with you holding the King of Diamonds, your partner is promising the Ace–Queen and probably the Jack, so you will have six Diamond tricks plus two Heart tricks for sure. If they lead a Club, you're in.

Hand 2: Pass. The Diamonds aren't going to come in because you can't fill in your partner's Diamonds. If you bid 3 No Trump, Hearts may be a problem and you will certainly lose the Ace of Clubs. You have four losers for sure: Ace of Clubs, Ace–King of Hearts and the Diamond, and maybe more if your opponents play the Hearts correctly.

Hand 3: 3 No Trump. Take a chance on a Heart lead and bad split. Maybe you'll get a Club lead into your Ace–Queen.

Hand 4: Pass. Even though you have the Ace of Diamonds for six Diamond tricks, there are too many holes in the hand. You could get killed in both Clubs and Hearts. Forget game and let your partner play it in 3 Diamonds, which should give you a pretty good score.

Hand 5: Pass. You almost certainly are going to get a lead of a major suit, and if it's Hearts you're probably dead meat. If you get a Club lead you can run off all the tricks before they get in to cash their major suit tricks, but this hand is too risky.

Responses to an Opening of 2 No Trump

As we've seen, an opening bid of 2 No Trump shows that your partner has 20 to 21 points and No Trump distribution. Stayman applies over a 2 No Trump open just as it applied over a 1 No Trump open. The only difference is that you need fewer points to respond.

Always assume when your partner opens 2 No Trump that she has 20 points. Then add to that the HCP you have in your hand. If they total 25, you should be in game somewhere. That means that you can bid with as few as 4 to 5 points.

The problem is that you don't really have the room to make an invitational bid, so you must make a decision based on your hand and what you know about her hand.

If you have 5 HCP but no four-card major, you respond 3 No Trump. Know why? Sure. She has at least 20 points in her hand. You have 5. 20 + 5 = 25, game in No

Trump. So, the point to remember is that when your partner opens 2 No Trump, you must respond with a much weaker hand than when she opens 1 No Trump. Against a 1 No Trump opening you had to pass unless you had a long major suit or at least 8 points. With a 0- to 7-point hand and no five-card major, you pass. When your partner opens 2 No Trump, you can pass only if you have 0 to 4 points. You must bid with 5 points or more.

Always Keep Your Goals in Mind

When you play Rubber Bridge (a form of Contract Bridge), which is what you are learning here, you have several goals.

1. When bidding, reach game if possible.

2. When it is determined that a game is not possible, stop at as low a level as possible.

3. When playing, maximize the number of tricks you take, whether you are defending or declaring.

The Least You Need to Know

◆ After a 1 No Trump opening, if you hold a balanced hand …
Pass with 0 to 7 points.
Bid 2 No Trump with 8 to 9 points.
Bid 3 No Trump with 10 or more HCP.

◆ When raising No Trump, only count HCP.

◆ Bid 2 Clubs (Stayman) to investigate for a major suit fit.

◆ Stayman promises at least one four-card major and 8 or more HCP.

◆ A jump to 3 of a minor is invitational to game showing a broken six-card suit.

Chapter 10

Simple Responses to Opening 1 Bids in a Suit

In This Chapter

- ◆ How to evaluate your hand for a response to a suit opening bid
- ◆ How to describe your strength
- ◆ The most important bid in bridge: Pass

Responding to opening 1 No Trump bids is much easier than responding to an opening of 1 in a suit because a 1 No Trump opening is such a specific bid. You know your partner has between 15 to 17 HCP and No Trump distribution. When she opens 1 of a suit, however, all you know is that she has 13 to 21 points, including distribution, and, if she opens a major, that she has at least five cards in that suit.

When you respond to an opening of 1 No Trump, you become the captain of the pair because you know so much about your partner's hand. When you respond to an opening of 1 in a suit, however, this is not the case because your partner hasn't told you enough for you to be able to take control. So, instead of taking control and placing the contract, you must communicate with your partner what you have in your hand. She's told you she has an opening hand, but not the requirements for a 1 No Trump open; so, she's asking you for a description of your hand. This chapter will tell you how you start this communication.

Reading Your Partner's Strength Quickly

When your partner opens the bidding, she tells you approximately how many points she has. If she opens in a suit, however, her bid isn't as specific as when she opens 1 No Trump. Basically all you know about her hand is that she has between 13 to 21 points and the minimum number of cards in the suit she bids. You don't know her distribution. If she opens 1 Club it could be 4–3–3–3 or it could be 0–1–4–8. You just don't know. All you know, if she opens a minor, is that she has at least three cards in that suit. If she opens a major she has at least five cards in that suit. In a nutshell, when your partner opens, this is what you know about her hand:

♦ She has at least three cards in the suit if she opens in a minor suit.

♦ She has at least five cards in the suit if she opens in a major suit.

♦ She has between 13 to 21 points.

Not much to go on, is it? But that's what you've got. And actually, it's quite a lot. You know she has at least 13 points, you can start determining what cards they are by listening to the bidding of your opponents. But now your job is to tell her what you have.

Evaluating Your Hand

As you've seen, when you open the bidding you count shortness. But in responding to a suit opening, you can't count shortness unless you have a trump *fit*. You can estab-

lish a trump fit quickly by your partner's opening bid. If she opens 1 Spade and you have three Spades in your hand, you have a trump fit.

When your partner opens the bidding with 1 of a major, she's promising you that she has the following:

♦ At least 13 points

♦ At least five cards in the suit bid

Lingo

A **fit** occurs when you and your partner have the preponderance of the cards in the suit. Generally, if you have at least eight cards between you, you have a fit.

So if your partner opens 1 Spade and you have three Spades, you know that she has at least five Spades, so you have a fit and, as a result, you can use shortness in determining your first bid, your response to her opening bid.

When you know you have a trump fit, you give yourself more points for shortness than when evaluating your hand for the purposes of making an opening bid. When you're making an evaluation to open the bidding, you have no idea if your partner has a fit for you in your suit, so you count your shortage points, or shortness, as I have discussed: 3 points for a void, 2 points for a singleton, and 1 point for a doubleton. But when you respond, you know what your partner has. So if you have a fit, you can give yourself more points, as follows:

Distribution	Points
void	5
singleton	3
doubleton	1

Tricks of the Trade

Why do you need a trump fit to count shortness? Simple. Shortness is only an asset if you can use it to ruff losers. If you're playing in Spades and you have four losing Diamonds in your hand but dummy has a singleton, you can ruff three of your losers in dummy, but only if dummy has enough trump. Without a trump fit, the shortness is not an asset because you don't have enough trump to take advantage of it.

You Must Bid with 6 Points

If you have at least 6 points, you *must* bid if your RHO passes. If you pass your partner's bid when your RHO has passed, you are telling her specifically that you have less than 6 points in your hand.

Why are you required to bid with 6 points when your RHO has passed? Because your partner can open a 15 to 21 point hand with an opening bid of only 1 of a suit.

You've already learned that a 20-point hand is opened 2 No Trump. However, there are specific suit distribution requirements for a No Trump bid, remember? What if your partner has 20 points, but a singleton? She can't open up 2 No Trump. She can't open up 2 Clubs because that requires 22 points. So what's she to do?

She can't lie to you, so she's left with opening up the hand with 1 of a suit. Even though you only have 6 points, you must keep the bidding open for her, in the event she has a strong hand. Look at the following:

♠ AKQ75
♥ 874
♦ AKQJ
♣ 7

That's a 21-point hand. But it can't be opened at 2 No Trump for two reasons. First, it contains a singleton. Second, it only has 19 HCP. So, she must open 1 Spade. But, look at the hand. She has seven sure tricks if Spades is trump. If you have three Spades in your hand, she probably won't lose a Spade trick, so she has nine sure tricks. That means she only needs one outside trick from you for game. Look at your possible hand:

♠ J86
♥ KQ
♦ 8532
♣ 9765

That's 6 points. But, can you see that game is cold? She's not going to lose a Spade trick, she has four cold Diamond tricks, and you give her a sure Heart trick. So, when she opens this hand, all she's waiting for is for you to give her an absolute minimum response of a simple raise in her suit, and she's jumping to game. If you pass because you don't like your 6 points, your LHO is probably going to pass, too.

Tricks of the Trade

Believe it or not, passing seems to be the hardest call to learn and conquer. For some reason, when someone's partner opens the bidding, people feel an almost irresistible urge to respond, no matter how weak the hand. Don't feel this. Remain unemotional. If your hand doesn't meet the requirements for a minimum response, pass.

Why? Count the HCP. You have 6, she has 19. That leaves 15 spread between both of your opponents. Your LHO would have to have 80 percent of the remaining points to have a bid at the 2 level. (You'll learn about bidding over opening bids, called *overcalling*, in Chapter 16.) Although it's possible that your LHO will make overcall, it's unlikely, and you can't take the chance that you'll leave your partner in the lurch with a big hand by passing.

Just remember, when your partner opens a suit bid at the 1 level, and the bid is passed by your RHO, you *must* make a bid if you have 6 points, regardless of your estimation of the quality of those points.

Pass

That said, the first call you learn is *Pass.* This tells her, "Partner, I really have a lousy hand—less than 6 points. Don't count on me for much help." It's important that you pass at your first opportunity if you have less than 6 points; then if you join the bidding later, your partner will know that you're just competing to interfere with your opponents, and have no thought of making a very high contract.

When I was still learning (actually, I'm always learning!), I was playing with one of the best players in Los Angeles, Earle Ziskin, *kibitzing* me. My partner opened 1 Club. I had 3 points, two Clubs, but four Spades. I bid 1 Spade. After the hand, Earle said, "Tony, you misbid that."

Lingo

To **kibitz** is to watch a game as a spectator without being a participant. Kibitzers must keep their mouths shut and not comment on anything.

"But I had such a terrible hand," I replied. "I was afraid she was opening up with only three Clubs. If it's passed out, she's playing in a 3–2 trump fit."

Earle replied, "You don't have your bid. You don't have enough points. Think about what might happen next. You only have 3 points. Someone might have a lot of points, and it might be your partner. She might be sitting over there just waiting to hear from you. All of a sudden she makes a jump shift, bidding 3 Diamonds. That's a forcing bid. You *have* to bid. What are you going to say?"

I didn't have anything to say to that. I knew I was in trouble in this discussion, so I kept quiet and listened.

Earle continued, "The worst thing that could happen would be that your partner would be playing the hand in a 3–2 trump fit in a 1 Club contract. So what? She has to have some values to open. She's going to take a few tricks. So you're down a few in 1 Club. That's not a disaster. What would be a disaster is playing the hand in 3 No Trump, doubled, down 3. *That* would be a disaster. One Club isn't going to be doubled, so that might be your best contract in this hand."

I've never forgotten that lecture. Don't feel you're forced to bid when your partner opens a minor and you have a very weak hand with no support for the suit she opens. Just bid your hand. If you pass and the bid is passed out, your opponents probably have the majority of the points between them and have probably missed some sort of partscore, if not game. Maybe they could have made 3 Hearts. So if your partner plays it in 1 Club down 2, you've probably traded 100 points above the line to keep your opponents from getting 140 below the line. I'll take that any day of the week.

Bridgebit

An apparently true story about a kibitzer in New York involved a 5-level minor suit contract that was doubled. At the tenth trick declarer spread his hand and claimed the balance, making his contract. The opposition agreed, but before the cards were thrown in, the kibitzer pointed out a defensive play that would set the contract. A bitter argument ensued and the dispute was referred to the club's committee. The committee ruled that declarer be credited with making his contract doubled, the defense be credited with defeating the contract one trick, and the kibitzer be ordered to pay the difference! Everybody laughed, and the kibitzer learned to keep his mouth shut.

Also, if your partner has the aforementioned huge hand, with 20 points, she's going to listen to your response, remember that when you responded you *guaranteed* that you have 6 points in your hand, and might jump to game. When your hand comes down and she goes set, you'd better hope the game never ends, because the conversation afterward isn't going to be a walk in the park on a nice spring day.

Want to know how that conversation will go? Read on:

> *Partner (dripping in ice):* You didn't have your bid.
>
> *You (sickly smile):* I thought you'd like to know I had four Spades.
>
> *Partner (venom in her voice):* You didn't have your bid.
>
> *You (starting to sweat):* I didn't want you to be in a 3–2 trump fit.
>
> *Partner:* You didn't have your bid, and if you make another bid like that, you won't have your partner.

The moral of the story: *Pass.* I think Pass is the best bid in Bridge. Learn it. Don't forget it.

Describing Strength

You want to tell your partner as much about the strength of your hand as possible in one bid. This is easier if your hand is weak. The most descriptive bid you can make is 1 No Trump. This tells your partner two things:

 ◆ You have at least 6 points, not more than 9 points, specifically limiting your hand.

 ◆ It denies a four-card suit higher ranking than the suit your partner opened. If your partner opened 1 Diamond and you responded 1 No Trump, you deny having either four Hearts or four Spades.

Your first obligation if you have a weak hand when your partner opens is to show a fit. So if you have 6 to 9 points and at least three cards in her opening major suit, you should simply raise her bid to the 2 level. If your partner opens in a minor, you cannot raise her suit unless you have five cards in it. Why? Because she only promises three cards in the suit when she opens a minor.

Your next obligation is to tell her whether or not you have a four-card suit higher ranking than the suit she opened. If she opens 1 Heart and you have 6 points and four Spades without at least three Hearts, your response is 1 Spade.

If your partner opens 1 Heart, and you don't have at least three Hearts, but you have 6 points with less than four Spades, your response is 1 No Trump. Knowing this, respond with the following hands to your partner's opening bid of 1 Club:

Tricks of the Trade

With a very weak hand your *first* obligation is to tell your partner if you have a fit in her major suit opening bid. So if she opens 1 Heart and you have 6 to 9 points and at least three Hearts, you should immediately raise her bid to the 2 level by bidding 2 Hearts. This shows her your fit.

1. ♠ AK85	2. ♠ 9865	3. ♠ AKQ	4. ♠ K64	5. ♠ 86
♥ Q74	♥ AKQ	♥ 863	♥ K65	♥ KJ972
♦ 854	♦ 832	♦ 9652	♦ Q98	♦ 853
♣ 987	♣ 742	♣ 874	♣ 9653	♣ 872

Hand 1: 1 Spade. This is a clear bid. You have 9 HCP and four Spades.

Hand 2: 1 Spade. Your strength is in Hearts, but you only have three of them. Your partner is looking for an eight-card fit. Because she can't open a major suit unless she has five of them, she must open a minor suit with only four cards in the majors. Your bid of 1 Spade tells her that you have four Spades. If she has four Spades, you have an eight-card trump fit, which is what you're looking for.

Hand 3: 1 Diamond. Despite your HCP strength in Spades, you only have three of them. You do have four Diamonds, even though they're weak.

Hand 4: 1 No Trump. You have 6 to 9 HCP, but you do not have a four-card suit of higher rank than the suit your partner opened. This bid tells her that information specifically.

Hand 5: Pass. Sure, your Hearts look okay, but you don't have enough points to bid. If you bid this hand, and your partner has a very strong hand, she could make a forcing bid, requiring you to bid again (more on this later), and you could find yourself at a much higher contract than you should be.

Which Suit to Show First

If you have a five-card suit and a four-card suit, which do you bid? Generally, your *longest suit is your strongest suit.* To take the most extreme example, xxxxx is stronger than AKJT. If your partner opens 1 Club and you have five Spades and four Hearts and enough points to bid, you bid the Spades, even if your Hearts are AKQJ and your Spades are Qxxxx.

Bidding with Two Four-Card Suits

If you have two four-card suits, the rule is simple: Bid the lower-ranking suit first. This is called bidding *up the line.*

If your partner opens 1 Club and you have four Diamonds and four Hearts, you bid 1 Diamond. If you have four Hearts and four Spades, you bid 1 Heart. This allows your partner to bid 1 Spade if she has four of them. If you were to bid 1 Spade and your partner should have four Hearts, it would force her to the 2 level to bid them, and she probably would not want to bid a four-card suit for the first time at the 2 level unless she had a very strong hand.

A new suit bid by responder is forcing on opener. This means that opener must bid again if his partner responds to his opening with a new suit.

Bidding with Two Five- or Six-Card Suits

If you have two five- or six-card suits, you should *not* bid them up the line. Rather, you should bid the higher ranking first, or bid *down the line*, and then rebid the other if your partner doesn't support you.

> **Lingo**
>
> Bidding a lower-ranking suit before you bid a higher-ranking suit is called bidding **up the line.** Conversely, bidding a higher-ranking suit before you bid a lower-ranking suit is called bidding **down the line.**

Why? There are several reasons. These are suits that demand they both be mentioned. If you bid them up the line, you might have to go to the 3 or 4 level to mention the other at the second bid. For instance, if you have five Diamonds and five Hearts and your partner opens 1 Club, if you were to bid up the line you'd bid 1 Diamond. Then if your partner bids 1 Spade or 1 No Trump or 2 Clubs, you have to bid 2 Hearts. A new suit bid by responder is forcing on opener for one round, so your partner must bid again. Basically you're asking her to make a choice, and whatever she chooses she has to go to the 3 level.

If, on the other hand, you bid the higher ranking first in response to her 1 Club opening, the bidding could go like this.

Partner	You
1 Club	1 Heart
1 No Trump	2 Diamonds

If she's got a minimum hand with Heart support, she can express her preference by bidding 2 Hearts, staying at the lower 2 level.

Another reason to bid down the line for two five- or six-card suits is that this is the only way you can indicate your length to partner. If you bid them up the line, how is she to know how many you have in your first suit? You could only have four. So if you bid a higher-ranking suit first, like Hearts, and then bid a lower-ranking suit at your next opportunity, you might only have four of the lower-ranking suit, but for sure you have five of the higher-ranking suit, which was your first bid suit.

Responding at the 2 Level

To respond at the 2 level to your partner's opening bid of 1 in a suit, you must have the following:

- ◆ At least 10 HCP
- ◆ A five-card major suit, or a four-card minor

If your partner opens 1 Spade and you have five Clubs and 10 HCP, you can respond with a bid of 2 Clubs. Whenever you make a 2 level response to your partner's opening 1 level bid, you are promising her at least 10 HCP.

Bidding 2 Clubs over a 1 Spade open does *not* deny that you have trump support (which would be at least three cards in Spades). So if you have at least 10 HCP and five Clubs, along with three Spades, you can, and should, bid 2 Clubs first, then support your partner's Spades at your next bid. Your first bid shows the strength of your hand, that you have more than a minimum. Don't forget, when you, as responder, bid a new suit, it is 100 percent forcing on opener to bid again; you can't be passed out at 2 Clubs. When your partner bids again, no matter what she bids, you can bid Spades to show her that you have Spade support.

This information is important to her, because if you just bid 2 Spades over her opening bid of 1 Spade, she would think that you had a minimum hand (see discussion in next section), maybe only 6 points, and might pass. But if you show her that you have at least 10 points and at least four Clubs first, when she learns that you *also* have three Spades, she can better evaluate where to place the contract.

Raising Your Partner's Major Suit Opening

The one exception to this rule of a 2 level response to partner's opening 1 level bid is if you raise your partner's suit. For example, she opens 1 Spade and you respond 2 Spades. A raise of your partner's opening major suit bid promises the following:

♦ 6 to 9 points

♦ At least three cards in your partner's suit

Next to responding 1 No Trump, this is the *weakest* positive bid you can make. Responding 1 No Trump is weaker because it denies trump support. Raising her suit promises at least three cards in the suit, and therefore informs her that you have trump support for her—information she can use to further evaluate her hand. This is a bid that definitely limits your hand. You can't make this bid with three trump and 10 points. Responding 2 Spades to your partner's opening bid of 1 Spade tells her you don't have more than 9 points.

Raising Your Partner's Minor Suit Opening

Note that I emphasized that you may support your partner's major suit opening if you have three cards in it. This is definitely not true for a minor suit opening by your partner. Why?

♦ When your partner opens in a major suit, she's promising at least five cards in that suit. So if you have three, you have the desired eight-card fit.

♦ When your partner opens in a minor suit, she's only promising three cards in that suit. So if you have three, and she only has the three she promised, you are in a dismal six-card fit and disaster is looming.

Because of this, you cannot support your partner in a minor suit opening unless you have five cards in the suit. Occasionally you will be in a fix where you can't respond 1 No Trump and only have four of your partner's minor suit; then you are forced to give her a raise with only four. But try to avoid this. Of course, when you raise your partner's minor suit opening, you're giving her the weakest response possible. If she opened on a three-card suit, and you're raising on a four-card suit, she'll probably pass, unless she opened a strong hand. That's the beauty of the auction. Each bid means something. When she opens a minor, it means she doesn't have a five-card major. If you respond by raising her suit, it means you not only don't have a four-card major, but your hand is weak and her suit is your strongest suit. So even if she only has three, if she's on just a standard opening hand, nothing special, she will probably pass. You shouldn't be in too much trouble playing in a 3–4 fit at the 2 level.

Enough talking, let's bid some hands. Your partner opens 1 Club:

1. ♠ 98743		**2.** ♠ AKQ4		**3.** ♠ AKQ		**4.** ♠ J865	
♥ AKQ6		♥ 8764		♥ 9754		♥ 76	
♦ 64		♦ 863		♦ 872		♦ AJ765	
♣ 54		♣ 85		♣ 984		♣ 75	
5. ♠ 64		**6.** ♠ A64		**7.** ♠ 876		**8.** ♠ K873	
♥ AK98		♥ K98		♥ J86		♥ Q985	
♦ AJ952		♦ 854		♦ AJ		♦ JT86	
♣ 87		♣ 8754		♣ 97652		♣ 7	

Hand 1: 1 Spade. Your Hearts are terrific, but you only have four of them. You must bid your longest major and that's Spades.

Hand 2: 1 Heart. Your Spades are terrific, but when you have two major suits of equal length, you bid the lower ranking first, bidding up the line.

Hand 3: 1 Heart. You have 9 points and four Hearts.

Hand 4: 1 Diamond. It's the longest suit, and therefore your strongest.

Hand 5: 1 Diamond. You have enough points to bid twice. Remember that when you bid a new suit it *forces* opener to bid again. So you bid your 1 Diamond. No matter what your partner bids, you can bid your Hearts at the 2 level, describing your hand as more than 10 HCP with five Diamonds and four Hearts.

Hand 6: 1 No Trump. You have 7 HCP and both major suits stopped once and only have four Clubs. You're not promising stoppers in all three unbid suits when you respond 1 No Trump, so the fact that you don't have Diamonds stopped doesn't preclude you from responding 1 No Trump.

Hand 7: 2 Clubs. This is pretty clear. You have 7 HCP, no stoppers in the majors, and five Clubs.

Hand 8: 1 Diamond. You bid suits of equal length up the line. You don't deny a four-card major by bidding 1 Diamond in response to your partner's 1 Club opening.

Your partner opens 1 Heart:

1. ♠ J643	2. ♠ AKJ	3. ♠ 742	4. ♠ K8	5. ♠ QT65
♥ AK4	♥ 752	♥ A5	♥ 862	♥ 65
♦ 753	♦ 85	♦ J632	♦ Q62	♦ 98
♣ 752	♣ K8653	♣ Q964	♣ JT754	♣ J7642

Hand 1: 2 Hearts. Your Spades are too weak to not show your very strong Heart support immediately.

Hand 2: 2 Clubs. You have 11 points and a five-card Club suit. You show your Heart support at your next bid.

Hand 3: 1 No Trump. You have a minimum hand without Heart support, even though you have the Ace. If your partner bids another suit at the 2 level, you can bid 2 Hearts, showing a minimum hand with 2 Hearts.

Hand 4: 2 Hearts. This is a bare minimum hand, but you do have 3 Hearts. You must tell your partner what you have, and a simple raise of your partner's opening suit only promises three trumps and 6 points. That's what you've got. Any other bid she makes will be her problem, because you've warned her that your hand stinks. But you have an obligation to keep the bidding open with 6 points. Why? Your partner might have opened a 20-point hand with a bid of 1 Heart. All she needs to know is that you have 6 points and three Hearts and she'll bid game. This is a classic hand where your partner must be able to trust you to bid correctly.

Hand 5: Pass. Only 4 points, no Heart support. You don't want this to get any higher. You must show your partner your weakness. You might have a 4–4 Spade fit, but if you don't, what are you going to do when your partner bids 3 Diamonds at her next call, a forcing bid?

Responses Over Interference

So far we've been talking about bidding when your opponents docilely pass at their turn. Alas, this doesn't always happen. When your opponents are bidding, it changes the meanings of your responses.

You have two obligations in responding to your partner's opening bid:

1. Tell her what you have as quickly and accurately as possible.

2. Keep the bidding open for your partner if you have at least 6 points in case she opened at the 1 level with a huge hand. This obligation is removed if you have less than 6 points.

Your first obligation doesn't change when your opponents interfere. Your second obligation does.

When your opponents interfere, you're relieved of one of responder's obligations: the commitment to keep the bidding open for your partner. Why? Because when your RHO passes, you don't know what your LHO is going to do. He might pass, too. If this happens, you must bid if you have 6 points so that your partner, whose hand is basically undefined unless she's opened 1 No Trump, will get another chance to bid. She might have opened a 20-point hand at the 1 level because she didn't have anything else to bid. She's just waiting to find out if you have 6 points to place the contract in game.

But when your RHO bids, this obligation to bid with at least 6 points is removed because your partner will definitely get another chance to bid, even if you pass. So if you take a bid right after your RHO bids, it's called a *free bid* because you have no obligation to bid.

Free Bid of a Suit at the 1 Level

A free bid of a new suit at the 1 level tells your partner that you have a better than minimum hand. So with 6 or 7 points, you should pass. If you take a free bid after your RHO bids, you're telling your partner that you have one of the following:

◆ At least 8 points with a four-card suit

◆ At least 7 points with a good suit

If you pass, you're denying one of these holdings and telling your partner that if she bids again she can't count on much help from you.

Free Bid of a Suit at the 2 Level

This promises the same 10 points it promises without interference, but implies game interest. Why? Because opponents have shown a biddable hand and some points. You're telling your partner that despite the fact that opponents may have some points and a good suit, you think the contract should be yours and want to explore it more. This is 100 percent forcing on your partner to bid again.

Free Bid of No Trump

A free bid of 1 No Trump over RHO's overcall promises the following:

- 8 to 10 HCP

- A stopper in RHO's suit

So, if your partner opens 1 Club and RHO bids 1 Spade, look at the following hands:

1.	♠ Q65	2.	♠ 86	3.	♠ 86	4.	♠ KT65
	♥ K97		♥ K94		♥ K94		♥ T94
	♦ 865		♦ Q842		♦ Q84		♦ Q82
	♣ Q975		♣ Q752		♣ Q9752		♣ J97

Hand 1: 1 No Trump. You can properly respond 1 No Trump because you have 8 HCP and a stopper in Spades. It's not a great stopper, but it is a stopper.

Hand 2: Pass. This tells your partner that you have a minimum hand, 0 to 9 points, without a stopper in opponent's suit. Had your RHO overcalled 1 Heart, your pass would also tell your partner you did not have four Spades, because with 8 to 9 points and four Spades, you should bid your Spade suit over RHO's *overcall* of 1 Heart. You can't make a simple raise to 2 Clubs because your partner might only have three cards in the suit.

Hand 3: 2 Clubs. You have 8 points. Even though your partner opened a Club, she may only have three cards in the suit, so you need five Clubs to make a simple raise. You have five Clubs and eight points. This bid effectively tells your partner that she can count on you for only 8 to 9 points and five Clubs.

Hand 4: Pass. You would have bid 1 Spade without interference, but your RHO bid it first! Even though you have a good Spade suit, you only have 6 points. A free bid of 1 No Trump would tell your partner you have a stronger hand. A pass tells her you have less than 8 points. If she has extra values, she'll bid again. Then, if she makes a forcing bid, you can tell her about your Spades. (For example, if your partner doubles to get you back in the bidding,

Lingo

An **overcall** is any bid after an opponent has opened the bidding. So, if your pair opens the bidding and opponents make a bid, it's an overcall. If your opponents open the bidding and you or your partner make a bid, it's an overcall. Overcalls are covered in Chapter 16.

you'd bid 1 No Trump.) If your partner has a minimum opening hand, it would be better to defend opponents in 1 Spade than to bid to a contract where you might have a lot of trouble, given your weak hand.

RHO Bids Your Strong Suit

If you have a very good suit and RHO beats you to bidding it after your partner has opened, what do you do? What if your partner opened 1 Club, your RHO bid 1 Spade and your hand was the following:

♠ AK987
♥ K64
♦ 75
♣ 865

You have three possible calls here:

- **Bid No Trump.** Here your hand is so strong you could jump to 2 No Trump to tell your partner that you have 10 HCP and your RHO's suit stopped twice.

- **Double for penalty.** Your partner opened the bidding, so you know she has at least 13 points. You have 11 points with your doubleton. That's 24 points, plus you have a very strong Spade suit, with at least two sure tricks to make the contract. But, your partner has power enough to make an opening bid, and you have a good enough trump suit to be playing the hand in Spades yourself. Ask yourself, "If my RHO didn't bid, would I think that my partner and I could make 1 Spade?" If so, you should double. This is especially true because you're sitting behind the declarer.

- **Pass.** If you're playing *negative doubles*, which you will learn about in Chapter 18, you can't make a penalty double because a double in this situation means something else. So you would pass and hope your partner would proceed as set forth in Chapter 18.

Your pass over opponent's interference generally means one of two things:

- Your hand is too weak for a convenient bid over the specific interference that occurred, or

- Your RHO bid your suit and you're not strong enough to double for penalty or bid 1 No Trump.

Your partner should be aware that your pass after interference means one of these two things.

The Least You Need to Know

- After your partner opens with 1 of a suit, you must respond if you have at least 6 points.

- Bid your longest suit first, provided you can still bid it at the 1 level. With two five- or six-card suits, bid the higher-ranking suit first.

- With four-card suits, bid the lowest ranking, if possible, at the 1 level. Suit quality is unimportant; length is the primary factor.

- After your partner opens a major, raise bidding to the 2 level with 6 to 9 points and at least three of her suit. You need at least four, and preferably five or more, to raise partner's minor suit opening. Raising to the 2 level also shows 6 to 9 points.

- With 6 to 9 HCP, bid 1 No Trump if you don't have a higher-ranking four-card suit to bid at the 1 level.

- A suit response at the 2 level shows 10 or more points and at least a four-card suit. It doesn't deny support for your partner's major suit opening bid.

11

Glad Tidings of Great Joy! Jump Responses

In This Chapter

- ◆ Limit raises
- ◆ Jump shifts
- ◆ Jumps to No Trump
- ◆ Responses by a passed hand

Sometimes you open your hand and start looking for your calculator so you can add up all the points you hold; next thing you know you hear your partner open the bidding! How can this be? You have a lot of points yet she's already bidding. What now?

Obviously you want to describe this good fortune to her as soon and as accurately as possible. But how?

This is where *jump bids* become useful. In this chapter, you learn how to use jump bids to describe hands that are better than what is communicated by a simple response.

Limit Raises

A *limit raise* is a raise that shows a hand with trump support and not less than 10 points, but not more that 12 points. It's called *limit* because the bid confines the hand to these parameters. There are other bids you can make if your hand is not within these boundaries. This section describes the various types of limit raises.

Your Partner Opens a Major

What if you have four of opener's major suit opener, 10 points, but don't have a suit to bid at the 2 level? Take a look at the following hand, after your partner has opened the bidding at 1 Spade:

♠ KQJ5
♥ A76
♦ J96
♣ 984

Not a bad hand, but what do you bid? If you just raise her 1 Spade bid to 2 Spades, she'll think you have a minimum and will almost certainly pass. (It's possible that she had to open a 20-point hand with a bid of 1 Spade because her distribution did not allow her to open it 2 No Trump. If she has such a strong hand, she will quickly jump to 4 Spades when she finds you have at least 6 points.) You are too strong to just reply with 2 Spades, but what do you bid?

You give her a limit raise. A limit raise in your partner's opening major suit is a bid that says you have the following:

- ◆ 10 to 12 points
- ◆ Three or four cards in opener's major suit

How do you make a limit raise? You jump your partner's suit. A *jump* is a bid that passes a level available to you. For example, if your partner opens 1 Spade, you could bid 2 Spades, but that would show a fairly weak hand. If you bypass bidding at the 2 level, and make a bid of 3 Spades, instead of 2 Spades, it's called a jump. If you play that a jump in your partner's opening major suit at your first opportunity is a limit raise, then it shows at least three-card support and 10 to 12 points.

This is a very good bid because it tells your partner so much. It limits your hand to no more than 12 HCP, but promises at least 10 HCP, and it promises at least three-card trump support. It's one of the most specific bids in Bridge, even more specific than the opening of 1 No Trump. From your limit raise, your partner should be able to determine if she should bid game. If she opened with a minimum, she'll pass and the contract will be 3 Spades. With more than a minimum, she'll bid at least a game.

Limit Raise When Your Partner Opens a Minor Suit

When your partner opens a minor suit, there are slightly different conditions when you make a limit raise. In the first place, because your partner has opened with a minor, you don't know how many she has. Because of that limitation, a limit raise in a minor suit should promise five cards in the suit. If you give a limit raise with a four-card suit and she has opened a three-card suit, you could find yourself playing at the 3 level on a 3–4 fit—not an attractive prospect.

Further, you should not make a limit raise of a minor suit opening if you have a four-card major. The requirements for a limit raise in a minor are as follows:

- No four-card major
- 10 to 12 points
- Five-card support

If your partner has opened a three-card suit, looking for a major suit fit, and you give her a limit raise in her minor suit opening, she'll probably either pass your limit raise and play it in 3 of the minor, or try 3 No Trump if she has strength in the other suits.

Jump Shift Responses

As we've seen, a jump is a bid that passes a level available to you. A shift is a change of suit. So a *jump shift* occurs when you make a jump bid in a suit different from the suit your partner opened. For example, if your partner opens 1 Club, you could bid any other suit at the 1 level. If you bid a new suit at the 2 level, when you could have bid it at the 1 level, it's called a jump shift. So if your partner opens 1 Club and you bid 2 Diamonds instead of 1 Diamond, you've made a jump shift. There are two ways to play a jump shift response. A lot of players generally play them weak. However, most Rubber Bridge players play them strong. That's what you're going to learn here, strong jump shifts. In Chapter 24, weak jump shifts will be explained, but learning them is optional.

Strong Jump Responses

Many good players play jump shifts as strong. A strong jump shift shows a very good hand and is game forcing on your partner. If you open 1 Diamond, your LHO passes, and your partner bids 2 Spades, that's a jump shift. She could have bid 1 Spade, but she skipped the 1 level and jumped to the 2 level. Also, she shifted suit, from your suit of Diamonds, to a new suit, Spades.

When your partner does this, you must keep the bidding open until you've reached game. Then, and only then, can you pass. The following chart shows what each bid means.

Partner	You	Meaning
1 Heart	2 No Trump	13 to 15 HCP, balanced hand, stoppers in the three unbid suits, denies four Spades
1 Heart	3 No Trump	16 to 18 HCP, balanced hand, stoppers in the three unbid suits, denies four Spades
1 Heart	2 Spades	16 or more points, game forcing, looking for slam, does *not* deny four Hearts, could be totally unbalanced

When I started playing Bridge again, after a hiatus of several decades after college, I was playing the game I played at UCLA—Strong Two bids and strong jumps. One day I picked up my cards and saw that I had 22 points. I was ready to open 2 Spades, which is game forcing on my partner. But my RHO opened 2 Hearts. I was stunned. How could she have a strong enough hand to open 2 Hearts when I had more than half the points in the deck in my hand? I thought about it a while and decided to pass, thinking that we could get them for a good set. Alas, my opponent was playing Weak Twos, so they stole the bid and we got a terrible result. That was my introduction to modern Bridge. So just be aware if you're playing Strong Twos and strong jump shifts, your opponents might be playing Weak Twos and weak jump shifts. So when an opponent jumps the bidding and you don't know what they're playing, always ask what the bid means before you assume you know.

Alert

You can always ask what an opponent's bid means when it's your turn to bid by asking the bidder's partner. (You must ask the bidder's partner because a bidder isn't allowed to say what his bid means.) He must give you an accurate and complete description of the meaning of his partner's bid. You can't be forced to bid without an explanation of a bid you don't understand.

Preemptive Jump to Game

Look at the following hand, after your partner has opened the bidding with 1 Spade:

♠ QT863
♥ 8
♦ Q653
♣ JT4

What's your bid? You have nice Spade support for your partner, but there's not much else that looks good except the singleton Heart.

Regardless of what your RHO does, this is a hand that requires a jump to 4 Spades. You can make a preemptive jump to game with a hand that satisfies the following requirements:

◆ Your partner opened a major.

◆ You have five-card or longer trump support for her.

◆ You have between 6 to 10 points.

◆ You have a singleton or void.

The reason for this is that your partner will have a fair chance of making the contract because you have so many trump between you. If she goes set it shouldn't be more than 1 or 2. And you want to stifle your opponents' ability to communicate with one another to find the game they might have. You have only 5 HCP. Your partner might be opening up a minimum with five Spades, a singleton, and 12 total points, which would translate to 10 HCP. That means that your opponents would have approximately 25 HCP between them. They might very well have a Heart game between them. If you jump immediately to 4 Spades, they don't have the time to communicate.

The prospects in this hand are twofold. You might very well have a game between you. If not, your opponents might very well have a game between them, and you've kept them from finding it or bidding it. You might have traded 100 points above the line to keep them from getting 120 below the line and 300 or 500 points above the line. Or your opponents might bid 5 Hearts, which might be one trick more than they can make.

Tricks of the Trade

The preemptive jump to game isn't strictly limited to a major suit opening. But it's riskier in a minor because you must take all but two tricks. Opponents will be more inclined to double a jump to a 5-level contract than a jump to a 4-level contract.

Also by making a quick preemptive strike you've prevented your opponents from communicating more to see if they have enough power between them to double and penalize you for your bid. Any double by them at this point would be a guess, because you obviously have a distributional hand.

Another thing to remember is that your opponents are listening to your bidding, too. If they are knowledgeable players, they'll know that your bid is preemptive. So you might be doubled for penalty, especially if your RHO has made an overcall and your LHO has a good hand. But that's just the chance you take. If you only go down 2 doubled and they can make game in their suit, you will have made a good bid—a "save" against their game.

Jumps to No Trump

Several jump bids to No Trump don't fit any of the patterns so far discussed. Generally, all jumps to No Trump show a strong hand.

CAUTION **Alert** _____

When you're jumping from a suit into No Trump, remember that you only count HCP, not shortness points, in evaluating your hand for this bid into 2 No Trump or 3 No Trump.

Remember also, when you bid No Trump as a qualitative bid, that is to suggest playing the hand without trump, you designate your partner as captain of the hand. This applies to responses and rebids as well as opening bids.

Jumps to No Trump After a Minor Suit Opening

A jump shift to 2 No Trump after a minor suit opening by your partner promises the following:

- Between 12 to 15 HCP
- No four-card major
- Stoppers in all suits unbid by your partner
- No Trump distribution

This is a very good bid because you already know that you have more points than they do. If your partner opened the bidding, she has at least 13 points and you know that you have 12 to 15 HCP, so you have at least 25 total points between you. Of course, at this time you don't know if your partner's points are HCP or distribution points, but you'll find that out when she bids.

This bid also tells your partner that you can't have an eight-card major fit between you. Can you figure out why?

Answer: This shows how you deduce what you have between you by what *wasn't* bid. Because your partner opened a minor, she probably doesn't have a five-card major, or she would have opened by bidding it. Because you jumped to 2 No Trump over her minor suit opening, you don't have a four-card major.

If she doesn't have a five-card major, you can't have an eight-card fit unless you both have a four-card major. but your bid denies a four-card major. Therefore, if she doesn't have a five-card major and you don't have a four-card major, you can't have eight cards in a major between you.

So you both know that if you have game it will probably be in No Trump. This puts it in opener's corner because only she knows whether her points are HCP or distribution points.

Finally, what if you have 12 to 15 points, no four-card major, but an unstopped, unbid suit? In this instance you must make a 2 over 1 response to tell your partner what you have. Look at the following hand:

♠ 872
♥ K4
♦ AQ76
♣ KT86

If your partner opens 1 Diamond, you don't have a four-card major to bid and you can't jump to 2 No Trump because Spades is unstopped. In this instance you must respond 2 Clubs. This tells your partner that you have at least 10 points, at least four Clubs, and no four-card major. It's forcing your partner to bid again; you'll have a better idea of where to play it when you learn more about her hand. Also, when she bids again, you can tell her that you have more than 10 points. You don't have to tell everything in one bid. It's nice when you can, but sometimes you can't.

Tricks of the Trade

If your opponents get into the bidding they might overbid. You can get a good score if they play the hand in a contract they can't make because they aren't powerful enough.

Also never forget that Bridge is a game of *communication* and *cooperation* between partners. You don't have to make unilateral bids. *Trust your partner!* (Have you heard that before?)

Alert

Don't forget—you shouldn't jump to No Trump over your partner's minor suit open if you have a four-card major.

Jump to 3 No Trump over a Minor Suit Open of 1

A jump to 3 No Trump over a minor suit open of 1 shows the next level, 16 to 18 HCP, and also denies a four-card major. There is sound arithmetic reasoning behind this. If you have at least 16 HCP and your partner has at least 13 points, you should probably be able to make 3 No Trump. If she has 2 or 3 shortness points, which is a possibility, that still leaves her with at least 10 HCP; this, when added to your 16 HCP, should offer a good play for 3 No Trump (which generally needs 25 points between you). As I said previously, if you don't have a four-card major, and your partner with an opening hand doesn't have a five-card major, there's no hope of an eight-card fit in a major. That said, if you are going to be playing the hand in game, it should probably be in 3 No Trump. If your partner opened a terribly distributional hand, like 6–5 in the minors, she can jump to game in the appropriate minor because your bid promised at least two cards in each suit.

The following shows the HCP requirements for jumps to No Trump after your partner makes a minor suit open of 1 of the suit:

Response	HCP
2 No Trump	12–15
3 No Trump	16–18

Responses When You Are a Passed Hand

When your partner opens the bidding in third or fourth seat, it means that you have passed at your first opportunity to bid, so you don't have an opening hand. Some of your responses remain the same, but some change when this occurs. You must remember that the standards for opening in third seat are less than they are for opening in first or second seat. Now that you are responder, you must remember the standards you learned for opening the bidding in third seat and follow those standards here.

Lingo

Opening light refers to when you open a hand with less than 13 points.

Your partner could have a perfectly good opening hand, one that she would have opened in the first or second seat. But, then again, she might not. She might be *opening light*.

When you have 6 to 9 points, your responses are the same, you bid your four-card majors. You bid up the line. And if you don't have a four-card major and can't support your partner, you bid 1 No Trump.

Jump Shift by a Passed Hand

When you're a *passed hand*, a jump shift obviously doesn't mean that you have a hand strong enough to make a game-forcing bid, as you learned earlier in this chapter. If you had an opening hand with the values to make a strong jump shift, you would have opened!

When your partner opens a minor, you make a jump shift when you are a passed hand to show that you have a six-card near independent major suit. If your partner opens 1 Club or 1 Diamond and you have the following type of holding in Hearts or Spades with nothing else, opposite a singleton or void, you should make a jump shift to your long suit:

> AQT9xxx
>
> AKTxxx
>
> AJT9xx

Lingo

A **passed hand** is one that could have opened the bidding but passed instead of making an opening bid.

This bid invites your partner to pass. If she opened with a minimum 13 to 14 point hand you'll be better off playing the contract in your suit, even if she has a void in your suit. You are specifically describing a hand that you feel should be played at the 2 level in your suit.

Unless she makes a forcing bid at her next turn to call, you have told her that you intend to pass. It's up to her to place the contract. And your strong suggestion is that she place the contract by passing and allowing you to play it at the 2 level in your suit. Any action she takes after this bid is on her shoulders. You have done the best you can to describe your hand.

The Least You Need to Know

- A jump raise in your partner's opening suit is called a limit raise. It shows 10 to 12 points and invites your partner to bid a game.

- A limit raise contains three or more cards in your partner's opening suit after a major suit opening and five or more cards in your partner's opening suit after a minor suit opening.

- After a minor suit opening, a limit raise denies a four-card or longer major.

◆ A jump shift shows 16 or more points and is at least invitational to slam. A jump shift is 100 percent forcing to game.

◆ A jump shift to a major suit by a passed hand after a minor suit open shows a strong six-card major suit with no high-card strength in any other suit. Partner is invited to pass.

Part 4

Rebids, Overcalls, and Doubles

After you and your partner have made your initial bids, you continue to communicate and describe your hands to one another. This section will teach you how to complete your communication and make a determination whether to play or defend.

If your opponents open the bidding, you still have a chance to bid by making an overcall or a takeout double. You'll learn about overcalls, takeout doubles, and responses to your partner's overcalls and takeout doubles.

Just because your opponents get the contract, you aren't finished. If you don't think they can make it, you can challenge them by doubling! You'll learn how to do this here, along with learning the risks and rewards of making a penalty double.

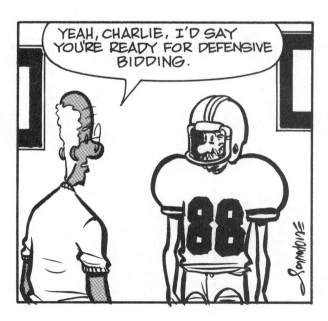

Aye, Aye, Sir! Rebids by No Trump Opener

In This Chapter

- ◆ How opener rebids after partner responds to an opening bid of No Trump
- ◆ How opener rebids when partner bids Stayman
- ◆ Rebids after your partner responds over interference
- ◆ Rebids over interference after your partner responds

As you learned in Chapter 5, when you open the bidding with any No Trump bid, you designate your partner as captain of your pair. You have specifically described your hand as one that is balanced and contains a number of HCP within a very narrow range: 15 to 17 HCP for a 1 No Trump open, and 20 to 21 for a 2 No Trump open.

Your partner has heard you and has responded, either by asking you a question or by describing her hand to you. This chapter tells you how you respond, depending on what's in your hand and the question she has asked.

Rebids When You Get an Invitation

You've opened the hand with 1 No Trump, which means that you have a balanced, 15 to 17 HCP hand. Your partner bids 2 No Trump. What do you do?

This is pretty easy. Your partner has said "maybe" by making an *invitational* bid. She has 8 to 9 HCP and a balanced hand. You don't know where her HCP cards are, but you know she has them. This is sheer arithmetic. Your partner, who is the captain at this point, has given you a specific instruction. She has said, "Partner, if you're at the top of your bid—17 points, or a good 16 points—bid 3 No Trump; otherwise, pass."

Why? Simple arithmetic. If she has 8 points, the minimum she could have, and you have 17 points, the maximum you could have, you have 25 HCP between you; that's usually enough for game. However, even if she's just 1 point below her maximum, when added to your 17 points this only totals 24 points. That's generally not enough for game, so you should pass.

This little game of math works remarkably well. Generally when I ignore the arithmetic and go to game with a bad 16-point hand, I get burned, because I've been set the one trick that the math said I couldn't get. Sometimes you can make 3 No Trump with 24 points or less, but the percentages are very much against you.

Lingo

Eights, Nines, and Tens are called **body cards**.

What constitutes a "good" 16? Although you only give yourself points in counting the hand for honors of the rank of Jack and above, Eights, Nines, and Tens have values because they can often take tricks. For example, look at the following holdings:

North
♠ K2

West
♠ Q43

East
♠ A765

South
♠ JT98

Which hand is the most powerful? Answer: South, even though South has the least number of points. When you lead your Jack of Spades, West covers with the Queen, you cover with the King from North and East takes the trick with the Ace. After this trick, South's Ten, Nine, and Eight of Spades are all winners.

This shows that when you evaluate a hand, especially when playing in a No Trump contract, you should take into consideration your Tens and cards just below honor rank. A good 16 points will be a hand that includes lots of Nines and Tens, like the following:

♠ AT93
♥ KJT
♦ AT95
♣ AT

This hand has only 16 points, but it's one that should accept an invitational bid of 2 No Trump by partner and go on to bid 3 No Trump. Even though you don't have 17 points, you have all four Tens, and the hand contains only two cards below the rank of Nine! This hand is worth a bid of 3 No Trump because this is a good 16 points.

Look at the following hand, which appeared in a national tournament:

♠ AT95
♥ KT4
♦ AQ7
♣ JT7

This hand has 14 HCP, but many experts opened it 1 No Trump because they elevated it to 15 HCP due to the *body cards*, which include three Tens and one Nine. The hand contains only four cards that aren't honors or body cards. Compare it with the following hand:

♠ A432
♥ A32
♦ A32
♣ A32

This is called *Aces and spaces*, and it can be a disaster because you only have four tricks, the four Aces. You would still open this hand 1 No Trump because you must describe your hand to your partner. But you're going to cringe and sweat until the bidding is over, just praying that it's not passed out and you're not stuck playing it in 1 No Trump. The hand with the body cards, but only 14 HCP is far more powerful than Aces and spaces. Sometimes you have to be flexible in counting your points and analyzing your hand.

Change the former hand by making the Seven of Clubs the Queen, so it looks like this:

♣ AT95
♥ KT4
♦ AQ7
♣ QJT

This is a good 16 HCP, which would accept an invitation to game by bidding game. In the Aces and spaces hand, the invitation should be declined.

Let's look at some *maybe* hands, where your partner responds 2 No Trump to your 1 No Trump opening bid:

1. ♠ J32	2. ♠ KJ7	3. ♠ AQ2	4. ♠ A2
♥ J432	♥ KJ8	♥ 543	♥ K32
♦ AQ32	♦ AQ87	♦ KQ6	♦ AQJ54
♣ AK	♣ K87	♣ KQ65	♣ Q65

Hand 1: Pass. Simple arithmetic prevails. You have 15 HCP. Partner has said, by her 2 No Trump response, "Pard, if you have 17 HCP, go to 3. Otherwise pass because I only have 8 or 9 HCP." With 15 HCP in your hand and a maximum of 9 HCP in your partner's hand, you have a maximum of 24 HCP, not enough for game.

Hand 2: 3 No Trump. You are at the top of your bid, 17 HCP. Even if your partner has her minimum, 8 HCP, 8 + 17 = 25, which is enough to bid game.

Hand 3: Pass. This is the tempting hand, but it's not a good 16 points. "Well," you say to yourself, "I'm only 1 point shy. If my partner is at the top of her bid, 9 HCP, we have 25 between us and that's enough for game." Don't succumb to this temptation. You must assume that your partner is at the bottom of her bid, 8 HCP, and 8 +16 = 24, not enough for game. Better to bid 2 and make 3 than to bid 3 and make 2!

Hand 4: 3 No Trump. Did you miss this one? You only have 16 HCP, but you have a very good five-card suit that should give you four tricks by itself. When you have a five-card suit headed by at least one of the top three honors, and you receive an invitation from your partner, accept it and take it to game. A good five-card suit is valuable when playing in No Trump.

Rebids When Your Partner Gives a Weak Response

When you open 1 No Trump and your partner bids a suit other than Clubs directly at the 2 level, it's a sign-off bid, and you should pass. She's telling you that she has a weak hand with either five or more Diamonds, Hearts, or Spades, and that the contract should be played in her suit.

Rebids When Your Partner Gives an Invitational Response in a Suit

When your partner bids 2 Clubs (Stayman), and then bids a suit different than the one you bid, she's telling you that she has an invitational hand, 8 to 9 points, and a five-card suit. Suppose the bidding goes like this.

You	LHO		Partner	RHO
1 No Trump	Pass	2 Clubs	Pass	
2 Diamonds	Pass	2 Spades	Pass	

Your 2 Diamond bid tells her that you don't have a four-card major. Her 2 Spade bid tells you that she has at least a five-card Spade suit with 8 to 9 points. Your response should be along the following lines:

♦ Pass if you have a minimum hand with three Spades.

♦ 2 No Trump with minimum hand and only two Spades.

♦ 3 Spades if you have at least three Spades and 17 points or a good 16.

♦ 3 No Trump if you have only two Spades but a maximum hand with 17 points or a good 16. If she has six Spades, she'll bid 4 Spades because she knows you should be playing in game in the major suit if you have an eight-card fit. Your bid of 3 No Trump tells her that you have a maximum hand but only two Spades.

Rebids When Your Partner Jumps to 3 No Trump

If responder has bid 3 No Trump, opener *must* pass. It doesn't matter if you are head over heels in love with your hand, if you have a long suit, if you are at the maximum, whatever. You have described your hand to your partner so she knows, within a couple of points, what you have. You must trust her. She's telling you that based on what she knows about your two hands 3 No Trump is the proper contract—no more, no less. So when you hear your loving partner say, "3 No Trump," you say, "Pass."

Responding to Stayman

When your partner bids 2 Clubs she's asking you if you have a four-card major. If you do, bid it. But what if you don't? What if you have a good four- or five-card minor in Clubs? Do you raise her 2 Club bid to 3?

Not in this lifetime. If you don't have a four-card major, you *must* bid 2 Diamonds. A bid of 2 Diamonds is conventional and denies a four-card major. It says nothing about your Diamond suit. When your partner bids 2 Clubs (a conventional bid, saying nothing about Clubs) in response to your opening bid of 1 No Trump, she's asking, "Do you have a four-card major?" You can answer one of two ways:

- 2 Hearts or 2 Spades ("yes")

- 2 Diamonds ("no")

If your hand contains two four-card majors, you respond Hearts first. If you respond 2 Spades to 2 Clubs, you're showing four Spades and denying having four Hearts. However, the response of 2 Hearts to 2 Clubs guarantees having a four-card Heart suit but does not deny having four Spades.

Also, remember that when you open 1 No Trump you have designated your partner as the captain of your team for this hand. So her first question may be to find out if you have a four-card major. When she discovers the answer to this question, she'll either place the contract, or tell you something about her hand by making an invitational bid. Then it will be up to you to place the contract. But so far, you don't know much about her hand, except that she has a four-card major. So you just answer no by saying 2 Diamonds and leave the rest of it up to her. Let's look at some hands and see how you'd respond after you opened 1 No Trump and your partner responded 2 Clubs:

1. ♠ A32	2. ♠ A432	3. ♠ A43	4. ♠ AKJ9
♥ KJ9	♥ KQ6	♥ KQ3	♥ 5432
♦ KJ8	♦ KQ5	♦ KQ92	♦ A9
♣ K984	♣ K32	♣ K98	♣ AT9

Hand 1: 2 Diamonds. No four-card major. Your answer is "no."

Hand 2: 2 Spades. You have one four-card major, Spades, so you bid it. This rebid absolutely denies a four-card Heart suit.

Hand 3: 2 Diamonds. This is a strong hand with 17 HCP. Despite that, you must respond 2 Diamonds. Your partner is now the captain for this hand. She has asked one simple question, "Do you have a four-card major?" That's all she wants to know. She doesn't care, at this point, whether you have 15 HCP or 17 HCP. All she wants to know is whether or not you have a four-card major, and your answer is "no."

Hand 4: 2 Hearts. You have two four-card majors, consisting of a terrific Spade suit and a terrible Heart suit. You *must* bid the Heart suit first. That's your agreement. She has at least one four-card major. It might be Hearts. You'd rather play in a 4–4 Heart fit with your Hearts than a 4–2, or worse, Spade suit with your Spades, wouldn't you? If you wouldn't, you'd better go back and reread the chapters on suit bids and responses. Also, remember that bidding your four-card Heart suit does not deny a four-card Spade suit. If you bypass the Hearts to bid the Spades, however, you'll be lying to your partner, telling her that you don't have four Hearts. If she then bids 2 No Trump, telling you that her four-card major is Spades, not Hearts, you can rebid 4 Spades to tell her that you have four Spades as well as four Hearts. Because her bid of 2 No Trump is invitational, and you have enough to play in game in a suit (your doubleton Diamond gives you 17 points in a suit contract), you must bid game. If you bid 3 Spades, your partner is allowed to pass.

Like it or not, when you open 1 No Trump you are giving up power. You are just putty in your partner's hands. She is in control and should either place the contract, or, after she's found out as much about your hand as she can, give you a clue about her hand so you can decide where to play the contract. So just relax, answer the questions, and enjoy it.

Rebidding over Interference When Your Partner Responds

Two types of interference can occur when your partner responds to your opening bid of 1 No Trump. Interference can occur *before* your partner bids, or it can occur *after* your partner bids. We've already covered how responder handles interference before she bids, but how does opening bidder respond when interference occurs after her partner bids?

Bidding over Opponent's Suit Bid After Your Partner Bids Stayman

Opponents take a chance in bidding a suit after your partner has bid 2 Clubs, Stayman. This gives you information about their hands and cards that you would not otherwise have.

For example, your partner bids Stayman, asking if you have a four-card major, and RHO bids 2 Hearts. If you have four Hearts, you probably don't want to be playing this hand in Hearts. If you have Hearts well-stopped, and don't have four Spades, you can respond 2 No Trump, telling your partner that she needn't worry much about Hearts if you play the hand in No Trump. But you might want to double for penalty. Look at the following auction.

You	LHO	Partner	RHO
1 No Trump	Pass	2 Clubs	2 Hearts
?			

1. ♠ AQ65	2. ♠ A72	3. ♠ 5432	4. ♠ KQ2	5. ♠ 32
♥ 32	♥ AQ	♥ AJ9	♥ 98	♥ AQ65
♦ KJ9	♦ KT73	♦ KJ8	♦ AJ98	♦ KJ9
♣ AQ98	♣ QJ98	♣ KQJ	♣ KQ64	♣ AQ98

Hand 1: 2 Spades. You bid what you would have bid had there been no interference. If your partner's suit is Hearts, she can bid 2 No Trump or 3 No Trump depending on the strength of her hand. If her suit is Spades, then you've found your fit and she'll place the contract or give you an invitational bid of 3 Spades.

Hand 2: 2 No Trump. You don't have four Spades, but you do have the Heart suit well-stopped. That's what this bid tells your partner: "Don't worry about Hearts, pard, because I can take care of them."

Hand 3: 2 Spades. Your Spades are terrible, but you do have four of them. If that's your partner's suit, you'll be okay because you'll be in a 4–4 fit.

Hand 4: Pass. You have a minimum No Trump opening, no Heart stopper, and you don't have four Spades. Both you and your partner have bid and have nice hands, but this does not mean you have to continue in the auction and play the hand. If your partner doesn't have any Hearts, you could lose six Heart tricks off the top in No Trump. On the other hand, if your partner just has two Aces, the Ace of Clubs and the Ace of Spades, or one Ace and the King or Queen of Diamonds, you have a good chance to set a bid of 2 Hearts. Your pass is non-committal, and it's up to your partner to decide whether to play or defend.

Hand 5: Double for penalty. Your Hearts are terrific. You're telling your partner that you have no fear of opponent's Hearts and you're willing to defend. It will be up to your partner to decide whether to defend or play. You'll learn about penalty in Chapter 18.

The Least You Need to Know

◆ With a maximum hand, you rebid game after an invitational bid by your partner.

◆ With less than a maximum hand, you play at the lowest level available.

◆ Respond to Stayman by bidding your lowest-ranking four-card major or 2 Diamonds if you don't have a four-card major.

◆ Pass if your partner jumps to 3 No Trump.

◆ If responder bids Stayman and then a major, she's showing a five-card suit.

Chapter 13

We Can Work It Out: Rebids by 1 of a Suit Opener

In This Chapter

- ◆ Rebids with a minimum hand
- ◆ Rebids when your partner passes
- ◆ Rebids when you have more than a minimum opening hand
- ◆ Rebids over interference after your partner responds
- ◆ What a reverse is and what it means

Opener's first rebid is the bid that many experts feel is the most descriptive and most important bid in the auction. When you open 1 of a suit, you tell your partner only that you have between 13 and 21 points. It's with your first rebid that you more specifically describe your hand to your partner.

An Introduction to the Reverse

You're going to be reading about reverses throughout this chapter, so I'm going to define it up front. A *reverse* is when opener rebids a suit at the 2 level that is higher ranking than the suit that she opened at the 1 level. Example: You open 1 Club. Your partner responds 1 Spade. You bid 2 Diamonds. Diamonds is higher ranking than Clubs, and you have bid them at the 2 level, so you have reversed.

A reverse promises that you have at least 17 points and is *forcing* on your partner for one round. In other words, if you reverse, your partner *must* bid again, no matter how weak her hand. I'll go into more detail later in this chapter.

> **Bridgebit**
>
> One of my partners, LuAnne Leonard, was trying to explain the concept of the reverse to her boyfriend, who was just learning. When he was having a hard time understanding, LuAnne turned to another of my partners, Marilyn Mitchell, and asked her to explain it. Marilyn gave one of the best definitions I've heard: "It's a helluva hand!" she said.

> **Lingo**
>
> **Forcing** means that your partner must bid if her RHO passes your bid.

> **Lingo**
>
> The term **extra values** refers to a hand that is more powerful than the minimum indicated by your partner's open. If your partner opens a suit bid at the 1 level, her minimum values are 13 to 15 points. So if she has opened up a hand that has more than 15 points, she has extra values.

Now I'm going to give you a caveat. Many Rubber Bridge players don't know the concept of the reverse. Just to give you an example: when I started playing Bridge again several years after graduating from college, I met a law school classmate of mine, Wall Street attorney Peter Kalat, to play in a regional tournament in Pasadena. Peter had been playing since law school and was a very good, experienced player.

We sat down at one table and the bidding proceeded. I was dummy and when I laid my hand down I noticed that all three players looked at me quizzically. After the hand Peter asked me, "Do you know who those two guys were?" I said no. He said, "Alfred Sheinwold and Frank Stewart, two of the best players in the world."

Then he said, "You reversed." It was like he was speaking Martian, but the tone in his voice told me I had done something wrong. I had no idea what he was talking about.

Peter explained what a reverse was, and then gave me an article on reverses that explained them in more detail. But the reason they all looked at me so funny when I put my hand down as dummy was that, by reversing, I had promised at least 17 points and I only had 13 points.

At this point I had been playing Rubber Bridge several times a week for a couple of years, and nobody with whom I had been playing would have recognized a reverse if it slapped them in the face. However, playing reverses is very good bidding procedure, so you should learn them and be aware of them. Try to avoid reversing unless you have the proper hand. You will be a better player for it.

What Type of Hand Do You Have?

Basically, when you open 1 of a suit, you can have three types of hands.

Type	Points
Minimum	13–15
Extra values	16–18
Big	19–21

Rebidding a Minimum Hand

If your partner bids a new suit, even if it's only at the 1 level, you're required to bid again. If your partner doesn't describe a hand with extra values by making some sort of jump response, you have to describe your hand as minimum. This is how you do it.

Partner Responds with a Bid of 1 of a Suit at the 1 Level

If your partner bids a higher-ranking suit than the suit with which you opened and stays at the 1 level, her hand is basically undefined. All you know for sure is that she has at least 6 points and at least four cards in the suit she bid. That could be all she has, but she could have a lot more. Therefore, you must describe what you have to her.

Bidding a Second Suit as a Rebid

Your first choice as a rebid is generally to bid a higher-ranking second suit at the 1 level if you have it. When you bid a second suit in your first rebid, you're generally promising that you have at least four cards in that suit. You're not sticking your neck out much because your partner can't support opener's second suit unless she has four cards in that suit.

A very important rule that you must remember is that *responder may not support opener's second suit unless responder has four cards in that suit.* If you're responder and you only have three cards in opener's second suit, you can't support it. This should be imprinted on your brain.

Supporting Your Partner's Suit

If your partner bids a new suit at the 1 level after your opening bid and you hold a minimum without a higher-ranking four-card suit, you may support it *only if you have four cards in her suit.* You may not support your partner's new suit response with only three-card support. Why? Because she can bid a four-card suit. You're looking for an eight-card fit. You don't know whether she has four cards in the suit or more. But, if your first rebid is to support her suit, you're absolutely promising her that you have four cards in her suit.

Rebid When You Can't Support Your Partner's Suit

If you don't have four cards in her suit, you have three possible rebids:

♦ **1 No Trump.** You may do this with a balanced hand. It tells your partner that you have no singletons or voids and probably only one doubleton at most. It also tells her that you have a minimum hand, and implies stoppers in the unbid suits.

♦ **Rebid your opening suit.** Rebidding your suit usually implies that you have six cards in it, but sometimes you have no choice but to rebid a five-card suit.

♦ **Bid a new suit at the 2 level that is lower ranking than your opening suit.** For example, if you open 1 Heart and your partner responds 1 Spade, you may rebid 2 Clubs if you have a four-card Club suit. This bidding sequence would generally show that you had five Hearts and either four or five Clubs.

> **CAUTION**
>
> **Alert**
>
> In bidding a second suit at the 2 level in your first rebid, you must be careful not to reverse.

If you make a rebid at the 2 level of your second suit lower ranking than your opening suit, you are asking your partner to make a choice between the two suits you bid. If you opened a major and rebid a minor she should go back to the major if she has two cards in your major suit, even if she has four cards in your minor suit.

Here's a summation of your rebids when you open 1 of a suit and your partner responds by bidding 1 of a higher-ranking suit:

Your Holding	Rebid
13–15 points, a four-card suit higher than your partner's suit	Bid your higher-ranking four-card suit at the 1 level.
13–15 points, less than six cards in your suit, less than four cards in responder's suit, balanced hand	1 No Trump.
13–15 points, six cards in your suit	Rebid your suit at the 2 level.

Your Holding	Rebid
13–15 points, less than six cards in your suit, a four-card suit lower ranking than your opening suit	Bid your lower-ranking four-card suit.
13–15 points, less than six cards in your suit, but four cards in your partner's suit	Raise your partner's suit to the 2 level.

Okay, let's look at some hands. You open 1 Diamond and your partner responds 1 Spade. What's your rebid?

1. ♠ 7
   ♥ KQJT
   ♦ A973
   ♣ K874

2. ♠ KQ8
   ♥ 65
   ♦ AQJ42
   ♣ J98

3. ♠ 4
   ♥ KQJT
   ♦ AQJ84
   ♣ AK3

4. ♠ QT84
   ♥ 3
   ♦ AQJ74
   ♣ AQ6

5. ♠ QT84
   ♥ K86
   ♦ A832
   ♣ A9

6. ♠ 86
   ♥ KQ83
   ♦ KJT7
   ♣ A83

Hand 1: 2 Clubs. You may not rebid 1 No Trump with a singleton. A new suit here lower ranking than your first bid suit shows a minimum, but does not deny extra values. It tells your partner to choose between the two suits you have bid.

Hand 2: 2 Diamonds. This hand poses a very difficult decision for you. Your Spades, although only three, are very good. You would like to have four-card support, but this is a hand with which you could bid 2 Spades instead of 2 Diamonds and your partner would not have much to criticize. She'll undoubtedly play you for having four Spades if you raise her, but you're giving her two of the top three honors, so this will mute most of her objections if she bid a four-card Spade suit, which is all she's promising. Either bid would be acceptable and would show a minimum hand.

Alert

I want to reemphasize here that the Rubber Bridge players you encounter might not know what a reverse is. Therefore, they might not recognize it as forcing. Similarly, they might unknowingly reverse with a weak hand. To guard against misunderstandings, when you play with a new partner, ask if she plays reverses.

Hand 3: 2 Hearts. This is a classic reverse by you and shows a hand with extra values. After opening 1 Diamond, you rebid 2 Hearts, a higher-ranking suit bid at the next level. The bid implies that your second bid suit, Hearts, is shorter than your first bid suit, Diamonds. Here you open with the five-card suit and rebid the four-card Heart suit. It's forcing on your partner to keep the bid open for at least one more round.

Hand 4: 3 Spades. After you reevaluate your hand by giving yourself 3 points for your singleton now that you know you have at least a 4–4 trump fit, you have 17 points. The jump in your partner's suit shows a hand with extra values. You'll learn about jump rebids later in this chapter. The bid is invitational only to game. Your partner may pass you.

Hand 5: 2 Spades. This is what you were looking for, a 4–4 fit in your major suit. But, you only have a minimum hand, so you just make a minimum raise to the 2 level. In Chapter 14 you'll learn how your partner proceeds from here.

Hand 6: 1 No Trump. You can't support your partner's Spades with only two. You can't rebid your Diamonds because you only have four. You can't bid Clubs because you only have three. You can't bid Hearts because that would be a reverse, showing extra values. You may bid 1 No Trump. You have a minimum hand, no singletons or voids, and have all the other suits stopped.

Finally, look at these hands when you open 1 Club and your partner responds 1 Diamond:

1. ♠ AQ76	2. ♠ 54	3. ♠ 87	4. ♠ 94
♥ 8642	♥ 7642	♥ AKQ	♥ A6
♦ 87	♦ AKQJ	♦ 87	♦ A953
♣ AK7	♣ A64	♣ KQT983	♣ KQJT3

Hand 1: 1 Heart. You bid your higher-ranking four-card suits up the line, so even though your Spades are much stronger, you rebid 1 Heart. Your partner might have five Diamonds and four Spades. If so, she'll respond with a bid of 1 Spade and you can still find your 4–4 Spade fit.

Hand 2: 1 Heart. You could support Diamonds, but you're looking for a major suit fit. You must tell her you have four Hearts. If you were to support Diamonds at your first rebid, you would be denying a four-card major.

Hand 3: 2 Clubs. You have a six-card suit and don't have a four-card major you can bid at the 1 level over her 1 Diamond response.

Hand 4: 2 Diamonds. Your Clubs are nice, but she might not have any. Because you have four cards in her suit, and you don't have a higher-ranking four-card suit to bid, and you don't have Spades stopped, 2 Diamonds is your only call. Incidentally, this is *not* a reverse because, even though you're bidding a higher-ranking suit at the 2 level, it's in support of your partner's suit. This takes it out of the realm of reverses.

Your Partner Responds 1 No Trump

When your partner responds to your opening bid of 1 of a suit with a response of 1 No Trump, she's denying that she has a four-card suit higher ranking than the suit you opened. If you opened a four-card suit, then you can't have a hand with two doubletons, although you could be 4–4–4–1. In any event, if you open a four-card suit you can't rebid it. If you open 1 Diamond and your partner responds 1 No Trump, she has denied four Hearts or four Spades. If she had five Diamonds she probably would have raised to 2 Diamonds. So she must have at least three Clubs in her hand. If you don't like your chances in No Trump after the bidding has gone 1 Diamond–1 No Trump, you can chance a rebid of 2 Clubs if you have four of them in your hand. This is telling your partner that you have a minimum hand but don't want to play in No Trump and asking her to pick which suit she would like to play at the 2 level, Diamonds or Clubs.

If you have a balanced hand without any voids or singletons and no more than one doubleton, you should pass her bid of 1 No Trump and let her play it there. She's telling you that she has a weak hand. Keep it at a low level before you get in trouble in a contract you can't make.

Your Partner Makes a Simple Raise of Your Opening Bid

If your partner raises your 1 bid to the 2 level, you should pass if you have a minimum opening. Why? You have no more than 15 points in your hand. She has no more than 9 points in her hand. The mathematics are simple, 15 + 9 = 24. You have little chance for game, so why go on?

Your Partner Responds in a New Suit at the 2 Level

Finally, your partner is showing a hand that is better than the minimum. In all the examples we've seen so far, your partner has either shown a minimum hand, by making a simple raise or by bidding 1 No Trump, or made an ambiguous bid of a suit at the 1 level that might be minimum—or it might not.

But when she responds in a new suit at the 2 level, she's promising at least 10 points, maybe more. If you have a minimum, you have to tell her this. Her bid is forcing on you to bid again. You can't pass.

Look at the following hands where you opened 1 Heart and your partner responded 2 Diamonds:

1.	♠ A7	2.	♠ AQ	3.	♠ KJ	4.	♠ A3
	♥ KQJT3		♥ KJ865		♥ KQ963		♥ KQT963
	♦ Q7		♦ J42		♦ 84		♦ 874
	♣ JT74		♣ QT8		♣ AK93		♣ AK

Hand 1: 2 Hearts. You're not strong enough to bid 3 Clubs. Your Heart suit is good and you show a minimum hand. If you were to bid 3 Clubs you would show a hand with extra values, which this hand does not possess.

Hand 2: 2 No Trump. You could raise Diamonds, but the 2 No Trump bid is a better description of your hand. It also shows a minimum and allows your partner to pass. At this point you may be asking yourself, "What's the difference between Hand 1 and Hand 2 that allows you to rebid 2 Hearts in Hand 1 but says you should bid 2 No Trump in Hand 2?" You rebid 2 Hearts in Hand 1 because of the quality of the Heart suit and the unbalanced nature of the hand. You only have one Spade stopper and one Club stopper. You bid 2 No Trump in Hand 2 because the Heart suit isn't as good as it is in Hand 1—you have two Spade stoppers, and the hand is more balanced, with only one doubleton. Both bids, however, tell your partner that you have a minimum hand, and this is the vital information that you want to convey.

Hand 3: 3 Clubs. This is a hand with extra values, unlike Hand 1. When you raise the level of the bidding with a new suit in your rebid you are showing extra values. This bid is forcing on partner to keep the auction open to game.

Hand 4: 3 Hearts. Again, this shows extra values and at least six Hearts.

Here's a summary of what you've just learned. If your partner bid a suit.

Your Holding	Rebid
13–15 points, a five-card opening suit, less than three cards in your partner's major suit or less than four cards in your partner's minor suit, unbid suits stopped, no singletons or voids	2 No Trump.
Same, but with support for your partner's suit	Raise your partner's suit.

Here's a summary of what to do if your partner responded 1 No Trump.

Your Holding	Rebid
13–15 points, balanced hand	Pass.
13–15 points, with a singleton or void	Bid a lower-ranking four-card suit at the 2 level or rebid your five-card opening suit.
13–15 points, less than six cards in your suit, but four cards in your partner's suit	Raise your partner's suit to the 2 level.

Rebidding After Your Partner Passes

If your partner passed, what does that tell you? It tells you several things:

◆ If there was no intervening bid between you and her, she does not have 6 points.

◆ If there was an intervening bid between you and her, she might have more than 6 points but your LHO might have bid her suit. However, if she passes after an intervening bid, then either one of two situations exist:

  ◆ Your LHO bid her suit.

  ◆ She has less than 6 points.

One thing you can count on is that you probably don't have an eight-card trump fit. It's possible she has three cards in your suit but less than 6 points, but you can't count on it. If she passes, you should assume she has less than 6 points and less than three cards in your suit. If you make these assumptions, you're not going to get hurt by rebidding based on a false expectation of support when she indicated none. Hope springs eternal, but it shouldn't in Bridge. If your partner says "Pass," take her at her word and don't count on her for anything. Unless you have more than a minimum, shortness in opponents' suit, or some other reason to bid, if your opponents have bid and it's passed around to you, you should pass.

How to proceed when you have opened and your partner has passed is an important aspect of the game. Let's look at some minimum hands after the following bidding.

You	LHO	Partner	RHO
1 Heart	Pass	Pass	2 Clubs
?			

1. ♠ K43	2. ♠ AJ75	3. ♠ 86	4. ♠ 98	5. ♠ 4
♥ AK763	♥ QJ872	♥ AKJ943	♥ JT9854	♥ KJ9753
♦ A6	♦ A	♦ K84	♦ AQJ9	♦ K83
♣ 863	♣ 984	♣ 74	♣ A	♣ AQ9

Hand 1: Pass. You don't have anything else to bid. You can't rebid your Hearts because you only have five and you don't have a four-card suit to bid. Further, your partner has denied 6 points and probably doesn't have Heart support. If you take another bid you're just going to get in trouble.

Hand 2: Pass. Again, you shouldn't rebid your weak five-card Heart suit. You can't bid Spades because that would be a reverse showing at least 17 points, which you don't have. Anyway, if your partner had 6 points and four Spades, she would have responded 1 Spade to your 1 Heart opening. Remember this before you fall in love with your Spades. Your partner's pass tells you a lot.

Hand 3: Pass. You might rebid your Heart suit if you're not vulnerable. But this hand looks like trouble. Your partner doesn't have much help for you and you don't have any outside source of tricks. What are you going to do for tricks, especially if your LHO has the Ace of Diamonds? You'll probably take five Heart tricks only for down 3. So even though you have six Hearts and could rebid them, pass would be the prudent move. However, if your Nine of Hearts was a Ten of Hearts instead, you might be tempted to take a 2 Heart bid. Do you know why? Because you would have *100 honors*, four of the five honors in the trump suit, which would give you 100 points above the line if you get the contract in Hearts. So, even if you were to get the bid and go down 2, undoubled, you would break even. They'd get 100 points above the line, but so would you for your 100 honors. However, don't succumb to this temptation. You shouldn't make a bad bid simply because you have 100 honors.

Hand 4: 2 Diamonds. Your six-card Heart suit is woeful to rebid when your partner passes, but this distributional hand could be nice if you find your partner with four Diamonds in her hand. If it's passed to your partner, it's up to her to make a preference at this point between Hearts and Diamonds. You will clearly pass no matter what she does.

Hand 5: 2 Hearts. Your Heart suit is not terrific, but you do have six along with a singleton Spade and sources of tricks in both Clubs and Diamonds. Even without much help from your partner you should compete at the 2 level. If they go to three, however, and your partner remains silent, let them have it.

There are several points I want you to take from this exercise:

- **Listen to your partner.** If she passes without an intervening bid, in considering your rebid you should assume she has the minimum, nothing.

- **You should strain to rebid a six-card suit.** This is crucial information for your partner. If she has two of your suit she knows that with a maximum pass in her hand, 5 points, she might be able to compete to the 3 level in your suit, something she'd never do if she thought you only had a five-card suit. Further, in a distributional hand you want ruffing power. In Hand 5, you have a good chance of getting two Club tricks, depending on the location of the King, regardless of what's trump. You want to be able to ruff Spades with your little Hearts!

- **Count your tricks.** Even if you have a terrific six-card suit, like you do in Hand 3, if you have no outside source of tricks and your partner has no help, you could be in big trouble if you rebid your suit.

What Does Your Partner's Response Mean?

If she responds, she's telling you a lot. First, if she supports your major suit opening she's telling you a couple of things:

- She has at least three cards in your suit.

- She has a minimum hand, not more than 9 points and not less than 6 points, and will probably not bid again unless you force her. But even if she bids another suit, she doesn't necessarily deny support for your suit. She might just be telling you she has another suit, or the number of points in her hand before she tells you she has support.

If she bids a new suit, it is 100 percent forcing on you to bid again. This means that you may pass your partner's response to your opening bid only in the following three instances:

- She bids 1 No Trump in response to your opening suit bid.

- She raises your opening suit bid to the 2 level.

- Your RHO makes an intervening bid.

These things should be going through your mind when you hear your partner bid and it comes back to you to make a rebid.

Analysis of Your Partner's Response

When your partner bids a suit, refer to Chapters 10 and 11 on responses and you'll see what your partner has told you. To recap, if she bids at the 1 level, she's promising only a minimum hand and four cards in the suit she bid. If she bids at the 2 level without a jump, she's showing at least 10 points and five cards in the suit if she bids a major but only four cards in the suit if she bids a minor. If she jumps, she's showing a more powerful hand.

Let's say you open 1 Club and she bids 1 Spade. What do you know about her hand? She has at least 6 points and at least four Spades. Anything else? You know at least two more things about her hand. What are they?

Answer: Her Hearts and Diamonds are not longer than her Spades. Remember, you bid your longest suit in response to your partner's opening bid, and if two suits are four cards equal in length you bid the lower ranking, or *up the line*. If you have two five-card suits, you bid the higher ranking, or *down the line*. So you know for an absolute fact that your partner has at least 6 points, at least four Spades, and not more cards in each of Hearts and Diamonds than she has in Spades. That's quite a lot to know from one bid, don't you think?

What if you open 1 Diamond and she bids 2 Clubs? This time she's telling you a little more. First, she is promising you more points, at least 10. Second, she's telling you that she has at least four Clubs and that her Clubs are longer than her Hearts and her Spades.

What if you open 1 Heart and she bids 1 No Trump with no intervening bid? Well, you know three things for sure:

◆ She has at least 6 points. She shouldn't bid unless she has at least 6 points.

◆ She doesn't have four Spades. If she had four Spades she would bid 1 Spade after your opening bid of 1 Heart, with one exception. The one exception is if she has an absolute minimum hand with four Spades and three Hearts. In that event she would only have one bid she could make and it should be to support your Hearts, so she'd *bypass* her four-card Spade suit to bid 2 Hearts.

◆ She doesn't have three Hearts. If she had three Hearts, she would support you immediately, especially if she had a minimum hand.

So, with that one bid of hers, you can forget about trying to find an eight-card fit in a major if you opened a five-card suit!

The point of all this is that bidding requires deductive reasoning—listening to what your partner has *not* bid to determine what she has in her hand. You must take negative inferences.

Analyzing for a Rebid

You shouldn't open if you don't have a rebid. As I said in Chapter 6 on opening bids of 1 of a suit, when considering opening, you should always ask yourself, "What am I going to bid if my partner bids thus and so?" "Thus and so" being the worst response you could hope for with your hand, probably bidding your singleton or void. If you don't have a rebid, you shouldn't open.

When I was just a Bridge tyke I had heard this maxim. One day I looked at a 14-point hand and didn't see a rebid, so I passed and the hand was passed out. When we looked at the cards it was clear that we could have made game because my partner had 12 points and we had a fit. They asked me why I didn't open. "I didn't have a rebid," I replied. They all laughed … and they weren't laughing with me.

A 14-point hand always has a rebid. Remember that. And often it's 1 No Trump.

Rebidding 1 No Trump

What does 1 No Trump rebid by opener tell partner? Several things:

- Opener has no more than 14 points.
- Opener has a balanced hand.
- Opener doesn't have four cards in responder's suit.
- Partner becomes captain of the hand, just as if opener opened with 1 No Trump (which would, of course, show a stronger hand than a rebid of 1 No Trump).

You can't make a 1 No Trump rebid as opener if you have a singleton or void. If you have a singleton or void, however, you must have at least two four-card suits, so your rebid would be your lower-ranking four-card suit, if you can't support your partner's response. Let's look at some hands, all of which you open 1 Club and your partner responds 1 Heart:

1. ♠ AK74	2. ♠ AK7	3. ♠ QT94	4. ♠ K8	5. ♠ 85
♥ 74	♥ 7532	♥ AK9	♥ Q7	♥ KJ
♦ Q84	♦ 983	♦ 75	♦ K932	♦ KJ3
♣ A832	♣ AK9	♣ A942	♣ AT432	♣ AJT643

Hand 1: 1 Spade. You have four Spades. When you open 1 Club you generally deny having as many as five Spades, so you're telling your partner that basically you have a maximum 18-point hand with four Spades. She might have bid a four-card Heart suit up the line and have four Spades, too.

Hand 2: 2 Hearts. Sure, your Hearts aren't pretty, but you have the correct number, four, so you will be in a 4–4 at worst if you play in Hearts.

Hand 3: 1 Spade. You certainly have nice Heart support, but you don't have four cards in the suit. So tell her about your Spades now. Her hand might be a minimum. She might have four Spades. She might have five Hearts or more. You just don't know. The best thing to do is to describe your hand as accurately as possible and let her take it from there.

Hand 4: 1 No Trump. You can't support Hearts. You can't bid Diamonds because it would be a reverse. (Didn't I tell you this word would be used a lot during this chapter?) You shouldn't rebid your Clubs because you only have five cards in your Club suit. A 1 No Trump rebid says that you have a minimum hand and denies four of your partner's suit.

Hand 5: 2 Clubs. You have a six-card suit and nothing else to rebid. Again, this tells your partner you have opened up a minimum hand.

But look at these hands:

You	Partner
♠ 82	♠ KQ96
♥ AKQJ9	♥ T72
♦ J85	♦ K976
♣ Q54	♣ JT

How would you bid it, as opener and responder? Before looking at how it should be bid, go ahead and bid it, assuming no intervening bids.

Okay, here's how it went. You opened 1 Heart, right? You have 14 points, so you couldn't open 1 No Trump. Responder bid 1 Spade. That's correct. Responder has 9 HCP and four Spades, a perfect bid.

So what's your rebid? You could rebid your strong Hearts, although you only have five. Your better response is what we've been discussing, 1 No Trump. You have 14 points, but 10 of them are in Hearts. So you let your partner know that you're basically a minimum open with a balanced hand. Your partner clearly can't take another call. Her response was minimum. Unless you make a forcing bid, she has to pass whatever you bid. It was passed out at 1 No Trump and that's what it made, exactly 1 No Trump.

Rebidding with Better Than a Minimum Hand

When you open a hand with extra values, a big hand, your rebids must communicate the strength of your hand to your partner. You should make a bid that she can't pass.

Reverses

As explained at the beginning of the chapter, a reverse is when opener bids a higher-ranking suit at the 2 level than the suit she opened with at the 1 level. Example: You open 1 Club. Your partner responds 1 Spade. You bid 2 Diamonds. Diamonds is higher ranking than Clubs, and you have bid them at the 2 level, so you have reversed.

To repeat, a reverse promises that you have at least 17 points and is forcing on your partner for one round. In other words, your partner *must* bid again, no matter how weak her hand, if you reverse.

Generally, a reverse also tells your partner that you have more cards, at least five, in the suit you opened and less cards, usually four, in the suit to which you reverse. So, in the previous example, you would have five Clubs and four Diamonds, or, rarely, six Clubs and five Diamonds.

If you play reverses, and most good players do, it causes problems when you have merely an opening hand with a longer, lower-ranking suit. For example, look at this hand:

♠ 98
♥ 75
♦ AK84
♣ KQ983

Normally, from what you've learned so far, this would clearly be a hand that you would open 1 Club, because you have five Clubs. But—and this is another rule you've already learned, but that you should have ingrained in your head—*when you open the bidding, be sure you have a rebid*. If you don't have a rebid, you shouldn't open the bidding. This hand illustrates this rule if you are playing reverses.

And this is why. If you open 1 Club and your partner responds with 1 Heart or 1 Spade, which, due to the perverse nature of the Bridge gods, she is almost certain to do, given the shape of your hand, you have no rebid! Why? Because you can't rebid 1 No Trump because you don't have the other major stopped. You can't rebid 2 Diamonds because your hand isn't powerful enough. A rebid in 2 Diamonds after your partner responds 1 of a major over a 1 Club open would be a reverse showing at least 17 points. You could rebid 2 Clubs, but it's not a great description of your hand.

So, in this instance, you should open this hand 1 Diamond. Then when your partner responds with 1 Heart or 1 Spade, you can rebid 2 Clubs, showing a minimum hand. This is one of the few times when you may open a shorter, higher-ranking suit instead of a longer, lower-ranking suit.

Let's look at some hands that we examined earlier. When we first looked at these hands you had opened the bidding with a bid of 1 Heart, your partner passed, and your RHO bid 2 Clubs. This time, however, let's say that you still open 1 Heart, but your partner bids 2 Clubs. (Please note that Hand 1 has been altered somewhat.)

1. ♠ K43	2. ♠ AJ75	3. ♠ 86	4. ♠ 98
♥ AK763	♥ QJ872	♥ AKJ943	♥ JT9854
♦ 64	♦ A	♦ K84	♦ AQ76
♣ K63	♣ 984	♣ 74	♣ A

What's your rebid?

Hand 1: 2 Hearts. You can't bid 2 No Trump because you don't have Diamonds stopped. This hand is as weak as it can be and still have enough points to open.

Hand 2: 3 Clubs. This hand is very weak. You can't bid 2 Spades, your other four-card suit, because that would be a reverse, and you are far too weak to make a reverse. Your supporting partner's suit here shows a minimum hand and invites a pass.

Hand 3: 2 Hearts. You have six Hearts and nothing else to bid. Again, this describes a minimum hand.

Hand 4: 2 Diamonds. Your Hearts are terrible. You are just asking your partner to take a preference. You're going to pass whatever she does unless she makes a forcing bid.

If you have a minimum hand with a higher-ranking four-card suit over your opening five-card suit, you have four choices when your partner responds by bidding a new suit, and you can't reverse because your hand isn't strong enough:

◆ Bid a new suit at the 1 level.

◆ Raise your partner's suit at the lowest level.

◆ Rebid your own suit at the lowest level.

◆ Rebid No Trump at the lowest level, but you must have No Trump distribution. You can't rebid No Trump if you have a void or singleton.

Strong Rebid Jump to Game

If you open a hand at the 1 level and your partner responds in a suit you can support and you have 20 points, you should immediately jump to game. Look at the following hand:

♠ AT92
♥ AK8
♦ A
♣ K7632

The bidding goes like this.

RHO	You	LHO	Partner
Pass	1 Club	1 Diamond	1 Spade
2 Diamonds	4 Spades		

The bidding went on, and we'll discuss it later in Chapter 15. The point to remember here is that when your partner gives you a minimum response, you jump to game immediately with this hand. Why? Because all you need for game in a major suit is 26 points. Your partner has absolutely promised you two things by her bid:

◆ She has at least four Spades.

◆ She has at least 6 points.

That's all you need for game in Spades. You know that you have at least an eight-card fit in trump and you know you have at least 26 points between you. (Actually you know you have at least 27 points because when you find that you have a trump fit your singleton is reevaluated upward by an extra point.)

Lingo
A **sign-off bid** is one intended to close the auction.

So when she responds with these promises, you jump to game. This is *not a sign-off bid*. With extras, your partner may bid on to slam.

This bid is a strength-showing bid, asking your partner to continue bidding to explore slam if she has the values. When you make this bid you're promising your partner that you have at least 20 points.

Opener's Jump to No Trump

If opener jumps to No Trump after partner has bid a new suit at the 1 level, the requirements are as follows.

Rebid	Requirements
2 No Trump	18–19 points, all unbid suits stopped
3 No Trump	20–21 points, all unbid suits stopped

Opener's Jump Shift

If you skip a level of bidding that is available to you and bid a new suit at the same time, you have made a jump shift, and have shown a hand that is between 19 to 22 points. A jump shift that skips a level is forcing to game. Look at the following hand:

♠ A
♥ A8
♦ K76534
♣ AK83

The bidding is as follows.

You	LHO	Partner	RHO
1 Diamond	Pass	1 Spade	Pass
?			

You can't jump in No Trump because you have a singleton in your partner's suit. You can't reverse into Hearts, a two-card suit. A rebid of 2 Clubs would show a minimum hand. You want to make a forcing bid to find out more about your partner's hand. What to do?

The answer is to make a jump shift to 3 Clubs. It's 100 percent forcing on your partner to bid. She can't support you unless she has at least four cards in the suit. By this bid you are telling your partner that you have a big hand but are groping for where to play it. You need more information from her.

The difference between a jump shift and a reverse is that when you reverse you do not skip a level of bidding that is available to you. 1 Club–1 Spade–2 Hearts is a reverse; it does not skip a level available to you. 1 Diamond–1 Spade–3 Clubs is a jump shift because it skips a level available to you, 2 Clubs. It shows a bigger hand than a reverse.

Both a reverse and jump shift are forcing, and therefore both could be just short of a Strong Two opening. They are distinguished only because a jump shift must arrive in game, whereas a reverse sequence may stop short, because a reverse is forcing for one round only.

To summarize …

Bid	Points	Result
Reverse	17+	Forcing for one round
Jump shift	19+	Forcing to game

Evaluating Your Partner's Bid over Interference

If your partner has bid over another bid by your LHO (her RHO), it tells you something different than if she bids without interference. If she bids 1 No Trump over your opening 1 bid without interference, it tells you, simply, that she doesn't have a four-card major higher ranking than the suit you opened, and that she has between 6 to 10 HCP. If she bids 1 No Trump over an interfering bid by her RHO, however, it also promises that she has a stopper in the interfering bidder's suit.

When you open 1 Diamond and your LHO overcalls 1 Heart, if your partner responds 1 No Trump, it tells you three things: First, she has 8 to 10 HCP; second, she doesn't have four Spades; and, third, she has Hearts stopped at least once.

There is a defensive value to straining to support your partner's suit over interference. This is especially true if your opponents are going to be forced up a level if they want to bid their suit again. So if your partner opens 1 Spade and your RHO overcalls 2 Clubs, if you raise to 2 Spades, your LHO will have to go to the 3 level to bid a suit other than Clubs.

You're telling your partner that you are minimum, so you don't have to worry that she'll over evaluate your hand by this bid. Basically, you're just competing, and your partner should know this and shut up if your opponents compete to the 3 level in Clubs. Unless she has extra values in her hand, she should let them play at the 3 level. You will have a better chance of setting them at the 3 level than you would have playing a 3 Spade contract with your weak hand.

The Least You Need to Know

◆ If you have a minimum hand, your rebid should show the values by bidding a lower-ranking suit at the next level, No Trump, or supporting your partner's suit.

◆ You must have four cards in the suit to support your partner's suit.

◆ A reverse is a bid of a higher-ranking suit at a higher level than the suit you bid at your opening bid and shows a minimum of 17 points.

◆ A jump shift changes suit and skips a level of bidding available to you and shows a minimum of 19 points.

Chapter 14

Rebids by Strong Opener and Responder

In This Chapter

- ◆ Rebids by Strong Two Diamonds, Hearts, or Spades opener
- ◆ Rebids by Strong Two Club opener
- ◆ How responder rebids when opener supports her suit
- ◆ How responder rebids when opener doesn't support her suit and shows a minimum

This chapter consists of two parts. The first part deals with rebids by a Strong Two opener. This topic is fairly straightforward, so it doesn't need a lot of space. The second part of the chapter covers responder's first rebid.

As with the first rebid by a 1 of a suit opener, the first rebid by a Strong Two opener is very important. And responder's first rebid really completes the first phase of communication between the partners and sets the stage for concluding the final contract.

When someone opens with a Strong Two, this bid determines how much information the opener can give to responder. Initially, responder only knows that opener has a very strong hand. With the opener's rebid, the auction is moved to the next level. Responder's rebid is extremely important because it basically determines whether or not you're going to play in a partscore, game, or slam.

Rebids by Strong Two Opener in Diamonds, Hearts, or Spades

If you open with a Strong Two in one of these suits and your partner gives you a negative response of 2 No Trump, you let her off the hook if you rebid your opening suit at the 3 level. If you do rebid your suit, your partner may pass. This is the only time that your partner may pass when you open with a Strong Two in these three suits.

It's axiomatic, therefore, that if you bid a new suit, it's forcing on your partner to make another response. For example, suppose the bidding goes as follows.

You	Partner
2 Spades	2 No Trump
3 Clubs	3 Spades
4 Clubs	4 Spades
5 Diamonds	?

You must bid. Anytime a Strong Two opener bids a new suit, responder must bid again. This is especially true when, as here, opener made a bid after you bid game in her suit.

This bid is not called a *two demand* for nothing. Unless you rebid your opening suit, your partner must keep the bidding open until you reach game.

Following is a hand that shows some of the problems encountered by a Strong Two opener:

♠ A
♥ AKJ832
♦ A7
♣ AKT8

Bidding.

You	Partner
2 Hearts	3 Diamonds
?	

The first thing to remember here is that when your partner gives you a positive response, which is any bid other than 2 No Trump or raising your suit a level, she is making a game-forcing bid. You don't need to worry about her passing you out short of game. You can rebid your Heart suit here without thinking that you are allowing her to pass. If you go straight to 4 Hearts, you could find your partner with a void. Your Heart suit is not strong enough for this.

The better bid here is to bid your four-card Club suit. Your partner should know that you may only have four. The problem with this is that it bypasses 3 No Trump. However, you could be very uncomfortable if you were to bid 3 No Trump and find that your partner doesn't have a Spade stopper.

> **Tricks of the Trade**
>
> A bid of 4 Hearts in this situation is weaker than a bid of 3 Hearts. Why? Because after a positive response from your partner, a jump to game by a bid of 4 Hearts would be a *sign-off*, whereas a bid of 3 Hearts asks your partner for more information.

Your partner has told you that she has better than a minimum, however, because she bid 3 Diamonds instead of 2 No Trump. This told you two things about her Diamond suit:

- She has at least five Diamonds.

- She has two of the top four Diamond honors with at least the King.

Those two honors could be the King–Jack, so you don't have total control of any suit. In a contract of 3 No Trump without a Spade stopper in Dummy you could be set by more than one with a Spade lead.

So you're trying to find a fit. If your partner has two Hearts, she should just close out in 4 Hearts.

As it happened, because your partner had four cards in your second suit, she supported it by bidding 5 Clubs. You know by that that your partner has four Clubs because she can't support your second suit without at least four cards in it. With the strength of your hand and your partner's initial positive response by bidding a new suit, you should probably bid 6 Clubs and try for the slam.

Here's how the bidding actually went.

You	LHO	Partner	RHO
2 Hearts	Pass	3 Diamonds	Pass
4 Clubs	Pass	5 Clubs	Pass
6 Clubs	Pass	Pass	Pass

Partner's hand:

♠ Q83
♥ Q
♦ KQ954
♣ J532

Initially, that looks like a pretty weak 10 HCP, with only one King and no Aces. But when you have opened with a two demand, your partner's honors become much more powerful. If she has 10 HCP and you open with a two demand, she knows that you must be in game and should be thinking about slam.

Remember, when you bid a new suit, 4 Clubs, your partner is forced to make another bid. If she had only three Clubs but had two Hearts, she should probably just bid 4 Hearts. But because she had four Clubs, she could support your second suit.

Alert _____

Slam bidding is covered in Chapter 15.

After she has shown you a positive response with her initial bid of 3 Diamonds, you are well within your rights to make a try for 6 Clubs, a small slam. You have 26 points and she has given you a positive response.

Following is the layout of all the hands and how it was played. Again, I suggest you lay the hands out and play it yourself and see how you do.

Dummy
♠ Q83
♥ Q
♦ KQ954
♣ J532

LHO
♠ JT962
♥ 9754
♦ J2
♣ 94

RHO
♠ K754
♥ T6
♦ T863
♣ Q76

You
♠ A
♥ AKJ832
♦ A7
♣ AKT8

Here is the play. L means that card led; * means that card won the trick.

	LHO	Dummy	RHO	You
1.	J ♠ L	3 ♠	7 ♠	A ♠*
2.	7 ♥	Q ♥*	6 ♥	2 ♥ L
3.	4 ♣	J ♣ L	Q ♣	K ♣*
4.	9 ♣	2 ♣	6 ♣	A ♣*L
5.	6 ♠	3 ♣	7 ♣	T ♣*L
6.	4 ♥	8 ♠	T ♥	A ♥*L
7.	5 ♥	Q ♠	3 ♦	K ♥*L
8.	9 ♥	4 ♦	6 ♦	J ♥*L
9.	2 ♦	5 ♦	8 ♦	8 ♥*L
10.	J ♦	9 ♦	4 ♠	3 ♥*L
11.	9 ♠	K ♦*	T ♦	7 ♦L
12.	T ♠	Q ♦ L	5 ♠	A ♦*
13.	J ♠	5 ♣	K ♠	8 ♣*L

Because the Queen of Clubs is favorably positioned and because your partner has the singleton Queen of Hearts, it makes seven. This is a slam that should be bid, even though you are playing in a 4–4 fit in a minor suit at the 6 level. You get more points by playing a minor suit slam than a major suit game.

Rebids by Strong Two Club Opener

There are only a few possibilities for responses you'll get from your strong opening of 2 Clubs. The most common response you'll get, more than 90 percent of the time actually, is that your partner will bid 2 Diamonds, a waiting bid.

What did 2 Diamonds tell you? Did you say, "nothing, idiot, it was a waiting bid"? If so, go to the corner and put on the dunce cap.

Although it's true that 2 Diamonds is a waiting bid in response to a strong opening of 2 Clubs, it most definitely tells you something. One of the great things about Bridge is that it teaches you to draw inferences from things. This is a good example. You're saying, "Well, 2 Diamonds is a waiting bid, isn't it? It's just keeping the bidding open and asking partner to further describe her hand. Isn't that correct?"

Sure, that's correct. But don't forget that responder has choices. Although 2 Diamonds is the most common response to a Strong Two Club opening, it is not her *only* bid.

Remember, I said that if responder has a good five-card suit she should bid it? Well, if she bids 2 Diamonds in response to your 2 Club open, what does that tell you about her hand? It tells you that she does *not* have a good five-card she wants to bid. Isn't that good information for you? Of course it is.

Further Distribution Description

So the first thing you want to do now is to tell your partner what kind of distribution you have in your hand. Did you open a balanced hand with 22+ points? Or did you open a hand that has strong Clubs. If you opened the former, you rebid 2 No Trump.

Making Sure Your Partner Doesn't Pass Out Too Soon

One thing with which you must concern yourself is the possibility of your partner passing you before you get to your contract. When you open a Strong Two Club bid, you must prepare yourself for what your partner is going to do when you make a rebid. So this gets to the questions of how you bid your hand, and can you bid anything other than a 2-level bid when your partner responds 2 Diamonds.

Allowing Your Partner to Quit at the Right Time

If you have opened up a balanced 22- to 24-point hand, you know that you need *something* from your partner to make game, even in No Trump, because your points are just not enough. Although it's rare to hold a Yarborough (no card higher than a Nine) when you have at least 22 HCP in your hand, there is a much greater possibility of your partner having a Yarborough than if you open up a hand with 15 HCP or less.

You don't want to be in game if you don't have it. That's the purpose of the 2 No Trump rebid. It tells your partner that she has the right to pass if she thinks there isn't game between you.

Lingo

Systems on means when you make a No Trump bid that is not an opening bid, you are still playing the normal responses that come after a No Trump opening, like Stayman.

No Trump Rebid

When you rebid 2 No Trump, it's like opening No Trump. It means *systems are on*, so you can bid Stayman.

If you open 2 Clubs, your partner responds 2 Diamonds, and you bid 2 No Trump, and your partner bids 3 Clubs, she's asking if you have a four-card major. When you rebid 2 No Trump, you are once again making her the captain of the team and leaving it up to her where you play the contract. You are, in effect, inviting her to bid Stayman if she can. If she doesn't, that tells you something about her hand. When you rebid 2 No Trump, she must then evaluate her hand as if you had opened 2 No Trump but with a minimum of 22 points instead of 20 to 21 points. This means that *systems are on*.

Respecting Your Partner's Opinion

When you open up 1 No Trump, you have a good hand, 15 to 17 points. But you've learned that when you do this you appoint your partner captain of your hand. You surrender power to her, even though you probably have the better hand of the two of you.

This isn't so difficult to do with a 15- to 17-point hand. But when you have a hand containing 22 points or more, it's much harder to pay attention to what your partner is telling you. You have more than half the points in the deck. You've got the power. Your partner is sitting over there with virtually nothing. Who is she to tell you what to do?

Ah, but you need her because she could have the few points you desperately need for game. She could very well have a Yarborough. You must listen to her and respect what she tells you. If you have a balanced hand, and have less than 25 points, you need her advice and opinion. You need her help. So you tell her what you have and listen to what she says she has. If the points she tells you she has in her hand don't total game when added to yours, pass it out at the lowest level possible.

Rebids by Responder

The second part of this chapter is how a responder rebids. When it comes time for you to make your first rebid as responder, you have heard your partner bid twice, so you should have a much better idea of how many points she has in her hand and what her suits are. It's up to you to make some decisions.

Partner Opens a Minor, You Bid a Major, and Opener Supports You

The bidding goes, for example, 1 Diamond–1 Heart–2 Hearts. What do you do? There is a very specific series of bids that defines your response.

◆ If you, as responder, have four Hearts and 10 points or less, pass.

◆ If you have four Hearts and 11 to 12 points, bid 2 No Trump. If your partner is at the top of her bid (at least 14 HCP), she goes to game. If she has 13 or less points, she closes out in 3 Hearts. This bid of 2 No Trump is a very limited bid. It tells your partner specifically the hand you hold. It says nothing about playing the hand in No Trump. It is inviting one of two bids, either 3 Hearts or 4 Hearts.

◆ If you have four Hearts and 13 to 15 points, bid game, 4 Hearts.

◆ If you have five Hearts and 10 points, bid 3 Hearts.

◆ If you have five Hearts and 11 to 12 points, bid game.

This is a standard bid but my experience is that very few players use it. If you use it you must have a firm understanding with your partner about what the bids mean. But you will find that you will arrive at the correct contract much more often than others who get these types of hands. Look at the following hands when your partner opened 1 Diamond, you responded 1 Spade and your partner rebid 2 Spades:

1. ♠ AT43	2. ♠ AT432	3. ♠ AT43	4. ♠ AT43
♥ KQ7	♥ K73	♥ K32	♥ T43
♦ J87	♦ QT5	♦ K73	♦ KQ7
♣ 963	♣ T5	♣ JT4	♣ A83

Hand 1: Pass. You have 10 points and four Spades. Even if your partner has a maximum hand at 15 points, you don't have enough for game unless you're lucky.

Hand 2: 3 Spades. This describes your hand specifically. You have 10 points and five Spades. It invites your partner to bid 4 Spades if she's at the top of her bid.

Hand 3: 2 No Trump. This also describes your hand specifically. You have 11 to 12 points and four Spades. You are asking your partner to bid 3 Spades if she has 13 points, 4 Spades if she has 14 or better. She can't pass 2 No Trump unless she violated your partnership agreement and supported you with only three Spades.

Hand 4: 4 Spades. Don't get excited and think about slam just because you both have opening hands and a major suit trump fit. Your partner has told you that she has a minimum hand by her simple raise of your major suit bid. You have a 4–4 fit and probably a maximum of 29 points. Forget slam and be content with a fairly safe game.

Captaincy

When it comes time for you to make a rebid as responder, you have the advantage of having a lot of information at your fingertips. You know much more about the potential of your hands than your partner. Your partner's opening bid, as you remember, just got the ball rolling, and probably described a hand that has between 13 points and 21 points (unless she opened No Trump).

Your response, unless it was a limit raise or a jump, just told her that you had at least 6 points and a minimum number of cards in the suit you bid.

By her rebid, she described her hand much more specifically to you. She should have told you whether or not she had a minimum, or more, and gave you a pretty good indication of her distribution.

Knowing this, you have so much information, that at this point you are in control of the hand. It's up to you to tell her whether or not you want to play in a partscore, a game, or try for a slam.

Opener Shows a Minimum Without Supporting Your Suit

If you make a bid in response to your partner's opening bid, you will basically have one of several types of hands:

- ◆ **6 to 9 points, a minimum.** If you are at the bottom of your range, 6 to 7 points, you should pass any response by your partner that doesn't force you to bid again. If you are at the middle or upper range of your bid, 8 to 9 points, you can give her another bid if she encourages it. Under no circumstances do you have the flexibility to pass a forcing bid, like a reverse. But if the bidding goes like this …

Partner	You
1 Diamond	1 Heart
2 Clubs	?

  …your partner is describing a minimum to medium opening and is telling you to take your pick between Diamonds and Clubs. If you feel Clubs is a better contract, pass. If you like Diamonds, then bid 2 Diamonds. Your bid of 2 Diamonds is pretty much a drop-dead bid to your partner, telling her that you don't have much, but that you prefer that she play the hand in Diamonds rather than Clubs. You shouldn't have to worry about her bidding on.

- ◆ **10 to 12 points.** This is a good hand with game potential. So you must be certain that your first response is one that does not allow your partner to pass. You can't respond 1 No Trump or make a simple one over one raise of her suit, because those bids describe minimum hands that invite a pass. Your rebid will be something that tells your partner that you're interested in game and does not invite a pass. For instance, if you were to rebid your suit at the 2 level, you would be telling her that you had a minimum hand, didn't like either of her two suits and were satisfied playing it in your suit at the 2 level. A rebid of your suit would not describe a hand of 10 to 12 points, but would, rather, invite your partner to pass.

- ◆ **13+ points.** This is a hand that you know you want to play in game, so you must make a forcing bid on your partner that she may not pass, either by jumping or bidding game yourself. You have to tell her your strength now because it must be decided whether or not you will be satisfied just playing in game or whether you want to try for slam.

With these as guidelines, refer to the chart later in this chapter showing how to respond to opener's second bid after you have a better idea of what opener's hand is like.

Consider the following auction.

Partner	You
1 Diamond	1 Heart
2 Clubs	?

How do you bid the following hands?

1. ♠ K74	2. ♠ K74	3. ♠ K74	4. ♠ K74	5. ♠ KJ74
♥ QJ743	♥ KQ8643	♥ KJ86	♥ KJ863	♥ KJ86
◆ Q74	◆ 74	◆ 87	◆ 87	◆ Q82
♣ 72	♣ 84	♣ J832	♣ 862	♣ JT

Hand 1: 2 Diamonds. Your partner has asked you to choose between Diamonds and Clubs and you like Diamonds better because you have three, headed by an honor.

Hand 2: 2 Hearts. You have a minimum hand with a six-card suit. You don't like Diamonds or Clubs especially. Because you have six Hearts headed by two of the top three honors, you prefer to try playing in the major at the 2 level. Whatever your partner does next, unless it's a forcing bid, which is unlikely given her minimum rebid in Clubs, you're telling her you're going to pass.

Hand 3: Pass. You have minimum, but your Clubs are clearly better than your Diamonds. Better to play in 2 Clubs. Any other bid would mislead your partner into thinking you are stronger than you are. You shouldn't raise Clubs just because you have four of them. Your hand is too minimum.

Hand 4: 2 Diamonds. Your hand is very minimum. It's possible that your partner is 4–4 in Diamonds and Clubs, or 5–5, but you should assume that she has five Diamonds, anyway, and it would be better to play in a 5–2 fit in her opening suit than a 4–3 fit in her second suit.

Hand 5: 2 No Trump. You have 11 HCP and good body cards. 2 No Trump promises your partner that you have the unbid suit, Spades, stopped, and tells her that you have more than a minimum. It invites her to bid game if she has anything but a bare minimum.

Opener	Your Hand	Your Rebid
13–15 points	6–9	Pass.
		Support partner's suit at the 2 level.
		Rebid your good five-card suit or six-card suit at the 2 level.
	10–12	2 No Trump if balanced.
		Support partner's suit at the 3 level or bid your suit at the 3 level.
	13+	Bid game in a suit in which you have a fit or 3 No Trump.
		Bid a new suit, forcing partner to bid.
16–18	6–7	Pass as soon as possible!
		Support partner's suit with a simple raise.
	8–9	Rebid your suit if it has six cards in it.
	10+	Bid game in a suit in which you have a fit or 3 No Trump.
		Bid a new suit, forcing partner to bid.
19+	6–7	Support partner's suit if possible.
		Rebid a suit in which you have a fit.
		Rebid your own five-card or longer suit.
		Bid No Trump at the cheapest level available.
	8+	Support partner's suit.
		Rebid a suit in which you have a fit.
		Jump to 3 No Trump.
		Bid a new suit forcing partner to bid.

These bids are based on simple arithmetic. In the bids where your minimum hand and your partner's minimum hand show that you have enough points for game, you must either bid the game or make a bid that forces your partner to bid again. However, when you add your points to your partner's minimum hand and don't get enough for game, you have to let her decide by giving her the information on your hand. At that point you make an invitational bid to her, which tells her that you are above your minimum, and if she is also above her minimum you should be in game, but it's up to her to bid it. She knows that if you had a hand that, when added to her minimum hand, would make game, you would either bid game or make a forcing bid. So if you make a bid that allows her to pass, you are telling her that your hand, when added to her minimum hand, will not make game.

Let's look at some hands.

Hand	Bidding	
Hand 1	*Partner*	*You*
♠ T	1 Heart	2 Diamonds
♥ 8	2 Spades	?
♦ AQT754		
♣ KT863		
Hand 2	*Partner*	*You*
♠ A9872	1 Club	1 Spade
♥ A4	2 Spades	?
♦ QJ76		
♣ AQ		
Hand 3	*Partner*	*You*
♠ 8652	1 Diamond	1 Heart
♥ KJ73	2 Clubs	?
♦ 73		
♣ A43		
Hand 4	*Partner*	*You*
♠ K8	1 Diamond	1 Heart
♥ Q9875	1 Spade	?
♦ Q72		
♣ JT5		

Hand 1: 3 Clubs. You have 13 points with a very distributional hand. Rather than rebid your six-card Diamond suit, it's better to mention your five-card Club suit at the 3 level to show your partner your strength and distribution. Your partner, who has reversed, showing at least 17 points, may not pass a new suit by responder at the 3 level.

Hand 2: 3 Diamonds. You've already established a trump fit in a major suit, Spades. So your bid of 3 Diamonds is at least game invitational and forcing on your partner to bid again. When you, as responder, rebid a new suit after establishing a fit in a major suit, it means that you have a better than minimum hand and you should consider game, at least. When you have a major suit fit, there's no reason to bid a new minor suit unless it is to tell your partner something about your hand. Here you have 17 points and are sniffing for slam. Your bid of a new suit is absolutely forcing on your partner to bid again.

Hand 3: Pass. You have a minimum. Your partner doesn't have four Spades or she would have bid them. She must have a distributional hand or she would have bid 1 No Trump. You have the *Ace third* of her second suit. You can't get hurt too much in 2 Clubs and it can't be much worse than 2 Diamonds, even if she is 6–4 in Diamonds and Clubs. She's basically asking you to take your pick between Clubs and Diamonds. If you had three little Clubs you should take her back to Diamonds, because that was her first suit and she probably has at least five of them. But because you have the Ace of Clubs with two others, I'd leave her in 2 Clubs.

> **Lingo**
>
> **Ace third** means that you have three cards in the suit headed by the bare honor. Any card followed by a number, like third or fourth, means that you have that card plus that number of cards in the suit. So *King fourth* means that you have Kxxx in the suit.

Hand 4: 1 No Trump. Your five-card Heart suit is too weak to rebid at the 2 level and your hand is too weak to go to the 2 level without a more encouraging bid from your partner. You know that your partner doesn't have five Spades or she would have opened 1 Spade, so you don't want to leave her in a 4–2 fit. 1 No Trump describes your hand well here, weak and fairly balanced. This is a bid that says that you might have a little more than the minimum, but not much more, and allows your partner to pass.

The Least You Need to Know

♦ A 2 Diamond, 2 Heart, or 2 Spade opening bid begins a game-forcing auction if responder doesn't bid 2 No Trump.

♦ After a 2 No Trump response, the responding hand must continue bidding as long as the opener changes suits. If opener rebids her original suit or bids 3 No Trump, responder may pass.

♦ Responder's bid of 2 Diamonds after an opening bid of 2 Clubs is a waiting bid and denies a five-card or longer suit headed by at least the King–Jack.

♦ If a 2 Club opening bidder rebids No Trump, she shows a balanced strong hand and does not promise a Club suit.

♦ If your partner's rebid shows that you have enough points between you for game, you should either bid game yourself or make a forcing bid that your partner can't pass.

Going for the Gold: Slam Bidding

In This Chapter

- Definition of a slam
- How to evaluate for slam
- Blackwood
- Judgment

I've alluded to slams before. Essentially, a *slam* occurs when you bid a contract to take either all tricks but one, which is a *small slam*, or all tricks, which is a *grand slam*. So you must make a contract to take 12 of the 13 tricks, and do so, to make a small slam, and you must make a contract to take all 13 tricks, and do so, to make a grand slam.

This chapter explains how to evaluate your hand for slam and how to bid to a slam.

How You Find a Slam

You look for slam through arithmetic. Basically, the points required for slam are as follows:

Small slam   33 points

Grand slam   37 points

The bonuses involved are wonderful. They are as follows.

Bid	Not Vulnerable	Vulnerable
Small slam	500	750
Grand slam	1,000	1,500

Clearly, these are bonuses not to be discarded lightly. The question is, can you make it? This is especially important when you're vulnerable because if you have a cold vulnerable game, you are forsaking at least 600 points to try for the slam.

How Do You Find Slam Potential?

When you count up the points in your hand and find that you have an opening hand and then hear your loving partner open the bidding, you will generally think, "Hmmm. I've got an opening hand. She does, too. Maybe we have a slam!"

Not so fast. Two opening hands only equal 26 points, just enough for a game in a major suit or No Trump. You shouldn't start thinking slam until your partner jumps the bidding.

Alert

Two opening hands opposite one another do not equal slam.

A jump bid always indicates extra values. So if one partner opens and responder jumps, that's when you start thinking about slam. If one partner opens, the other partner responds, and opener jumps, responder may start thinking about slam if she has an opening hand herself.

This is the theory behind jump responses. They make your partner aware that you not only have most of the points between you, but that at least one of you has extra values. This alerts her to the fact that you think that game is pretty clear and that you should explore the possibility of slam.

How to Evaluate Your Hand for Slam

The optimum idea is to reach agreement on trump as soon as you can. Why? Because there are two basic ways to explore the specific cards in your hands to see if you can make slam. One is by the use of *Blackwood*, which is explained later in this chapter.

A second way to explore for slam is through the use of *cue bids*, which are discussed in Chapter 24. The vast majority of Rubber Bridge players use Blackwood. If you were to try to use a cue bid with the average Rubber Bridge player, however, you'd feel like a pair of brown shoes at a party for tuxedos.

But before you get to Blackwood, you need to communicate with your partner to see whether the hand has the potential for the use of Blackwood.

Analysis by Opener When Responder Jumps

If your partner just makes a standard response showing a minimum hand, like responding 2 Diamonds over your 1 Spade opening, you aren't thinking slam. It's when she does something other than a standard bid that gets your small gray cells working.

If your partner jumps the bidding, she's showing you a specific number of points in her hand. So remember what a jump means.

	You	Partner	Meaning
Hand 1	1 Heart	2 No Trump	13–15 HCP, balanced hand, stoppers in the three unbid suits, denies four Spades
Hand 2	1 Heart	3 No Trump	16–18 HCP, balanced hand, stoppers in the three unbid suits, denies four Spades
Hand 3	1 Heart	2 Spades	16 or more points, five Spades, game forcing, looking for slam, does *not* deny four Hearts, could be totally unbalanced

Let's say you open a 13- to 15-point hand with a bid of 1 Heart. How should you respond to your partner's jump bids set forth above?

Hand 1: 3 No Trump. You have a maximum of 30 points between you. That's not enough for slam, even if you're at the top of your bid.

Hand 2: If you have your minimum, 13 or 14 points, you should pass. However, if you have 15 points you should continue, probably with a *quantitative* bid of 4 No Trump, asking your partner if she's at the top or bottom of her bid. You'll learn about quantitative bids shortly in this chapter.

Hand 3: If you're at the bottom of your bid and have three Spades in your hand, bid 4 Spades. This is a minimum response that denies slam interest, but shows three card support. Your partner's minimum hand is 16 points. She could have more. So you must describe your hand so she can evaluate slam potential. If you're at the top of your bid, you should either bid 3 Spades or bid a new suit if you have one with some power.

When your partner makes a game-forcing bid at a level where you can bid her suit short of game, if you jump the bidding to bid game directly, it's a weak bid, showing no slam interest. When she makes a jump shift to 2 Spades, your bid of 4 Spades directly shows weakness. If you were to bid 3 Spades, you would be telling her that you have a good hand and it would be an invitation to slam.

Why? Because the bid she makes requires you to keep the bidding open to game. It allows you to communicate with one another without fear of either of you passing short of game. If you make a jump bid to game, you're telling her that you don't have anything further to tell her and you're not much interested in anything she might want to tell you. If you make a bid in her suit short of game, you're telling her that you want to hear more about her hand.

If you have more than a minimum opening and responder jumps to anything other than 2 No Trump or a limit raise, you clearly should explore for slam. Your more than minimum opening would show a hand of 16+ points. Any other jump by your partner would indicate that you probably have enough points for slam and you should proceed by going to Blackwood. Take a look at the following hand you hold in first seat—a minimum hand that you open 1 Club:

♠ 654
♥ A4
♦ K4
♣ KQ6432

Following are your responses to various bids by your partner after you open this hand at 1 Club.

Partner	You	Meaning
2 No Trump	3 No Trump	Your partner is showing 13–15 HCP. You have 12 HCP, enough for game. Plus you have a nice six-card Club suit. Slam shouldn't even enter your mind because your partner has limited her hand.

Partner	You	Meaning
3 No Trump	Pass	Again, your partner has limited her hand to a maximum of 18 HCP. Add your 12 to that and you get 30, not enough for slam.
2 Diamonds	3 Clubs	You are conveying to her that you have a minimum. She's shown five Diamonds and at least 16 points, but you must tell her that your hand is a minimum with a long Club suit as its best feature. Now it's up to her to further evaluate.

Following is your partner's actual hand:

You	*Partner*
♠ 654	♠ AT
♥ A4	♥ K2
♦ K4	♦ AQJ86
♣ KQ6432	♣ AJ85

She has 19 HCP and 21 total points. Added to your 14 points, that's 35 points and a Club slam is cold. But that's up to your partner to determine after you've told her your hand is minimum and you have a Club suit.

Analysis by Responder When Opener Shows Extra Values

The other way you can find slam is when you give your partner a standard response and she reverses or jumps the bidding, showing extra values.

To refresh your memory, your partner opens 1 of a suit, you respond and your partner reverses or jumps. Opener's bids mean the following.

Opener's Second Bid	Meaning
2 No Trump	18–19 points, all unbid suits stopped
3 No Trump	20–21 points, all unbid suits stopped
Reverse	17+ points
Jump shift	19–22 points

Again, your responses are based on simple arithmetic. If your response was a minimum 6- to 9-point hand, here's how you should respond.

Opener's Jump Bid	Your Response
2 No Trump	Pass if 6 points. For balanced 7+ points, you should bid 3 No Trump because you should have a game, given your partner's promised minimum of 18 points.
3 No Trump	Pass. You don't have slam because your partner has a maximum of 21 and you have a maximum of 9. That's only 30 points, not enough for slam.
Reverse	If the bidding is passed to you by your RHO, you *must* make another bid. A reverse is forcing on you for one round. Either rebid your five-card suit, support the suit of your partner that you can, or bid No Trump to deny support for either of your partner's suits and to indicate a weak hand.
Jump shift	A jump shift is forcing to game so you must continue bidding if your RHO passes until you have bid to the game level. If your hand stinks, just make the weakest bid you can, supporting your partner's suit in which you have the best support or rebid your own suit if it's adequate.

Blackwood—The Easiest Convention of All

If both you and your partner have communicated to each other that you have good hands, the thought will start to germinate that maybe you can bid and make slam. So far, however, you've just been communicating how many points each of you has in your hand and how many cards you have in the trump suit.

When you start to consider slam, you start to realize that you need to know exactly what cards each of you has, and, specifically, how many Aces and Kings and which ones.

This is where *Blackwood* comes into play.

Blackwood is very simple. When your partner bids 4 No Trump she's asking one question: How many Aces do you have in your hand? You tell her by bidding suits, as follows.

> **Bridgebit**
>
> *Blackwood* was devised by Easley Blackwood in 1933, and has been almost universally adopted as the standard for asking for Aces and Kings.

Bid	Number of Aces
5 Clubs	0 or 4
5 Diamonds	1
5 Hearts	2
5 Spades	3

Is that easy, or what?

If your partner then bids 5 No Trump, she is telling you something and asking you something:

♦ She's telling you that you and she hold all four Aces. This is an absolute promise. After bidding 4 No Trump asking for Aces, she cannot bid 5 No Trump asking for Kings if your pair is lacking one Ace. So if you respond, for example, 5 Diamonds, telling her that you have one Ace, and she comes back with 5 No Trump asking for Kings, you can take it to the bank that she has the other three Aces in her hand.

♦ She's asking you how many Kings you have. You answer in exactly the same manner as you answered for Aces, only you're up one level.

Bid	*Number of Kings*
6 Clubs	0 or 4
6 Diamonds	1
6 Hearts	2
6 Spades	3

That's Blackwood. When she has your answers to her questions, she places the contract. If she places the contract somewhere, you must accept her decision and pass. For example, if your agreed that trump is Spades and she bids 4 No Trump after you bid 4 Spades, let's say you respond 5 Diamonds, showing one Ace. She then bids 5 Spades. She's saying, "Okay, partner, you've told me your holding and we don't have enough, so let's just play it in 5 Spades. You must pass. She knows more about your two hands than you do. You must trust her.

When You Shouldn't Use Blackwood

Blackwood is a terrific convention if your slam depends on the location of all the Aces. But there are two instances when Blackwood shouldn't be used.

The first is when the bidding has been opened in 1 or 2 No Trump. Look at the following bidding.

You	Partner
1 No Trump	4 No Trump

A bid of 4 No Trump here would not be Ace asking. When a hand is opened 1 No Trump and you look like you're going to play it in No Trump, a bid of 4 No Trump is called a *quantitative bid*.

In this instance, 4 No Trump is quantitative because it isn't conventional—that is, it doesn't ask for Aces. What, you may be inquiring, is it asking? Good question.

Lingo

A **quantitative bid** is a bid that is natural, limited, and nonforcing.

Obviously there must be some meaning to it because 3 No Trump is game and bidder has bypassed 3 No Trump. What it's asking is simple. In this bidding sequence, or any sequence when the bidder goes from any No Trump bid directly to 4 No Trump, bidder is asking partner to go to slam, 6 No Trump, if she's at the top of her bid, but to pass if she's not at the top of her bid.

So in this situation you have shown your partner a balanced 15 to 17 HCP hand. She probably has 16 HCP herself. So she's asking you whether you opened a 15-point hand or a 17-point hand. Because 32 HCP should be very close to making a small slam, she's just saying to you, "If you have 17 HCP or a good 16 HCP hand, go to 6 No Trump. If you have 15 HCP or a bad 16 HCP hand, pass and we'll play it in 4 No Trump." Again, it's just arithmetic.

The second situation in which you shouldn't use Blackwood is if you have a void in your hand and don't need that Ace for slam. If you have two Aces and a void in your hand, what good does it do to discover that your partner has one Ace? If it's the Ace in which you have a void, it won't do you any good at all. So if you have a distributional hand with a singleton or void, you should examine slam potential through the use of cue bids, which is explored in Chapter 24.

How to Get Out of Blackwood

Sometimes you get in Blackwood and discover that you don't want to be in slam but you want to play the contract in 5 No Trump. Look at the following bidding sequence where your partner has only 1 Spade and two Aces.

You	LHO	Partner	RHO
1 Club	Pass	2 Hearts	Pass
3 Clubs	Pass	3 Hearts	Pass
4 Clubs	Pass	4 No Trump	Pass
5 Diamonds	Pass	?	

After your 5 Diamond bid she wants to play it in 5 No Trump. But if she bids 5 No Trump directly you will think she's telling you that you have all the Aces between you and is asking for Kings. How can she get it so you can play in 5 No Trump?

The answer is to bid the unbid suit. In this situation she would bid 5 Spades. This says nothing about Spades. It merely asks you to bid 5 No Trump, which she will pass.

So the rule is: If you are in Blackwood and want to play the contract in 5 No Trump, bid the unbid suit, asking your partner to bid 5 No Trump. This is obviously a tactic that can only be used by the player who first bid 4 No Trump.

Making Responder Captain

Now I'm going to focus on a hand I discussed previously in Chapter 13. Look at your hand:

♠ QJ643
♥ 95
♦ 9
♣ AQJ85

Here's how the bidding went.

LHO	Partner	RHO	You
Pass	1 Club	1 Diamond	1 Spade
2 Diamonds	4 Spades	Pass	?

By this time you should know what your partner's bid means. Do you remember? Is it a sign-off, or something else?

If you remember what you learned in Chapter 13, you remember that this bid by your partner shows a 20-point hand. Why? Because you are only promising her 6 points by your bid. If you have a four-card Spade suit and 6 points, you can bid 1 Spade to show that you have at least 6 points and at least four Spades. But your partner jumps to game! She can only do that if she adds up all the points and determines that from your minimum bid she can make game. And the only way she could make that determination is if she has enough points in her hand to make game. You showed at least 6. So she must have 20 points in her hand to make this bid. What do you do?

What you do *not* do with this hand is meekly pass. You have 13 points. She has 20 points. 13 + 20 = 33. How many points do you need for a small slam? 33. How many points do you have? 33. Should you pass your partner's 4 Spade bid?

Lingo

Onside means that a card is placed so that if you take a *finesse*, the finesse will be successful. A **finesse** occurs when you take advantage of a higher-ranking card in opponents' hand. It will be discussed in detail in Chapter 19.

You have two alternatives. One is to just bid 6 Spades. The other is to bid Blackwood. Blackwood is correct because you might be missing two Aces, in which case you don't want to bid 6. Following is your partner's hand:

♠ AT92
♥ AK8
♦ A
♣ K7632

If you passed 4 Spades and laid down your hand, which is cold for six (it makes seven because the King of Spades is *onside*), you won't be able to find a closet far enough away to hide.

Following is a layout of all four hands:

North (you)
♠ QJ643
♥ 95
♦ 9
♣ AQJ85

West
♠ 75
♥ T7642
♦ KQT842
♣ void

East
♠ K8
♥ QJ3
♦ J7653
♣ T94

South (partner)
♠ AT92
♥ AK8
♦ A
♣ K7632

So when your partner makes a bid like this, jumping to game after you've made a minimum response, she's not saying, "Pass, partner, I want to play this in game and that's why I bid game." No, she's saying, "I've got a big hand. I want to be sure we play in game because with your minimum bid I have enough in my hand to make game. If you have more than your minimum bid, bid on. Maybe we have slam."

In essence, she's making you the captain of the team again, because you know a lot more about her hand than she knows about yours.

A Slam Try When Your Partner Preempts

What if you look at a huge hand and hear your partner open a preemptive bid? Look at the following hand after you hear your partner open up with a bid of 4 Spades:

♠ A
♥ KT32
♦ KQ965
♣ K54

Wow! You were getting ready to open 1 Diamond and then reverse into 2 Hearts. And you hear your loving partner open the bidding with 4 Spades! Are you sniffing slam? You bet you are.

But hold on a minute. What's your partner telling you when she opens the bidding with 4 Spades? Right. She's virtually yelling at you, "Partner, my hand is *weak!*" She's got *less* than a minimum opening hand. Does that change your orientation? It should.

Your bid here is clearly "Pass." Sure, you have 15 HCP and 17 points if you count your singleton Ace. But the singleton Ace is in your partner's trump suit. So, even though it's nice that you have the Ace of trump, the fact that it's a singleton doesn't make your hand any better at all. In fact, it makes it worse.

Further, your Heart suit is pretty weak. If your LHO has the Ace, your King isn't worth much. And your Club suit only has one trick.

Even if the vulnerability is unfavorable, which would mean that your partner was overbidding her hand by only two tricks, you only have three quick tricks in your hand, the Aces of Clubs and Spades and the King–Queen of Diamonds. If that's the case, you will make one overtrick. Pass.

As it was, you were wise to pass. Here's your partner's hand, followed by your hand:

Partner
♠ KT876532
♥ 94
♦ A7
♣ 9

You
♠ A
♥ KT32
♦ KQ965
♣ K54

You lose a Club and a Heart even with a 2–2 trump split, which is only a 40 percent chance. Never forget. When your partner preempts, she has a weak hand, even if she's preempting in game.

Investigating for the Correct Slam

When your partner opens and you have a huge hand, you're going to be tempted to jump the bidding immediately to tell your partner and the world that you have a terrific hand. You don't need to do this.

If you know you have the preponderance of the points in the hand, it's much better to proceed slowly so that you can communicate with each other to determine the correct contract. Jumping the bidding squeezes you and takes away bidding space you might need. Look at the following hand after your partner opens the bidding with 1 Club:

♠ AK65
♥ AK96
♦ AQ6
♣ KJ

That's a 24 HCP hand and your partner has opened? You're going to have to be tied down to keep from jumping, nay, leaping! But you don't need to leap or even jump. Your correct bid is 1 Heart!

1 Heart? Are you kidding? I've got 24 HCP, my partner opens the bidding, and I just show her a minimum 6-point hand? Are you nuts?

No, I'm not nuts. Remember that your 1 Heart bid is 100 percent forcing on your partner to bid again. You want to find out what she has. Does she have four Hearts? Does she have four Spades? What does she have? If you jump to something like 3 No Trump, for example, how is she going to respond? As long as you make a bid that forces her to bid again, you've done what you want to do. You want to find out about her hand at the lowest level so you know whether you're going to play this hand in Clubs, Hearts, Spades, or No Trump. A jump to 3 No Trump does *not* force your partner to bid again.

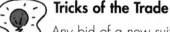

Tricks of the Trade

Any bid of a new suit by responder is 100 percent forcing on opener to bid again for one round.

So you bid 1 Heart and your partner responds 1 No Trump. What do you do?

Now you know what you want to know. Your partner doesn't have four Hearts or she would have supported you. Your partner doesn't have four Spades or she would have bid 1 Spade. Your partner has a balanced hand with no voids or singletons. She has shown 13 points and you have 24 HCP. That's 37 points, enough for a grand slam. You should bid 7 No Trump immediately. There's nothing more you need to know.

Maybe you won't make 7 No Trump every time with this hand, but you've got the points for it and should bid it. The key to the hand is that you kept your head and didn't jump. You made a forcing bid at the lowest level possible, then determined the correct contract and bid it.

Lingo

A **one-over-one** bid is when you bid a suit at the 1 level after your partner has bid a different suit at the 1 level.

Just remember this rule: *A one-over-one bid by responder to partner's opening bid is 100 percent forcing on partner to bid again.*

Knowing When Not to Bid Slam

Just as important as finding the proper slam is knowing when you should not bid a slam. Staying out of improper slams is probably more difficult than finding the right slam and bidding it. Look at this hand after your partner opens 1 Club:

♠ AQ75
♥ KQ73
♦ AQ62
♣ 8

That's 17 HCP. What do you bid? Again, you want to make the lowest bid you can make that forces your partner to bid again. So you bid the lowest ranking of your three four-card suits, 1 Diamond. Your partner responds 1 No Trump. What now? Do you have slam?

Your partner has told you that she has a balanced hand that is no more than minimum. Her maximum holding is 14 points. You have 17 HCP. In No Trump your singleton isn't worth anything. Your partner does not have four Hearts or four Spades or she would have bid them. That's the end of the story. You have a maximum of 32 points and that's not enough for slam. Bid 3 No Trump, a bid that is a sign-off, and play it there.

> ### Tricks of the Trade
>
> Frank Stewart, one of the best Bridge writers and players around, gives a good rule that you should follow for any bidding, but especially when considering slams: *If you are considering a contract and partner must have just the right cards, forget it!*

Sometimes your partner will have a hand that results in your taking all but one trick here. But you must trust your arithmetic. If your points don't add up, don't try to project something into your partner's hand that you don't know is there. Don't bid speculative slams.

Deceptive Bidding

Sometimes you lie to everybody. When you really trust your partner, you can fool your opponents and lure them into a foolish double or a foolish act. But it requires total confidence in your partner. Look at the following bidding.

You	LHO	Partner	RHO
2 Spades (1)	Pass	2 No Trump (2)	Pass
3 Hearts (3)	Pass	3 Spades (4)	Pass
4 Clubs (5)	Pass	4 Spades (6)	Pass
5 Diamonds (7)	Pass	5 Hearts (8)	Pass
6 Diamonds (9)	Pass	6 Spades (10)	Pass
7 No Trump	Double	Pass	Pass
Redouble			

Here's what it means:

(1) I have a huge hand. Keep the bidding open.

(2) My hand stinks. Please let me pass.

(3) I have a huge hand. Do you prefer Hearts or Spades? Please bid again.

(4) Spades. Please, please, let me pass.

(5) Not yet. We have now agreed that Spades will be Trump. However, I also have the Ace of Clubs. Do you have any Aces you want to bid? Please bid again.

(6) No, all I have is minimal support in Spades. Please. Let's play this here. My hand is awful.

(7) Not yet. I also have the Ace of Diamonds, at least a first round stopper. How do you like them apples? Please bid again.

(8) I got plenty of nothin'! I hope this will put an end to this foolishness! My hand is terrible. However, I do have minimal support in Hearts. Because I have to bid, and because you already know about my Spades, I thought I might as well mention it here.

(9) Thanks. That's nice to know. Not so fast. I not only have the Ace of Diamonds, I also have the King of Diamonds. Because we've agreed that Spades is going to be trump and I'm bidding Diamonds, I want you to bid again. I want to hear more.

(10) Okay, my Spades are better than my Hearts and my whole hand stinks. Stop while we have a chance.

Responder's hand was the following:

- ♠ 8642
- ♥ Q83
- ♦ 7632
- ♣ 64

7 No Trump? Look at declarer's hand:

- ♠ A
- ♥ AK
- ♦ AK
- ♣ AKQ98754

Tricks of the Trade

Advanced players often use a bid of an unbid suit after a trump fit has been agreed upon as a **cue bid** showing *first round control* of a suit. **First round control** is either an Ace or a void. Rubber Bridge players generally don't use cue bids.

Declarer never bid Clubs as a suit, which was his real suit. He knew he had 7 No Trump cold from the start. But he went through the bidding process hoping he could get a double of 7 No Trump. If he had just opened at 7 No Trump it would have been passed out. But from the bidding, where it looked like his two suits were Spades and Hearts, he whetted the appetite of his opponents and sucked them into a double of a cold, cold 7 No Trump contract.

The point of this exercise is not that it's okay to lie to your partner. On the contrary, you should *not* lie to your partner. The point of this exercise is that both partners had such wonderful trust in one another that they complied with their agreements and continued to bid.

Declarer could bid all these false suits in the sublime confidence that he was in total control of the hand because he trusted his partner to continue bidding and not take some unilateral action to pass him out in one of his one- or two-card suits. He didn't care what his partner had. All the bidding was to create a false impression on opponents. He knew he was in control, that his partner would keep bidding so long as he demanded another bid, and that the final contract was going to be 7 No Trump, regardless of the cards held by his partner and regardless of his partner's responses.

And his partner trusted declarer to know what he was doing and continued to bid despite the abysmal cards he held. The result was an awful lot of points. 7 No Trump doubled and redoubled is the most you can make offensively in Bridge.

The Least You Need to Know

- You need 33 points for a small slam, 37 points for a grand slam.

- In Blackwood, a bid of 4 No Trump asks partner to respond with the number of Aces in her hand.

- Partner responds to Blackwood by bidding 5 Clubs with zero or four Aces, 5 Diamonds with one Ace, 5 Hearts with two Aces, and 5 Spades with three Aces.

- Don't bid a slam if your partner must have specific cards for you to make it.

Chapter 16

Not So Fast! Overcalls and Takeout Doubles

In This Chapter

- ◆ Requirements for making an overcall
- ◆ Takeout doubles
- ◆ Balancing seat overcalls
- ◆ Overcalling preemptive bids

Up until now we've been talking about how you open the bidding or respond when your partner opens the bidding. But half the time your opponents open the bidding and you are in the position of *overcalling* your opponents' opening bid. This chapter discusses what you need to overcall and how you do it. It also explains what a *takeout double* is and how you do that.

Why Overcall?

When opponents open the bidding, you know that at least one person at the table is sitting there with a pretty good hand, and it's not your loving partner. So when should you overcall, and, better question, why?

Because we know that you need 13 points to open the bidding and there are 40 total HCP in the hand, that leaves a maximum of 27 points, plus some distribution points, spread among the three other players. If you subtract the points in your hand from that 27, it tells you approximately how many points you can expect from the other two players.

If you have 12 points, that's 25 total points accounted for. Which means that there are approximately 15 points left to be distributed between your LHO and your partner. To make game in No Trump you need 25 points. You have 12. That means that your partner must have 13 of the 15 unaccounted for points for you to make game.

Lingo

An **overcall** is a bid by either partner after an opponent has opened the bidding. A **takeout double** is a low-level double asking partner to bid an unbid suit.

All this leads up to the question, why overcall? If we can't make game, why say anything?

Four reasons …

- **You might make game.** You have to tell your partner what you have. You know what the possibilities and the probabilities are. What you don't know are the *facts.* Tell her what you have and let her tell you what she has. The way to do that is to make an overcall within the parameters upon which you and your partner have agreed.

- **You might make a partscore.** Don't just roll over and play dead because you think your opponents might have better hands than you. If you have a bid, make it. You and your partner might be able to make 3 Diamonds, for instance. If your opponents can make 2 Hearts, but not 3 Hearts, you should bid to 3 Diamonds. If they bid to 3 Hearts and you set them, you score points that you wouldn't have made had you not overcalled.

- **You tell your partner something about your hand to help her defend the contract if opponents win the auction.** Without your bid, she has no clue as to what's in your hand and she will probably assume you don't have much. With an overcall at the 1 level you tell her what your preferred suit is and that you have at least 8 points.

- **You crowd the bidding a little for opponents.** If they open 1 Club and you can overcall 1 Spade with an 8-point hand and five Spades, it means that they will have to go to the 2 level to communicate and that might be difficult.

With those reasons in mind, if you have a hand to overcall you turn the auction into a *competitive auction*, and that makes it more unlikely that your opponents will bid to game than if you were not competing with them.

Lingo

A **competitive auction** is one where both pairs are bidding and competing to get the contract.

Suit Length Requirements

Back when I was on the beginning side of the learning curve, my RHO opened 1 Heart and I overcalled 2 Clubs with a 10-point hand and a five-card suit. We were vulnerable and the bidding went Pass–Pass–Double-pass out. I was down two for a terrible result.

After the hand, my LHO, Arlen O'Hara, who has since become one of my partners, knew that I was relatively new to the game, so she gave me some advice. "I never," she said, "overcall at the 2 level unless I have an opening hand or a six-card suit."

That sounded good to me, so I adopted that. I called it *Arlen's rule*. I played by Arlen's rule for awhile until I learned more specific point and suit length requirements for overcalls, which you'll learn shortly. It kept me out of a lot of trouble.

So the first question you ask yourself is, how long must my suit be to overcall, regardless of how many points I have in my hand. Answer: *You must have at least a five-card suit to make an overcall.* Look at the following hand, when your RHO opens 1 Club:

♠ KQ86
♥ K8
♦ KQ98
♣ 873

Not a bad hand. What? You have 13 HCP, 14 total points. This is a hand you would clearly open 1 Diamond. But your RHO opened 1 Club. Can you overcall 1 Diamond or 1 Spade? Not in this lifetime, you can't. When you overcall you *promise* your partner you have five cards in the suit you bid. It doesn't matter that you are only bidding at the 1 level. Overcalling is not like responding to your partner's opening bid. It's more like making an opening bid. But you don't have the luxury of being able to open a three-card minor

Lingo

A **passed hand** is one that is limited to being below the requirements to open the bidding. If you fail to open you are a passed hand. If you fail to overcall, you're not a passed hand because you might have a hand you could have opened, but not one that you could overcall.

when you only have a four-card major. So when you make an overcall you must have five cards, at least, in the suit you bid.

This is a very instructive hand because it illustrates a principle that you should never forget. When your LHO opens the bidding, the fact that your partner passes doesn't say that she has a bad hand. She just might not be able to bid what she has. In such an event, she will be counting on you to *balance*, which is explained later in this chapter.

So your partner's failure to overcall by passing doesn't make her a *passed hand*.

Point Requirements

This is pretty simple black letter law. You may overcall in accordance with the following rules:

- To overcall at the 1 level you should have no less than 8 points and no more than 15 points. This is flexible and according to partnership agreement. For example, some people play 7 to 17.

- To overcall at the 2 level …

    - With a five-card suit, you must have no less than 11 points and no more than 16 points.

    - With a six-card suit, you may overcall at the 2 level if you have at least 10 points.

If you overcall at the 1 level with an 8-point hand, however, you should have a very good suit. It would not be wise to bid a poor five-card suit with only 8 points. Look at the following two hands:

1.	♠ JT984	**2.**	♠ AKT84
	♥ A87		♥ J98
	♦ K83		♦ 873
	♣ 73		♣ 73

Hand 1: What's the point of overcalling 1 Spade? You have 9 points, but your Spade suit is terrible. If your partner is on lead, she's going to trust you and lead a Spade, even though she might have a better lead in her hand (Maybe she has the KQx of Hearts and would normally lead the King of Hearts). You would be misleading your partner.

Hand 2: You have a wonderful Spade suit. So even if your partner doesn't have Spade support and the opponents get the contract, you want your partner to lead

Spades so you can cash your two Spade tricks. Further, if your partner has a doubleton, you might get your two Spade tricks plus allowing your partner to ruff the third Spade. So in Hand 2 you have every right to overcall 1 Spade, but in Hand 1 it would be a big mistake.

Let's look at some more hands after your RHO opened the bidding at 1 Heart as dealer:

1. ♠ AT964
   ♥ Q4
   ♦ AQ93
   ♣ 32

2. ♠ A863
   ♥ KQ5
   ♦ 83
   ♣ A873

3. ♠ K983
   ♥ 7
   ♦ T74
   ♣ KQJ52

4. ♠ QJ976
   ♥ J6
   ♦ T97
   ♣ AJ4

5. ♠ K983
   ♥ 7
   ♦ Q74
   ♣ KJ752

And look at the following hand after RHO opened the bidding at 1 Spade as dealer, and you are vulnerable:

6. ♠ void
   ♥ KT9873
   ♦ J98
   ♣ KJ84

Hand 1: 1 Spade. This is a clear hand. You would open it. It's got a five-card major. You have 14 points. No problem.

Hand 2: Pass. You shouldn't make a takeout double this hand because, as you will learn later in this chapter, a double promises tolerance for all unbid suits. You can't tolerate a Diamond bid.

Hand 3: 2 Clubs. This is a minimum hand to overcall at the 2 level. You have 11 points and five Clubs. Your Club suit is good enough to serve as a lead directing call if your partner is on lead. If vulnerable you should probably pass.

Hand 4: Pass. You have 10 points, but a weak Spade suit. Really the only trick you have in your hand is the Ace of Clubs. Forget it. At equal or unfavorable vulnerability, pass and let your partner carry the ball. With favorable vulnerability, overcall 1 Spade.

Hand 5: Pass. This hand is identical to Hand 3 except that your Club suit lacks the Queen and your Diamond suit has the Queen. The points are identical. But you should pass this because your Club suit is not strong enough and isn't good enough to serve as lead directing for your partner.

Hand 6: Pass. Remember, on this hand, RHO opened 1 Spade. This is a shot in the dark. Against good players the bidding could go as follows.

RHO	You	LHO	Partner
1 Spade	2 Hearts	Pass	Pass
Double	Pass	Pass	Pass

Result? Down two for 500 points above the line for the bad guys. Even though you have 11 points and six Hearts, your Heart suit is far too weak to overcall at the 2-level vulnerable (or even nonvulnerable unless opponents are vulnerable). From the bidding you're going to get the sinking suspicion that the Hearts are sitting behind you and that you're going to get killed. This is a hand that mediocre players often rush in where good players fear to tread. In the direct seat you must always take into consideration the possibility of this type of bidding, to which we have referred earlier, the *reopening double*, and which is explained in detail in Chapter 18. To overcall at the 2 level without opening-hand values, you must have control of your trump suit (see the next section).

Goren gives a very good rule: *Don't overcall at the 2 level unless you can promise you will not lose more than two trump tricks.* You should adopt that rule. This hand does not promise that, even though it has six cards and two honors.

Second Position Overcalls

If dealer opens and you are in second position, your overcalls should be disciplined. The reason is that your partner's hand is undefined. If you overcall with a weak hand, 8 points, and she's sitting there looking at a 12-point hand, she's going to be thinking game. So in second seat you shouldn't overcall, even at the 1 level, unless you have at least 10 points. Look at the following hand after dealer, your RHO, opens 1 Spade:

♠ 3
♥ AK9863
♦ J96
♣ 832

Like your Hearts? You have six of them. And a singleton Spade. Are you tempted to overcall 2 Hearts? I don't blame you. I know a lot of people who would. Now take a look at your LHO's hand:

♠ J74
♥ QJT74
♦ Q85
♣ 97

Your RHO opened 1 Spade so you know that he has an opening hand. How do you think you're going to fare in 2 Hearts with all those Hearts sitting behind you? If you're up against savvy opponents, this is how the bidding will go.

RHO	You	LHO	Partner
1 Spades	2 Hearts	Pass	Pass
Double	Pass	Pass	Pass

You'll probably be set two or three and your partner will be seething. This is the danger of overcalling on a good 1 suit with nothing else. The two hands behind you are unknown. If you're lucky, your partner will have the holding shown above in your LHO's hand. But there's at least as good a chance that it will be your opponent and you'll be in for a long, long hand.

However, look at the next hand after your RHO opens 1 Club as dealer:

♠ 73
♥ QJT6543
♦ A
♣ T52

What do you think? This is a seven-card suit, but it's not as good a suit as the six-card suit led by the Ace–King. The answer is that you have 10 points and long, long suit, and you should overcall 1 Heart.

Third Position Overcalls

You can be more aggressive when you're in third position. You've already heard from your partner and she's passed, telling you that she does not have an opening hand. (Remember, when you're in third seat, your partner is the dealer and opening bidder.) You need have no fear that if you bid her eyes will light up and immediately think of game. It's here that you can bid your 8-point hand with the good suit. This bid tells her, "Partner, I have a nice suit. If you can support it, let me know and we will compete. If you can't support it, this is the suit you should lead if you are on lead."

Also in third position you're in a perfect spot to try to foul up your opponents' communication. So you have three incentives to make an overcall in third position:

♦ Tell your partner you have a good hand, good suit, or both.

♦ Give your partner a lead direction.

♦ Interfere with opponents' communication.

Fourth Position Overcalls

You can be aggressive here, too. In fourth position both your partner and one of your opponents have passed. However, it matters who opened the bidding. If dealer opened and your partner passed, she could have a good hand that she couldn't overcall. So she will be relying on you to make a bid. I'll talk about this shortly when I discuss balancing.

If your RHO opened the bidding in third seat, you know that both your LHO and your partner do not have opening hands. If you bid, you'll be interfering with your LHO's ability to respond to his partner's opening bid. This is another situation where you have an incentive to interfere with a weak hand. This is especially true if you can elevate the level of bidding so that your LHO will be forced to respond at the 2 level. For instance, if your RHO opens 1 Diamond and you can overcall 1 Spade, it makes it difficult for your RHO to tell his partner he has four Hearts with a minimum 6-point hand. If you can overcall 2 Clubs it's even better, because that eliminates your LHO's ability to communicate any four-card major he might have to his partner at the 1 level.

> **Lingo**
>
> The **direct seat** is the seat immediately to the left of the opening bidder. The **passout seat** is the seat immediately to the right of the opening bidder after it has gone "Opening bid, Pass, Pass," and if that person passes, the contract will be passed out to the opening bidder.

No Trump Overcalls

If your RHO opens the bidding and you overcall 1 No Trump, it's the same as opening the bidding with 1 No Trump. A 1 No Trump overcall shows 15 to 17 HCP, no voids or singletons, and no more than two doubletons. This is only true if you are in the *direct seat* (immediately to the left of the opening bidder).

> **Lingo**
>
> A **balancing call** is a bid or takeout double made to keep the bidding open after opponents have opened and there have been two consecutive passes, so that if you pass, the auction will terminate.

Balancing

A *balancing bid* is only made in the *passout seat* (immediately to the right of the opening bidder). So an overcall in the balancing seat could be a bid to keep the bidding open for one of two reasons:

- You don't want to let opponents play the hand at a low level.

◆ You're protecting your partner in the event she was forced to pass what might be an opening hand because her RHO opened before she could bid.

Look at your partner's hand:

♠ KQ8
♥ K85
♦ KQ98
♣ 873

This is your partner's hand when her RHO opened the bidding with 1 Club. She shouldn't bid, but she has 13 points. She is relying on you to balance if the bidding is passed around to you. If you don't have a five-card suit to bid yourself, then you can make a takeout double, which I will explain later in this chapter. This doesn't say much about your hand. But you know that your RHO, opener's partner, can't have more than 5 points in his hand or he would have been forced to respond when your partner passed. So you count the points in your hand, add five to it, add 14 to that, and you come up with a reasonable expectation of what your partner has in her hand. Take a look at your hand:

♠ A9532
♥ 763
♦ J3
♣ K92

The bidding has gone 1 Club–Pass–Pass to you. What do you do? Following is the way you can fairly reliably determine where the points are in this hand:

You	8 points. You know this for sure because you can see them and count them.
RHO	A maximum of 5 points. He passed after your partner passed. If he had 6 points he would have bid.
LHO	Probably 14 points. He opened the bidding at one of a suit. It's possible he's got a big hand, 17 points or more, and is just waiting to jump or reverse, but that occurs less frequently. You can feel fairly certain that he's got a maximum of 14.
Total	8 + 5 + 14 = 27
Partner	40 – 27 = 13

That's 13 points in your partner's hand. What does that mean? That means you have the preponderance of the points. You can't let opponents play this in 1 Club unless your partner is sitting there with a lot of Clubs.

So what you do is bid your five-card suit, even though your hand is minimal and your suit isn't great. You know that your partner's hand is going to be a source of some tricks for you, even if she only has two Spades, so you aren't taking much risk in bidding a weak five-card suit when you know your RHO has dreck. You aren't selling out at the 1 level when you and your partner have 22 points between you. And you're protecting your partner. When you bid with this kind of hand in the passout seat you give your partner the confidence to pass her 14-point hand without a five-card suit when her RHO opens the bidding because she knows she can rely on you to balance to *protect* her.

> **Lingo**
>
> **Balancing** is called **protection** in England, which is probably a more descriptive term for what you're doing.

What if your hand were the following?

♠ A952
♥ K763
♦ J432
♣ 9

> **Alert**
>
> You must be absolutely certain that you and your partner are on the same wavelength on the meaning of a 1 No Trump overcall in the passout seat. If she thinks you're showing 15 to 17 HCP when you only have 12 HCP in your hand, you could find yourself in a 3 No Trump contract real fast, down two.

You have 10 points and can support all unbid suits. I discuss takeout doubles later in this chapter. For the purposes of overcalling and balancing, however, I introduce this concept here just to point out that if you have 10 points, as you do here, and you know that there's a very good chance that your partner has as many as 13, you must make a bid with this hand. Because you don't have a five-card suit, and because you can support any other suit bid by your partner, you make a takeout double. There's a possibility that your partner's suit is Clubs and if she has enough points, she might leave it in for a spirited hand at 1 Club doubled. That's where defense really gets to be tense and fun.

Balancing No Trump Overcalls

When your LHO is dealer and opens the bidding and it's passed around to you in fourth seat, your No Trump overcall is different than if you make it in the direct seat. As you remember, if you make a 1 No Trump overcall in the direct seat, you're promising a standard 15- to 17-point hand that you would have opened 1 No Trump had you been the opening bidder.

But when you're in the passout seat, your No Trump overcall can be made with three less HCP in your hand. In the passout seat, your bid of 1 No Trump promises 12 to 14 HCP, not 15 to 17.

Overcalling Opponents' Opening Bid of 1 No Trump

If your RHO opens 1 No Trump, you know that at least 15 HCP are in his hand. But if you have an opening hand, too, and a good five-card suit, there's no reason why his 1 No Trump open should intimidate you and keep you from bidding. The fact that you're sitting behind him makes your hand valuable because you're in a good position to take his high cards with your high cards.

You can overcall an opponent's opening bid of 1 No Trump if you have an opening hand and a good five-card suit. Your LHO may have a Yarborough and you and your partner could have game. If your RHO's hand is a balanced 15 HCP and his partner has a Yarborough, you and your partner have 25 HCP between you and probably some distribution points, too; you could have game. You should bid your hand, even if opponents open with 1 No Trump.

Overcalling Preemptive Bids

When opponents make a preemptive bid and it's your turn to bid in the direct seat, you shouldn't bid unless you have extra values. This means that if you have a mere opening hand, 13-14 points without a good five-card suit, and your RHO opens 3 Diamonds, you pass. You will be relying on your partner to make a balancing bid in the passout seat if it's passed around to her with a subminimum hand of 11 points. Look at the following hands after a 3 Diamonds opening by your RHO:

1. ♠ AK73	2. ♠ AK732	3. ♠ KQ4	4. ♠ KQJ732
♥ KQ83	♥ KQ8	♥ JT98	♥ 94
♦ 87	♦ 87	♦ 87	♦ 9
♣ 943	♣ JT3	♣ AK86	♣ KQ84

Hand 1: Pass. You have a minimum opening hand with no five-card major. You'd ordinarily open this 1 Club. If your partner doesn't have enough to make a balancing bid or double, you'll be in trouble in three of anything.

Hand 2: Pass. You have a nice five-card Spade suit, but what if your LHO has a lot of Spades? Do you want to start off at the 3 level with this hand? I don't. Again, it's a minimum opening hand; you don't want to start bidding with a minimum opening hand at the 3 level. Also, you can support your partner on anything she bids, if she bids. Two hands are unknown, your LHO's and your partner's. If the remaining points are evenly distributed between the two hands, it's a crapshoot whether anybody can make a three bid. In that event I'd rather defend. Wait until you know the lay of the land, which will be after your LHO bids. If he passes, your partner will have the opportunity to bid or make a balancing double. Then you'll be able to bid more confidently.

Hand 3: Pass. This is another minimum opening hand that can support your partner if she bids. Don't go searching for a fit with minimum points unless your partner asks you to.

Hand 4: 3 Spades. Finally, a bid! This is a good hand with which to overcall a preemptive bid. You've got a nice six-card Spade suit, and nice distribution with a singleton and a doubleton. Plus, your Clubs will give you at least one trick.

When you're in the passout seat, the rules change. If the bidding has gone 3 Diamonds–Pass–Pass to you, you must protect your partner in the event that she has passed with one of the opening hands above. So in the passout seat, you should bid with a subminimum opening hand. If you have 11 points, or 10 points with a six-card suit, you should make some sort of call—either bid a suit or double if you can support all the unbid suits. The rules in the passout seat are that you should bid with the following minimum holdings:

- At least 10 points and a fair six-card suit (two of the top four honors), bid your suit.

- At least 11 points and a good five-card suit (two of the top three honors), bid the suit if you can bid it at the 3 level.

- At least 11 points and 4–4–4–1 distribution with the singleton in the preempted suit, double. Your partner will either bid her longest suit, or, if she has a good hand and at least four cards in the preemptive suit, will leave the double in for penalty.

- At least 11 points and 4–4–3–2 distribution with the doubleton in the preemptive suit you can double because you can support your partner in anything she bids. If she bids your three-card suit, you can pass.

For more on this, refer to Chapter 17 to see how you and your partner interact in this situation.

Overcalls by a Passed Hand

What if you are dealer and the bidding goes, Pass–Pass–Pass–1 Diamond. You're a passed hand. What should you do? Obviously you don't have at least 13 points.

An overcall by a passed hand shows between 8 to 12 points and a five-card suit. If you're doing it with 8 points, it should be a very good five-card suit. And if you're doing it at the 2 level, you should have a six-card suit and no less than 11 points.

Don't forget, you don't have many values in this hand because you know your partner doesn't have an opening hand, either. Making an overcall when you are both passed hands can be risky business, indeed.

Jump Overcalls

A jump overcall (like 1 Club–2 Hearts) shows a very big hand, more distributional than for you to overcall 1 No Trump. It promises at least six cards in the suit and at least 16 points. Following is an example of a typical hand where you would want to make a jump overcall:

♠ AKT964
♥ AK6
♦ 864
♣ 7

Tricks of the Trade

The modern trend is for jump overcalls to be weak. Goren recognized this in his last book and taught preemptive jump overcalls as a part of his standard system.

This is a hand that is close to game with no help. If trump splits favorably and your partner has trump support, you have eight tricks.

A jump overcall requests help from your partner in outside suits. You're telling her, "Don't worry too much about my trump suit. If you have help in other suits, let's keep bidding."

If your partner has two quick tricks in outside suits, she should jump to game, even without much trump support. She can jump to game even if she only has a singleton honor in your suit. It's the cards in her hand that are outside your trump suit that you're interested in.

Jump Overcalls in Balancing Seat

By now, you should be aware that rules change when you're in the balancing seat, and that's true for jump overcalls, too. If you are in the direct seat, a jump overcall is very strong. But in the balancing seat, a jump overcall shows 14 to 15 points and a six-card suit.

Defensive Value of an Overcall

To show how valuable an overcall can be in defending a hand, look at the following, which I played recently. My RHO opened 1 Heart and I held the following:

♠ 832
♥ K43
♦ AQ983
♣ A4

This is a no sweat 2 Diamond overcall, so that's what I did. The auction went like this.

RHO	Me	LHO	Partner
1 Heart	2 Diamonds	2 Spades	Pass
3 Hearts	Pass	3 No Trump	Pass
Pass	Pass		

My partner, the aforementioned Arlen O'Hara, was on lead, so she led the Ten of Diamonds. Dummy came down with the following hand:

♠ Q4
♥ AQJ953
♦ J5
♣ K63

What a terrific lead by her! I had a strong suspicion that declarer had the King of Diamonds with three small Diamonds. He was in a terrible position because Arlen's lead, which she would have never found had it not been for my overcall, set up my hand totally. My Nine of Diamonds became very powerful because she led the Ten and the Jack was on the *board* in dummy's hand.

Lingo

The **board** is another name for the hand in dummy, which is exposed.

Declarer played low from the board. I ducked. I was in terrific shape. He had no hope of making this hand solely because of Arlen's lead. We had four cold Diamond tricks because all he was going to get was his King. I had two sure entries, the Ace of Clubs and the King of Hearts. He held up on taking his King, so Arlen led her other Diamond, the Six. Dummy played the Jack. I covered with my Queen and he was forced to take his King. I now had the two top Diamonds out, the Ace and the Nine. (The King, Queen, Jack, and Ten had all been played.) He had two Diamonds left, but they would fall on my Ace and Nine, setting up my fifth Diamond. That's four Diamond tricks plus the Ace of Clubs and the King of Hearts.

The only reason we set this hand was because my 2 Diamond overcall told Arlen what to lead and she led her top Diamond. You'll learn more about leads in Chapter 21. The point here is to show the value of an overcall on defending the hand. Arlen actually had a Yarborough, so they had 27 HCP between them. We set them because of the overcall. With any other lead they make 3 No Trump easy.

Lingo

A **marked card** is one that is known to be in a certain hand because of previous play or bidding.

Downside of Overcalling

As with anything you do in Bridge, there's a downside to overcalling. You give information to your opponents that they otherwise would not have. If you overcall 2 Hearts, for example, over a 1 Spade opening, it gives your opponents a pretty good hint as to where the Heart honors are if they play the hand. If you overcall and your partner remains silent, the honors will be *marked* in your hand for the missing power. It will make it easier for them to play the hand.

So while you're giving your partner information, you're giving your opponents the same information. It's generally worth the risk to give your partner information she can use on defense.

Takeout Doubles

Previously I have referred to a bid called a takeout double. It occurs, under partnership agreement, when one partner doubles an opponent's bid, asking partner to bid. Your partner has the option of bidding or leaving the double in for penalty if your LHO passes. You are not doubling for penalty. You are doubling to tell your partner that you have values and asking her to describe her hand. She can't leave the double in for penalty unless she has a lot of cards in opponents' suit.

Distribution Is More Important Than Points

Generally speaking, a takeout double at the 1 level is telling your partner that you have some values and are short in opponent's bid suit, but that you don't have the requirements to make a bid on your own. For example, you might only have a four-card major, but have an opening hand. You can't overcall on a four-card major, so if the opponents have bid the other major, you can double to tell your partner that you not only have opening or near opening values, but you also have four cards in the unbid major.

For a normal takeout double, you must have the ability to support any suit your partner bids. You shouldn't double for takeout if you can only support two of the unbid suits. For example, if you hold the following …

♠ AK43
♥ 872
♦ 94
♣ KQ87

and your RHO opens 1 Heart, you have an opening hand but cannot overcall 1 Spade because you only have four Spades. It might appear to you that this is a good takeout double, but it's not because you cannot support your partner if she bids Diamonds—you only have two Diamonds.

Remember, your partner is forced to bid if your LHO passes your double. She must bid even if it's only a four-card suit. Sometimes, in rare but very uncomfortable circumstances, you find yourself having to bid a three-card suit in response to your partner's takeout double. Look at the following hand:

♠ 984
♥ 943
♦ JT83
♣ 543

In the prior bidding sequence, where your RHO opened 1 Heart, if you were to double with your four Spades and four Clubs but only two Diamonds, if your RHO passes, your partner would have to bid 2 Diamonds with this hand. What would you do? You'd have to pass. So you'd be in a terrible contract with no hope of making it. If you were against good opponents you will probably be doubled and you have nowhere to run. So, remember this rule: *In order to make a takeout double you must be able to support all unbid suits.*

Following are requirements for a takeout double:

◆ Shortness, no more than two cards, in suit bid by opponent

◆ Support for all unbid suits

◆ Minimum of 10 HCP

What is *support?* Ideally it would be at least four cards, but this is impractical. Sometimes you will have a 4–4–4–1 hand and your RHO will bid your one-card suit, but more often you have two four-card suits and a three-card suit. If you have sufficient HCP, you can make a takeout double with 4–4–3 in the unbid suits because if your partner bids the suit in which you have three cards you can pass and you'll only be at the 2 level. So playing in a 4–3 fit won't be a disaster.

Doubling and Then Bidding Your Own Suit

There is another use of the takeout double, and that's to show a big hand. If you have a hand that's too big for an overcall with a good suit, the way you show it is to double whatever your opponents bid, then, regardless of what happens, you bid your suit at your second opportunity. This shows a hand bigger than the maximum hand you need for an overcall. Generally you need at least 17 points and a good five-card suit.

In a nutshell, the requirements for bidding your own suit after doubling are as follows:

◆ Not less than 17 points

◆ A good five-card suit headed by three of the top five honors

Shortness in the suit bid by opponents is not a requirement for this bid.

The reason you double and then bid your suit is so that you have a way to tell your partner the size of your hand, which you can't do with an overcall. Look at the following hand:

♠ AKJ76
♥ 54
♦ A7
♣ KQ54

If your RHO bids 1 Club, what are you going to do? Overcall 1 Spade? Okay, but what does that tell your partner? You can overcall in this auction with a good five-card Spade suit and 8 points. How does your partner know whether you're overcalling a minimum hand or a huge hand?

The answer is that there's no way she can know this unless you have a way to bid big hands in a manner different than an overcall. And that way is to double the 1 Club bid first. Then bid your Spade suit at your next opportunity, regardless of what your partner bid or what your opponents bid. Your hand is strong enough to bid your Spades up to the 3 level. You could have game if your partner has the following minimum hand if Spades are properly positioned:

♠ 432

♥ 862

♦ T983

♣ A76

If you were to overcall 1 Spade with this hand your partner would undoubtedly pass. Whereas if you've told her that you had a hand that contains at least 17 points, she might make a bid here after you bid your Spades. And if the Spades split 3–2 and your RHO has the Queen of Spades, you can make 4 Spades, even with your partner's dismal hand. And it's a hand with which she'd never respond if you just overcalled 1 Spade.

Let's look at some hands. Your RHO opens 1 Diamond. What's your bid with the following?

1. ♠ KQT9	2. ♠ KQT	3. ♠ KQT6	4. ♠ K7
♥ QJT7	♥ QJT7	♥ 74	♥ QJT7
♦ 5	♦ KJT	♦ KQT6	♦ A84
♣ A863	♣ Q84	♣ AQ8	♣ KJ73

5. ♠ K7	6. ♠ AKJ75
♥ QJT7	♥ KQJ6
♦ AQJ5	♦ A8
♣ AK4	♣ 74

Hand 1: Double. You can support all the unbid suits plus you have an opening hand.

Hand 2: Pass. You have an opening hand but you shouldn't make a takeout double for a couple of reasons. First, you have too many cards in opponents' suit. Second, you have minimal support in two of the unbid suits. With these deficiencies, the fact that you have a minimum hand suggests that you pass.

Hand 3: 1 No Trump. You have enough points for a No Trump opener. You have the opponents' suit stopped. You have a balanced hand. A 1 No Trump overcall in any seat other than the balancing seat guarantees No Trump opening values and a stopper in opponents' suit.

Hand 4: Pass. You have too many Diamonds and not enough Spades. With a minimum hand you must have support for every unbid suit to make a takeout double.

Hand 5: Double. It is okay to make a takeout double without support for every suit as long as you have more than 16 points. If your partner bids Spades (remember, she must bid something!), you will then bid No Trump at the lowest possible level. This will tell your partner that you have 18 to 20 HCP, a balanced hand, and opponents' suit well stopped.

Hand 6: Double. This is a classic hand for doubling and bidding your own suit. If your partner responds to your double with a bid of 2 Clubs, which is likely because you're short in that suit, you can freely bid 2 Spades to show her that you have at least 17 points and a good Spade suit.

Doubling RHO's Opening Bid of 1 No Trump

A double of your RHO's opening bid of 1 No Trump promises your partner that you have a hand that you could have opened 1 No Trump yourself, 15 to 17 HCP, no voids or singletons, and no more than two doubletons.

The Least You Need to Know

- To overcall at the 1 level, you must have at least five cards in the suit and between 8 and 15 points.

- To overcall at the 2 level, you must have at least five cards in the suit and between 11 and 15 points; with six cards in the suit you need only 10 points.

- To make a takeout double, you must have all support in all unbid suits and at least 10 points.

- To double and bid your own suit, you must have at least 17 points, a five-card suit and three of the top five honors.

Chapter 17

Responses to Overcalls and Takeout Doubles

In This Chapter

- ◆ Responding to an overcall by your partner
- ◆ Responding to a takeout double by your partner
- ◆ Responding when RHO bids

When your partner overcalls, you are in a relatively ticklish position because of the large disparity between her minimum and her maximum. As you learned in the last chapter, when she overcalls, her upper maximum is 15 points, but her minimum is just 8 points. That's a lot less than the minimum for an opening 1 bid. This chapter discusses how you respond when your partner makes an overcall.

What Do You Know?

When you are the partner of an overcaller, you have a lot of information at your fingertips. First, you know where at least half the points in the hand are. Opener, one of your opponents, has at least 13. Your partner has at least 8. That's 21, minimum. So you can look at your hand and evaluate it with much more confidence than if there had been no bidding.

Further, you know that if your partner bid a suit, she has at least five cards in it. That's very valuable because it means that if you have three cards in her suit, you have at least an eight-card fit.

Responding to Major Suit Overcall with Support

If your partner made a major suit overcall and you have three-card support, here's how you should respond:

6–10 points	Make a 1 level raise.
11–13 points	Make a jump (limit) raise.
14–17 points	Jump to game.

Look at these hands after the bidding has gone as follows.

LHO	Partner	RHO	You
1 Club	1 Heart	Pass	?

Here are the hands to evaluate:

1. ♠ KJ7	2. ♠ JT98	3. ♠ A98	4. ♠ AQ973	5. ♠ J973
♥ 9832	♥ A82	♥ 32	♥ 8632	♥ 3
♦ A87	♦ 943	♦ K832	♦ KQJ	♦ KQJ4
♣ K84	♣ J83	♣ KJ43	♣ 9	♣ T965

Hand 1: 3 Hearts. You make the same bid you'd make if she opened 1 Heart, a limit raise showing 11 to 13 points and at least 3 Hearts.

Hand 2: 2 Hearts. Don't mess around showing a weak four-card Spade suit. You only have one bid and your first obligation should be to tell your partner that you have a trump fit. The advantage you have in an overcall situation is that you know at least one of your opponents is sitting there with an opening hand, at least 13 points. You want to get to your trump fit as quickly as possible. If you respond with 1 Spade and partner has a minimum overcall, she won't rebid her Hearts and you'll miss your fit. Your hand is too weak to bid Spades and then bid Hearts later. A simple raise to an overcall supporting your partner's suit shows 6 to 10 points.

You really have no hope for game here, but you want to bid for two reasons:

- ◆ You have safety because of your trump fit, so you can't be hurt too badly if you get the contract.

- ◆ You make it a little more difficult for your opponents to bid because you're raising the level for opener to bid if he has a fairly big hand.

Hand 3: 1 No Trump. You have 11 HCP and opponents bid Clubs. You can't support her Hearts with only two. And you have their Clubs stopped twice. A 1 No Trump response to an overcall shows 8 to 11 HCP.

Hand 4: 4 Hearts. You have a five-card trump support with 14 points. Again, you don't want to mess around with a 1 Spade bid. Get to game without any further communication between your opponents.

Hand 5: Pass. Just because you have Diamonds well stopped, that's no reason to bid without a fit. Your partner is limited to 15 points and it is unlikely that there is a game here. Don't bid to "save" your partner.

Responding by Bidding a New Suit

When you are responding to an opening bid, a new suit bid by you is forcing on opener. However, when responding to an overcall, a new suit bid by you is *not* forcing. Before I give you some examples, you should know the reasoning behind this.

When you respond to an opening bid, you're looking to make game, and it's a real possibility because you know your partner has at least 13 points. However, when responding to an overcall, game is much more unlikely because you know that one of your opponents has an opening bid in his hand. While game may be possible, it's not probable.

So your goal in responding to an overcall is to quickly find an area where you can compete. The requirements for responding to an overcall are similar to responding to an opening bid. And it's very important that you bid a new suit at your first opportunity, if you are going to bid a new suit at all.

The requirements for responding to an overcall with a new suit follow:

- ◆ If you are at the 1 level, you should have at least 8 points and a good five-card suit.

- ◆ If you are at the 2 level and have only 8 points, you should have a six-card suit.

♦ If you have three-card support for your partner's major suit overcall, you shouldn't bid a new suit unless you have opening hand values or a good six-card suit. The idea is to quickly find a fit in which to compete. If you have a fit in your partner's major suit, you should tell her immediately. Because a new suit by you is not forcing, she might pass your bid of a different suit and you could find yourself in a terrible fit when you could have had an eight-card fit had you just supported her at your first opportunity.

Points to consider in responding to your partner's overcall with a new suit include the following:

♦ Your partner may pass your bid, so you must be certain that you will be willing to play the hand in your suit if your partner cannot support you.

♦ You partner is going to consider leading your suit if she's on lead. So it's not a good idea to bid a new suit unless it's a good suit that could give you some defensive tricks if you are on defense.

♦ Beware of introducing a new suit if opponents have shown power. If opener's partner has bid a new suit over your partner's overcall, for example, they probably have the majority of the points in their hands. If you were to bid the fourth suit here, you could be getting into a world of hurts.

♦ Don't respond to your partner's overcall by bidding a new suit at the 3 level unless you have a good six-card or longer suit and at least 11 points. A "good" suit is one with three of the top five honors with at least the King.

Responding to Your Partner's 2-Level Overcall

When your partner makes an overcall at the 2 level, you know that she either has at least 11 points with a five-card suit or a six-card suit with at least 10 points. Therefore, you know that she's stronger than if she overcalled at the 1 level.

Let's take a look at some hands when partner overcalls at the two level. The bidding has gone as follows.

RHO	You	LHO	Partner
		1 Spade	2 Diamonds
Pass	?		

Here are the hands to evaluate:

1.	♠ K4	2.	♠ KQT	3.	♠ 86	4.	♠ 7	5.	♠ 7
	♥ 9863		♥ T974		♥ AQJT7		♥ AK		♥ AJ5
	♦ QJ86		♦ K843		♦ 96		♦ T8763		♦ Q954
	♣ 964		♣ KJ		♣ T642		♣ JT974		♣ JT974

Hand 1: Pass. Even with support, there is little hope of game. Because of the 1 Spade bid, your King of Spades rates to be of little use.

Hand 2: 3 No Trump. Because this hand is balanced and you have Spades well stopped, 3 No Trump is more likely to make than 5 Diamonds.

Hand 3: 2 Hearts. You have minimal values but a good suit. It is possible you have game in Hearts.

Hand 4: 5 Diamonds. Your extra trump, Spade shortness, and long Club suit should make this a good game.

Hand 5: 4 Diamonds. A distributional limit raise. Never less than four trumps and not a lot of HCP. Remember that a 2-level overcall by your partner promises a stronger hand than a 1-level overcall. So this 10-point hand is game invitational if your partner is at the top of her bid.

Responding to an Overcall After a Raise by RHO

When your RHO makes a simple raise of opener's suit over your partner's overcall, he is showing weakness, so you can be more assertive. If you have a good six-card major suit, you can even bid it at the 3 level in this situation. But you must either have length or shortness in the opponents' suit.

Why? Because length would strongly indicate that your partner has shortness. If you're bidding at the 3 level, you can only lose four tricks. You don't want to start right off with two losers in opponents' suit, which is what might happen if you have a doubleton. If you have three or four, it's highly likely that your partner has no more than a singleton.

Look at the following hands and determine how you are going to respond to your partner's overcall. The bidding has gone as follows.

RHO	You	LHO	Partner
		1 Club	1 Spade
2 Clubs	?		

Here are the hands to evaluate:

1.	♠7	2.	♠843	3.	♠74	4.	♠QJ
	♥KJ53		♥A74		♥KQ532		♥KJ9
	♦QJ73		♦QJ73		♦A64		♦AQT986
	♣K873		♣J98		♣JT3		♣74

Hand 1: Pass. You can't support your partner with only one Spade. Even though you have all the other suits stopped you can't bid 2 No Trump because you have a singleton in your partner's suit. If opponents get the contract you have a good defensive hand.

Hand 2: 2 Spades. You have three-card support, even though the rest of your hand isn't too good. But you do have scattered values. You should assume your partner had opening hand values and make the bid you'd make if she opened, which is 2 Spades.

Hand 3: 2 Hearts. Your partner might have three Hearts. You're telling her that you have a good five-card or longer Heart suit and some values.

Hand 4: 2 Diamonds. You only have two cards in Spades, but they're both honors. But you have a terrific Diamond suit, and this might be the only opportunity to tell your partner about it in the event she is on lead. If she rebids Spades, you have support for her with your two honors. If she passes, you shouldn't be in too much trouble in 2 Diamonds because you have a six-card suit and three of the top five honors.

Responding to Minor Suit Overcalls

This is a good time to tell you that there are five basic game contracts into which you can enter. They are as follows:

- ◆ 3 No Trump
- ◆ 4 Hearts or 4 Spades
- ◆ 5 Diamonds or 5 Clubs

Two of these contracts are not favored. Can you guess which two? Because minor suit games require you to take all but two tricks, they can be extremely difficult. Further, 3 No Trump, 4 Hearts, and 4 Spades give you more points despite having to take fewer tricks.

So, if possible, you should exert every effort to play contracts in Hearts, Spades, or No Trump.

With that as a prologue, your responses to a minor suit overcall are the same when you have support for your partner's suit and your hand is the minimum 6 to 10 or 11 to 13. That is, with the former you give a simple raise, and with the latter you give a limit raise by jumping a level.

It's good to point out here the difference between responding to a minor suit overcall and a minor suit open. And it's a big difference. When responding to a minor suit open by your partner you don't know how many cards she has in the suit. She could have as little as three cards in the suit. So you can't respond by raising her suit with minimum support.

But when your partner overcalls in a minor suit, she is promising you that she has at least five cards in the suit. So you can confidently raise with three-card support.

> **Lingo**
> Goren referred to games bid in No Trump, Hearts, and Spades as **golden games.**

However, when you have the big hand, 14+ points, instead of jumping to a minor suit game at the 5 level, you should try to bid 3 No Trump, one of Goren's *golden games*, if you have stoppers in the other suits.

Responding in No Trump

You have a similar obligation to keep the bidding open for your partner's overcall as you do when your partner opens the bidding, if you have the point count and suit length requirements set forth previously. If however, your partner has overcalled at the 2 level, you may pass if your hand is 6 to 9 points without support. You should only bid without support if your hand contains 10 or more points.

Responding to a Takeout Double

If your partner makes a takeout double and there is no intervening bid by your RHO, you should bid your longest suit—unless you have a four-card major—regardless of the number of points in your hand. When responding to a takeout double you should prefer a four-card major to a longer five-card minor. In case there is a game in the hand, it's easier in a major than in a minor. Your partner's takeout double strongly implies four cards in unbid majors. Even if you have a Yarborough, you must bid. Remember, your partner will not make a takeout double unless she can support anything you bid. So you can rely on her to have at least three cards in all of the unbid suits.

If you have at least 10 points, you should make a jump response. This shows her that you have at least 10 points and at least four cards in the suit you bid. There are two exceptions to this requirement of bidding in response to your partner's takeout double:

◆ If you have a lot of cards in opponents' suit and you think you can set them, you can pass. This tells your partner that you're willing to defend the hand for penalty.

◆ If your RHO makes an intervening bid and you have less than 10 points and no five-card suit or no four-card major, your pass tells your partner that your hand is nothing to get excited about.

Look at the following hands after your partner has made a takeout double over her RHO's opening bid of 1 Diamond:

1. ♠ A873	2. ♠ K9873	3. ♠ A98	4. ♠ 986
♥ QT83	♥ K83	♥ K73	♥ 8975
♦ 8	♦ 87	♦ 87	♦ 963
♣ JT63	♣ A73	♣ JT873	♣ 742

Hand 1: 1 Heart. You bid your four-card suits up the line. You have less than 10 points, so you just bid your cheapest long suit, which is Hearts.

Hand 2: 2 Spades. You have more than 10 points and a five-card suit, so you make a jump response to show your points.

Hand 3: 2 Clubs. You must bid your longest suit. You're not jumping to go to the 2 level because the only way you can bid Clubs over Diamonds is to go up a level. This bid, not being a jump, shows that you have less than 10 points and that Clubs is your longest suit.

Hand 4: 1 Heart. You are forced to bid this stinkeroo. The best you can tell your partner is that you have less than 10 points. You're going to pass anything she does unless she makes another forcing bid, like 2 Diamonds.

The Least You Need to Know

◆ With support for your partner's suit you make a 1-level raise with 6 to 10 points, a limit raise with 11 to 13 points, and jump to game with 14+ points

◆ To bid a new suit at the 1 level, you must have a five-card suit and at least 8 points; to bid a new suit at the 2 level, you should have a six-card suit.

◆ If you have three-card support for your partner's suit, you should not bid a new suit unless it is a good six-card suit.

◆ You must bid if your partner makes a takeout double and your RHO passes unless you have a lot of cards in opponents' suit and want to leave the double in for penalty.

◆ Make a jump bid in response to your partner's takeout double if you have at least 10 points.

Doubles, Defensive Bidding, and Etiquette

In This Chapter

- ◆ Penalty doubles
- ◆ Negative doubles
- ◆ Etiquette

I've told you about doubles previously. In its pure form, a double is a defensive bid, saying to your opponents, "I don't think you can make your contract, and I'm so confident of that that I'm going to double you."

In this chapter, you learn about penalty doubles and negative doubles. Finally, you're going to learn how to deal with a partner who irritates you or whom you irritated and how to avoid such confrontations.

Penalty Doubles

A penalty double is like a double or nothing bet. If you double for penalty and your opponents don't make their contract, you get twice the penalty bonus for setting them and more than twice the penalty bonus if you set them more than one trick. If they're not vulnerable and they went down one, you'd ordinarily get 50 points above the line. If you double them and they go down one, however, you get 100 points above the line. On the other hand, if you don't set the contract, your opponents get a bonus for making a contract doubled.

Lingo

An **undertrick** means that declarer didn't make her contract, and each undertrick is the amount by which she did not make it. An **overtrick** is how many tricks declarer took over her contracted amount. So if she bid two and made four, she made two overtricks.

Redoubles

If a declarer is really confident, he can *redouble*. That means, "So you don't think I can make it? Oh, yeah? Well, I'm so confident I can make it that I'm going to *redouble*, which causes the *doubled* score to be doubled! Following is a chart showing what defenders and declarers get when they successfully double and/or redouble.

Scoring Penalty Doubles

Lots and lots of points result from doubles and redoubles. The following table shows how much you can make (or lose!).

Penalties

Not Vulnerable

Undertricks	Not Doubled	Doubled	Redoubled
1	50	100	200
2	100	300	600
3	150	500	1,000
4	200	800	1,600
5	250	1,100	2,200
6	300	1,400	2,800

Vulnerable

Undertricks	Not Doubled	Doubled	Redoubled
1	100	200	400
2	200	500	1,000
3	300	800	1,600

Undertricks	Not Doubled	Doubled	Redoubled
4	400	1,100	2,200
5	500	1,400	2,800
6	600	1,700	3,400

The following table lists the points given for overtricks.

Overtrick Points

Not Vulnerable

Not Doubled	Doubled	Redoubled
Trick value	100 per trick	200 per trick

Vulnerable

Not Doubled	Doubled	Redoubled
Trick value	200 per trick	400 per trick

Trusting Your Partner's Bidding

I've emphasized that you must not lie to your partner. Time and again I've told you how important it is that you be consistent in your bidding and refrain from making unilateral bids that are inconsistent with your partnership understandings, just because you might *like* your hand.

Now you'll learn one of the reasons why this is so important. When you or your partner make a penalty double, you are generally doing it as a result of the auction and what you've learned about your partner's hand, as well as the hands of your opponents. Let's say the auction went like this.

RHO	You	LHO	Partner
1 Club	1 Heart	1 Spade	2 Diamonds
2 Spades	Pass	3 Spades	Pass
4 Spades	?		

Your partner has made a bid that has told you that she has at least 10 points in her hand, and you have 10 points in your hand, and your opponents have bid a major suit game. You would be entitled to think to yourself, "Well, I have 10 points, and my partner has made a free bid at the 2 level and we've agreed that she can't do this without 10 points. They need at least 26 points to make game. If we have 20 points between us, there aren't enough points in the deck for them to have 26 between them, so there's a very good chance they won't make this contract." So you say, with confidence, "Double."

Now, what if during the play of the hand you discover that your partner does not have the 10 points she indicated she had in the bidding and they make 4 Spades doubled for a big score? You're not going to be very happy, are you? After the hand your conversation will probably go something like this:

You: I thought you had 10 points.

Partner: Well, I had such a nice Diamond suit.

You: How many points did you have?

Partner: I had such a nice Diamond suit.

You: How many points did you have?

Partner: Uh, er, my Diamonds were real nice.

You: How many points did you have?

Partner: Uh, well, I had the Ace–Queen of Diamonds and they were nice.

You: You had 6 points?

Partner: Yes, but my Diamonds were so nice, I thought you'd want to know about them.

You: I doubled on your having 10 points, which is what your bid said you had.

Partner: (embarrassed silence)

You need feel no guilt about being annoyed. Your opponents have received a big bonus for making the contract doubled. You were absolutely correct to take the chance on doubling the contract based on your partner's bid. But your partner didn't have her bid. *Don't lie to your partner!*

Listening to Your Opponents' Bidding

Doubling is a real art. It requires deductive reasoning and strict attention to the auction. If your opponents have made a preemptive bid, showing a weak hand but a lot of trumps, you have to take into consideration the possibility that one of them will be short in the suit in which you have your power.

If you're sitting there with Ace–King–Queen of Clubs and the Ace of Hearts, for example, and your LHO opens the bidding at 1 Spade, your partner overcalls 2 Clubs and your RHO makes a preemptive jump to game, should you double? You look at your hand and think you have four cold tricks. But your RHO has five Spades in his hand. It's very likely that his short suit is Clubs, because you and your partner have at least eight of them between you. You might only get 1 Club trick. For sure you won't get three Club tricks because the best the suit could split for you is 3–2 in your opponents' hands. This is not a hand to double on because you know that it's distributional, and if they have long Spades, they're short in some suits.

> **Lingo** _____
>
> The term **hit** is synonymous with double. So if someone says, "I was just waiting for you to bid 4 Spades because I was going to hit it," it means he was going to double you if you bid 4 Spades.

They Won't Be as Aggressive the Next Time

Another advantage of doubling, and of getting the reputation that you're not afraid to double, is that it can inhibit opponents' bidding. If you double them successfully, it hurts them, and they'll remember.

When you're playing people you know won't double you, you feel freer to take chances and bid to questionable games, knowing that the penalty will just be minimal if you don't make your bid. But if you're playing someone who has no fear of doubling and will *hit* (another term for double) you if you make a chancy bid, you are more reluctant to take the chance. So doubling has the extra added benefit of making your opponents more cautious in their bidding.

> **Lingo** _____
>
> In Duplicate Bridge, which you aren't learning here, a **director** is the person who runs the game. A Duplicate Bridge director is like an umpire in baseball or a referee in other sports, the font of all knowledge.

Negative Doubles

This is a terrific bid. I remember when I was first starting to play Duplicate Bridge, I was playing in a game at the Marina City Club and Cyma Aronow was the *director*.

She was playing as well as running the game because there weren't enough players. When I came to her table the bidding went 1 Diamond by my LHO, 1 Heart by my partner, Double by Cyma. I asked what that meant and she told me it was a *negative double.* I had no idea what it meant, so she explained it to me. Then she said, "You have the potential to be a good player, Tony, but you must learn negative doubles. All the good players play them."

So I learned them, and now I'm going to teach them to you, because it is another wonderful bid that communicates a lot to your partner in just one bid.

Alert _____

The negative double is another bid that most Rubber Bridge players don't play. If you want to play negative doubles, you must be absolutely positive that your partner is playing them, too, or you will end up where there's weeping and gnashing of teeth.

Basically a negative double is a double by you when your partner has opened the bidding, and RHO has overcalled to tell your partner that you have exactly four cards in the unbid major and a certain number of points. So let's say you're in third seat and the bidding has gone 1 Diamond by your partner, 1 Heart by your RHO, and you hold the following:

♠ KQ75
♥ T9
♦ J76
♣ 8732

Not wonderful, is it? But you do have four Spades and you do have 6 points. From what you've learned so far, you would just bid 1 Spade and let it go at that. But how does your partner know how many Spades you have? You could have five Spades, or you could have four Spades.

The negative double takes care of this problem for you. If you have at least five Spades and this hand, you bid 1 Spade. If you have this hand, with four Spades, however, you double!

This is another conventional bid that doesn't mean what it says. It's not a *penalty double.* You aren't saying to your partner, "Hey, pard, we got 'em. We can set this baby, so I'm doubling!"

No, it doesn't say that at all. Instead, it says, "Partner, I have at least 6 points and exactly four Spades in my hand. Not five Spades. Not six Spades. Not three Spades. Exactly four Spades."

The requirements for a 1-level negative double—that is, a negative double that allows your partner to make a bid and stay at the 1 level—are as follows:

♦ At least 6 points

♦ Exactly four cards in the unbid major

Negative Doubles at the 2 Level

The requirements become more stringent as you force your partner to higher levels of bidding. Look at the following hand:

♠ T97
♥ KQ85
♦ 73
♣ KT64

Bidding goes like this.

Partner	RHO	You
1 Diamond	1 Spade	?

Now from what you've learned, you know you can't bid a new suit at the 2 level without at least 10 points. If you were to bid this hand at the 2 level, you would be lying to your partner. And you don't want to have one of those conversations when she takes action on your promised strength only to find out you lied, do you? Of course not.

So what are you to do? Your hand isn't bad and you do have four Hearts, which your partner might like to know about. What to do?

Ah, you're probably way ahead of me. Negative double? Absolutely. In this hand you have four Hearts and 8 points, exactly what you need to make a negative double, which forces your partner to bid at the 2 level. The negative double is a terrific way to tell your partner what you have without lying to her.

Tricks of the Trade

You might have more than 6 points when you make a negative double at the 1 level and more than 8 points when you make it at the 2 level, but you are *promising* that you have *at least* 6 points at the 1 level and *at least* 8 points at the 2 level.

Again, I am going to stress that you cannot lie to your partner. If, instead of the hand above you had the following hand and the bidding went as above, 1 Diamond by your partner and 1 Spade by your RHO, what do you do?

♠ T97
♥ KJ85
♦ 73
♣ QT64

Well, one thing you do not do is make a negative double because if you did you would be forcing your partner to bid at the 2 level and you don't have 8 points. Your bid here would be to pass. Your partner has another bid, so you have no obligation to keep the bidding open. You can't bid at the 2 level because you don't have 10 points, and you can't bid 1 No Trump because you don't have Spades, your RHO's bid, stopped. So all you can do is pass.

I know a lot of players who would be tempted to make a negative double with this hand, even though they don't have enough points. But I hope you're not one of these. Don't lie to your partner. Have I said that before?

Following is a chart showing point requirements for negative doubles.

Level	Points
1	6
2	8
3	10

To recap …

- If your negative double will allow your partner to bid your suit at the 1 level, you can make a negative double with 6 points in your hand.

- If your negative double will force your partner to bid your suit at the 2 level, you must have 8 points in your hand.

- If your negative double will force your partner to bid your suit at the 3 level, you must have 10 points in your hand.

2-Level Negative Doubles with a Five-Card Major

If you have five cards in an unbid major in this situation, but not enough points to make a suit bid at the 2 level, you can utilize the negative double. Look at the following hand:

♠ T97
♥ KJ852
♦ 73
♣ QT6

Bidding is as follows.

Partner	RHO	You
1 Diamond	1 Spade	?

You can't bid 2 Hearts because you only have 7 points. But you do have five Hearts. What to do?

In this situation, I make a negative double. You don't have 8 points, but you do have five Hearts. So you can amend the rule a little to say that you can make a negative double, which forces your partner to bid your suit at the 2 level in the following circumstances:

- Four cards in the unbid major and at least 8 points, or

- Five cards in the unbid major and at least 7 points

Upper Limit for Making Negative Doubles

You can play negative doubles through any level you and your partner wish. I generally play them through 3 Spades. I recommend that you start playing negative doubles through bids of 2 Spades. If this is what you choose to do, any double of a bid over 2 Spades would then be for penalty. So look at the following hand you hold:

♠ 86
♥ KQJT
♦ A763
♣ 874

> **Alert**
>
> Negative doubles through 2 Spades is by partnership agreement. That's the way you should play it while you're learning. Many advanced players play them through 3 Spades. One of my partners, Diana Ayres, widow of film legend Lew Ayres, plays them through 4 Diamonds.

The auction goes as follows.

Partner	RHO	You
1 Spade	3 Clubs	?

You can't double the 3 Clubs bid here to show that you have four Hearts. If you double 3 Clubs, your partner will leave it in, probably, as a penalty double. (Remember, when playing negative doubles only through 2 Spades, if you double any bid over 2 Spades, you're doubling for penalty.)

Remember that a negative double promises four cards in the unbid major. So if the bidding goes 1 Club by your partner, 1 Diamond overcall by your RHO, you must have *two four-card majors* to make a negative double.

Negative Doubles and Five-Card Majors at the 1 Level

If you have a five-card major and sufficient points, you must bid the suit. If you have a four-card major and a five-card major, don't use a negative double to describe this hand, bid the five-card major. Your partner will be relying on you to bid a five-card major at the 1 level if you have it. If you're using negative doubles, bidding the suit at the 1 level over an intervening bid promises five cards. A double promises four cards.

Only One Four-Card Major

If your partner and your RHO have both bid minor suits, and you only have one four-card major, you can't use a negative double to describe your hand, because a negative double promises four cards in each unbid major suit. Look at the following hand:

♠ KQ75
♥ Q73
♦ 872
♣ 983

Your partner opens 1 Club, RHO bids 1 Diamond. You can't make a negative double. Your only bid is 1 Spade. If you made a negative double you'd be promising four Spades *and* four Hearts. Because you don't have four Hearts, you can't make a negative double.

If, on the other hand, your RHO had overcalled 1 Heart instead of 1 Diamond, then you could make a negative double because the only unbid major suit would then be Spades, and you have four of 'em, and at least 6 points.

The negative double is a terrific bid. I recommend that you learn it and use it.

Reopening Double

When you add any bid to your repertoire, you give up something. When you play negative doubles, you give up the ability to double some low-level bids by opponents for penalty.

Even a lot of experienced players aren't aware of the fact that the *reopening double* is an integral part of the negative double system. What if you're in third seat and the bidding goes 1 Heart by your partner then 2 Diamonds by your RHO? It's now your bid and you hold the following cards:

♠ A86
♥ 95
♦ AKJ86
♣ K42

You could bid 2 No Trump, but wouldn't you like to hit 2 Diamonds? Alas, you can't double it because that would be a negative double, wouldn't it? And it won't do you any good to make a negative double for two reasons. First, you don't have the bid. You don't have four Spades. Second, you want it to be a penalty double, not a negative double. So how can you defend 2 Diamonds doubled in this hand? You clearly cannot double because your partner will respond as she has to in the negative double system.

The answer is that if your partner opens the bidding followed by a bid at the 2 level by your RHO, and you pass, your partner *must* double with shortness in the suit bid by opponents and tolerance for the unbid suits, especially if your LHO passes. *Shortness*, in this context, means no more than a doubleton. So if your partner has two or less of your RHO's suit, she should double. To be specific, here's how the bidding goes.

Partner	RHO	You	LHO
1 Spade	2 Diamonds	Pass	Pass
?			

In the previous situation, your partner should protect you by doubling when it's her turn. Then you can either let it sit for penalty, which you would do with the above hand, or pull it by either bidding your partner's suit at the 2 level if you can, or making the best bid you have under the circumstances.

This is called a *reopening double* because it's made by the opening bidder, and she's reopening the bidding by doubling. If she doesn't bid or double, the auction is over.

Of course, you might have a legitimate pass, too. You might *not* be passing because you have opponents' suit. You might have the following:

♠ 862
♥ 75
♦ T96
♣ QT873

If you have this holding and your partner makes a reopening double, you should just pull the double and support your partner's opening suit, in which she'll have at least a 5–2 fit. Your partner anticipates this. Her double is just inviting you to let it stand for penalty if you have a lot of opponents' suit. If you don't, just retreat to the best contract. If you retreat, your partner will know you passed because you don't have much.

Requirements for a reopening double are as follows:

- A reopening double can be made only by opening bidder;

- After LHO has overcalled and there are two passes by your partner and your RHO.

- Opening bidder has two or less cards in overcalled suit.

- Opening bidder must have tolerance for all unbid suits.

- Opening bidder's hand cannot be distributional.

As to the last rule above, if opener has a long suit, six cards or more, or is 5–5–2–1, she should either rebid her six-card suit, in the former, or bid her second suit in the latter. Look at the following two hands:

1. ♠ J5
   ♥ AQT864
   ♦ 8
   ♣ AQT8

2. ♠ J75
   ♥ AKT864
   ♦ 8
   ♣ AK9

Bidding is as follows.

You	LHO	Partner	RHO
1 Heart	2 Diamonds	Pass	Pass
?			

How do you, as opening bidder, respond with each?

Hand 1: 2 Hearts. This is not a hand with which you should use a reopening double. True, you have a singleton in your LHO's suit. And, true, your partner is almost certainly sitting behind your LHO with a lot of Diamonds. But your hand has two shortcomings that make it inappropriate for a reopening double:

- You don't have tolerance for all unbid suits. Your Spade doubleton is insufficient for support if your partner responds to your double with a bid of 2 Spades. Remember, your partner might be short in your suit. So if you double and your partner doesn't want to sit for the penalty double at the 2 level, she has to either support your suit if she has two cards in it, or bid her longest suit. If she has five Diamonds but not enough to sit for the double, her longest suit might be Spades. She could be 4–1–4–4, so she would be forced to bid Spades, and you can't support her.

◆ Your hand isn't strong enough. You really only have two fairly certain tricks, your two Aces. Remember, you have to take six tricks to set them. Otherwise they're going to get a terrific score, making two or more, doubled!

Hand 2: Double. This is a very good hand with which to make a reopening double for two reasons:

◆ You have tolerance for both unbid suits, so if your partner can't support your Heart bid you have at least three cards in the unbid suits. The worst that can happen is that your partner will be playing in a 4–3 fit at the two level, not a disaster.

◆ You have a good hand, with two Ace–King combinations. In a defense you have good trick-taking capability.

Remember this: Just because you have an opening hand and shortness in LHO's suit, you don't automatically make a reopening double. Your hand must fit the requirements in addition to shortness and the appropriate bidding after your open.

Trust Your Partner—Partnership Etiquette

Bridge can be a difficult game on relationships. Whether you're playing with a friend, a spouse, a significant other, or someone who doesn't fit any of those categories, Bridge tests the limits of a relationship. Why? Because it goes to the essence of your being, the way you think and reason. When someone questions something you did, that person is questioning your intelligence, and the questioning can become destructive.

My experience has been that the area of penalty doubles is where many of the emotional problems arise. That's why I'm digressing a little here to discuss etiquette and to make some suggestions for getting along.

When you don't trust your partner to know what she's doing, and you take some unilateral action inconsistent with what she has done, you are communicating a lack of respect that can, in its most virulent form, destroy a relationship. The following story illustrates what can go wrong.

I was playing in a club championship with one of my best partners. We were good enough to have won a regional championship together. When we first played together, we had a problem because she continually pulled my penalty doubles. She, unilaterally, didn't think we could set our opponents; she didn't trust my doubles. I asked her to respect my penalty doubles.

We stopped playing for quite a while, and when we started again she exhibited more respect for my game. The first test of this was in a game where I doubled someone who had balanced. The bidding went as follows.

Me	LHO	Partner	RHO
1 Diamond	Pass	1 Heart	Pass
2 Hearts	Pass	Pass	3 Clubs
Double	Pass		

My partner thought for awhile and finally passed. We set them two for a score of 300. I thanked her for not pulling my double and felt more confident about our partnership.

We continued to play and did well, winning championships. Then we came to a club championship and, with us vulnerable and our opponents nonvulnerable, the bidding went as follows.

RHO	Me	LHO	Partner
1 Club	1 Diamond	1 Heart	Pass
4 Hearts	Double	Pass	

This was my hand:

♠ Q5
♥ KQJT
♦ KT876
♣ A8

I had three certain trump tricks and the Ace of Clubs. The only way I could be kept from setting them at least one was if the game were terminated by an earthquake.

My partner started thinking and I started getting worried. Finally, after long thought, she bid 4 Spades! Double by my RHO. I could do nothing but pass. As my partner played the hand, I saw that she was missing the Ace and King of Spades, as well as the

Queen I had in my hand. She was down three. Doubled. Vulnerable. So she took what was going to be a very nice hand for us, setting them at least one for a score for us of 100, and turned it into a fantastic hand for them, down three doubled and vulnerable for 800 for them above the line.

While she was playing the hand, I was talking to myself, saying, "Don't say a word, Tony. Just start the next hand and go on." But when the hand was over our opponents started talking and the devil got control of me and I asked, "Why did you pull my double?"

She leaned over the table and castigated me in a voice loud enough for everyone in the room to hear. Although I hadn't been abusive or abrasive, I felt bad because I had embarrassed her. Now I'll stop the story and lay down some rules:

- ◆ **You must trust your partner.** If you can't trust your partner's bid, you shouldn't play with her. My double was clearly penalty. She knew that I was a good enough player that I wasn't going to double unless I had a very good chance of setting them. And, from the bidding, I had to have it in my hand. I couldn't rely on anything in her hand because she hadn't bid!

  Sometimes you might pull a penalty double of your partner's if you have bid and you feel that you've made a mistake and your partner has misinterpreted the strength of your hand, especially if you are nonvulnerable against vulnerable. You have a logical argument if you misrepresented your hand and can say that you pulled it because you felt your partner was relying on something you didn't have.

  But here she hadn't bid. She had to trust me that I knew what I was doing. Further, we were vulnerable and they weren't. The worst that could happen was that they'd make it, doubled, and would get a bonus of 170 points. But if she pulled it, which she did, and went down three, which she did, because we were vulnerable they got 210 points more than they would have if she had left my double in and they made it. There was no logic or reason to her pulling the double, from a Bridge point of view. As it was, they would have been set at least one, so it was a difference in the score of 900 points.

- ◆ **Don't discuss hands or bids at the table.** When you question someone, it challenges their intelligence and ability to reason in front of others, which can be embarrassing and demeaning. I should have waited until the game was over and talked about it on the way home.

- ◆ **Don't be abusive.** Don't call your partner names. If you do discuss the hand, limit it to Bridge and try to discuss it calmly and logically, with the purpose being to avoid misunderstandings in the future. Don't make the discussion for the purpose of putting the person down.

◆ **Remember that your partner is trying to do the best she can.** If she makes a mistake or a bad play, it wasn't because she is trying to do something person-ally harmful to you—that would harm the partnership. If she makes a mistake, realize that she probably feels worse about it than you do, so try to minimize it at the time. You can talk about it later, the next day, if it's important enough to the partnership. The best way to strengthen a partnership is to be supportive when your partner makes a mistake. Instead of criticizing, give her a pat on the back and say, "Don't worry about it."

◆ **If your partner criticizes you, realize that Bridge is competitive, and your partner is competitive.** Partners are human. When they see you do something they think is incorrect, or, let's face it, stupid, they can react emotionally on the spur of the moment. There are very few saints, and most saints don't play Bridge. The Pope might have reacted emotionally to my partner's pulling my penalty double in that situation. So I reacted, even though I tried not to. When your partner reacts to something like that, and asks, "Why did you trump my Ace?" try to realize that it's just a human reaction of the moment and that she'll get over it. Turn the other cheek and let her get it out of her system by verbaliz-ing her frustration. If you felt it was offensive or embarrassing, talk with her about it later and express your feelings then, just by saying something like, "Please don't criticize me during the game. What you said embarrassed me. I'm sorry for what I did, but that wasn't the time to talk about it." Something as simple as that will bring it out in the open and keep it from festering. If your partner doesn't react with compassion and understanding, maybe it's time to consider taking a vacation from one another, which is what my partner and I did.

◆ **Take responsibility!** If you do something stupid or wrong or inconsistent with your partnership understanding, take responsibility as soon as possible. I was playing once with Mike Shuman, one of the giants of the game. I opened the bidding and he finally passed me out at 3 Diamonds. When he laid down the dummy, he said, "I apologize if we have game partner." Well, that completely disarmed me. What could I say? If we had missed game, he had taken all the responsibility, so I didn't have to say, "Why did you pass 3 Diamonds?" There was nothing to criticize. If my partner had said, "I'm sorry," after she saw my dummy and realized that she had pulled a perfectly good penalty double, it would have instantly relieved me of the anxiety I felt at having my wonderful double pulled. There's really not much you can say when your partner assumes full responsibility for a glitch and apologizes. Any partner who doesn't graciously accept such an apology is someone with whom I wouldn't want to play. Taking responsibility is the number one way to make sure a partnership runs smoothly and for a long time. And it's the best way to avoid contentious conversations and arguments at the table.

Tag line: We made up and continue to play to this day. So another thing to remember is to forgive and forget.

The Least You Need to Know

- ◆ You double for penalty when you think you can set opponents' contract, provided it is not a takeout double.

- ◆ A negative double promises four cards in the unbid major and 6 points if your partner can bid your suit at the 1 level, 8 points at the 2 level, and 10 points at the 3 level.

- ◆ Be considerate of your partners. Treat them as you would like to be treated.

Part 5

Defense, Play of the Hand, and Advanced Techniques

Bidding is one thing, but when it comes down to actually playing a hand, you may feel like a real dunce. Don't let this happen to you! Make sure you read this section carefully.

This section teaches you how to play or defend the hand once the bidding is completed. You'll learn how to play the hand as declarer, along with how to play some basic card combinations that arise again and again.

If your opponents win the contract, you're on defense. You'll learn how to begin your defense of the hand by your opening lead and some common techniques to use after the opening lead. You'll also learn how you communicate with your partner by the card you play, without even uttering a sound.

Finally, this section teaches you some advanced bidding and playing techniques that you might want to add to your repertoire after you've conquered the basics.

I KNOW I SAID TO FOLLOW ME, BUT I MEANT WHILE PLAYING BRIDGE.

Put Up or Shut Up: Declarer Play in No Trump

In This Chapter

- ◆ How to count winners
- ◆ Setting up a long suit
- ◆ Entries
- ◆ The finesse and hold up
- ◆ Ducking

Now you've got your contract. It's time to see if you knew what you were talking about when you said you could make this contract. If bidding is a team effort, playing the hand as declarer is entirely unilateral. It's up to you to play this hand by yourself. Your partner is dummy and can only sit and watch. Feel the pressure?

Your goal in any contract depends on the final contract you make. If you have contracted to make a 1 bid, you must take seven tricks, which means that you can afford to lose six tricks. If you have contracted to make a 4 bid, you must take 10 tricks, which means that you can afford to lose 3 tricks.

The first thing you do is set your goal and realize what your objective is. If you're playing in a 1 contract, your objective is to take seven tricks. It might be nice if you could take eight, or nine, or more. But you don't want to risk your ability to take seven by trying to take eight. Many times good players will try for the overtrick and fail to make their contract as a result. Always keep in mind that your goal is to make the contract. Overtricks are just bonuses. Don't risk your contract to try to make a bonus.

Playing a No Trump Contract

Playing No Trump is probably the most challenging task for a declarer, but it is also probably the most fun. In No Trump, all suits are equal and high cards dominate. That said, having the lead is all important in No Trump. Take a look at the following two opposing hands for which you are declarer in a No Trump contract:

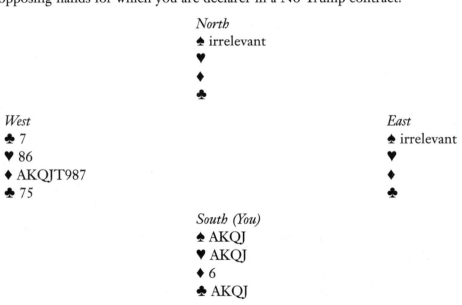

North
♠ irrelevant
♥
♦
♣

West
♣ 7
♥ 86
♦ AKQJT987
♣ 75

East
♠ irrelevant
♥
♦
♣

South (You)
♠ AKQJ
♥ AKQJ
♦ 6
♣ AKQJ

You look at your hand and think you should take 12 tricks. West, your LHO, looks at his hand and thinks he should take eight tricks. Who's correct?

He is! He is correct because he is on lead. And in No Trump, whoever has the lead is the monarch so long as he retains the lead. He runs his eight Diamond tricks and you must throw off seven of your winning tricks until he runs out of Diamonds and has to lead into you.

This also points out the fact that a long suit is a strong suit in No Trump.

Different Strokes for Different Folks

Your approach differs depending on the type of contract you are playing. When you're playing a No Trump contract, you count your winners. When you're playing a suit contract, you count your losers. That's the essence of planning.

When your partner lays down her dummy, the first thing you do is to put your two hands together in your mind's eye and count either your winners or losers, depending on the contract.

How to Count Your Winners

As you now know, in No Trump, having the lead is everything. If you have 13 Spades, you can't count them as 13 tricks unless you are on lead. If you are not on lead you have 13 definite losers. Because you have all of the Spades and you don't have cards in any other suit, there's no way you can get the lead.

If your RHO is declarer in No Trump and you have 13 Spades, however, you have 13 definite winners because you are on lead.

No Trump

When you're playing a No Trump contract, the winners you have are sure winners if you have the lead. If you don't have the lead, they aren't winners because your opponents could *run* one of their long suits and defeat your contract before you can take your winners.

Look at the following terrific hand between you and your partner:

Dummy
♠ 87
♥ T987
♦ KQT65
♣ AK

Declarer
♠ A6
♥ KQJ
♦ A87
♣ QJT98

Lingo

To **run** a suit means to take all the rest of the tricks in that suit without opponents having any way to stop you. This can occur either in No Trump when all the stoppers are gone or in a suit contract when opponents don't have any trump left to stop you.

You have winners galore. You have seven of the top eight Hearts. If you get a Spade lead and they take out your Ace and you then try to set up your Hearts by driving out their Ace, however, they will run their Spade winners and you'll be set before you get the lead back. You can't count any of your Hearts as winners because you don't have the Ace. They are *potential* winners, but they aren't sure winners, and that's what you have to count.

Lingo

To **set up** a suit means to *establish* it.

In this hand you have nine sure winners, five Clubs, three Diamonds, and one Spade. You should take them before surrendering the lead to the Heart Ace.

The rule for counting winners is *you only count winners that you can take without surrendering the lead.* So you can't count any card in any suit as a sure winner if you or your partner don't have the Ace of that suit.

Setting Up a Long Suit

One way to play a No Trump contract is to try to *set up* or establish your long suit. In analyzing the cards you control, one of the first things you do is count the number of cards you have in each suit and determine your longest suit. If you have, for example, two suits in which you have seven cards, if one of them is divided 4–3 and the other 5–2, the 5–2 suit is the one you should choose to develop, assuming equal strength and entries into the hand with the five-card suit. The five-card suit will give you more tricks than a four-card suit.

Tricks in No Trump

When you're playing a contract in No Trump, there are two kinds of tricks you can make. The first is tricks obtained through your high cards. It doesn't take a nuclear physicist to look at a hand with Ace–King–Queen in one suit to calculate that you'll probably be able to count on three tricks in that suit.

One place where the skill and fun comes in to play in No Trump contracts is when you have to take tricks by establishing a long suit. When playing in a suit contract, you can usually count on ruffing power for tricks. But in a No Trump contract, all suits are of equal power. If you don't have enough high cards to make your contract, you have to set up a long suit so you can take the rest of your tricks with low cards in that suit. Let's take a look at a hand to illustrate:

North
♠ K87
♥ 872
♦ QJT86
♣ 65

South
♠ AQ3
♥ AQ4
♦ 543
♣ KQ43

Even though you only have 23 HCP between you, you somehow ended up playing in 3 No Trump and you are South, which is declarer. How are you going to make this contract? Count your winners. You've got three Spade tricks, one or two Heart tricks, and one or two Club tricks. Even at a maximum, that's only seven tricks and you need nine.

To make this contract, you will need to set up your long suit, which is Diamonds, and establish your two needed tricks there. From looking at the hand in a vacuum, Diamonds appears to be your weakest suit. But actually, because you have eight total cards in it, and five in dummy, it's your strongest. Remember: *In No Trump, your longest suit is your strongest suit!*

With the above hands, you're lucky enough to get a Spade lead. You take it in South and immediately lead a Diamond to your Queen–Jack–Ten. It's better if West goes up and takes it, but it doesn't matter much because you're counting on a 3–2 split. No matter what they return, you lead a Diamond again. You might win or lose. Again, it doesn't matter. Because you're going to keep leading Diamonds until your Eight of Diamonds and Six of Diamonds are established, or *set up*, and become winners because they are the only remaining cards left in the suit.

Entries

When playing No Trump, it is essential that you keep entries into the weak hand if it has the long suit. An *entry* is simply a card that allows you to get the lead in that hand. In the referenced hand with the long Diamond suit, you had two sources of entries:

- The fact that you had three Diamonds in your hand to continue leading up to the dummy

- Your King of Spades

But let's change that hand a little:

North
♠ K4
♥ 872
♦ QJT96
♣ 652

South
♠ AQ32
♥ AQ4
♦ 54
♣ KQ43

Now, you take the opening Spade lead in your hand and then lead a Diamond, which they take. They return a Spade and you are forced to take it in dummy with your King. You lead a second Diamond, which they take. Now how are you going to get back to dummy to cash your winning Diamonds? Here's how the hand looks after these plays:

North
♠
♥ 872
♦ T96
♣ 652

South
♠ Q3
♥ AQ4
♦
♣ KQ43

You have no entry into dummy! Your Diamonds are good because your Ten and Nine will take the two outstanding Diamonds and then your Six is the only remaining Diamond, but you can't get there to cash them. You have admirably established your Diamonds, but you lost your entry to cash them.

The rule to remember from all this? Establish your suit *before* you lose your entries.

Choosing Which Suit to Establish

Sometimes you have suits of equal lengths and have to decide which one to establish. It might be axiomatic to say this, but you should attempt to establish the suit in which you could take the most tricks. If you have two suits in which you hold eight cards, but one is divided 4–4 between declarer and dummy and the other 5–3, for example, the suit in which you will probably take the most tricks is the one that is divided 5–3, if defenders' cards in those suits both split 3–2, and assuming relatively comparable high-card strength in both suits.

Timing

When you plan your play you not only determine your longest suit, but you know which suits in which your opponents have more cards than you. In those suits, your short suits, you should protect your stoppers. Don't lead those suits yourself because you'll just be helping your opponents establish their suits.

It's essential that you establish your suit before your opponents establish theirs. When playing No Trump it often comes down to a race. Who can establish their suit first, declarer or opponents?

Often it comes down to who is on lead. If you have their long suit stopped twice but you need two leads to establish your long suit, you're going to lose the race. Look at the following hand:

North
♠ 32
♥ AK93
♦ KQ98
♣ 532

West
♠ QJT984
♥ 65
♦ 763
♣ A4

East
♠ 765
♥ JT874
♦ J52
♣ K7

South
♠ AK
♥ Q2
♦ AT4
♣ QJT986

Opening lead: Queen of Spades

If you try to establish your six-card Club suit, you're going to lose this battle of timing. You take the Queen of Spades lead and immediately lead the Queen of Clubs.

East takes it and returns a Spade, which you take with your last Spade stopper in South. You lead the Jack of Clubs, which West takes with the Ace and runs his four remaining Spade winners. He has established his six-card Spade suit before you could establish your six-card Club suit because you only had two stoppers in his suit and you needed to drive out two losers in Clubs. The timing is against you in this hand.

Lingo

Off the top means that you take all your tricks before losing a trick to opponents.

The point is that you should see this after the opening lead and abandon all hope of establishing Clubs. You should look to see if there's any other way to make this hand in 3 No Trump, and there is. If defenders' Diamonds split 3–3, or if the Jack is a singleton or doubleton, you can make 3 No Trump *off the top* by taking the following cold tricks:

Two Spades

Three Hearts

Four Diamonds (because they split 3–3 or the Jack is a singleton or doubleton and falls setting up the rest of your Diamonds)

How to Play and Win Honors

As you've learned, honors in a suit consist of the Ace, King, Queen, Jack, and Ten. They are the most powerful cards in the suit. Generally honors are the cards that win the tricks. But an honor, unless it's an Ace, is not a sure trick.

If the King is sitting in front of the Ace, the King probably won't win a trick. If the Queen is sitting in front of the Ace or the King, it probably won't win a trick. Look at the following holdings in Spades:

North
♠ AT76

West
♠ K95

East
♠ J82

South
♠ Q43

The only winner in this hand is North's Ace. West's King is not a winner because it's sitting in front of North's Ace. Because North will play after West, North can take West's King when he plays it if he waits for it to be played. Similarly, South's Queen is not a winner because it's sitting in front of West's King. Same with East's Jack.

Now let's reverse East and West's holdings:

North
♠ AT76

West
♠ J82

East
♠ K95

South
♠ Q43

Now the situation is a horse of a different color. East's King will be a winner because it sits behind North's Ace. Unless East leads his King, which would certainly be fool-hardy, he shouldn't lose it because if North is dummy, East can see where the Ace is and play the King on a trick where the Ace has not been played. Similarly, if South knows the location of the King, her Queen is a winner because it is sitting behind East's King.

But the bottom line is that you can't count on these cards being winners until you know the location of the missing honors. Which leads us into the discussion of how to play honors so they win tricks.

When you don't know the location of the honors that are higher than your honor, you must *lead up* that honor. To lead up to a card means to lead a lower-ranking card in your partner's hand, or in the case of declarer, to lead a low card to a higher-ranking card in your other hand. For example, in the hand just displayed, if you wanted to try to win the Queen, you would lead a low Spade from North to South's Queen. If East has the King, you should win the Queen. Because if East plays low, you play the Queen, hoping that East had the King. Here, East did have the King so the Queen wins. But if East *goes up*, plays a high card when he has a choice of playing high or low because he's not on lead, with the King when you lead low from North, you play a low Spade from South. Although East has won the trick, you have set up the Queen as a definite winner because you hold the Ace and two additional Spades in North and the Queen and one additional Spade in South. You can play the Ace and play low from South, then lead a low Spade to the Queen, which is a definite winner because the King has already been played.

Lingo

To hold a card or cards **tight** means that you don't have any other cards in the suit but that card or those cards. Holding the Ace tight means that you have a singleton Ace. Holding the King–Queen–Jack tight means that those are the only three cards in the suit in your hand.

Sequential Honors

If all your cards in a suit consist of honors in a *sequence*, it doesn't matter whether you lead from the hand that contains the sequence, or if you lead up to them because you don't have any other low card to play. If you hold the King–Queen–Jack *tight* (meaning that those are the only three cards in that suit), even if you lead up to them and your LHO goes up with the Ace, you still have to play one of your honors on the Ace.

Further, it doesn't matter how or where you hold your sequential honors. Look at the following holding:

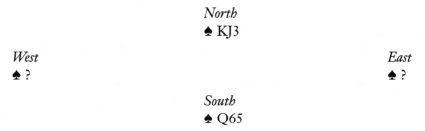

North
♠ KJ3

West   *East*
♠ ?   ♠ ?

South
♠ Q65

Unless you have an entry problem in one of your hands, it doesn't matter how you play these honors or how you lead. You're going to take two tricks and lose one to the Ace. It doesn't matter if you lead the Queen from South, or if you lead low. If you lead low and West goes up with the Ace, you will discard low and will still take two tricks.

Leading Up

However, what if you hold KQxx in a suit? How should you play it to maximize your trick taking power? You can count on this holding for one sure trick because if you lead the King or the Queen, it will lose to the Ace, but then the remaining card will be the top card out in the suit, a definite winner. But if you lead up to the King–Queen holding, you have a chance to win both cards if the King–Queen sit behind the Ace. Look at the following:

North
♠ KQ84

West   *East*
♠ A97   ♠ JT6

South
♠ 532

If you lead from South's hand up to North's hand and West ducks, you will win with either the King or the Queen. You then get back into South's hand and lead up to North again. If West ducks, you win with the remaining honor. If West goes up with the Ace, you play low and your King and Queen become sure winners.

However, if you were to lead the King from North's hand, it would lose to the Ace. Then the Queen would be the only winner you would get in the suit because after you play the Queen, East will win the next Spade trick with the Jack. So leading up to North gets you an extra trick.

Single Honors

Leading up is especially important when you hold a single, nonsequential honor. Look at the following:

$$
\begin{array}{c}
\textit{North} \\
\spadesuit \text{ K4} \\
\end{array}
$$

$$
\textit{West} \qquad\qquad \textit{East} \\
\spadesuit \text{ ?} \qquad\qquad \spadesuit \text{ ?}
$$

$$
\textit{South} \\
\spadesuit \text{ 53}
$$

If you lead the King or the Four from North, you aren't going to take a trick with the King. If you lead the four and East goes low, West will win with his lowest Spade. Then, any lead that produces the Ace will win your King. Obviously, if, instead of leading your Four you lead the King from North, opponent's Ace will win it.

The only way you can hope to win the King is to lead low from South to the King. If West produces the Ace, your King will win the next trick. If West goes low, you must play the King, hoping that West had the Ace. If he did, you'll win. If East has the Ace, you'll lose. When you have this holding you can count on the King as a half trick because you have a 50 percent chance that West has the Ace and you'll win the King and a 50 percent chance that East has the Ace and you'll lose the King.

Lingo

To **underlead** means to lead a lower card in a suit, instead of leading your highest card in that suit. To underlead an Ace means you have the Ace in your hand, but you lead a lower-ranking card of the same suit.

This holding also shows why you shouldn't do two things unless you have an awfully good reason for them:

- You should not underlead an Ace.

- You should not lead an Ace.

You shouldn't *underlead* an Ace because you make the King good. If either opponent underleads the Ace, your King will win if you play it. If you lead your Ace, especially if you are East, you just give up the chance of winning the King with it. Remember this axiom: *Aces were created to take Kings and Queens.* If you lead an Ace, it won't take either unless the King or Queen happens to be a singleton.

The Finesse

The *Official Encyclopedia of Bridge* defines a *finesse* as "the attempt to gain power for lower-ranking cards by taking advantage of the favorable position of higher-ranking cards held by the opposition." Say, what? If you know what a finesse is, I guess that's as good a definition as any. But if you don't know what a finesse is, that won't help you much.

An easier definition might be this: A finesse is any play that depends on finding a specific card in a specific place.

So if you're South and you make a play that depends on the King of Spades being in West's hand, that's a finesse. The best way to define a finesse is to show you one. Look at the following holdings:

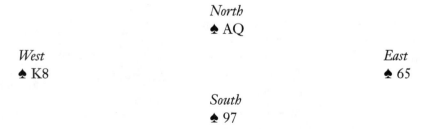

North
♠ AQ

West   *East*
♠ K8   ♠ 65

South
♠ 97

You are declarer and playing the South hand and South has the lead. You play West for the King of Spades. So you lead the Seven of Spades. If West plays the King you take it with the Ace, obviously. If West plays the Eight of Spades, however, you play the Queen, hoping that West has the King. If he does, as he does here, you win the trick with the Queen. That's a finesse. In this instance it works. If the East and West holdings were reversed and East held the King, the finesse wouldn't work. You'd play the Queen and East would take it with the King.

The lead must be up to the cards where you'll work the finesse. If the lead were in North, there would be no way for you to win both the Ace and the Queen, because if you lead the Ace, West will go low and then win your Queen with his King. If you lead the Queen, West will take it with his King. Either way, you only win one trick. But if you have the lead in the hand with the weak cards leading up to the hand with the strong cards, you can work the finesse.

Lingo

The Ace–Queen holding is called a **tenace** (pronounced like "tennis"), which is a holding of two cards, one of which is two levels below the other. Examples: Ace–Queen, King–Jack, Ten–Eight. If cards in between two cards have been played, the cards are said to be in a tenace position. So if the King, Queen, and Jack have been played, the Ace–Nine is a tenace (because the only remaining card between them is the Ten).

The Double Finesse

If you have alternating cards, you should usually finesse twice, no matter what happens the first time. Look at the following:

North
♠ AQT86

South
♠ 432

If you don't have any clue from the bidding or the play of the hand, you should first lead low from South and if West ducks (plays low), play the Ten of Spades. If that forces out the King from East, you'll be okay because both the Ace and the Queen will be good. That would mean that West has the Jack. If East had the Jack, he'd win the trick with the Jack, not the King. Because East won with the King, he doesn't have the Jack. If he doesn't have it and you don't have it in either of your hands, West must have it. But it doesn't matter because the Ace and Queen are now good.

If East wins your Ten with the Jack, however, the next time you get the lead you should finesse the Queen. The reasoning is that the odds favor the honors being split. Of course they won't be split all the time. But with no clue from the bidding you should try the finesse twice.

The Eight- and Nine-Card Finesse

This is a very common situation. It occurs when you're playing a contract, generally a suit contract, and you and your partner have eight or nine trump between you. This means that there are either four trump out against you or five trump out against you. You have the Ace, King, Jack, and Ten between your two hands. You need to find the Queen.

One axiom to remember is that *an odd number of cards tend to split evenly and an even number of cards tend to split oddly.* What does that mean? It means that the odds are in favor of five cards splitting 3–2. And the odds are in favor of four cards splitting 3–1, not 2–2. Surprised? Actually four cards will split 2–2 only about 40 percent of the time, whereas they'll split 3–1 about 49 percent of the time.

So if your Ace and your King are in different hands, and your Jack and your Ten are in different hands, and you have no clue from the bidding, you should pull a round of trump, leading low to the high honor and then back again. The advantage of this is that it gives you three plays from your opponents. One of them may be forced to drop the Queen because it's a singleton or doubleton. If not, then you have to decide whether or not to take the finesse. Look at the following layout.

North
♠ AJ98

South
♠ KT652

You have to find the Queen and there are four cards out against you. If you're in South, you lead the Deuce. If West plays the Queen (because it's a singleton), you're home free. If West plays low, you play the Ace. If East plays the Queen (because it's a singleton), you're home free. If East plays low you've won the trick with the Ace.

Now you lead the Jack back to South's hand. If East drops the Queen (either because it was a doubleton or because he's covering your honor to protect his partner because, not knowing the exact lay of the cards, he might think his partner had three to the Ten), you're home free. If East shows out and discards another suit, then you've lost this round because West has the Queen protected by three. If East plays low, then you have to decide whether the

> **Lingo**
>
> To play for the **drop** means to lead high-ranking cards hoping that a missing high card, lower-ranking than the cards you lead, will have to be played because holder is short in the suit. This can be done rather than finessing for it.

cards split 2–2, in which event you should play the King and watch the Queen fall, or 3–1, in which event you should play low and let the Jack win the trick.

There are some situations with which you are faced time and again. Trying to find the Queen when there are four cards out against you is one of them. As you can see, there are two views on how you should act. Goren says play for the *drop*. Others think you should take the finesse. Whichever way you want to go, I think you should be consistent. Don't play for the drop once and then take the finesse the next time. Decide which way is best for you and do it each time. If you vacillate between positions, the odds won't work in your favor. If you do it the same way all the time, you'll at least have the odds working for you. That's why I play for the finesse. I should be right 49 percent of the time, whereas if I play for the drop I'll only be correct 40 percent of the time.

Tricks of the Trade

Goren says when there are four cards out against you and you're looking for the Queen, you should play the Ace and the King, looking for the drop. If you do this, however, you should still play it the way described above to maximize the opportunity for a drop before you have to make a decision.

Eight Ever, Nine Never

This is another famous bridge axiom. It means that if you're missing the Queen and you have nine cards in the suit, you should play for the drop. If you have eight cards in the suit, you should take the finesse.

Although Goren advises to play for the drop when there are four out against the Queen, he doesn't advise you to play for the drop when there are three out against the King. And he has good reason.

Three cards will split 3–0 22 percent of the time, which means that they will be divided 2–1 78 percent of the time. This means that two thirds of the time they divide 2–1—the King will be protected. Look at the possible divisions with which you could be faced in a 2–1 split of three cards:

1. Kx	**2.** x	**3.** xx
x	Kx	K

So, Goren is correct. Two thirds of the time that the cards split 2–1, you're going to be looking at a protected King and your lead of the Ace playing for the drop is not going to work.

How to Play the Opening Lead

When you're playing a No Trump contract, how you play the opening lead often sets up whether or not you make the contract. Following are common holdings with which you will find yourself faced time and again:

1. *Dummy*
  ♠ Q4

Declarer
  ♠ A93

2. *Dummy*
  ♠ QT4

Declarer
  ♠ A73

3. *Dummy*
  ♠ Q74

Declarer
  ♠ A93

LHO leads a low Spade. What do you play? Your problem is to find who has the King: your LHO or your RHO.

Holding 1: You must play the Queen. If you play low, whether or not you win the trick with the Ace, your Queen will be sitting there naked. Opponents will play the King at their first opportunity. Further, your RHO, if he has any smarts at all, won't play the King even if he has it, knowing that playing it would give you an extra trick if you hold the Ace. The only chance you'll ever have to make this Queen good is now, hoping that your LHO underled the King. And the underlead of a King in a No Trump defense is a fairly common lead because a standard lead is fourth from longest and strongest suit, and this is often a suit headed by a King. You'll learn about opening leads by defense in Chapter 21.

Holding 2: Play the Ten. The hope is that your RHO holds King empty. If so, playing the Ten here will force out the King and you'll get two tricks in this hand. If your RHO does play the King, you take it with the Ace and your Queen is good. If the Ten forces the Jack from RHO, win the Ace and later lead up toward the Queen. If LHO had the King, your Queen will be a winner as you've learned in our previous discussion of leading up to a Queen when the Ace isn't a concern.

Holding 3: Play low. If RHO's opening lead was from JTxx, RHO will have to play the King or you'll win with the Nine. If RHO doesn't play the King, but plays the Jack or Ten, you can win with the Ace. You still have your Queen protected by a second card and can lead up to it. If your LHO has the King, your Queen will win then. If he doesn't, you're going to lose it anyway.

The Holdup

When your LHO leads your weakest suit on opening lead, a suit in which you only have one stopper, often you need to hold up taking your trick. This occurs when your LHO leads a suit in which you have Axx, for instance. You have two or three in dummy. You guess that your LHO has at least five, maybe six cards in the suit, and you hope he has no other entries in his hand. Instead of taking the trick immediately with your Ace, you play low and allow him to win the trick. He continues and you allow him to win the second trick. Only when he forces you to play your Ace with a third lead of the suit do you take the lead. The reason for all this is that you want to be sure that your RHO is out of his partner's suit, so if he gets the lead he can't return the suit to your LHO for him to run his remaining winning tricks in the suit. Look at the following hand:

North
♠ T9
♥ AQ73
♦ QT75
♣ Q53

West
♠ Q8753
♥ 985
♦ 83
♣ JT7

East
♠ KJ6
♥ KT6
♦ J92
♣ K642

South (you)
♠ A42
♥ J42
♦ AK64
♣ A98

Bidding is as follows ...

South	West	North	East
1 No Trump	Pass	2 Clubs	Pass
2 Diamonds	Pass	3 No Trump	Pass
Pass	Pass		

West's Opening Lead: Five of Spades

West leads the Five of Spades, fourth longest from a five-card suit, a standard opening lead as you'll learn in Chapter 21. East plays the King. What do you do? If you take the Ace, you're doomed to being set. You can't take nine tricks off the top. You can take four Diamond tricks and your three Aces. That's only seven tricks. You need to develop one or two Heart tricks or a Club trick. That means that you might have to surrender the lead twice. But if even one of your finesses fail, you're dead. Because you only had Spades stopped once, as soon as opponents get in they'll run off four Spade tricks, which will set you one trick. As the cards lay you'll lose your Heart finesse and East will return the Jack of Spades, which wins. Then he returns a low Spade to West's Queen, and the hand is history as West plays his two remaining low Spades, both of which are good because they're the only two remaining cards in the suit.

So you must hold up taking your Ace of Spades and plan on taking your Heart finesse into East. The idea is to surrender two Spade tricks at the outset. This loses two tricks, but what you want to do is drive East out of Spades so he can't get back to West to run his good Spades. So, after holding up on two rounds of Spades and then taking your Ace of Spades when East leads them a third time, this is what the hands look like:

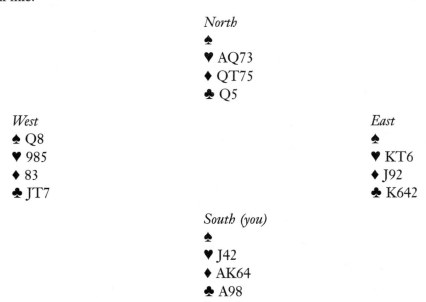

North
♠
♥ AQ73
♦ QT75
♣ Q5

West
♠ Q8
♥ 985
♦ 83
♣ JT7

East
♠
♥ KT6
♦ J92
♣ K642

South (you)
♠
♥ J42
♦ AK64
♣ A98

Now things look a little better. There's no way for West to get the lead again. You take your four Diamond tricks and then try the Heart finesse, which loses to East.

Under no circumstances do you want to take a finesse into West. The Heart finesse is safe because if West has the King you can always cover with the Ace. When West plays low, you go low and East shows up with the King and wins the trick. But what's East going to lead? He can't get back to West's hand. If he underleads his King of Clubs, which is about all that he can do, you won't know where the King is, so you'll go up and take it in your hand with the Ace. You'll then take your three remaining Heart tricks and that's nine tricks, one Spade, one Club, four Diamonds, and three Hearts. You've made your contract, but only because you held up on the first two rounds of Spades!

Ducking

It goes against your grain, but sometimes you have to lose a trick intentionally. This often occurs when you're playing a No Trump contract and you have a long suit in dummy with the only entries being in the long suit. Look at the following hand where you are South playing in 3 No Trump:

North
♠ 5
♥ AK7643
♦ T6
♣ 9732

West
♠ KQ9
♥ 982
♦ J8754
♣ JT

East
♠ T8743
♥ QJ
♦ Q3
♣ KQ65

South (you)
♠ AJ62
♥ T5
♦ AK92
♣ A84

Opening lead: Five of Diamonds.

Count your winners. You have six, the Ace–King of Hearts, the Ace–King of Diamonds, the Ace of Clubs, and the Ace of Spades. But that leaves you three tricks short of your contract. How are you going to make this?

Your only chance is to set up your Heart suit in dummy. But you've got a serious entry problem, because you only have two Hearts in your hand and no other entry on the board. How do you play it?

This is where you *duck*, lose a trick intentionally, to set up the Heart suit. You must lose the first Heart trick. So you take the opening lead in your hand with the King of Diamonds. Now you lead a low Heart to the board. West plays the Deuce. You play the Six, allowing East to take the trick! You are hoping for a 3–2 split in Hearts. East returns a Diamond which you take with your Ace. You then lead your last Heart to the Ace–King on the board. Hearts split 3–2 as you had hoped, and you can run your five Heart tricks.

The only way you could make this hand was to lose the first Heart trick by ducking. That took out two of opponents' Hearts and allowed you to pull the remaining Hearts with your Ace and King when you got back in the lead. If you don't duck, you have no way to get back to dummy without losing the lead when you try to take out the last Heart. If you lead to the Ace on your first lead of Hearts and then play the King, you're out of Hearts and North still has the Nine of Hearts, which will take the next Heart lead. Then there's no way for you to get back to dummy to cash your remaining good Hearts.

Further, if you lead to the Ace and then lead a low Heart, you still can't get back because you only have two Hearts in your hand and the second Heart will go on your second lead. So you must lose the *first* Heart trick.

Here's the layout of the hands after the first three tricks if you immediately play the Ace and King of Hearts:

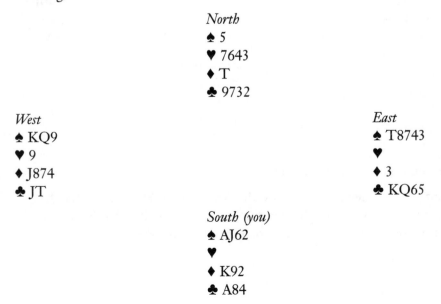

North
♠ 5
♥ 7643
♦ T
♣ 9732

West
♠ KQ9
♥ 9
♦ J874
♣ JT

East
♠ T8743
♥
♦ 3
♣ KQ65

South (you)
♠ AJ62
♥
♦ K92
♣ A84

Now what? You lead a Heart and West takes it with his Nine. You have no way to get back to the board to cash your three winning Hearts. This is what it looks like:

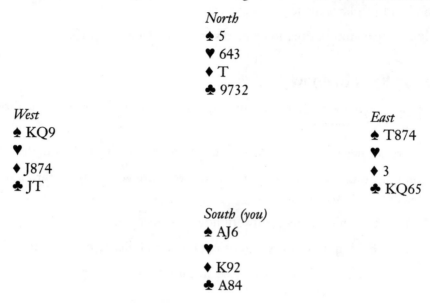

North
♠ 5
♥ 643
♦ T
♣ 9732

West
♠ KQ9
♥
♦ J874
♣ JT

East
♠ T874
♥
♦ 3
♣ KQ65

South (you)
♠ AJ6
♥
♦ K92
♣ A84

Sure you can get the lead again, no matter what West leads, but you can't get back to cash your three little Hearts. Now look at the holding after you lose the first Heart trick instead of taking it:

North
♠ 5
♥ AK764
♦ T
♣ 9732

West
♠ KQ9
♥ 98
♦ J874
♣ JT

East
♠ T8743
♥ Q
♦ 3
♣ KQ65

South (you)
♠ AJ62
♥ T
♦ K92
♣ A84

Now you're in great shape. No matter what East leads, you win in your hand and lead to the Ace–King of Hearts. When you cash them, your three remaining Hearts are good and you have made your contract.

This is a fairly common situation, and it's one where a lot of players misplay.

The Least You Need to Know

- When playing a No Trump contract, you start off by counting your sure winners.

- A sure winner is a trick you can take without fear of surrendering the lead.

- You must establish your long suit before you lose your entries, through ducking and the use of the finesse.

- You can't establish a long suit if timing is against you.

- You can hold up to protect against opponents' ability to establish their long suit.

- You can duck and intentionally lose an early trick to set up a long suit in your weak hand with few entries.

20

Declarer Play in Suit Contracts

In This Chapter

- ◆ Counting losers
- ◆ Drawing trump
- ◆ Setting up a long secondary suit
- ◆ The crossruff
- ◆ Safety plays

When you're playing in a suit contract, you have a huge basic difference between playing in a No Trump contract. That is, you have one suit that is all-powerful, the trump suit.

This allows you to take high cards in nontrump suits with low cards in the trump suit if you're void in the suit led. This makes playing a suit contract substantially different from playing in a No Trump contract where an Ace that is led will *always* take the trick, and where having the lead is so important.

How to Count Your Losers

If you're playing in a suit contract, you immediately count your losers. How? You must combine your hand and dummy in your mind's eye. Then you gather the high cards in each and see if they will eliminate losers in the other. For example, look at the following Spade holding in the two hands:

Dummy
♠ Q65

Declarer
♠ AK43

Declarer has two losers, the Four and the Three. Dummy has three losers, the unprotected Queen, the Six, and the Five. But when you put the two hands together you see that the Queen is not a loser at all, but a winner, because declarer has both the Ace and the King.

Then you look at the other losers. You see that one of the losers in declarer's hand is protected by the Queen in dummy. So that reduces the number of losers in declarer's hand from two to one.

Dummy still has two losers, the Six and the Five. But you see that they're protected by the Ace and the King in declarer's hand. So dummy has no losers when you combine the hands and declarer has only one potential loser, which may not be a loser if the suit splits 4–3–3–3 and trumps are drawn.

You count losers in the combined hands by two methods:

◆ Shortness in declarer's hand

◆ Missing high cards in both hands

Shortness in Declarer's Hand

Here are examples of counting shortness losers.

Dummy
♠ 6543

Declarer
♠ 87

You would have two losers because declarer can ruff dummy's extra losers after losing her Eight and Seven.

However, look at the following holding:

Dummy
♠ 43

Declarer
♠ 8765

In this holding, you would have to count four losers because shortness should only count in declarer's hand, unless dummy has at least the same number of trump as declarer. This rule is alleviated if dummy only has a singleton. Why? Because dummy should have at least three cards in your trump suit if you have bid the hand properly, so you should be able to trump losers quickly if dummy has only a singleton. However, you must be leery of being too sanguine about dummy's singleton, especially if you don't have the Ace of the suit and you're up against savvy players.

Any defender of quality who feels he and his partner have the bulk of the high cards in a suit, seeing a singleton in dummy will immediately attack trump by leading it. He does this to lessen dummy's ruffing power. So if you don't have the Ace, you'll have to lose a trick to get rid of your singleton. This will allow your opponents to lead trump to get rid of at least one trump in dummy.

Another disadvantage in counting shortness in dummy is that dummy's trump might consist of high cards you will need in pulling trump. Look at the following hand:

North (Dummy)
♠ T
♥ AQT4
♦ AKQ
♣ T7632

South (Declarer)
♠ J95
♥ 86
♦ 987652
♣ AK

Bidding is as follows.

North	East	South	West
1 Club	Pass	1 Diamond	Pass
1 Heart	1 Spade	2 Diamonds	2 Spades
5 Diamonds	Pass	Pass	Pass

North liked your Diamond bid, because she had the Ace, King, and Queen, so she jumped to a very questionable game. You'd like to use your Spade shortness in dummy to ruff your losers in your hand, but each time you ruff in dummy, you're taking away a high card that can win a trick on its own. If you were to ruff three Spades in dummy with the Ace, King, and Queen, you'd have two trump losers out against you, the Jack and the Ten. Clearly, the shortness in dummy doesn't help you much with your Spade losers because your trumps in dummy consist of high cards you're going to need to take tricks when you pull trump.

If you pull trump, and it takes three rounds because they're split 3–1, and you find that your Clubs don't set up, and you then lose the Heart finesse, opponents will switch back to Spades and you'll lose at least two more tricks because you're out of trump in dummy.

Moral: Shortness in dummy doesn't help you if you need all or most of dummy's trump to draw trump. You'll learn about drawing trump later in the chapter.

Missing High Cards

When you combine the two hands, the number of high cards that are missing is usually the number of losers you have in the suit. Look at the following hands and see if you can count the losers:

1. *Dummy*	2. *Dummy*	3. *Dummy*	4. *Dummy*
♠ Q32	♠ 542	♠ 432	♠ 432
Declarer	*Declarer*	*Declarer*	*Declarer*
♠ KJ8	♠ AQT3	♠ KJ8	♠ AQJ

5. *Dummy*	6. *Dummy*	7. *Dummy*
♠ T987	♠ 32	♠ Q2
Declarer	*Declarer*	*Declarer*
♠ J43	♠ K8	♠ K8

Hand 1: One loser. Combined, you have three cards in each hand and they include the King, Queen, and Jack. The Ace is the only loser.

Hand 2: Three losers. The Ace is the only winner. You could lose the others. You can't count shortness in dummy unless dummy is loaded with trump, which it usually isn't.

Hand 3: Three losers. The Ace and Queen could be sitting behind declarer. You could very easily lose all three tricks.

Hand 4: One loser, the King.

Hand 5: Three losers. You're missing the Ace, the King, and the Queen, and you have three cards in the suit in declarer's hand.

Hand 6: Two losers. The King is not supported by anything.

Hand 7: One loser. You have the King and the Queen and only two cards in the suit in each hand. You'll lose the Ace, but will win the next trick.

Trump

Trump is what distinguishes suit contracts from No Trump. In No Trump contracts, each suit has equal power. In suit contracts, the trump suit is all powerful. The Deuce of trump can take the Ace in any other nontrump suit. Therefore, how you manage your trumps is important.

However, what you've learned in playing the cards in the preceding chapter on No Trump contracts still applies. You must be aware of the position of honors and you'll still have to finesse occasionally. The difference is that you must manage your trumps.

Drawing Trump

Generally, and there are exceptions to this rule, the first thing you try to do in playing a suit contract is to establish your trump suit, sort of like you established a long suit in the preceding chapter. You're not necessarily going to take all the trump tricks, but you want to get rid of all the trump cards in your opponents' hands so they can't ruff any of your good nontrump tricks with their small trump. Look at the following hand:

North
♠ A853
♥ Q52
♦ J54
♣ Q98

West
♠ 74
♥ JT6
♦ AKT8
♣ T763

East
♠ QT92
♥ 83
♦ Q976
♣ K42

South
♠ KJ6
♥ AK974
♦ 32
♣ AJ5

You're in a contract of 4 Hearts. West leads the Ace of Diamonds, which he wins. He follows with the King of Diamonds, which he wins. He follows that with the Eight of Diamonds, and East covers North's Jack with the Queen. You, however, can win this trick because you are out of Diamonds by now, so you can ruff. This shows you the basic difference between a suit contract and a No Trump contract. In a No Trump contract, you're helpless when an opponent runs a long suit. But in a suit contract, you can put an end to it by ruffing and taking the trick.

As soon as you get the lead, you should rid the opponents' hands of trump. So, you should play the Ace and the King of Hearts from your hand and then go to dummy to win opponents' last trump with the Queen. You can then finesse East's King of Clubs and Queen of Spades and your contract is safely made. But the important thing is that you don't have to worry about losing one of your Club or Spade tricks through the opponents' trumping when they run out of the respective suit. That's why you play trump first, and arrange it so you are the only one who holds any remaining trump.

You should always have more trump combined than your opponents. Generally you will have eight or more trump between you and dummy, although occasionally you will find yourself playing a hand with only seven or less trump between you and dummy.

When Not to Pull Trump Immediately

Sometimes your losers are in your own hand and you're short in that suit in dummy. Let's change the previous hand a little, but you're still in a 4 Heart contract, meaning you have to take 10 tricks:

North
- ♠ A853
- ♥ Q52
- ♦ 5
- ♣ Q9875

West
- ♠ 74
- ♥ JT6
- ♦ AKT8
- ♣ KT32

East
- ♠ QT92
- ♥ 83
- ♦ Q9763
- ♣ 64

South
- ♠ KJ6
- ♥ AK974
- ♦ J42
- ♣ AJ

You have problems because you have three Diamond losers. Neither your Club nor your Spade suit is going to set up. If you pull trump, how are you going to avoid losing two Diamonds? The only way to make 4 Hearts in this hand is for the play to go as follows:

> West leads and takes the Ace of Diamonds. Seeing that the dummy is now void in Diamonds, he switches to a Spade, and you take East's Queen with your King.

If you were to draw trump now, you would be making a fatal error. Instead of drawing trump, you lead a Diamond from your hand and ruff it in dummy. You return to your hand by leading a low Spade from dummy and take it with the Jack of Spades in your hand. You then lead your last Diamond from your hand and ruff it in dummy. Voilà! You have rid yourself of your two Diamond losers and have made two small trump in dummy into winners. Now you can pull trump. Instead of taking five trump tricks, you've taken seven. Add to this your three Spade tricks and the Ace of Clubs and you make five.

But if you pulled trump immediately after getting the lead with the King of Spades, your hand would look like this:

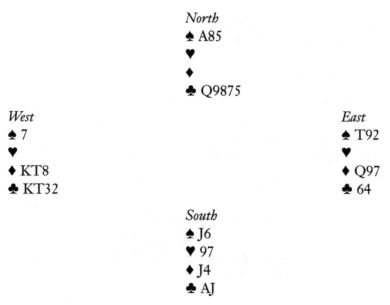

North
♠ A85
♥
♦
♣ Q9875

West
♠ 7
♥
♦ KT8
♣ KT32

East
♠ T92
♥
♦ Q97
♣ 64

South
♠ J6
♥ 97
♦ J4
♣ AJ

Now, what? How do you avoid losing two Diamonds, along with the King of Clubs, which you have to lose? Sometimes you have to ruff losers *before* you pull opponents' trump. This is the advantage of counting losers in a suit contract. You must know immediately where your losers are and how you're going to handle them before you start your play.

Discarding Losers on Winners

Another way to get rid of losers is to discard them on winners in a longer suit. Look at the following hand, in which you hold the South hand and the contract is 6 Hearts:

North
♠ J8
♥ AT3
♦ AJT65
♣ AT5

West
♠ QT764
♥ 5
♦ 742
♣ K962

East
♠ A9532
♥ 974
♦ Q983
♣ 8

South
♠ K
♥ KQJ862
♦ K
♣ QJ743

Count your losers. For sure you should lose one Spade. You lose no Hearts, maybe the Queen of Diamonds. A risky slam.

But you're lucky because West leads the Seven of Diamonds. East is very coy and plays low, but you have to go up and take it with your singleton King, which gives you a Diamond void in your hand. You draw trump and then lead the Ace of Diamonds from dummy. You discard your losing King of Spades and the contract is cold because the Club finesse is on.

Why can East play low on West's lead of the Seven of Diamonds? He can see that he has the Diamond Eight, Nine, and Queen and dummy has the Jack and Ten. So the only card that can take the Seven of Diamonds is the King of Diamonds. Playing the Diamond Eight, Nine, or Queen avails East nothing, so he plays low.

Ruffing Finesse

There's another finesse in this hand. Can you see it? You can see the Club finesse, but where's the other one?

You have what's called a *ruffing finesse* in Diamonds. It's not relevant to making this hand, but because it does appear in this hand I'm going to explain it to you because it is a tool you can use to make some contracts. After you draw trump and get rid of the King of Spades, the hands look like this:

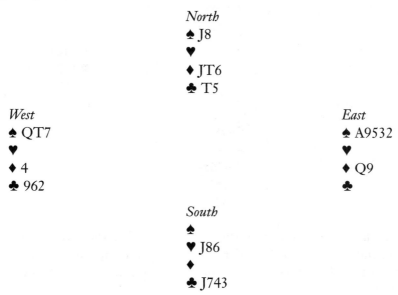

North
- ♠ J8
- ♥
- ♦ JT6
- ♣ T5

West
- ♠ QT7
- ♥
- ♦ 4
- ♣ 962

East
- ♠ A9532
- ♥
- ♦ Q9
- ♣

South
- ♠
- ♥ J86
- ♦
- ♣ J743

A ruffing finesse occurs in this situation. Look at your Diamond holding. There are three honors still out, the Queen, Jack, and Ten. You hold the Jack and Ten in dummy, opposite a void in your hand! So you lead the Jack. If East covers, you ruff it. If East plays low, you let it ride, discarding a Club, playing East for the Queen. If he has it, you win the trick. If West has it, you lose the trick. This is *a ruffing finesse*. Instead of having a higher card to cover the honor, you have a trump to cover it.

Again, there's no reason to use the ruffing finesse in this hand because it doesn't get you anything. But sometimes using a ruffing finesse is the only way you will have to make your contract. I mention it here so you'll recognize it when it arises.

Setting Up a Long Suit to Discard Losers

Another way to get rid of losers is to set up a long secondary suit. Look at this hand:

North
♠ 932
♥ AQJ
♦ K8
♣ K9643

West
♠ QJ86
♥ T93
♦ J96
♣ Q52

East
♠ AKT7
♥ K2
♦ Q542
♣ J87

South
♠ 54
♥ 87654
♦ AT73
♣ AT

You ended up in an extremely optimistic contract of 4 Hearts, playing South. You get a Spade lead and lose two Spades before ruffing the third Spade in your hand. You immediately lose a Heart finesse. Now your hand looks like this and you can't lose any more tricks:

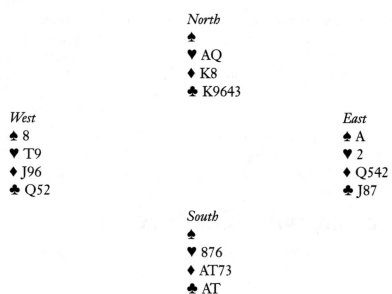

North
♠
♥ AQ
♦ K8
♣ K9643

West
♠ 8
♥ T9
♦ J96
♣ Q52

East
♠ A
♥ 2
♦ Q542
♣ J87

South
♠
♥ 876
♦ AT73
♣ AT

East returns a Diamond, which you should take with your Ace. Now what? You have Diamond and Club losers, even though you have the Ace–King of Clubs and the

King of Diamonds. Your only chance is to set up the Clubs and hope they split 3–3. So you take out trump, leaving you one in your hand. Then you lead the Ace of Clubs and the Ten of Clubs to the King. Now your hand looks like this:

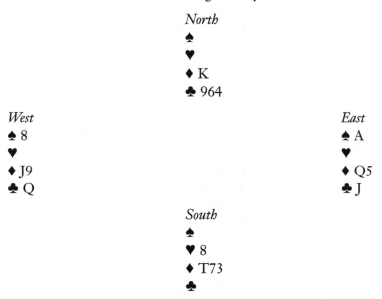

North
♠
♥
♦ K
♣ 964

West
♠ 8
♥
♦ J9
♣ Q

East
♠ A
♥
♦ Q5
♣ J

South
♠
♥ 8
♦ T73
♣

You lead the Four of Clubs and ruff it in your hand. You breathe much easier when you see both East and West discard Clubs. Now the only two Clubs left are on the board in North's hand and you have a lead to the King of Diamonds on the board. You have made a very difficult contract by setting up your Six and Four of Clubs as the winning tricks, discarding your losing Diamonds on them.

Tricks of the Trade _____

Remember the entry problem we spoke of in the last chapter? You have it here, too. You have to retain an entry to the board to get back there to make your two little Clubs good. That's why you took East's Diamond lead in your hand with the Ace, preserving the King of Diamonds as your entry to the board!

An even better example of a hand where you set up a long suit to make your contract occurred in the 1995 Worldwide Bridge Contest. This hand has the added value of also showing the importance of the duck by declarer. Following are the hands:

North
♠ A6
♥ 8762
♦ void
♣ Q976543

West
♠ Q953
♥ QT
♦ QT432
♣ K2

East
♠ T842
♥ J43
♦ AK95
♣ JT

South (you)
♠ KJ7
♥ AK95
♦ J876
♣ A8

Bidding:

West	North	East	South
		Pass	1 No Trump
Pass	2 Clubs	Pass	2 Hearts
Pass	4 Hearts	Pass	Pass
Pass			

Opening lead: Three of Diamonds.

Your partner has a tough decision to make when you open 1 No Trump. With only 6 HCP but seven Clubs, four Hearts, and a Diamond void, she should do something. She decided to bid 2 Clubs because she had a four-card major. If you responded in 2 Diamonds or 2 Spades, she would bid 3 Clubs as a sign-off bid and you'd play in her seven-card suit. When you responded with a fit in Hearts, she jumped to game because her void now became worth 5 points and her hand reevaluates to 11 points. But it doesn't look easy, does it?

The only way to make this hand is to ruff the Diamond in dummy. You then play the Ace of Clubs and another Club, losing to West's King, and breathe a little easier when Clubs split 2–2. You now have five good Club tricks on the board if you can get to them and get the trump out.

Defenders in this hand were two world champions. West chose to lead another Diamond, forcing you to ruff again on the board, leaving you with only two trump there. Now, what do you do? If you lead to the Ace and King of trump, opponents are left with the high trump. You will be out of trump on the board and the Ace of Spades is your only entry, which you will have to use now to get there. Here's the hand at this stage:

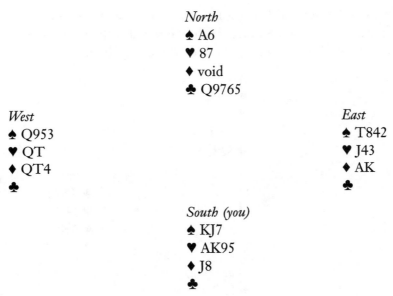

Lead is in North, dummy. If you play the Ace and King of Hearts, East will be left with the Jack. Here's the layout of the hand if you lead a low Heart to your Ace and then play the King:

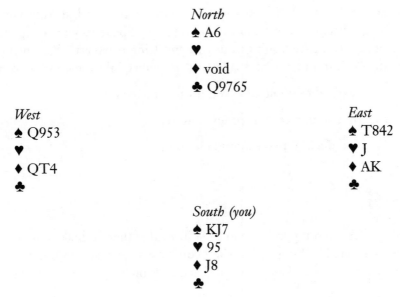

Now, what? Your only hope in this hand is to make all the Clubs good, but you can't lead over to the Ace of Spades and run the Clubs because East will ruff in and then play the Ace and King of Diamonds and you'll be set. Further, your Ace of Spades is your only entry to the board.

Instead of leading the Ace and King of Hearts, lead a low Heart and duck, allowing opponents to win. Now your contract is cold. Here's how the hands look after leading the low Heart and ducking, retaining the Heart Ace and King:

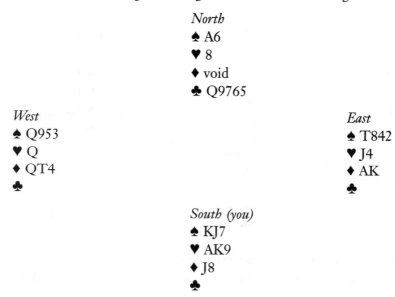

North
♠ A6
♥ 8
♦ void
♣ Q9765

West
♠ Q953
♥ Q
♦ QT4
♣

East
♠ T842
♥ J4
♦ AK
♣

South (you)
♠ KJ7
♥ AK9
♦ J8
♣

West leads another Diamond, which you have to ruff with your last trump on the board. But you get back to your hand by leading a low Spade to your King and then pull the remaining trump by leading your Ace and King of Hearts. You then go back to the board with a lead to the Ace of Spades and all your Clubs are good, making five!

This hand is a very good example of two things you have learned:

- How to set up a long suit in a trump contract
- How to use the duck to make a difficult contract

The Crossruff

I don't think there's anything more enjoyable in Bridge than to make a hand by crossruffing. What's a *crossruff*? Simply, it's when you have a short suit in dummy and a different short suit in your hand and you ruff back and forth. Look at the following hand:

North
- ♠ Q
- ♥ K98754
- ♦ QJ432
- ♣ 2

West
- ♠ KT963
- ♥ J
- ♦ 987
- ♣ Q954

East
- ♠ A542
- ♥ T
- ♦ AK65
- ♣ KJ87

South
- ♠ J87
- ♥ AQ632
- ♦ T
- ♣ AT63

East–West is vulnerable, you're not. You are South and the bidding went as follows.

You	West	North	East
1 Heart	Pass	4 Hearts	Pass
Pass	Pass		

You've gotten to a major suit game with only 20 HCP between you and your partner. How are you going to make this? South has three Spade losers, three Club losers, and a Diamond loser. North has a Club loser, a bunch of Diamond losers, and a Spade loser.

You're going to crossruff. Let's say they lead a Spade, which they win with the Ace. East switches to a Heart, which you win in your hand, and find that you have drawn trump because each of your opponents has a singleton trump. You immediately lead your Ten of Diamonds, surrendering your last trick. They switch to a Club, which you take with your Ace. Now your hand looks like this:

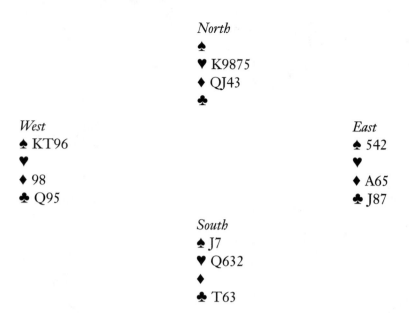

North
- ♠
- ♥ K9875
- ♦ QJ43
- ♣

West
- ♠ KT96
- ♥
- ♦ 98
- ♣ Q95

East
- ♠ 542
- ♥
- ♦ A65
- ♣ J87

South
- ♠ J7
- ♥ Q632
- ♦
- ♣ T63

You have five losers in South, two Spades and three Clubs. But you are void in both those suits in dummy and have five trump in dummy! Similarly, you have four losing Diamonds in dummy, but you are void in Diamonds and have four trump in your hand. It's a simple matter to just keep leading a nontrump suit from one hand and trumping it in the other. What a terrific feeling to take all those high honors with small little trump. With only 20 HCP, this hand makes five Hearts, solely through the use of the crossruff!

The Backward Finesse

Normally, there's no reason to take a finesse unless you're trying to set up a card. Look at the following holding:

North
A87

South
Q54

There is no earthly reason to lead the Queen up to the Ace. If West covers with the King, you don't hold the Jack, so what's the point? You're just setting up opponents' cards for sure tricks.

However, if you're holding a tenace position in lower cards, sometimes you can lead the unprotected honor if you can set up another finesse. Look at the following holding:

North
K87

South
AJ9

In this situation you could try a finesse hoping that West holds the Queen and East holds the Ten. With the lead in south, you lead the Jack. When West covers, you play the King. Now your Ace–Nine is a tenace because the only card out between them is the Ten. If East has it, you can finesse *back* by leading the low card to the Jack-Nine. If East ducks you play the Nine. If East has the Ten the Nine holds and you have taken three tricks! It works if the holding is like the following:

North
♠ K87

West
♠ Q65

East
♠ T432

South
♠ AJ9

You should have a compelling reason for making this play, which requires two cards well placed rather than just one for a simple finesse of the Jack. Perhaps, by the bidding, West is marked with the Queen of Spades, which would justify this.

Safety Plays

Sometimes you have to forego the finesse and play it safe. Let's say you have nine trump between you and dummy like the following:

North
♠ A976
♥ 652
♦ 532
♣ AK8

South
♠ QJT32
♥ AKQT
♦ AQ4
♣ 7

Bidding is as follows.

East	South	West	North
2 Diamonds*	2 Spades	Pass	4 Spades
Pass	4 No Trump	Pass	5 Hearts
Pass	5 No Trump	Pass	6 Diamonds
Pass	6 Spades	Pass	Pass
Pass			

* Weak Two Bid

Opening Lead: Seven of Diamonds.

You've learned that an opening bid in a suit at the 2 level shows a very strong hand, but many advanced players play Weak Twos, a system that uses an opening bid in a suit at the 2 level to show a hand with a six-card suit and 5 to 11 points. You'll learn about Weak Twos in Chapter 23. I've introduced it here so you'll know from the bidding that East promises six Diamonds in order to illustrate the point of the safety play.

If trump splits 2–2 and West has the King of Spades, you're okay. But sometimes you don't have the luxury of relying on this. You're South and you see dummy come down with three Diamonds. You hold three Diamonds. You know for an absolute certainty that West is leading a singleton Diamond.

How do you know it's a singleton? Because you know that East must have six Diamonds to open with a Weak Two. You have three and dummy has three. That's 12. West's Seven *must* be a singleton. Do you try to finesse the King of Spades through West?

No. Play low to the Ace and then back to your Queen–Jack–Ten. If you try to finesse West for the King and lose the finesse to East, East can come back with a Diamond. West is going to get at least one ruff, and you will not make your contract. But if you play the Ace of trump and then lead back to your Queen–Jack, there's no way that West can ruff a Diamond because if he has the three remaining trump he'll take his King but he probably can't get back to East to lead a Diamond because he's void. If trump splits 2–2, you'll complete your draw of trump with this lead and West won't have any with which to trump the Diamond. And if East has the three remaining trump, West will be out and won't be able to ruff. You lose the King of trump, but that's all. Following is the hand:

North
♠ A976
♥ 652
♦ 532
♣ AK8

West
♠ 54
♥ J987
♦ 7
♣ 965432

East
♠ K8
♥ 43
♦ KJT986
♣ QJT

South
♠ QJT32
♥ AKQT
♦ AQ4
♣ 7

If you were to try the Spade finesse, which seems to be the correct play, you'd go down. East would win the King of Spades and return a Diamond, which West would ruff and you'd be down one. But if you play the safety play, and win with the Ace and return a Spade, East wins his King, but when he returns the Diamond, West has no more Spades with which to ruff and you make your six Spades.

The Least You Need to Know

♦ When playing a suit contract, you should first count losers in your combined hands after you see dummy.

♦ If you have too many losers, see if it's possible to ruff some losers in your partner's hand.

♦ If you don't need to ruff losers, generally when you get the lead you draw trump before doing anything else.

♦ Look for a way to establish one of the nontrump suits in either hand. Then you can discard losers on that suit.

♦ If you have losers in both hands, sometimes you can crossruff, take tricks with individual trump in both hands.

Chapter 21

Defense of the Hand: Opening Leads

In This Chapter

- Fourth from longest and strongest
- Top connecting honors
- Standard leads
- Leading suits with Aces
- Leads against slams

After an auction is concluded the play of the hand is commenced by declarer's RHO making the first lead. This is called the *opening lead*. There are entire books devoted to how to make an opening lead. In this chapter, you learn the basics of how to make this important decision.

Opening Leads Against No Trump Contracts

As you've learned, the opening lead is made by declarer's LHO. So if declarer is on your right, you will make the opening lead.

Whenever you're defending a hand and must make the opening lead, the first thing you should do is *think!* The opening lead is the most important aspect of defense. There is a lot to consider. So before you just throw down a card to get the hand started, you should pause and think about how you're going to defend.

In defending No Trump your longest suit is generally your strongest suit. Keep that in mind throughout the following discussion.

Now forget about your hand for a moment. In defending No Trump, often you must try to determine what is in your partner's hand and play to her hand.

The first thing you should take into consideration is what you've learned from the bidding. Following are some clues you should consider before making your lead:

- Has your partner bid a suit?

- Has she made a double?

- Have your opponents bid any suits?

- Did the dummy bid a suit?

Let's take these in order.

When Your Partner Has Bid a Suit

First, if your partner bid a suit freely you know that she has at least five cards in it. How many cards do you have in that suit? If you have three or more, that suit is probably your strongest asset in defending this hand because you have at least eight cards between you.

If your partner has bid a suit, you must determine which card in her suit you want to lead. Here are the rules:

Lingo

A **connecting honor** is a holding of two consecutive honor cards in the same suit, like the King–Queen or Jack–Ten.

- If you have three or more to an honor, lead your lowest card.

- If you have exactly three cards in her suit but no honor, lead the highest card in her suit.

- If you have two in her suit, lead the higher card.

- If you have connecting honors, lead the top *connecting honor,* no matter how many cards you have in her suit.

What if you have a five-card suit yourself? Should you lead your suit or your partner's? Answer: *Lead your partner's suit!* Why?

- Make your partner happy. If you lead your suit and it's the wrong lead, your partner's first question will be, "Why didn't you lead my suit?" If you lead her suit and it's wrong, she can't criticize you. It might sound selfish, but it's the best way to keep your partnership on an even keel.

- From a Bridge point of view (yes, we do still think about Bridge in our partnerships!), it's better to lead *to* a suit than to lead *from* a suit. So if you lead to your partner's suit, it will force your opponents to lead to your suit, or will allow your partner to lead to your suit. Further, you know that she has a suit, so you know that leading her suit will help her. Leading your suit could work to your disadvantage because you're telling declarer where the power is in your suit. Keep that a secret for awhile. Because your partner has given you a lead, take it.

> **Tricks of the Trade** _____
>
> Interestingly, the selfish lead would appear to be to lead your own suit. In actuality, however, the selfish lead is your partner's suit because you don't want to be criticized. Listen, if you think this sounds silly, even the best players in the world think this way. Nobody likes to have their partner always yelling at them, "Stop eating your soup with a fork!"

Another thing to consider is when was No Trump first bid. Did declarer bid No Trump after your partner bid her suit, after their pair had been bidding suits? If so, it's a clear indication that declarer has stoppers in your partner's suit. If you lead the suit, one of the downsides you must consider is that you'll be leading right through her into the power in her suit. Let's say that the bidding went like this.

RHO	You	LHO	Partner
1 Heart	Pass	1 Spade	2 Diamonds
2 No Trump	Pass	3 Clubs	Pass
3 No Trump	Pass	Pass	Pass

Declarer is telling his partner (and you) that he has no fear of your partner's Diamond suit. But what else do you know about this hand from the bidding?

- RHO has five Hearts, no more. If he had six Hearts he would have rebid them. Because he opened 1 Heart he must have five, but not six.

- ◆ LHO has at least four Spades.

- ◆ LHO doesn't have three Hearts. If he had three Hearts, because he knows his partner has five Hearts, he would have placed the contract in 4 Hearts because of the eight-card major fit. Because he never supported Hearts and put the contract in 3 No Trump, he has a maximum of two Hearts in his hand.

- ◆ Your partner has at least five Diamonds and close to an opening hand because she bid at the 2 level after opponents had bid two suits.

- ◆ RHO has Diamonds stopped, probably at least twice.

- ◆ LHO has at least four Clubs, maybe five.

- ◆ RHO doesn't have four Spades. If he had four Spades, because he knows partner has at least four Spades, he would have supported Spades or placed the contract in 4 Spades after his partner bid 3 No Trump.

- ◆ LHO has at least 10 points, probably more.

Knowing this, you should have a pretty good picture of the structure of each of your opponents' hands:

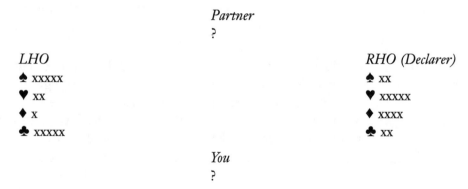

Partner
?

LHO
♠ xxxxx
♥ xx
♦ x
♣ xxxxx

RHO (Declarer)
♠ xx
♥ xxxxx
♦ xxxx
♣ xx

You
?

Your partner might have the following Diamond holding:

♦ KJT875

Declarer has said, twice, that he has no fear of your partner's Diamonds. Your hand looks like this:

♠ J74
♥ 9642
♦ 94
♣ QJ62

What should you lead? Your partner bid Diamonds, so that should be your first choice. However, declarer said he had no fear of Diamonds. Despite this, you must trust your partner. She has at least five, maybe six. This is why the opening lead is so important. If declarer only has Diamonds stopped twice, he could be using his first stopper on the first lead. So let's look at declarer's Diamond holding:

♦ AQ32

Anybody would be willing to bid No Trump over his RHO's Diamond bid with the Ace and the Queen behind the probable King. But if you start out leading the Nine of Diamonds, it starts to set up your partner's hand. So with all this thought, you lead the Nine of Diamonds. (Remember, if you have two cards in your partner's suit, lead the higher.) But you can only make this determination by thinking about what you know about the hands from the bidding and, finally, trusting your partner.

When You Can Lead Something Other Than Your Partner's Suit

Sometimes you don't lead your partner's suit. Two such instances follow:

- If you have a strong, self-establishing suit of your own. Let's say your partner bid Diamonds and your hand looks like the following:

  ♠ 974
  ♥ KQJ95
  ♦ 84
  ♣ K83

  With this holding you should lead your King of Hearts because you'll probably be able to take four Heart tricks here and you have another possible entry with the King of Clubs. So, with this hand, you have a good answer when your partner asks, "Why didn't you lead my suit?" But she probably won't ask that. She'll probably say, "Nice lead, Partner!"

- If you have a singleton in her suit and you have a suit you might be able to develop in your hand. If you have a basically worthless hand, however, you should lead the singleton because your partner's hand is your best line of defense, and that's her best suit.

When Your Partner Doubles the Final 3 No Trump Contract

If your partner doubles the final 3 No Trump contract for penalty, it's not just for penalty. *A double of a 3 No Trump contract asks partner to make a specific lead.* The rules for the specific leads requested by a double follow:

> **CAUTION**
>
> **Alert** _____
>
> The lead of the fourth highest card from your longest suit is a standard opening lead against a No Trump contract. You'll learn about it shortly in this chapter.

◆ If your partner (who doubled) has bid a suit, lead her suit.

◆ If you have bid a suit, lead your suit.

◆ If neither of you has bid, you should lead dummy's first bid suit *unless you have a better lead in your hand*. So you can use your own judgment here. If you have a holding like the Heart holding referred to above, KQJ94, you should lead the King of Hearts. But if you don't have a good lead from your hand, your partner's double asks you to lead the dummy's first-bid suit.

◆ If you have both bid, you should use your own judgment. But if you don't have a terrific suit, lead your partner's suit.

◆ If no suit has been bid by opponents and neither of you has bid, look at the following bidding.

LHO	Partner	RHO	You
1 No Trump	Pass	3 No Trump	Pass
Pass	Double	Pass	Pass
Pass			

By doubling, your partner is asking for an unusual lead, like a singleton, from your hand. She's saying that she has a long suit that, if you find it, will set the contract. In this instance, you forget all the standard leads, like fourth from longest, top of sequence, and so on and lead your singleton or the shortest suit in your hand.

When Opponents Have Bid a Suit

If the opponents bid suits, you want to stay away from leading any suit bid by declarer for your opening lead unless it's a very good suit and you're pretty confident that your holding is longer than declarer's. Leading declarer's suit, even if it's your best suit, means that you are *leading into strength*. Declarer will have the last play on the trick, so will generally be able to take it with a card that allows an extra trick. If you don't have cards in the suit bid by declarer, there's a fair chance that your partner will. And if she does, you'll be leading right through her into declarer's strength.

Generally, you try to lead a suit that hasn't been bid. If your opponents are bidding their suits and end up in No Trump, the longest suit you and your partner have is usually the unbid suit.

Leading Through Strength

Sometimes it's a good lead to *lead through strength*. This means that if dummy has bid a suit, it's sometimes a good lead to lead through that suit. This is especially true if you don't hold an honor in that suit. The reason is that dummy may have a suit with broken honors, like AQxx or KJxx. There is a possibility that your partner holds the missing honors. This is especially true if dummy was not the opening bidder and responded in a major that was not supported by opener. If you're short in that suit, there's a good chance that's your partner's suit.

Fourth from Longest and Strongest

When you're on defense against a No Trump contract, your strongest suit is your longest suit. So you're on lead against 3 No Trump. How do you choose your lead?

The standard lead against a No Trump contract is to lead the fourth highest card in your longest suit. Look at the following hand:

♠ AQ4
♥ 84
♦ 98642
♣ KT9

If you don't have any clue from the bidding, what should you lead against 3 No Trump? Well, I've already told you the answer. Your lead is the Four of Diamonds.

There's sound reasoning behind this lead, even though both your Clubs and Spades look like better suits. You want to set up one or two Diamond tricks. Diamonds may be split evenly. If so, the other three hands hold 3–3–2 in Diamonds. That leaves you with two good Diamonds if you get in after they've been led three times. And you have three possible entries into your hand, the Ace and Queen of Spades, and the King or Ten of Clubs. This is not counting the possibility that your partner might get lucky and take a trick then lead a Diamond. Even if opponents hold all the Diamond honors, if they're split, as anticipated, when you finally get in, you'll set 3 No Trump because you'll get two Diamond tricks and you have a good chance of getting two Spade tricks and a Club trick. And this isn't counting on partner for anything.

Count the Points in Your Partner's Hand from the Bidding

This brings up a good point. How many points do you think your partner has if you're defending 3 No Trump in this hand? Answer: not many. You have 9 HCP and opponents probably have at least 25 HCP. That only leaves 6 HCP for your partner. But that might be enough for her to get in once and lead a Diamond.

You must rely on your partner to trust you and lead a Diamond when she gets in, regardless of the holding in her hand. She might have five Hearts and want to set up her Hearts. But she must trust you and return a Diamond if you led a low Diamond. If she were to switch to a Heart, it would destroy your defense and render your good Diamond lead valueless. You're probably getting sick of hearing this, but *partners must trust one another.* Following is the entire hand:

North (partner)
♠ 632
♥ KJ632
♦ T3
♣ Q63

West (dummy)
♠ 9875
♥ T95
♦ KJ7
♣ A87

East (declarer)
♠ KJT
♥ AQ7
♦ AQ5
♣ J542

South (you)
♠ AQ4
♥ 84
♦ 98642
♣ KT9

The bidding went like this.

East	South	West	North
1 No Trump	Pass	2 Clubs	Pass
2 Diamonds	Pass	2 No Trump	Pass
3 No Trump	Pass	Pass	Pass

The play might go like this. You lead the Four of Diamonds. declarer plays low from dummy and your partner plays the Ten, which declarer wins with the Queen. Declarer tries a Club that loses to your partner's Queen.

This is the biggest play of the hand right here. What card your partner chooses to lead determines whether or not you're going to set the hand. She's going to be mighty tempted to switch to a Heart, her good, long suit and the weakest suit in dummy, but she must have discipline and trust you. She must then return a Diamond, despite her nice Hearts. It doesn't matter how declarer then plays the Diamonds because after your partner's lead, he only has one more Diamond stopper. When you *get in* (get the lead), you'll take it out and then when you get in again, you'll have the setting tricks in your remaining two Diamonds. If your partner were to switch to a Heart instead of returning your Diamond, however, you wouldn't have enough remaining entries to take out his two Diamond stoppers and he would probably make the hand.

Lingo _____
To **get in** means to get in the lead.

Tricks of the Trade _____
Goren says that every time the defense leads a new suit it averages to lose a half trick!

Further, when she switches, it will tell a savvy declarer that she's got the Heart honors and if he goes low from his hand, it will give him a Heart winner with the Ten on the board and another entry to the board to finesse through her.

When You Lead from a Weak Suit, You Must Have Entries

The only reason you would lead from such a weak five-card suit, however, is because you have entries in other suits that will allow you to get in and set up your Diamonds. If you have a Yarborough, or a hand without more than one entry, you should not lead the Diamond because it will give your partner a false hope that your opponents can be set up. And they can't if there's no way you can get the lead to take advantage of your long suit. So if you were without the Ace–Queen of Spades and the King of Clubs, you would lead something else, even though, as the cards lie, any other lead would be harmful.

Top Connecting Honors

Another lead is the top of connecting honors. But in No Trump this is often not a good lead unless they're internal connecting honors, like KJTx, leading the Jack, or a three-card sequence, like QJTx. Why? Because you give up a possible trick if opponents have the Ace, which they probably do.

What would you lead against a No Trump contract with the following Club holding?

♣ KQ74

You have two choices from the two rules you've learned. Do you lead the top connecting honor, or do you lead fourth from longest and strongest? Answer: Lead fourth. You give up a potential trick if you lead the King. Your partner might have the Ace or Jack. If she has the Ace, she can take the trick and return it and you might get four Club tricks off the top if they split 4–3–3–3. If she has the Jack, it will either force out the Ace or she can return it to you.

What would you lead from the following Club holding against a No Trump contract?

♣ KJT4

In this instance you should lead the top connecting honor, the Jack. Why? Because with your King on top of the Jack–Ten, whichever card you force out—be it the Ace or the Queen—makes the other two of the top three honors outstanding, which should result in a trick.

Standard Leads

The following list shows the standard opening leads when defending against a No Trump contract. The standard lead is bold and underlined:

Xx	xxx**X**
Xxx	xxxx**X**
A**K**Jx	A**Q**Jx
A**J**T9	AT**9**x
KQJx	KQ**T**9
K**J**Tx	K**T**9x
QJTx	Q**T**9x
JT9x	**T**9xx

There is one lead here that is a departure from the norm, so it bears explaining. It's the lead of the Queen from the holding of KQT9. Normally you'd think you'd lead the King or the Nine. You lead the Queen to ask your partner to jettison the Jack if she has it.

If you lead the Queen and she has the Jack, she'll know that you're leading from this specific holding. Otherwise the lead of the Queen in a No Trump defense would promise a holding of QJT. But if she has the Jack, you can't be leading from that, so you must be leading from KQT9. She must drop the Jack to keep her from *blocking* your suit.

If she holds Jxx in the suit, and you hold the King and follow with the Queen, it's taken by the Ace. If you get in again and lead the Ten, your partner will be forced to overtake with her Jack because it's the only card she has left in the suit. Now you can't win the Nine unless you have another entry into your hand. But if she plays the Jack at your first play of the Queen, your remaining cards are all good tricks after the Ace is played.

One of the points of a standard lead is that it tells your partner what you have in your hand. If she sees you lead the Ten, for example, she'll know that it promises the Nine and denies the Jack. If you lead the King, it means that you have either the Ace or the Queen and Jack along with it. But one thing to notice about these standard leads is that none of them consists of *top connecting honors when you only have two connecting honors*, which is a standard lead against a suit contract, as you'll see shortly. However, top connecting honors of three in a row is a good defensive lead against a No Trump contract.

Lingo

You **block** your partner's suit when your partner has several good cards remaining in a suit but you must take the trick because your only card in that suit is higher ranking than the remaining cards in her suit, and there's no way back into your partner's hand to allow her to cash her tricks. Unblocking is explained in Chapter 22.

Tricks of the Trade

Review the bidding and, without looking at your cards, try to come up with an opening lead just from the auction. Then look at your cards and determine what you want to lead.

Opening Leads Against Suit Contracts

When you're on lead against a suit contract, your defense is substantially different than when you're on lead against a No Trump contract. When defending against No Trump you're trying to set up a long suit. You can be patient to try to develop this suit.

When defending against a suit contract, however, you must take your tricks when you can. Because declarer has the ability to ruff Aces and Kings, you have to take them before declarer has been able to create a void, which renders your Ace or King valueless.

Alert

Setting up a long nontrump suit is a very rare defensive tactic because it relies on declarer running out of trump and you getting the lead to set up your suit. It happens, but not often.

When defending against a suit contract, however, you have different ways of attacking, only one of which involves setting up a long suit.

When defending against a suit contract you often have to take your tricks before declarer can get rid of losers and ruff your winners. If you have the Ace–King–Queen of a suit, for instance, they would be worth three cold tricks in No Trump. If declarer has a void in that suit, they're worthless against a suit contract.

The Best Lead Against a Suit

Louis Watson, author of the best book on play of the hand (called, not too surprisingly, *Watson's Play of the Hand*), says that the best lead against a suit contract is the King from the Ace–King holding. This is a great lead for two reasons:

♦ It almost definitely wins you the first trick.

♦ It allows you to get a view of dummy before making your next lead.

Unfortunately, it is not often that you're defending against a suit contract and you find yourself in the wonderful position of being able to lead from an Ace–King.

Leading Your Partner's Suit

When you haven't bid and you don't have a good lead from your hand, leading your partner's suit is usually a good lead and is generally safe. There are two theories about whether or not you should lead your highest card in a suit.

For years, when I was playing with Nancy Kelly and we were playing Standard American and no systems, which is what you're learning here, we played that you always led the top of your partner's bid and it worked wonderfully. Nobody else liked it, but I still like it because it gives your partner an instant idea of where the other cards in her suit are.

But the experts disagree and most insist that if you lead your partner's suit, the lead should be as follows:

+ **Low from an honor.** So if you have Q72 you would lead the Deuce.

+ **High from a doubleton.** You're trying to get a ruff and you want to tell your partner that you only have two. Of course, she won't know until the next time the suit is led whether or not you were leading a singleton or doubleton.

+ **A singleton.** This is a wonderful lead because if your partner has the Ace, which is presumable if she bid the suit, you're almost always assured that she'll return it and you'll get a ruff. Again, she has to determine whether or not you led a singleton or doubleton, but if she comes to the correct conclusion, you'll start out with two tricks.

+ **Middle card from three worthless.** This is called *MUD* for "middle-up-down." It gives your partner *count*, which I discuss in Chapter 22. If you lead a lower or middle card and the next card you play in the suit is higher, it indicates that you have an odd number of cards in that suit.

There's one time when you shouldn't lead your partner's suit: when you have a lot of cards in it. If your partner bid Hearts, for example, and you have five Hearts in your hand, the likelihood is that declarer will be void and your Heart lead will just turn the lead over to him without you taking a trick.

Lingo

Count tells your partner whether you have an even or odd number of cards in the suit led.

Top of Connecting Honors

You learned about this lead in the section on leads against No Trump contracts. Against No Trump, it's not a terrific lead unless you have a three-card sequence, like Queen–Jack–Ten. Top of two connecting honors is a better lead against a suit contract because it sets up a relatively sure trick. Remember, against suit contracts you always must be sensitive to taking your tricks in outside suits before declarer can ruff them. If your first lead is the King from King–Queen, if declarer has the Ace you have a good chance of getting your Queen before he can set up a side suit to rid himself of the loser in the led suit.

Leading a Singleton

The idea here is to create an instant void in your hand so that if the suit is led again before you are out of trump, you can ruff. However, it requires a firm partnership understanding that your partner will return your opening lead when she finally gets the lead herself.

When you're on defense and you're not on opening lead, if you get in you should *return* your partner's suit unless there's a very good reason not to do so.

You don't want to lead a singleton unless it has the possibility of giving you a trick you might not otherwise get. For example, if you have Q74 of trump, a singleton lead really doesn't do you much good because you have the Queen protected by two. If you are forced to use a small trump, your Queen will fall with the lead of the Ace and the King, so you really haven't gained anything. You had a good chance of cashing your Queen anyway, so even though your lead of your singleton allowed you to ruff in once, you didn't get your Queen.

Sometimes a lead of a singleton is a good lead; often it's not. If you have only small trump, it's okay because you might be able to take advantage of the trump.

That said, if your partner has bid the suit in which you hold a singleton, it's almost always the best lead you can make for obvious reasons.

> **Tricks of the Trade**
>
> There's little more frustrating than to lead a singleton, have your partner get the lead while you still have some trump in your hand, and see her lead a different suit. You sit there in helpless anguish while your brilliant lead becomes worthless.

Leading a Singleton Honor

This is a paradox that faces many players. Opponents have the contract and you have a singleton honor. Should you lead it? Answer: Unless your partner has bid the suit, *no*. You're going to have a good chance to win this card during the play of the hand if opponents try a finesse. But if your partner has bid the suit, it's a terrific lead. Not only will it set up a ruff in your hand, but it will probably help to set up your partner's suit.

Fourth from Longest and Strongest

You learned about this in the section on leads against No Trump, and it's a valid lead against a suit contract, too. It's a good, safe, standard lead.

Cards That Smile; Cards That Frown

On opening lead, the specific card you lead communicates specific information to your partner:

- **Leading a low card promises an honor in the suit.** So if you lead a Deuce you're promising your partner that you have an honor in the suit. The lead of the Deuce, Trey, or Four would promise an honor, with one exception. If the next card you play in that suit is lower than the one you lead (for example, if you lead the Four and then play the Trey), this tells your partner you led a doubleton.

- **The lead of a middle card denies an honor.** So if you lead, for example, the Seven, it tells your partner to forget about your having any help for her in this suit.

Leading Suits with Aces Against Suit Contracts

One of the oldest axioms in Bridge is *never underlead an Ace*. Why? Well, whenever you succumb to the temptation to underlead an Ace you see the singleton King come up on the board and you feel like an idiot, which is what I'm trying to keep you from feeling like here.

However, it doesn't matter whether it's a singleton King or a singleton anything else. If you underlead an Ace and declarer has a singleton in his hand or in the dummy, and if your partner doesn't have the King, you won't win your Ace on this hand. You've just given up a trick.

To make matters more confusing, *you shouldn't lead an Ace!* So where does that leave you? It means that against a suit contract below the slam level you shouldn't lead a suit in which you have an Ace unless you have the King to go with it (and, in the event of having an Ace–King combination, you should lead the King first) or unless your partner has bid the suit. But even if your partner has bid the suit, you shouldn't lead the Ace! More about this later in this chapter.

> **Tricks of the Trade** _____
>
> If you wonder about not leading an Ace, just remember this axiom: *Aces were created to take Kings or Queens.* As a general rule, you shouldn't play your Ace until you can use it to take a King or Queen. If your Ace happens to be the setting trick, however, you should take it immediately.

If you lead an Ace on opening lead, often you'll set up a King–Queen combination for opponents. If you wait to take your Ace when they play one of their honors to try to take a trick, you might get an extra trick (if, for example, your partner has the Jxx in the suit). You certainly will keep them from making both the King and the Queen!

So here are the rules relating to opening leads of suits with Aces:

◆ Don't underlead an Ace.

◆ Don't lead an Ace against a contract below the slam level unless you have the King (and then lead the King first).

Now I'm going to explain why you shouldn't lead an Ace even if your partner has bid the suit. You hold the following:

♠ AJ4
♥ 75
♦ 8643
♣ JT98

Your partner opens 1 Spade. RHO overcalls 2 Hearts. By now you should know that you should bid 2 Spades with this hand. LHO bids 3 Hearts, which is passed out. It's your lead. Do you remember what the first thing you do before leading? *Think!* What do you know?

1. How many Spades does your partner have and how big is her hand? Answer: five with a minimum. If she had six she would have rebid them, even with a minimum hand.

2. How many Spades do opponents have? Answer: five. Your partner has five Spades, you have three Spades. That leaves five.

3. Key question. You have the Ace. Who has the King—your partner or your opponents? Because your partner has a minimum, probably 13 points, and you have 6 HCP, opponents have 20 to 21 points. In this situation, more than half of the time opponents will have the King of Spades. Why? Because more than half the points outside of your hand belong to opponents, 21 for them, 13 for your partner.

Tricks of the Trade

If you have Ace doubleton, the Ace can be a very good lead against a suit contract. If your partner has the King and you lead the Ace and follow with another card in the suit, she should know you're leading a doubleton and return the suit for ruff, giving you three tricks off the top.

So there are two definite negatives to leading your Ace here:

♦ More than half of the time your lead of the Ace here will make the King a definite winner for opponents, because by leading your Ace you can't take their King;

♦ You give them an easy ruff of a Spade. Why? Because Spades will split one of three ways, 3–2, 4–1, or 5–0. In any of those situations if you lead the Ace and then the King wins for them, they will have a void somewhere which they can use to ruff a losing Spade before you've had a chance to reduce their trump holding.

Leading an Ace generally costs you half a trick, because if you don't lead a Spade you might be able to lead trump, drive them out of trump where they have their short Spades, and, as a result, end up taking three Spade tricks.

In time and as your wisdom grows, you might find an instance when you should lead the Ace. But for now you should adopt the following two rules:

♦ If you have at least three cards in the suit, don't lead an Ace on opening lead.

♦ Don't underlead an Ace on opening lead.

Period. End of story. Incidentally, I have not yet found the wisdom alluded to in the preceding paragraph and follow these rules religiously.

> **CAUTION**
>
> **Alert**
>
> Prohibition against underleading an Ace is only applicable when you're defending against a suit contract. It doesn't apply when you're defending No Trump contracts, when the preferred standard lead of your fourth from longest and strongest often requires you to underlead an Ace.

Leading Trump

"When in doubt, lead trump," is another ancient axiom of Bridge. Sometimes a trump lead is the best lead you can make. More often it's not. It's not a good lead when you or your partner are short in a suit and you'll want to ruff some tricks yourselves. It is a good lead in the following situations:

♦ When dummy might be short in a suit and declarer will want to ruff his losers

♦ When you and your partner have a lot of HCP in outside suits

The question is, how do you know? From the bidding! Following are situations in which a trump lead is advised.

- If all of the following are true …

    - You and your partner bid to game in a competitive auction, and

    - The ultimate declarer doubles you for penalty, and

    - His partner pulls the double and puts him in game in their suit

    You should lead trump because from the bidding you can deduce that declarer has a substantial holding in your suit whereas his partner is short. Ergo, the point of playing the hand will be for declarer to ruff in dummy the losers he holds in your suit. If you get off to a trump lead you'll be cutting down his ability to ruff.

- Your partner opens the bidding at 1 No Trump, but the opponents end up playing in a suit contract. The reason here should be obvious. Your partner has a good high-card holding and opponents are going to try to ruff or crossruff the hand. You should lead a trump to cut down this ability.

- If you make a takeout double and your partner leaves it in for penalty. You probably have only one trump and you should lead it.

- You and your opponents bid only one suit each, each partnership establishing a trump fit between them, and opponents end up in a partscore contract. You'll want to drive them out of trump in the hand where they're short in your suit.

Leading Doubletons

If you're leading a doubleton, you lead the higher card, then play the lower card at your next opportunity. This tells your partner that you only have two. It's called *going high-low*. The lead of a worthless doubleton is one of the worst leads in Bridge, but sometimes you have no choice.

The "when you have no choice" situation can appear if you hold a hand like the following defending a Heart contract:

- ♠ AQ73
- ♥ Q72
- ♦ 83
- ♣ Q843

You don't want to underlead your Ace–Queen of Spades, your Queen of Hearts or your Queen of Clubs. So your least-harmful lead is the Eight of Diamonds.

However, except in special circumstances, you shouldn't lead a doubleton when it's headed by an honor, like Kx, Qx, or Jx. You've got an opportunity to win a trick with your honor, so there's no reason to give that up by leading high-low from the doubleton, unless your partner has *freely* bid the suit.

If your partner has freely bid the suit, the lead of the King from Kx can be very profitable in two situations:

♦ If your partner has the Ace, a presumable prospect, you should win the King. She'll win your next lead of your remaining card in the suit with her Ace and return the suit for a possible ruff by you.

Lingo

To bid a suit **freely** means that partner was not forced to bid it by you making some sort of forcing bid, like a takeout double.

♦ If she's lacking the Ace, in all probability she'll have the Queen or Queen–Jack combination, so you'll be setting up her hand to win tricks by driving out opponents' Ace.

Standard Leads Against Suit Contracts

The following list shows standard leads when you are on opening lead against a suit contract. The standard lead is bold and underlined:

XX	XXX**X**
X**X**X	XXXX**X**
A**K**x	**T**9x
KQx	KJ**T**x
QJx	K**T**9x
JT9	Q**T**9x
KQT9	

Note the difference between opening leads against suit contracts and opening leads against No Trump contracts. In a No Trump defense, leading top connecting honors when you only have two connecting honors is not a good lead. But against a suit contract top connecting honors of two connecting honors is a very good lead.

Note also that when you have the Ace–King in a suit, you lead the King, not the Ace. The only time you don't do this is if your Ace–King is a doubleton. If you lead the Ace, then the King, you're telling your partner that you're now void in the suit, so if she gets in before trump is pulled, you might be able to get a ruff if she leads the suit. The converse is that if you lead the King, then the Ace, you're promising her that you have at least one more card in the suit.

Also note the difference in standard lead when you hold KQT9. In No Trump defense, you lead the Queen, asking your partner to jettison her Jack if she has it. Against a suit contract, you lead the King. Against a suit contract, you're trying to take your tricks before declarer can ruff them, so you're not trying to set up a long suit, as you would be if your were defending a No Trump contract. Also, against a suit contract you're not so concerned about blocking and unblocking.

Leads Against Slams

If you're playing against a grand slam and you have an Ace, it's probably going to be ruffed. Why would anybody in their right mind make a contract to take all the tricks without an Ace unless that Ace was of no concern to them?

The only reason the Ace would be of no concern to them is if they're void in that suit. If you lead an Ace, you're probably going to have it ruffed immediately. If so, you might be setting up a suit for them containing the King and Queen, giving them a better chance of making their contract. Don't lead an Ace against a grand slam contract in a suit for this reason.

To elaborate a little further on this, they might have to make a ruffing finesse to make the contract if they don't know where the Ace is. Look at the following Spade holding in a contract of 7 Hearts by East:

Partner
♠ 76432

West
♠ KQJT9

East (declarer)
♠ void

You
♠ A85

If you lead the Ace on opening lead, you set up West's Spades. If you don't lead the Ace and East has a loser, he has to jettison it on West's Spades. You're going to set the contract because East will have to take a ruffing finesse and it will lose.

However, against a small slam, many people like to lead an Ace, figuring that then they only need one trick. Probably not a good idea. Remember, Aces were created to take Kings and Queens. You're not going to take a King or Queen if you lead the Ace, so even against a slam the lead of an Ace is not a good idea unless it's the only trick in your hand and you can't see where you and your partner will take another trick. In that event you better take your trick while you can.

But it's generally better to keep declarer in the dark as to who has the Ace. You'll probably get to take it later and if declarer doesn't know where it is he might make a mistake if he has to guess on the location of an honor without knowing who has the Ace. Look at the following hand:

♠ 975
♥ T632
♦ 84
♣ A842

You're defending against a contract of 6 Diamonds and are on lead. Let's look at the entire Club holding:

	Partner	
	♣ Q74	
West		*East (declarer)*
♣ 532		♣ KJT6
	You	
	♣ A98	

Declarer is probably going to have to guess the location of the Ace and the Queen. Without any clue, he'll have to lead from the board into his hand. If he guesses correctly and plays the Jack you'll be forced to play the Ace and he'll make his slam. If he guesses incorrectly and plays the King, you win it with your Ace and your partner should get the Queen and you'll set him.

If you lead the Ace at your first lead, however, you take this guess away from him. His King will then be a cold trick and he'll probably correctly conclude from your lead that your partner has the Queen. This illustrates why the opening lead of an Ace is generally not a good idea, even against slam bids.

Leads Against Slams When Your Partner Doubles

A double of a slam by your partner should only be made as a lead-directing device. The reward of an extra 50 or 100 points simply isn't worth the penalty of having your opponents make a slam doubled. This is what the doubler, your beloved partner, is asking you to do when she doubles a slam:

1. Lead the first suit bid by dummy if dummy has bid a nontrump suit.

2. If dummy hasn't bid a suit other than trump but declarer has, lead the suit bid by declarer.

3. If opponents have bid no other suit but trump, lead anything but trump.

4. If you or your partner have bid a suit, don't lead it!

The Least You Need to Know

♦ When defending a no trump contract, generally the best lead is fourth from your longest and strongest suit;

♦ A double of a no trump contract asks for a specific lead;

♦ Don't lead or underlead an Ace when defending a suit contract;

♦ Lead trump if you think opponents will have to ruff losers to make the contract.

♦ Leading a low card against a suit contract promises an honor in the suit.

In the Trenches: Defense After the Opening Lead

In This Chapter

- ◆ Signals: Attitude and count
- ◆ Rule of 11
- ◆ Second hand low
- ◆ Third hand high
- ◆ Unblocking

Defense, for me, is the most fun part of Bridge. You have to communicate with your partner, without speaking, through the cards you play. When you click and get together to set a contract, it's just a wonderful feeling.

Play by Opening Leader's Partner to First Trick

The card played by the partner of the player making the opening lead to the first trick can set the tone for the entire defense of the hand. The player making the opening lead, I'll call her opening leader, is doing the best she can by paying attention to the bidding and correlating the bidding to her hand.

> **Lingo**
>
> **Attitude** refers to the interest, or strength, you have in the suit your partner led. **Count** refers to the number of cards you have in the suit your partner led; you're usually limited to telling her whether you have an even or odd number of cards.

But she's leading with only the bidding as her knowledge. After she leads, the dummy is exposed and at that time everyone knows where 26 of the 52 cards in the deck are located—the 13 in their hand and the 13 in dummy.

If your partner is on opening lead, your first opportunity to communicate with her is in your play to her lead. There are two ways to communicate with your partner when she makes the opening lead. You can either give her *count* or you can give her *attitude*.

Cards That Convey Your Attitude

You learned that opening leader can use cards that frown and cards that smile by the denomination of the card she leads. Small promises an honor, so it smiles, whereas medium denies an honor, so it frowns. *Attitude* is the interest you have in the suit your partner led.

> **Tricks of the Trade**
>
> More advanced players sometimes reverse smiles and frowns, with a high card indicating displeasure and a low card being encouraging. There are even more esoteric ways of indicating attitude, none of which you need to worry about yet because very few Rubber Bridge players use them.

However, when playing to your partner's opening lead, you indicate your pleasure or displeasure in just the opposite manner:

- A small card played to your partner's opening lead frowns because it says that you don't like the suit and have no help in it.

- A high card played to your partner's opening lead smiles because it tells her that you do like this suit and probably have an honor in it.

Count

Count is the number of cards you have in the suit your partner led, usually limited to telling her whether you have an even or odd number of cards. Some players prefer to have count indicated on the first trick, rather than attitude. This is the way you indicate count:

◆ If your first two cards played to the trick are low to high, you have an odd number of cards in the suit. So if your first card is the Trey and your next card is the Seven, you have an odd number of cards in the suit, probably three or five.

◆ If your first two cards played to the trick are high to low, you have an even number of cards in the suit. So if your first card is the Seven and your next card is the Trey, you have an even number of cards in the suit, probably two or four.

Tricks of the Trade

Whether your first play to your partner's trick conveys count or attitude is strictly a function of partnership agreement. Before you start playing, make certain you have this understood. I prefer attitude. Others prefer count. There is no right or wrong. The important thing is that you agree.

Rule of 11

This is a wonderful rule. It applies when your partner has led fourth from longest and strongest. You, as opening leader's partner, simply subtract the value of her opening lead from 11. That tells you how many higher cards are in all three hands other than opening leader's. Understand? Look at the following hands:

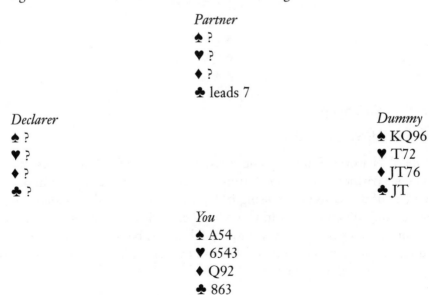

Partner
♠ ?
♥ ?
♦ ?
♣ leads 7

Declarer
♠ ?
♥ ?
♦ ?
♣ ?

Dummy
♠ KQ96
♥ T72
♦ JT76
♣ JT

You
♠ A54
♥ 6543
♦ Q92
♣ 863

Your partner leads the Seven of Clubs through dummy to you. What's the Club holding? Before you look at the answer, try to figure it out. Your partner led fourth from longest and strongest, so you should have knowledge of the configuration of the Club holding by using the rule of 11. Have you figured it out?

Subtract 7 from 11. You get 4. That means that there are only four cards higher than the Seven in the three hands other than opening leader's. That includes your own. So you have one card higher than the Seven (the Eight). That leaves three cards higher than the Seven in declarer's hand and dummy's hand combined. You can see that dummy has two cards higher than the Seven. That means that declarer only has one card higher than the Seven in his hand. Following are the actual hands:

Partner
♠ JT7
♥ 98
♦ A43
♣ AK972

Declarer
♠ 832
♥ AQJT
♦ K86
♣ Q54

Dummy
♠ KQ96
♥ K75
♦ JT75
♣ JT

You
♠ A54
♥ 6432
♦ Q92
♣ 863

Contract: 2 No Trump

Opening Lead: Seven of Clubs

The rule of 11 works. I'm not going to explain how or why, but it does. If you can rely on your partner to lead fourth from longest and strongest, you can determine where most of the cards are by using it. You really don't need to understand why it works, do you? When you get in with your Ace of Spades and return the Six of Clubs, your partner is going to win four Club tricks, because when she plays her Ace and King, the other two honors will fall and the rest of her Clubs will be good, and your partnership will be cemented.

Second Hand Low

This is an axiom that is probably as old as the game. It means what it says; when you're defending and the lead is from your right, you play a low card unless the card led is an honor or there's some other good reason to play high. The reason is that it puts declarer on the guess as to where the high cards are. Your partner will have the last play, and declarer won't know what she has until she plays. If you play high, it simply takes this obligation to guess away from her.

Unless there's a reason to play high, playing high by second hand just gives away a trick uselessly. Look at the following holding with dummy as your RHO and on lead:

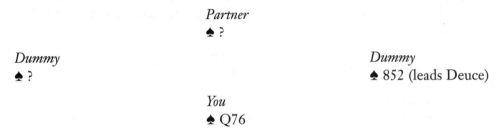

Partner
♠ ?

Dummy
♠ ?

Dummy
♠ 852 (leads Deuce)

You
♠ Q76

Opponents lead the Deuce from dummy. If you play the Queen, it will probably lose to the Ace or King. What's the point of going up with such a high card when declarer has to play behind you and your partner plays behind him? He doesn't know which hand has the missing cards. If you voluntarily play your highest card, it removes the guess from him. If you play high, he *knows* where that card is! It just goes against common sense. Whenever you're second hand, your partner has the last play. Keep declarer in the dark until your partner plays.

This might seem elementary, but you should always put declarer to the guess. The time when most people are tempted to play high as second hand is when they hold an Ace and the King is in the dummy to their left. Look at this holding:

Partner
♠ ?

Dummy
♠ KJ7

Declarer
♠ leads 4

You
♠ A832

Declarer leads low to the King–Jack. If you go up with the Ace, it makes the King a winner for sure. Worse, it takes the guess on the Queen away from him. If you play low, declarer must guess both the Ace and the Queen. If he guesses you for the Queen and your partner for the Ace, he'll play the Jack and your partner will win the Queen. You'll end up with two tricks, your Ace and your partner's Queen. If you play the Ace, you take part of this guess away from him and give him a sure trick with the King. If your partner has the doubleton Queen, you'll be giving opponents two Club tricks by going up high as second hand, if declarer then plays for the drop.

When to Play High in Second Hand

Sometimes you must go against the axiom and play high. This occurs when you have connecting honors and to play low could give opponents a deep finesse and a gift trick. Look at the following where you're holding second hand, playing behind declarer:

Partner
♠ ?

Dummy
♠ AT7

Declarer
♠ leads 4

You
♠ QJ7

Declarer, sitting as your RHO, leads a low Spade. You're not sure, but there's a good possibility declarer has the King of Spades. If you play low, he could play the Ten of Spades, which will win the trick if declarer has the King. Then declarer plays the Ace and goes back to his hand for the King and you have lost all three Spade tricks.

However, if you play high as second hand here, and go up with your Jack, you force out the Ace. That way you have a third round winner in your Queen because it's protected by the Seven of Spades and you're sitting behind the King.

But there's an exception to this rule, too. If you're sitting with the following, you should not go up with the Jack:

Partner
♠ ?

Dummy
♠ AKT

Declarer
♠ leads 4

You
♠ QJ7

Why? Because declarer might be able to figure out that you went up with the Jack because you also had the Queen and he'll just come back to his hand to finesse you again. He has absolutely nothing to lose to come back to his hand and try another finesse because if you have a doubleton it will fall. If you don't have a doubleton, but your partner has the Queen, he's going to lose it anyway unless it was a Queen doubleton. But that's unlikely because why would you voluntarily play the Jack if your partner is short in the suit? That would mean you have several cards in the suit. It just doesn't make sense. So if you play the Jack he's definitely going to come back to his hand and finesse again. In this instance you should go low and hope that declarer will figure you don't have both the Queen and the Jack (or you would have played the Jack) and will go up with the King. You don't have much to gain by going up with the Jack here, and you have a trick to gain if you go low and declarer guesses wrong.

Covering an Honor

Generally, second hand should cover an honor if it is led. There are exceptions to this rule however. Second hand should not cover an honor in the following circumstances:

◆ If the honor is led from a sequence. Consider the following holding in dummy, your RHO:

Hand 1:

	Partner ♠ ?	
Declarer ♠ ?		*Dummy* ♠ QJ73 (on lead)
	You ♠ K64	

Hand 2:

	Partner ♠ ?	
Declarer ♠ ?		*Dummy* ♠ JT3 (on lead)
	You ♠ Q87	

In both instances, if you hold the King in Hand 1, or the Queen in Hand 2, you should *not* cover the honor the first time it's led. If your partner can take the trick, she will. If she can't take the trick, you can cover the second honor. You will have lost nothing because the only way you will have a trick in the first hand is if your partner has Txx. And if she does, you protect her by covering the second honor. In the second hand, if your partner can't take the first trick, you're out of luck in this suit because opponents have four of the top five honors. It's just a matter of time before they capture yours.

◆ If your honor is going to be good if you don't cover it. This occurs when declarer only has a certain number of times he can finesse you, and you have more cards than that to protect your honor. Consider the following:

Partner
♠ ?

Declarer
♠ ?

Dummy
♠ Q5 (leads Queen)

You
♠ K743

You would be foolish to cover the Queen if it's led because you can protect your King. Look what happens. The Queen is led. You play low and the Queen wins. Then the Five is led and you go low again. declarer wins with the Jack. declarer plays the Ace. You can discard your third card and retain your King. The only way declarer can get your King is if you voluntarily play it.

Which Honors to Cover

If you are in a situation that calls for you to cover an honor, you should cover *any* honor with your honor. So if the Jack or Ten *empty*, meaning it's the top of several unconnected cards, is on the board and the Jack or Ten is led, you should cover if you have the King.

Why? Look at the following:

Hand 1:

Partner
♠ JT6

Declarer
♠ A982

Dummy
♠ Q5 (leads Queen)

You
♠ K743

Hand 2:

Partner
♠ T96

Declarer   *Dummy*
♠ AJ82   ♠ Q5 (leads Queen)

You
♠ K743

Hand 1: If you don't cover the honor, declarer gets two Spade tricks he'd never get. Your partner is sitting with the Jack and the Ten, both of which will be winners if you cover the Queen. If you don't cover the Queen, declarer will let it ride and your partner can't take it. The Queen will emerge as a winner in addition to declarer's Ace. If you cover the Queen, declarer takes the Ace and your partner's Jack and Ten are now the two highest cards in the suit.

Hand 2: This is a very common occurrence. If you don't cover the Queen immediately, declarer makes three Spade tricks because the Queen wins, then he finesses the King and the Ace wins, too. If you cover, it makes his Jack good, but then your partner takes the Ten. So if you cover, you save a trick.

Third Hand High

This is another axiom that's been around since creation. It means that if your partner leads low, you play as high a card as you can as long as it's higher than the card played by dummy.

Bottom of a Sequence

You should play the bottom card of your highest sequence. For example, your partner led the Three of Clubs and your RHO plays low, and you hold the following:

♣ QJ75

You should play the Jack. If opponents take the trick with the King, it indicates to your partner that you might have the Queen. However, if you were to play the Queen it would absolutely promise your partner that you did *not* have the Jack.

Finesse Against Dummy When You Can

What does this mean? Finesse against dummy? How? Okay, look at the following holding. This is a situation that occurs again and again. Even good players misplay it:

Partner (on lead)
♦ 3

Declarer   *Dummy*
♦ ?   ♦ K54 plays the 4

You
♦ AJT

What do you play? If declarer has the Queen, he'll take the trick. If it's a singleton, you won't ever get your Ace. Should you take your Ace or play low, hoping your partner has the Queen? If your partner has the Queen, you can wait until she gets the lead again. She'll lead through the King again, and the King will never win a trick. If you play your Ace, you make the King a sure trick. What to do?

Answer: Your partner led fourth from longest and strongest. That means that she has a maximum of five Diamonds. You have three. dummy has three. declarer must have at least two. That means you should play the Ten because you should still get your Ace, even if declarer has the Queen.

If you're playing in a suit contract and you think that declarer has a singleton honor, however, you should take your Ace. This would occur if, in the above situation, your partner had led the Deuce and both you and dummy had four Diamonds instead of three each. That pretty much marks the suit as 4–4–4–1, with declarer having the singleton. In this instance, take your Ace while you can.

Unblocking in No Trump

When defending a No Trump contract, especially one in game, you are working with fewer HCP than your opponents. When you know your partner is trying to set up a long suit, you sometimes have to *unblock* by discarding a high card, maybe a potential winner, in order to allow your partner to run her long suit. To understand this concept, let's look at a hand where you're defending a contract of 3 No Trump:

Your partner leads the Four of Diamonds. dummy plays the singleton Ace. You must unblock by discarding the Jack of Diamonds. Here's how unblocking works.

Partner
- ♠ 9853
- ♥ T2
- ♦ Q9843
- ♣ 85

Declarer
- ♠ KQ2
- ♥ AK7
- ♦ T752
- ♣ Q73

Dummy
- ♠ AT74
- ♥ 9863
- ♦ A
- ♣ AJT4

You
- ♠ J6
- ♥ QJ54
- ♦ KJ6
- ♣ K962

If you were to play the Six on the first trick, then when you subsequently get on lead with your King of Clubs you will play your King of Diamonds, which wins. Then you return your last remaining Diamond, the Jack. That's the only entry into your partner's hand. But if your partner overtakes with the Queen, declarer has the suit stopped with his Ten. Following is the layout of the cards if you originally play the Six and then win the losing Club finesse (after your opponent wins the Ace of Diamonds, he goes to his hand with a Heart and then leads the Queen of Clubs, which you win with your King), after you have cashed your King of Diamonds:

Partner
- ♠ 9853
- ♥ T
- ♦ Q98
- ♣ 8

Declarer
- ♠ KQ2
- ♥ A7
- ♦ T7
- ♣ 73

Dummy
- ♠ AT74
- ♥ 98
- ♦
- ♣ AJT

You
- ♠ J6
- ♥ QJ5
- ♦ J
- ♣ 962

You lead the Jack of Diamonds. If your partner lets it ride, there's no other way into her hand to allow her to cash her two remaining Diamond winners. So she has to overtake, which leaves declarer's Ten of Diamonds as the highest card outstanding in the suit. He takes your partner's Diamond lead and cashes his remaining winning tricks to make the contract. But look how the cards lay if you originally sluff the Jack of Diamonds under the Ace in dummy on your partner's opening lead:

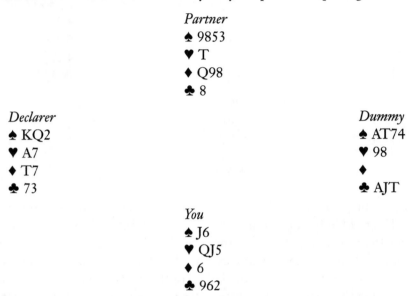

Partner
♠ 9853
♥ T
♦ Q98
♣ 8

Declarer
♠ KQ2
♥ A7
♦ T7
♣ 73

Dummy
♠ AT74
♥ 98
♦
♣ AJT

You
♠ J6
♥ QJ5
♦ 6
♣ 962

See what a big difference that makes? You now lead your Six of Diamonds through declarer's Ten. Declarer can't win because if he plays low, your partner will win the trick with the Eight and then pull declarer's Ten with his Queen. If declarer plays his Ten, your partner wins with her Queen and runs her remaining Diamond winners. If you unblock on your partner's opening lead by discarding your Jack and keeping your little Six, you defeat the contract. If you just discard the Six on her opening lead, you can't defeat the contract.

As an additional bonus to the discard of the Jack instead of the Six, it signals your partner to continue the suit because you have help.

The opportunity to unblock usually arises in the following circumstances:

♦ When you have three cards in your partner's suit

♦ When you also have high cards in your partner's long suit, but only one low card

You must preserve that low card as an entry back into your partner's hand.

What Card to Return to Your Partner

When defending a No Trump contract, there's another unblocking rule you should follow when you hold three in your partner's suit to the Ace. After you win the Ace, you should lead your highest card back to her. For example, if your original holding was Ace–honor–low and you took the trick with the Ace, return the Honor, not the low card. This has several desirable effects:

◆ It leads through declarer and possibly finesses him.

◆ It informs your partner where the missing high cards in the suit are located. If you take the Ace and return the Ten, she should know that you don't have the cards in between the Ace and the Ten. So she can mentally remove the cards she sees in dummy and the cards she sees in her own hand and place the missing cards in declarer's hand.

◆ It unblocks your suit for your partner. If you lead low and your partner wins and returns a lower card than your remaining honor, you win, but can't get back to her.

Return Lead with Four Cards in Your Partner's Suit

When you have four cards in your partner's suit, and you know that your partner has led fourth from longest and strongest, you need not be too concerned with unblocking, because you have between you the majority of the cards in the suit.

When you have three cards in your partner's suit it's important that you return your highest card, as explained in the preceding section. However, what card should you return when you started out with four cards in your partner's suit?

The answer is that you should return the card you would have led had you been on lead—the card that was originally your fourth highest. Look at the following holding between you and your partner defending a No Trump contract:

Partner (on lead)   *You*
♣ KT652   ♣ Q743

Your partner leads the Five; you play the Queen, which loses to the Ace. Declarer loses a finesse to you. What card do you now play to return to your partner? Right, you return the Three, the card that was your fourth highest in the suit originally. Now, if you have agreed that when you have three cards you return the highest remaining card, your partner knows that you started with either four or two cards in her suit. Why? Because the three is the lowest outstanding card in the suit. If you had three cards in the suit, you would have returned a higher card.

Now your partner should be able to determine the exact holding in her suit by looking at dummy and looking at the card you returned. But there's still a remaining question. Your partner wins with the Ten and comes back with the King, dropping opponents' remaining Jack. What card to you play now? Here's another unblocking situation, and you must be alert for it. If you were to just play low now, you have the Seven and the Four left, your Seven will take your partner's next lead, which will be the Six. Here's the holding after your partner gets in with the Ten:

Partner	*You*
♣ K62	♣ 74

When your partner leads the King, you have to choose between playing the Seven and the Four. Here's the holding if you play the Four on her King:

Partner	*You*
♣ 62	♣ 7

When your partner leads the Six next, your only remaining card is the Seven, which will win the trick. Now you're out of Clubs while your partner is sitting across from you with a good Club trick in her hand and no entry. Is she upset? Are you going to get up and run away from the table as soon as this deal is over?

As you can see, this is an unblocking situation. When your partner leads her King, you drop your Seven of Clubs, retaining your Four. Here's the holding if you play the Seven on her King instead of the Four:

Partner	*You*
♣ 62	♣ 4

Then when she leads her Six, you play your Four, leaving her in the lead to cash her Deuce and set the contract. Is she smiling?

Leading After the Opening Lead

Ah, those axioms. Here's another in iambic meter that generally holds you in good stead:

When the dummy's on the right,

Lead the weakest suit in sight!

If you get the lead after the opening lead, and you're sitting in front of declarer, so that the dummy is your RHO, you have the advantage that you don't have on opening lead of seeing the cards in dummy. The corollary to this is that it's unwise to lead into a tenace composed of honors, like the Ace–Queen in dummy. Look at the following holding in dummy after you win the opening trick with your singleton King of Clubs, so you can't return your partner's lead:

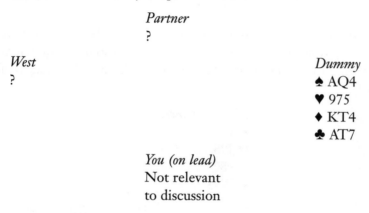

Partner
?

West
?

Dummy
♠ AQ4
♥ 975
♦ KT4
♣ AT7

You (on lead)
Not relevant
to discussion

If you lead a Spade, you take the guess on a possible finesse from declarer and put your partner in a terrible spot. If she has the King, it renders it fairly useless because the Queen will win if she ducks and the Ace will take it if she plays the King.

If you lead a Diamond, it once again removes a possible guess from declarer. You might not know where the Ace is. If your partner has it, declarer won't know either. Why make life easier for him? If you lead a Diamond, he'll play low and your partner will have to either take the Ace, making the King good, or duck, making the King good.

Hearts is the weakest suit in sight, and that's what you should lead because you're leading through declarer. If he has broken honors, he has to guess what to play with no help from dummy. As an example, look at the actual Heart holding:

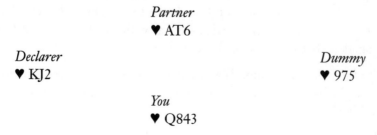

Partner
♥ AT6

Declarer
♥ KJ2

Dummy
♥ 975

You
♥ Q843

You lead the Three of Hearts. What's declarer to do? Play the Jack? Play the King? Play low? If he plays low, your partner will win with any card higher than the Nine.

If he plays the Jack and your partner has the Queen, he's going to lose. If he plays the King and your partner has the Ace, he's going to lose. As the cards lay, his correct play is the Jack, which will force out your partner's Ace. But he has to guess. Make him.

The Holdup

You learned about the holdup, the refusal to win a trick, as declarer where you used it to cut off communication between defenders' hands. It's also useful in defense to keep declarer from getting to the spot where his long suit is located. Look at the following hand:

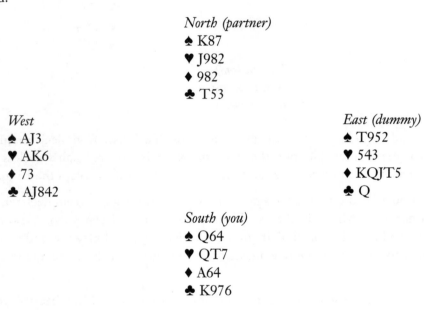

North (partner)
♠ K87
♥ J982
♦ 982
♣ T53

West
♠ AJ3
♥ AK6
♦ 73
♣ AJ842

East (dummy)
♠ T952
♥ 543
♦ KQJT5
♣ Q

South (you)
♠ Q64
♥ QT7
♦ A64
♣ K976

West reached an optimistic contract of 3 No Trump and your partner led the Deuce of Hearts. West took your Queen with his Ace. It's clear that the only chance he has to make this hand is to set up his Diamonds and take four Diamond tricks. He should take two Club tricks and with the three tricks he has with the Ace–King of Hearts and the Ace of Spades, that would make his contract.

If he leads low to his King of Diamonds and you take it with your Ace immediately, he'll get the lead right back on whatever you lead next and will get back over to dummy and run his Diamonds.

But if you hold up on his Diamonds, it's unlikely he'll be able to get back there after you take your Ace. Let's look at it. He takes the Ace of Hearts and leads low to the

King of Diamonds, which you allow him to take. He then leads the Queen of Diamonds, which you also allow him to win. When he leads the Jack, you're forced to take it because your Ace is the only remaining Diamond in your hand. Now the hands look like this:

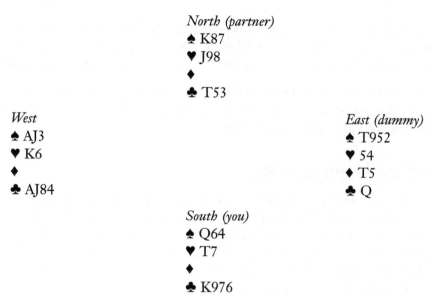

North (partner)
♠ K87
♥ J98
♦
♣ T53

West
♠ AJ3
♥ K6
♦
♣ AJ84

East (dummy)
♠ T952
♥ 54
♦ T5
♣ Q

South (you)
♠ Q64
♥ T7
♦
♣ K976

So far he's taken three tricks and you've taken one. He can take two more Clubs, a Heart, and a Spade, maybe two. Unless he can get to the dummy to cash his two good Diamonds, he's history. As you can see, there's no way he can now get to the board. By holding up you destroyed his transportation to the board and assured the defeat of the contract. Had you taken your Ace of Diamonds at the first trick, making his contract would have been a piece of cake.

Signals

When a suit is led and you have no more cards in it, you can use this as an opportunity to communicate to your partner what you have in your hand, and what you want her to lead if she gets the lead.

High-Card Discard Is Encouraging

There are several methods of discarding to communicate with your partner. The standard way is to discard a high card in a suit you want her to lead. Look at the following holding in your hand:

♠
♥ KQ92
♦ 872
♣ 752

Spades is trump and your opponent is pulling trump. Your partner still has one Spade in her hand, so your opponent leads another high Spade to pull your partner's last trump. You should use this opportunity to tell your partner about your hand.

A good discard here would be the Nine of Hearts, telling your partner that if she gets the lead you want her to lead Hearts. Discarding a high card in a suit that was not led tells your partner that you like that suit.

Low-Card Discard Is Discouraging

If you discard a low card, you discourage your partner from leading that suit. So if you were to discard the Deuce of Clubs or the Deuce of Diamonds, you'd be telling your partner that you don't want her to lead those suits because you don't have much in them. If you discard your Deuce of Clubs, however, she can't tell which of the other two suits you want led. So if you can discard high without harming the holding, you should make an encouraging discard.

Sometimes, however, it's inconvenient to discard a high card, and it's better to discourage another suit, implying that you like your good suit. Let's assume that the hands look like this:

Partner
♠ ?
♥ ?
♦ ?
♣ ?

West (dummy)
♠ 8
♥ J32
♦ QJ9
♣ AK

East (declarer)
♠ ?
♥ ?
♦ ?
♣ ?

You
♠ void
♥ KQ2
♦ 872
♣ 752

East is declarer and is pulling trump. As mentioned, there's still one out in your partner's hand, so East leads the Ace of Spades. What do you discard?

You don't want to discard the Queen of Hearts, because that's an extremely important card that you can't intelligently give up. You can't discard the Deuce of Hearts because that would be discouraging.

But there's a good way in this hand to tell her to lead a Heart without throwing away a good Heart trick. Because you clearly wouldn't want her to lead a Club with the Ace and King on the board, you should discard the Deuce of Diamonds. That tells her that you don't like Diamonds. Your partner can look at the dummy and determine that you clearly shouldn't like Clubs much either. So by discarding the low Diamond in your hand, you're telling her that you want her to lead a Heart.

This concludes your introduction to basic Bridge. The following three chapters introduce you to some advanced techniques that can enhance your skills and knowledge of the game.

The Least You Need to Know

♦ If you give attitude to your partner's opening lead, a low card tells her you don't like the suit and a high card says you do like the suit.

♦ If you give count to your partner's opening lead, your first two plays are high to low to show an even number of cards in the suit. If your first two cards are low to high, you show an odd number of cards in the suit.

♦ Using the rule of 11, if your partner leads fourth from longest and strongest, you subtract the number of the card she leads from 11 and the result is the number of cards higher than the card led in the three hands other than opening leader's.

♦ If you're second hand, you should generally play low, unless you're covering an honor.

♦ If you're third hand, you should generally play high.

23

Opening Weak Two Bids and Responses

In This Chapter

- ◆ When you may open a hand that doesn't meet the requirements for opening at the 1 level

- ◆ Requirements to open a Weak Two bid

- ◆ Opening a Weak Two in first and second seat versus third and fourth seat

- ◆ The Strong Two Clubs bid

Until the early 1960s, most players played an opening at the 2 level as strong, the system you learned in Chapter 7. This Strong Two bid is called a demand bid and generally requires the partner to keep the bidding open to game, regardless of the strength of her hand.

Although the Weak Two was used in Auction Bridge and was a part of the Vanderbilt Club System, it was not used much. Howard Schenken, who is thought by many to be the best player of all time, is credited with developing and popularizing the Weak Two system most players use today.

Weak Two Bids

It used to be that if you opened two of a suit you were showing a huge hand. As discussed in Chapter 7, there is a better way to show your strong hands. You can open them with 2 Clubs, which gives your partnership more room to bid.

If, instead of proceeding as explained in Chapter 7, in which every opening bid at the 2 level showed a huge hand, you can use a 2 Clubs opening bid to show all of your big hands (this includes big balanced hands and strong hands with long suits and good distribution), even those that contain major suits with five or more cards, you now have your other opening 2-level bids available for something else. It took awhile to figure out the best treatment, but with time one became available and has become popular with almost everyone. Curiously, it is the exact opposite of Strong Two bids. The replacement is Weak Two bids.

What Is a Weak Two Bid?

A Weak Two bid is a relative of a Weak Three bid. The primary difference is that when you open with a 2 bid in Diamonds, Hearts, or Spades, you promise exactly six cards in the suit. There are different HCP requirements, depending on your vulnerability:

- **Not vulnerable.** 6 to 10 HCP
- **Vulnerable.** 7 to 11 HCP

Here are some rules you should know about Weak Two bids. In first or second seats, your Weak Two bids must follow these guidelines. The reason is that your partner is not a passed hand. If your partner has a good hand and chooses to bid, she must be able to count on you to have certain values.

Values Required to Make a Weak Two Opening Bid in First or Second Seat

The following list details the values required to make a Weak Two opening bid in the first or second seat.

- ◆ **A six-card suit.**

- ◆ **A good suit.** The question that has been debated for years is how good the suit should be. Some players say you need three of the top five honors, others say that virtually any six cards headed by the Ace, King, or Queen is okay. Others take a middle ground. Experts generally suggest that you bid aggressively.

- ◆ **No side four-card major.** You may miss a good major suit fit if you have four cards in a major.

- ◆ **No side five-card minor.** Your wild distribution will be too big a surprise for your partner to judge the hands well.

- ◆ **No void.** If you have a void, it means that you have good trump support for other suits. It may be that another suit would be a better trump suit.

- ◆ **No seven-card suit.** Your seventh card will be unexpected and this extra card will cloud your partner's judgment.

CAUTION

Alert

If you make a Weak Two bid, even if it is a little less than classic, your partner will have a better idea of what your side can make than either of the opponents. Because it is very hard to bid against preempts, you have a lot to gain when you open a Weak Two bid and not that much to lose. Winners preempt a lot. Be a preemptor.

When You Are Not Vulnerable

Consider the following: You are in first or second seat and not vulnerable. You get to open the bidding if you want. Remember that a Weak Two bid not vulnerable shows 6 to 10 high-card points:

1. ♠ QJ9843	2. ♠ KT7632	3. ♠ AQJ874	4. ♠ KJ9732
♥ K3	♥ Q8	♥ J983	♥ 32
♦ K2	♦ Q8	♦ 73	♦ A762
♣ 873	♣ J63	♣ 3	♣ 8

5. ♠ 73	6. ♠ 7
♥ KQT8763	♥ AQT984
♦ Q84	♦ 8743
♣ 6	♣ 94

Hand 1: 2 Spades. When you bid a Weak Two, your partner learns you have a six-card suit and 5 to 10 points. The points you have are nice quality and your Spade suit, even though missing the Ace and King, is nice. All you need from your partner is two of them, or perhaps, the Ten spot to make this a playable trump suit. That is not asking for too much. Keep in mind that if you pass and later bid Spades, your partner will not know you have six of them. She will suspect that you have five. Further, by passing first, you have given the opponents room to do some cheap bidding.

Hand 2: Pass. You have poor Spade spots and importantly, you have high cards on the side that may be useless.

Hand 3: Pass. This has a perfect Spade suit for a Weak Two bid, and it has the right number of points but it has four Hearts. That is a serious warning sign.

Hand 4: 2 Spades. All of its points are working and it has nice distribution.

Hand 5: 3 Hearts. This is not a 2 Heart opening bid. Don't make a Weak Two bid with a seven-card suit.

Hand 6: 2 Hearts. This is a rare 6-point Weak Two. When you make a Weak Two on a minimum hand, be sure you have all of your points in the trump suit.

When You Are Vulnerable

Consider the following situation: You are in first or second seat, vulnerable. You get to open the bidding if you wish. Remember that a Weak Two bid vulnerable shows 7 to 11 HCP

1. ♠ 74	2. ♠ AJT864	3. ♠ KJ8753	4. ♠ 82
♥ KQJ874	♥ 2	♥ K42	♥ 83
♦ Q8	♦ KT5	♦ 42	♦ AKJ876
♣ K32	♣ K52	♣ 82	♣ 83

Hand 1: 2 Hearts. This is a maximum Weak Two bid. Note, however, that the quality of the eleven HCP is not that good. The Queen of Diamonds is suspect because it's a doubleton, so it does not indicate trick-taking capability unless your partner has the Ace or King or Jack fourth. If not, you could have two immediate Diamond losers and no winners.

Hand 2: 1 Spade. When you have a really nice 11 points plus good distribution and a fine six-card suit, your hand is really worth close to 13 points. Open with a 1 bid.

Hand 3: Pass. This is tempting but being vulnerable, caution is acceptable. Nonvulnerable, you'd open this in 2 Spades in a flash.

Hand 4: 2 Diamonds. You have close to a minimum in terms of HCP but your suit is outstanding. Note that if you pass you may not get to bid your Diamonds later.

Lingo

High cards that have no obvious value such as Qx or Jxx are called **soft points** or **bad points.** When you preempt, you want to have as few bad points as possible. You would rather have six good points than four good points and four bad ones.

Weak Two Bids in Third Seat

In third seat, you are in a different situation. Your partner has passed, so you know she does not have a good hand. If you have a weak hand yourself, you can count on your LHO being ready to bid something. In third seat, it is a proven strategy to open aggressive Weak Two bids. In fact, if you are willing to take some chances, you might try opening a Weak Two bid with a good five-card suit and the appropriate number of points. Do not try this in any seat except for third seat. This is a very effective ploy.

Weak Two Bids in Fourth Seat

This is an odd situation. If the bidding is passed to you in fourth seat, you do not really have a reason to open a weak hand. You can pass it out and avoid getting a negative score. If you do open with a 2 bid other than clubs, the hand you show is dramatically different. Instead of being weak, your 2 bid is descriptive, saying that you have a six-card suit and about 11 to 14 points. The reason for this is that you get to describe your hand exactly while at the same time making it hard for the opponents to have second thoughts. One example of a fourth seat 2 bid is as follows:

♠ 83
♥ KQJ984
♦ KJ4
♣ QJ

This hand has 13 HCP, but they are not terribly good ones. If you open 1 Heart, your partner may get you too high or perhaps the opponents can bid Spades or Clubs. By opening 2 Hearts, you tell your partner exactly what you have and at the same time you suppress the opponents' bidding.

Responding to Weak Two Bids

Responding to a Weak Two bid is totally different from responding to a 1 bid. Here are some rules that will get you off to a good start; you can respond to a two Weak Two bid …

♦ If you bid a new suit. If you bid a new suit, it is a forcing bid. You tend to deny support for partner's suit and you show enough points that you hope for a game. This means you need around 15 HCP and a good suit.

♦ If you have a fit and enough for game. Bid game if you have game points. Keep in mind that your partner has a six-card suit. You can raise to four of partner's major with only two-card support.

♦ If you have a fit and you think there could be a slam. You may be able to bid slam directly or after asking for aces. It is possible that you can bid 2 No Trump and discover more about your partner's hand.

♦ If your hand is invitational. If you are not sure whether you have enough for game and want to find out more about your partner's hand, you can bid 2 No Trump to ask the opener for more information. There are many ways to do this, but this is the simplest. You are asking partner to bid an Ace or a King in a suit outside the trump suit, if she has it, regardless of what else she has in her suit. So if she has opened 2 Hearts in Hand 1 above, and you bid 2 No Trump, she would respond 3 Clubs, showing she had the King of Clubs. If she has no outside Ace or King, she rebids her trump suit.

> **Lingo**
>
> When you play that a 2 No Trump response to a Weak Two opening asks for an Ace or King outside the trump suit, the Ace or King is called a *feature.* When you play that any suit bid other than a raise is forcing, it's called **RONF,** which is an acronym for *raise is the only nonforcing* bid.

After you have become familiar with Weak Two bids, you can add something to your methods. Instead of saying that a 2 No Trump bid asks for a feature, the 2 No Trump bid can be used to get more detailed information. A little judgment is needed, something that you will want to develop. In response to a 2 No Trump bid, opener bids as follows:

♦ If opener has a minimum hand she rebids her suit even if she has an Ace or King on the side.

♦ If opener has a maximum, at least 1 point better than average, she shows an Ace, King, or Queen if she has one.

♦ If opener has a maximum but does not have an outside value to show, she raises to 3 No Trump, which implies a very good suit.

♦ If you know your side does not have a game. In this case, you usually pass. If you have support for partner, however, you can raise to the 3 level if you have three- or four-card support. In fact, if you have four-card support and two doubletons or four-card support and a singleton, it is wise to bid game in the expectation that the opponents may have a contract of their own. The reason for this is that if you don't have much, you're just cooperating with partner's preempt by squeezing opponents further and giving them less room in which to communicate. If partner opens 2 Spades and you raise to 3 Spades, opponents must start communicating at the 4 level.

Consider the following hand: Your partner opens 2 Hearts with no one vulnerable. She has 6 to 10 points. With these hands, what do you respond?

1. ♠ QJ873	2. ♠ A84	3. ♠ QJ3	4. ♠ 8
♥ K	♥ J83	♥ 8	♥ Q873
♦ KQJ	♦ Q8762	♦ AKQJ872	♦ KT987
♣ K878	♣ 72	♣ AJ	♣ 873

5. ♠ AK3	6. ♠ AQJ986
♥ T3	♥ 3
♦ AT87	♦ 8
♣ KJ64	♣ JT875

Hand 1: Pass. You have 15 points, but they are poor-quality points. You have only one Heart, so the hands are something of a misfit. Best is if you pass smoothly. Perhaps the next opponent will decide to bid something. You would like it if he bid Spades.

Hand 2: 3 Hearts. The idea is that you are making the bidding a little more difficult for the opponents.

Hand 3: 3 No Trump. You do not want to play in Hearts but you would like to take a chance on game. Bid 3 No Trump without showing diamonds and without asking questions with 2 No Trump.

Hand 4: 4 Hearts. You won't make it, but you won't be down a lot either. The idea is that you are making life very tough for the player on your left.

Tricks of the Trade

One of the very best things you can do at the table is to exude confidence. You do not have to know what you are doing, but if you can manage to act confidently about your bids and plays your opponents will be impressed and that will affect their play. This is analogous to putting on a poker face.

Hand 5: 2 No Trump. You have a good hand that is not quite good enough to bid game. Bid 2 No Trump and find out whether your partner has the King of Diamonds or the Ace of Clubs. If so, you should bid 4 Hearts knowing that her six Hearts and your two Hearts are fine for game. If not, pass her 3 Hearts rebid.

Hand 6: Pass. 2 Spades would be forcing. You need around 15 good points to bid a new suit. Your partner, remember, may not pass your bid. It is forcing, and she will always bid again compounding your problems if you have bid with a weak hand.

Strong Two Clubs Bid

Because the modern trend is to use an opening bid at the 2 level as weak, a bid at a reasonable level was needed to show a very strong hand—stronger than 1 No Trump, stronger than 2 No Trump. So the 2 Clubs open was reserved for a strong hand.

Requirements for a Strong Two Clubs Open

The requirements for a hand to open 2 Clubs are as follows:

- ◆ 22 or more HCP; or
- ◆ $8\frac{1}{2}$ tricks

So a Strong 2 Clubs bid either shows a lot of points, or an unbalanced hand with enough trick-taking capability that you're assured of taking more than eight tricks in your own hand. Look at the following hands—all of these hands qualify for an opening bid of 2 Clubs:

1. ♠ AK74	2. ♠ AKQJ643	3. ♠ Q8653	4. ♠ AK
♥ KQJ6	♥ AK	♥ AKQJ	♥ 865
◆ AK	◆ Q43	◆ AKQJ	◆ KQJ2
♣ QJ6	♣ 3	♣ void	♣ AKQJ

Hand 1: Contains 23 HCP and is balanced.

Hand 2: Contains only 19 HCP, 21 total points; if Spades is trump, however, you have nine tricks in your hand, so that qualifies.

Hand 3: Contains 22 HCP and 3 distribution points.

Hand 4: Contains 23 HCP, 24 total points. Regardless of the terrible Hearts, this is a 23-HCP hand and must be opened 2 Clubs.

The 2 Clubs open is an *artificial* bid. That means that it says nothing about the suit bid, Clubs. So you can open all four hands 2 Clubs, even though Hand 2 only has one Club and Hand 3 is void of Clubs.

Responses to Strong Two Club Opening

You must remember two rules when you're responding to your partner's opening bid of 2 Clubs:

◆ When your partner opens 2 Clubs, you are required to keep the bidding open to either 2 No Trump or until she bids one of her suits for the second time. So even if you have a Yarborough, you must keep bidding if your partner opens 2 Clubs, until she either gets to 2 No Trump or bids one of her suits a second time.

◆ Whenever your partner bids a new suit, you must bid again. Bidding a new suit by your partner who has opened 2 Clubs is *forcing for one round* on responder. Of course, if your RHO interferes and bids before you, you need not bid. Your Pass will tell her something about your hand.

This is true regardless of the weakness of your hand.

What Is Your Partner Telling You?

Don't pass! That's the main thing she's telling you. There's a famous story about the police being called to a Bridge club to find a player dead, shot through the heart. The police asked what happened and one of the players responded, "The deceased's partner opened 2 Clubs and the bidding went Pass, Pass, Pass, Bang! Bang! Bang!" Don't let this happen to you. If you pass a Strong Two Club opening, you had better have a bodyguard available when the hand's over. If not, you could be shot through the heart; if there are any Bridge players on the jury, your partner will probably get off with justifiable homicide.

Your partner's telling you she has a huge hand and she's not just interested in game, she's interested in slam if you have any kind of support at all.

Patience Prevails

Another thing she's telling you by her bid is that you should bid slowly and communicate. There's absolutely no reason for you to give some kind of a jump response telling her about your hand. You have time. Although the 2 Clubs opening crowds the bidding a little, you haven't given up much space, and you still have a lot of time to talk to each other.

So just be patient. Use the system you've agreed on to describe your hands to each other. What you're learning here is the most standard system used by players. It's the one I use. But there are a lot of different systems that require different responses to an opening of 2 Clubs. Although you might be aware of them, you shouldn't concern yourself too much with what they are because the system you're learning works just fine.

Waiting Bid

The first thing you should know is, unless you have a strong five-card major, or a balanced hand with 7 or more points, you *must* bid 2 Diamonds when your partner opens 2 Clubs. This is called a waiting bid. It's conventional, in that it says nothing about Diamonds. You must bid 2 Diamonds even if you're void in Diamonds. All it says to your partner is, "Okay, partner, I hear you. You have 22+ points or $8^1/_2$ tricks in your hand. Tell me more."

Weak Response

Because your first bid is relatively preordained, you really have no choice but to bid 2 Diamonds (unless you have a good five-card major or good six-card suit, or at least 7 points, which I cover shortly), it tells your partner that you haven't died since she opened her hand. It also allows her to breathe a sigh of relief that you didn't pass her out.

So how do you tell her your hand stinks? What if you have a Yarborough? How can you tell her if you're required to bid?

Cheaper Minor

The answer to this question is that, at your next bid, if you bid the cheaper minor available to you at the 3 level, it tells her that your hand has 3 points or less in it.

So if she opens 2 Clubs and you respond 2 Diamonds, and she bids 2 Spades, what do you think you bid to show her a terrible hand?

Answer. Your bid is 3 Clubs (artificial). That's the *cheaper minor*—that is, the lowest minor suit you can bid at that point.

Rules for responding with cheaper minor are as follows.

Partner's First Rebid	Your Response
2 Hearts or 2 Spades	3 Clubs
2 No Trump	Pass
3 Clubs	3 Diamonds
3 Diamonds	3 No Trump

All of these responses show a bad hand with no more than 3 points.

This is the basic, standard way to show a weak hand. There are alternatives. Some people play responder shows a weak hand by bidding 2 No Trump. Others play that the response to show a weak hand after partner's first rebid is 3 Diamonds is to bid 3 Hearts, the cheapest suit available. I recommend you start playing it the way shown above. As you become more advanced, you may want to change. For the record, the way I'm teaching it is still the way I play.

Positive Response

But you don't absolutely, positively *have* to bid 2 Diamonds in response to your part-ner's Strong Two Clubs opening. There are times when you have something, too, and you want to let her know about it as soon as possible. The following are allowed responses:

- ◆ **2 of a major or 3 of a minor.** This shows you with a good five-card suit or a six-card suit and at least 6 HCP. A *good* five-card suit should be one headed by two of the top three honors, or three of the top five honors. Don't forget that your partner is the one with the big hand. She probably has a suit she wants to promote. So you don't want to tell her that you have the suit in which you should be playing unless it's a very good suit. A five-card suit headed by the King–Jack, for instance, just isn't good enough.

- ◆ **2 No Trump.** This shows at least 7 HCP and denies a four-card major with no voids, singletons, and not more than two doubletons.

- ◆ **Jump to 3 of a major.** This shows at least a six-card suit with three of the top four honors.

Bidding When Opponents Open a Weak Two Bid or Higher Preempt

When your RHO opens a Weak Two bid, you will often have the urge to bid something. Certain care has to be taken when bidding against a preempt because it is forcing you to bid at a high level, and at the same time it is warning you that there could be some bad distribution to contend with. Here are some general guidelines.

If you are thinking of making a takeout double, you need proper shape with support for the unbid suits and at least the following:

- 12 HCP if you are doubling a Weak Two bid.

- 14 HCP if you are doubling a 3 bid.

- 16 HCP if you are doubling an opening 4 bid. Note that a double of a 4-level preempt can be played as penalty or takeout. The better view is to play double is takeout. You will gain many times with this treatment and will lose out only occasionally.

If you are thinking of overcalling in a suit, you need a good suit in all cases. Following are point requirements for bidding at the various levels, in addition to having at least five cards in the suit:

- **2 level.** 13 good-quality HCP

- **3 level.** 15 good-quality HCP

- **4 level.** 17 good-quality HCP, and usually a six-card suit

All No Trump overcalls at the 2 or 3 level against a preempt are natural. If they open a Weak Two bid and you bid 2 No Trump, you are showing 15 to 18 HCP with a stopper in their suit. This is *not* an unusual No Trump overcall. With 19 or more balanced points, you usually bid 3 No Trump, although a double first is fine if you have good distribution for it. If they open with a 3-level preempt, you can bid 3 No Trump with a variety of hands. Typically you have at least 16 HCP. This is not always a safe bid, but they have made life difficult for you and the only way to get what you deserve is to take an occasional risk. However, if you do this, you should have at least one stopper in their suit, preferably two.

Balancing When Opponents Open a Weak Two Bid or Higher Preempt

If your LHO opened the Weak Two and the bidding is passed around to you, you can be aggressive to the extent that you need 2 fewer points for your bid. Previously it was suggested that you can double a Weak Two bid with 13 HCP and proper distribution. If a Weak Two is passed around to you, it is acceptable to double with 2 fewer points, 11 in this case, as long as you have support for the missing suits. You can deduct 2 points for the requirements for balancing at the 3 and 4 levels as well (13 HCP for the 3 level and 15 HCP for the 4 level). Be careful that you do not deduct more. If you get in the habit of being aggressive on the theory that the opponents are showing a weak hand, you will be caught speeding now and then and there will be a stiff price to pay.

When you make a balancing double with a weak hand, it is essential that you have support for all three unbid suits. If you do it with a doubleton in an unbid suit, your partner could find herself playing in a 4–2 fit and she won't be happy.

The Least You Need to Know

- ◆ Weak Two bids can be made in Diamonds, Hearts, or Spades in suits that contain six cards, 5 to 10 HCP, and two of the top three honors.

- ◆ In first or second seat, you shouldn't have a side four-card major, or a side five-card minor or a void.

- ◆ A response of 2 No Trump to a Weak Two opening asks for a feature in an outside suit, either a King or a QJx.

- ◆ 2 Clubs is a strong artificial opening bid promising 22+ points or $8^1/_2$ tricks.

- ◆ A 2 Clubs opening is forcing to 2 No Trump or until the opener bids one of her suits for the second time. You must bid if your opponents have not intervened.

- ◆ A response of 2 Diamonds is a waiting bid in response to a Strong Two Clubs opening, saying nothing about the Diamond suit.

Chapter 24

For Advanced Idiots

In This Chapter

- ◆ The strip and end play and the principle of restricted choice
- ◆ Blackwood and interference
- ◆ Weak jump responses and lead-directing doubles
- ◆ Cue bids and splinter bids
- ◆ Jacoby Transfer

The goal of this book is to quickly teach you how to play Bridge and to show you that it's easy to master the basics. But Bridge is a constant learning process. Now that you know the basics and should be able to sit down and play a respectable game, I want to introduce you to some slightly advanced elements. These are introduced in no particular order. Some are playing techniques, and some are bidding techniques.

The playing techniques are methods you can use immediately when you master them because they only involve you and the way you play your cards. The bidding methods must be used with someone who has the same understanding of them as you do.

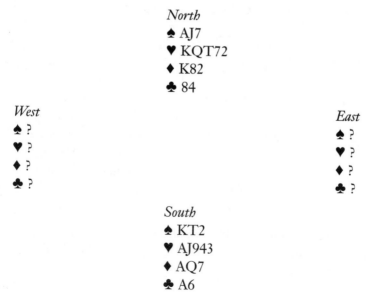

Lingo

Strip means to take away the opponents' cards that they can safely lead without giving you a trick. These cards are called *exit cards*. **End play** means to put the opponents in the lead in a situation in which anything they lead will gain you a trick.

The Strip and End Play

Although this sounds like something you might see in a Madonna movie, it's actually an ingenious way to make an extra trick. One of the hands in which it works is where you have to find a missing honor, like the Queen, and you have the appropriate distribution in declarer and dummy. For instance, a *strip* and *end play* would work if your hand and dummy's have mirror distributions of 3–5–3–2. You have a problem of finding the Queen of one of the suits and the contract depends on your locating the Queen. If you don't take the Queen, you'll go set. Do you finesse? Or is there a way to play it so that there is absolutely no guess? Let's look at the following hand which South is playing in 6 Hearts:

North
♠ AJ7
♥ KQT72
♦ K82
♣ 84

West   *East*
♠ ?   ♠ ?
♥ ?   ♥ ?
♦ ?   ♦ ?
♣ ?   ♣ ?

South
♠ KT2
♥ AJ943
♦ AQ7
♣ A6

You have 11 cold tricks and the success of the contract depends on your ability to locate the Queen of Spades. You could guess and leave it up to luck. Or, you could play it in such a way that the contract is cold. Which would you prefer? Before you learn how, can you figure out how to play this hand without any possible chance of not making six?

The answer, as you might have guessed, is to execute a strip and end play. It doesn't matter what cards your opponents hold or lead. You can't lose this contract if you play it correctly. You are in total control. Have you figured it out yet?

For those of you who haven't, here's what you do. You pull trump, even if it takes three rounds. Then you take your three Diamond winners and the Ace of Clubs. This leaves you with the following holding:

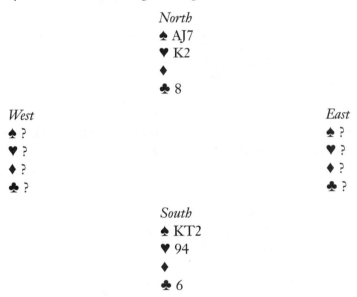

North
♠ AJ7
♥ K2
♦
♣ 8

West
♠ ?
♥ ?
♦ ?
♣ ?

East
♠ ?
♥ ?
♦ ?
♣ ?

South
♠ KT2
♥ 94
♦
♣ 6

What now? Well, what you don't do is guess your finesse. What you do now is lead a Club, which you will obviously lose. But now look at your situation. Your opponents are out of trump, so they can't lead Hearts. If they lead Spades, they lead right into you because you can take it in the fourth seat. So a Spade lead obviates the need for a finesse. You are void in both Diamonds and Clubs in both hands at this point, so if they lead either of those suits, you get a *ruff and a sluff*, throwing off your losing Spade and ruffing in the other hand. That way you can trump your losing Spade in the other hand. Look at the situation after they lead a Club or a Diamond and you sluff the Two of Spades in South and ruff the Club in North:

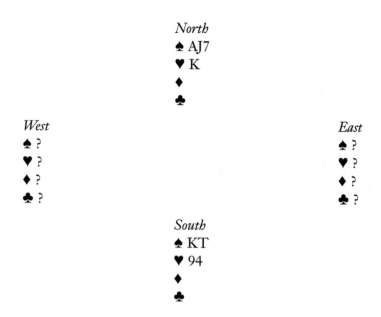

See? Now you can't lose. You lead the Seven of Spades to the King. Then lead the Ten of Spades to the Ace. Now your holding is as follows:

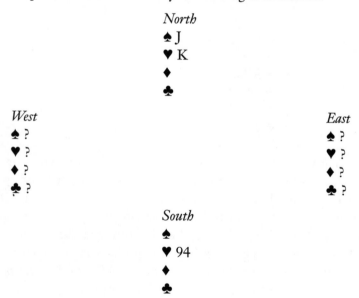

You can ruff the Seven of Spades in South, so the contract is made. You can't go set if you recognize a strip and end play and execute it properly.

The key to a strip and end play is to lose a trick at a time when any lead by opponents will either give you a ruff and a sluff or will force them to lead into your tenace.

Which leads into another aspect of the strip and end play, placing the lead in the opponent who will be forced to lead into your tenace. Look at the following situation at the end of your playing a Spade contract, after you have drawn all the trump:

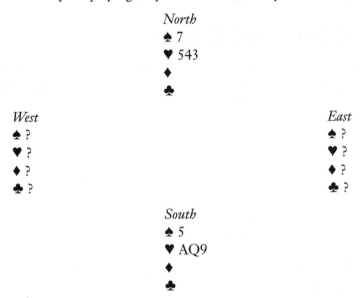

North
♠ 7
♥ 543
♦
♣

West
♠ ?
♥ ?
♦ ?
♣ ?

East
♠ ?
♥ ?
♦ ?
♣ ?

South
♠ 5
♥ AQ9
♦
♣

How do you make three of the last four tricks? If you play it correctly, you can't fail. Your opponents have no good defense against the correct offense. From what you now know, you should be able to figure it out. No matter what they do, if you know what you are doing, you have three of the last four tricks cold if you have the lead in North.

You lead a low Heart from the North hand. If East goes low, you play the Nine. That leaves West to take the trick and lead into your Ace–Queen. If he leads a Diamond or Club, he gives you a ruff and a sluff. He's helpless.

Even if East goes up with the Ten or the Jack, you have it cold. Why? Because if East plays the Ten, let's say, and you play the Queen and West wins with the King, your Ace–Nine is now in a *tenace position* because the only card out between them is the Jack. So the Ace–Nine is now basically the same card holding as the Ace–Queen had been prior to the play.

The essentials of the strip and end play are as follows:

1. Strip your hand of two nontrump suits.

2. After you've stripped your hand (or with the lead that completes the strip), lose a trick and put opponents into the lead.

The Principle of Restricted Choice

Although it's a little more complicated than this, the *principle of restricted choice* decrees that if one of your opponents drops an honor, you should play his partner for the other honor. I'll show you by an example. Following are your cards:

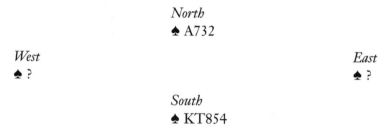

North
♠ A732

West   *East*
♠ ?   ♠ ?

South
♠ KT854

You play the Ace, East follows with the Six and West plays the Queen. Assuming you have no clue from the bidding, what do you do? Play for the 2–2 split, or finesse the Ten? Even though it's a guess, the correct play is to finesse the Ten. Why? Because of the *principle of restricted choice*.

The theory is that if he has both, he could have played either, but if he only has one he's limited to playing it. So the odds favor the proposition that he only has one and if you lead low to South's hand and East goes low (with the Nine, which is the only other card out except the Jack), you should play the Ten. The odds are somewhat like 2–1 in your favor that East holds the other honor in this situation.

Blackwood and Interference

There are two methods of dealing with interference. In the first, if your partner bids Blackwood and your RHO bids a suit, you use a convention called *DOPI* (Double = Zero, Pass = One). If you don't have any Aces, you double. If you have one Ace, you pass.

So look at the following two hands:

1. ♠ KQT9   2. ♠ AQT9
   ♥ QJT   ♥ QJT
   ♦ 983   ♦ 983
   ♣ QJ9   ♣ QJ9

Lingo _____

DOPI stands for "Double = Zero, Pass = One."

Your partner has bid 4 No Trump but before you can bid you hear your RHO bid 5 Hearts. What do you do?

Hand 1: Double. That tells your partner that you have no Aces. It says nothing about your ability to defend and set a contract of 5 Hearts by opponents. Your partner won't take this as a penalty double and will just bid her hand as she sees fit, knowing that you don't have any Aces.

Hand 2: Pass. This tells your partner that you have one Ace. There's no chance of the hand being passed out because your partner still has another chance to bid since her LHO bid.

The second method of dealing with interference by your RHO after your partner has bid 4 No Trump asking for Aces is to just bid up the line starting with the next available bid. So in the example above, where your RHO bid 5 Hearts, a bid of 5 Spades by you would say you had no Aces. Because it's the next available bid, it would be equivalent to your bidding 5 Clubs. If you had one Ace you'd bid 5 No Trump. Two Aces would be shown by 6 Clubs. Well, you get the picture. Frankly, I don't like this method because it gets you too high and it precludes your partner from asking for Kings with 5 No Trump. But it's a method of which you should be aware.

Weak Jump Responses

You have learned that all jump responses show a strong hand. However, the modern trend is for jump responses to show a weak hand. Most Rubber Bridge players play them strong, which is the reason you were taught that they are strong. But you should be aware that most advanced players play jump responses as weak. This is the way they work.

A weak jump shift is called a *preemptive jump shift*. There are three requirements for this bid:

- You must have at least six cards in the suit.

- You must have less than 6 HCP.

- You must not have three cards in your partner's suit if she opens in a major.

A final corollary to these rules is that *you must not bid again unless your partner makes a forcing bid that requires you to bid again.*

A preemptive jump shift (PJS) tells your partner that you have a terrible hand, but a long suit and asks her not to bid again. Unless she has an unusually strong hand, she should pass, even if she's void in your suit. The exception to this is if she is void and has a six-card major suit of her own, in which event she might rebid her opening suit. Whatever she does after you've made a PJS, she knows that you will not bid again.

Don't try to save your partner. After you've described your hand accurately, you must trust that she wants to play the hand in a contract of whatever she bids in her rebid if it's not a forcing bid. Remember, you've already told her, "Partner, this is my hand and this is my only bid. Anything you do after this is at your own risk because I'm going to pass, pass, pass every time it's my turn."

I tell all my partners, "Don't ever try to save me. I generally know what I'm doing and you must trust me. If you have accurately described your hand to me, let me make the decision." I've been burned more times than I would like to remember by partners who thought they had a terrible hand and that I was in big trouble so they bid something trying to save me, only to end up in a worse predicament than I would have been in.

If you have described your hand and made a bid that says, "I'm not going to bid again," you must trust your partner to know what she's doing. Think of the downside. If you save her and get a terrible result, she's going to have the right to criticize you for taking her out of a less damaging contract. But if you let her go ahead with her bid after you've said you're not bidding again and she gets in trouble, she can't criticize you at all. Maybe that's a selfish way to look at a partnership, but it's realistic. Trust your partnership agreement. Don't deviate from it. The person who does is the one who will get criticized. The one who complies with the agreement can't be reproached. Generally your partner should know what she's doing, so just assume that she does. After you've made a PJS, the bidding is out of your hands—you're off the hook.

Finally, a word of explanation. Why is a PJS made with a weak hand? The answer is simple. When you and your partner have the bulk of the points in your hand, you want to keep the bidding low so you can communicate. It makes no sense whatsoever to make a jump bid, because you are preempting yourselves. The point of a jump bid should be to crowd the bidding for your opponents, to make it more difficult for them to communicate when they have the bulk of the points. So, when your partner opens and you don't have much, your PJS does two things:

- ◆ It tells your partner exactly what you have; not much.

- ◆ It crowds the bidding for your opponents, who probably have a lot more than you and your partner have. They will have to start their conversation at, probably, the 3 level, when, without your PJS they could have started at the 1 level.

On the other hand, when you have the bulk of the points, keep the bidding low for as long as you can so you and your partner can converse back and forth and tell each other what you have and where you have it.

Lead-Directing Doubles

This usually occurs after an opening by your LHO of 1 No Trump and a conventional bid by your RHO, like 2 Clubs, Stayman. Let's say you have a good Club suit headed by two of the top three honors or three of the top five, so you want a Club lead if they're playing the contract in No Trump. You tell your partner what to lead by doubling the 2 Clubs bid. This generally only works when opponents are making conventional bids.

If you're going to play lead-directing doubles, be certain that your partner is playing it, too, and knows that when you make a double of a conventional bid it's only for lead-directing purposes.

Cue Bids

The Encyclopedia of Bridge defines a cue bid as "a forcing bid in a suit in which the bidder cannot wish to play." The easiest understood cue bid is a bid of opponent's suit. Very few Rubber Bridge players use cue bids. If you were to throw one into your bidding, probably everybody at the table would think you had lost it. I'll explain a few types of cue bids.

Cue Bid Limit Raise

When you've passed or not made a bid, if your partner opens the bidding or makes an overcall, you can tell her that you have a limit raise by cue bidding the suit bid by opponents. For example, take the following hand:

- ♠ KJ8
- ♥ A63
- ♦ QT83
- ♣ 743

Bidding is as follows.

LHO	Partner	RHO	You
1 Club	1 Spade	Pass	?

From what you know right now, you have a limit raise, so you'd make a jump bid to 3 Spades, right? That's the correct bid. However, if you're playing a cue bid limit raise you have a much better bid that keeps the bidding lower. You can bid 2 Clubs, opponents opening bid suit! This shows your partner that you have a limit raise in the suit she overcalled.

> **Alert**
>
> People who play cue bidding usually have the understanding that the bid shows that you have a limit raise *or better* in your hand. So you can make a cue bid with a huge hand, knowing that it forces your partner to bid and you'll get another bid.

The advantage of this is that you don't know if she overcalled with an opening hand or a minimum 8-point hand. By cue bidding, you tell partner what you have, but keep it at a lower level so if she made a weak overcall she can close it out in 2 Spades. If she had a weak overcall and you weren't playing cue bid limit raises, you would have to jump to the 3 level, and if she's weak she might only be able to make 2 Spades.

Another advantage of this bid is that you can then make a jump bid to show a weak hand with a lot of Spades. Look at the following hand:

♠ J732
♥ Q8
♦ K93
♣ 8732

It's probable that opponents have a Heart fit. You have four Clubs and only two Hearts. If you weren't playing a cue bid limit raise, the best you could do with this hand would be to bid 2 Spades, leaving 3 Hearts available for opponents. If you have the cue bid limit raise in your arsenal, however, you can make a preemptive jump to 3 Spades. Now what are opponents going to do? Bid 4 Hearts without Hearts ever having been bid? Unlikely. You have shut off their communication.

Cue Bidding First Round Control

After trump is established, many people play a bid of another suit shows first round control of that suit, either an Ace or a void. This doesn't require that you bid opponents' suit. Look at the following bidding.

Partner	RHO	You	LHO
1 Spade	Pass	3 Spades	Pass
4 Clubs	Pass	4 Diamonds	

You have already agreed on trump. Your partner's bid of 4 Clubs is a slam try, probably telling you that she has a good Club suit and asking you to further describe your hand. Your 4 Diamond bid tells her that you either have the Ace of Diamonds or a Diamond unbid suit after you have agreed upon a trump suit. Clearly you aren't going to introduce Diamonds as a possible trump suit after you've agreed that Spades, a major, is going to be trump. So a cue bid doesn't necessarily have to be a bid of opponents' suit.

There are other types of cue bids. One of their big advantages is that they force your partner to bid because she can't pass you out in a bid of opponents' suit or a previously unbid suit after an agreement on another suit as trump. But it can be dangerous unless you have a firm partnership agreement and understanding about what your cue bid means.

Splinters

This is an advanced bidding technique, but it's such a nice descriptive bid that I'm going to teach it to you. It doesn't come up often, but when it does it describes your hand to a "T."

A *splinter* is a bid by responder (generally, although opener may splinter, also) that shows four-card trump support, a singleton or void and opening hand values. It's generally made in response to a major suit opening, although it may be made in response to a minor suit opening.

Let's say your partner opens 1 Heart and you hold the following:

♠ KQJ
♥ A987
♦ 4
♣ KT987

That's a pretty good hand, don't you think? It's one you'd open. If you didn't have a specialized bid, you'd probably bid 2 Clubs, then jump to 4 Hearts, depending on your partner's response. However, is there a way to tell your partner that you have a singleton Diamond? Can you think of a way? Maybe kick her twice under the table?

Okay, that's illegal, so you don't want to do that. How do you tell your partner that you have an unusual hand here and describe it in one bid?

Give up? The answer, as you might have guessed, is that you make a splinter bid. I love this bid. How do you splinter? You make a *double jump* shift bid and bid your singleton (or void, as the case may be).

So in response to your partner's opening bid of 1 Heart, you bid 4 Diamonds (skipping 2 Diamonds and 3 Diamonds)! That tells your partner three things in one bid:

♦ You have a singleton or void in Diamonds.

♦ You have at least four cards in her opening bid, Hearts.

♦ Your hand has opening values, at least 13 points.

All that information in one bid! Is that terrific, or what? The bid is obviously game forcing and it's exploring for slam.

The problem with the bid is that if you're not used to it, your partner could misinterpret it and pass. Then you're playing the contract in your singleton. That's not much fun. So if you decide you want to play splinters, and there's a little more to them than this, be sure you and your partner are on the same wavelength.

That's all I'm going to say on splinters. Actually, that's all I knew about them when I started playing them. You have to start. Then when you bid a splinter and you get into it, something will come up and you'll say to yourself, "Gee, I wonder how we should handle that?" You'll look into it or ask someone and you'll learn something new. The worst way to learn something new is to try to learn *everything* about it immediately. So I'm not going to teach you everything. Just learn this much and try it. It doesn't come up often, but when it does you'll try it and when it works you'll feel wonderful.

Just remember, when you open the bidding and your partner skips not one, but two levels of bidding in her first response, she's doing something very unusual and that should alert you that this is a splinter and that she's telling you she has a singleton or void.

The Jacoby Transfer

Contrary to what you may be thinking, this is not a new rock group. In fact, this is one of the most ingenious conventions in Bridge, and one of the easiest to learn. This is a convention that a lot of Rubber Bridge players don't play, so you should be prepared to play Stayman only. But this is a great bid, and I'm including it here so you'll know what it is and be able to play it with people who know it.

Have you ever envied Svengali? Have you ever wished you could train someone like Pavlov trained his dogs? In short, have you ever wanted to have total control over someone? The Jacoby Transfer will give you a taste of what Svengali and Pavlov experienced. Maybe your partner won't drool, but if you play the Jacoby Transfer, you can control exactly what she says by what you say.

What if you heard your partner open with 1 No Trump and looked at your hand and saw that you had only 2 points, but six Spades? Your partner, by opening 1 No Trump, has told you several things:

- She has 15 to 17 points, no more, no less.

- She has a balanced hand with no voids or singletons, and no more than two doubletons.

You have a maximum of 19 points between you, your 2 and her maximum of 17. Because you need 25 points to make game, you aren't going anywhere. But you know that the best place to play this contract is in 2 Spades because you are assured of at least an eight-card trump fit in Spades (because your partner couldn't have opened 1 No Trump without at least two cards in each suit; remember, no singletons or voids when you open 1 No Trump).

If you pass and your partner plays it in 1 No Trump, she could be set; if you could play it in 2 Spades, however, you'd have a much better chance of making the contract. However, if you bid 2 Spades, you have two big problems:

- First, your partner won't know the size of your hand. Do you have 2 points or 10? Does she pass or bid on after you bid 2 Spades?

- Second, if you end up playing in Spades, you'll be playing the contract and your partner will put her hand down as dummy. What's so bad about this? Well, everyone at the table knows that your partner has 15 to 17 points. If you're playing in 2 Spades, they also know that you don't have much. They can see the dummy and know fairly well what's in each other's hand. Ergo, they can easily defend, knowing that what's not in their hand is probably in their partner's hand.

So the problems are: How to tell your partner you don't have much, and, at the same time, tell her that you have six Spades, and, communicate both bits of information to her in a way that results in her playing the hand so your hand is dummy!

Hard problem? It was until Mr. Jacoby came along with a better idea. The gist of the Jacoby Transfer is that when your partner opens 1 No Trump …

- ◆ If responder bids 2 Diamonds, opener must bid 2 Hearts.

- ◆ If responder bids 2 Hearts, opener must bid 2 Spades.

In the previous hand, you would bid 2 Hearts, your partner would bid 2 Spades and, because your hand stinks, you would then pass and she'd play the hand in 2 Spades. Opener has no choice here. If you bid 2 Hearts in response to her 1 No Trump opening, opener *must* bid 2 Spades.

Tricks of the Trade

One final caveat, however, before you move on to the next section: *Both partners must be playing Jacoby Transfer for it to work!*

Remember that when one partner opens 1 No Trump, the other partner becomes the captain of the hand. *You have to trust your partner!* The responder knows opener's hand as a specific, balanced 15 to 17 points. Responder's hand is undefined, so responder places the contract. One of the beauties of the Jacoby Transfer is that responder makes the decision. With six Spades and 2 points, the contract is played by opener in 2 Spades.

Any time you have a five-card major and your partner opens 1 No Trump, you can transfer. Even if you have no points, it would be better to play in 2 of your major, with an assured seven-card trump fit, than to force your partner to play in a more questionable 1 No Trump.

Responder's Bid After Partner Accepts Transfer

Going on, if you have an invitational hand (8 to 9 points) and five cards in your suit, you bid 2 No Trump in response to your partner's bid. That tells your partner exactly what you have. If she has three cards in your suit and is at the top of her range, she goes to 4. If she isn't at the top of her range with three cards in your suit, she closes out at the 3 level. If she only has two cards in your suit and a maximum, she goes to 3

No Trump. If she only has two cards in your suit and not a maximum, she passes 2 No Trump.

With six cards or more, and a 7- to 8-point invitational hand, you, as responder, bid 3 of your major in response to her 2 bid. With a six-card suit and 10 points, you go to game in your major in response to her 2 bid. With less than 8 points, you pass her 2 bid. Following is a chart showing responder's rebid.

Responder's Hand	Responder's Rebid
Less than 8 points	Pass
Five-card suit, 8-9 points	2 No Trump
Six-card suit, 8-9 points	3 of your suit
Five-card suit, 10+ points	3 No Trump
Six-card suit, 10+ points	4 of your suit

Why is the fact that opener might have three cards in the suit to which responder is transferring so magical in the discussion of Jacoby Transfer? Because responder might be transferring with a five-card suit. At responder's first bid, opener doesn't know how many cards responder has in her suit. Responder tells opener how many she has by her next bid. If her next bid is No Trump, she only has five. If she rebids her suit, she has six or more. At that point, the captaincy changes back to opener because she now knows a lot about responder's hand and the decision where to play the hand and at what level is opener's responsibility. Opener knows that responder either has five or six (or more) cards in her suit. After responder's rebid, opener also knows she either has 7-8 points or 10 points. Opener places the contract based on how many points she has (15 to 16, or 17) and how many cards she has in responder's suit. Following is a chart showing opener's third bid.

Responder's Rebid	Opener's Hand	Opener's Rebid
2 No Trump	Two cards in responder's suit, 15–16 points	Pass
2 No Trump	Three cards in responder's suit, 15–16 points	3 of responder's suit
3 of a suit	15–16 points	Pass
3 of a suit	17 points	4 of responder's suit
3 No Trump	Two cards in responder's suit	Pass
3 No Trump	Three or more cards in responder's suit	4 of responder's suit

The Least You Need to Know

- The strip and end play allows you to force opponents to either lead into a tenace or give you a ruff and a sluff.

- A preemptive jump shift tells your partner that you have 5 points or less in your hand, a six-card suit, and you don't have three cards in any major suit she bid.

- D0P1 is used to tell your partner how many Aces you have when opponents interfere with Blackwood and stands for "Double = Zero, Pass = One."

- A cue bid can be a bid of opponent's suit promising a limit raise or better, or a bid of an unbid suit at a high level after agreement on trump showing first round control.

- A splinter is a double jump shift that shows four-card trump support, opening hand values, and a singleton in the suit bid.

- Jacoby Transfer requires a partner who opens 1 No Trump to bid the next higher-ranking suit when responder bids 2 Diamonds or 2 Hearts.

Chapter 25

For More Advanced Idiots

In This Chapter

- Roman Key Card Blackwood, Defensive bids against No Trump, and New minor forcing

- Two over one

- Reverse Drury and semiforcing No Trump

- Two-suited hands

- Western Cue bid

Although the principles covered thus far in this book will allow a new player to learn the game and compete without apology in a normal game of Bridge, quite a few advanced techniques can greatly increase your competency. The bidding methods presented in this chapter are used widely by experienced players. Although they are not absolutely necessary, and although you can play a perfectly acceptable game of Bridge without them, if you learn them and play with a partner who also plays them, you will find your abilities and enjoyment of the game substantially enhanced.

Roman Key Card Blackwood

One of the finest conventions in use is the Blackwood convention, in which 4 No Trump is used to ask your partner how many Aces she has. For game bidding, this information is unimportant; for slam bidding, however, you do not want to see the opponents take the first two tricks with Aces.

Blackwood does have a drawback. The following hand raised some eyebrows when it came up. You have the West hand and are lucky to hear your partner open with 1 Diamond. You bid 1 Spade and partner raises to 2 Spades. Depending on what your partner has, you may be able to take as many as 13 tricks. So you ask for Aces and your partner bids 5 Diamonds, showing one. What now?

West	*East*
♠ AQ763	♠ T842
♥ 4	♥ AKQT
♦ K2	♦ QJ83
♣ AKJT3	♣ 8

The player holding this hand bid 6 Spades and found that it was too high. The defenders took their Ace of Diamonds and even though the Spade finesse worked, declarer lost a trick when South had the KJ9 of Spades. Bad slam.

A new version of Blackwood has been uncovered that addresses problems like this one. It is called *Roman Key Card Blackwood*. It works like this. Instead of the 4 No Trump bid asking responder for Aces, it asks responder how many key cards he has. A key card is defined as one of the four Aces and the King of trumps, a total of five key cards. Here are the responses to 4 No Trump:

　　5 Clubs: shows 0 or 3 key cards

　　5 Diamonds: shows 1 or 4 key cards

　　5 Hearts: shows 2 key cards without the Queen of trump

　　5 Spades: shows 2 key cards with the Queen of trump

If your bidding has not established a trump suit, then the last bid suit is treated as the trump suit in responding to 4 No Trump. For example, if the bidding has gone ...

North	East	South	West
1 Spade	Pass	2 Hearts	Pass
3 Diamonds	Pass	4 No Trump	Pass

North responds as if Diamonds is trump, so the key cards are the four Aces and the King of Diamonds. If, on the other hand, you have agreed on trump, like 1 Spade–Pass–3 Spades–Pass–4 No Trump, trump is, obviously, Spades, and the key cards are the four Aces and the King of Spades.

In the previous hand where West bid to slam and went down, East would bid 5 Diamonds, showing one key card. West would know that two key cards were missing and would stop at 5 Spades.

When responder bids 5 Hearts or 5 Spades, the 4 No Trump bidder knows about every important card, including the Queen of trumps.

When responder bids 5 Clubs or 5 Diamonds, the 4 No Trump bidder is not sure about the Queen of trumps. If she wishes to learn more, she can do so by making the cheapest available bid that is not 5 of the trump suit:

1 Heart	3 Hearts
4 No Trump	5 Clubs
?	

In this case, the bid that asks for the Queen of trumps is 5 Diamonds. Responder bids as follows.

- If she does not have the Queen of trumps, she returns to the trump suit as cheaply as possible. In this case, she would bid 5 Hearts.

- If she does have the Queen of trumps, and no other Kings, she bids 5 No Trump. Otherwise she bids 6 of the suit in which she has the King if that King is lower ranking than the trump suit. If she has the Queen of trumps and a King that is higher ranking than trump, she bids 5 No Trump and lies about having a King.

Bridgebit

Roman Key Card Blackwood is a good convention that is not widely used yet. If you want to play this convention, be very sure that you have talked about it. Here is one rule you must follow: Never bid 4 No Trump unless your partner knows what suit is trumps. A sensible rule to follow is that if you have a fit, that is the trump suit. If you do not yet have a fit, the trump suit is the last-bid suit. You do not want to ask for key cards thinking Hearts are trump and have your partner thinking Clubs are trump.

Defense Against No Trump

When opponents open 1 No Trump, it effectively squeezes your ability to describe your hand to your partner. You could make an overcall, but you're at the 2 level and if you have a two-suited hand, you might be at the 3 or 4 level before you can mention your second suit. This is why the various *conventional bids* were devised for use when opponents open 1 No Trump.

Lingo

A **conventional bid** is one that doesn't mean what it says, like when you bid 2 Clubs in response to an opening 1 No Trump bid. Your 2 Clubs bid does not show that you have Clubs, but says something completely different. It is a request for your partner to bid a four-card major suit, if she has one.

Alert

Assuming you give a 1 No Trump opening bid a little respect, it is wise to have the policy that bidding against it is a good idea. If you let your opponents have the bidding to themselves, it is much easier for them to bid accurately. You can do a lot to inconvenience their bidding by bidding.

However, you must remember the purpose of defensive conventional bids. They are not necessarily to get you to the correct contract. They are basically to disturb the bidding of the opponents, one of whom has 40 percent of the available HCP in his hand.

When an opponent opens 1 No Trump, showing 15 to 17 HCP, your side is probably outgunned. But you should not assume that you should be quiet. There are many reasons for bidding. First, you may actually be able to make something. If so, you do not want to be shut out. Second, even if you can't make a contract if you are able to make a bid, you may be able to bother your opponents' bidding enough that they misjudge the hand.

One obvious thing you can do is double, which usually means that you have a hand at least as good as theirs. You should not double with less than 15 HCP. Also it helps if you have a good suit to lead.

The other thing you can do is bid something if you have a good suit and distribution. Note that because the opener has promised 15 to 17 HCP, your side should not be thinking of bidding games unless you find a very good fit. Take a look at the following hands after your RHO has opened 1 No Trump:

1. ♠ AJT874	2. ♠ KQ874	3. ♠ AJ984	4. ♠ K2	5. ♠ QJ3
♥ 3	♥ K8	♥ 3	♥ A76	♥ K543
♦ QJ87	♦ QJ8	♦ KQT64	♦ AQ7	♦ AK
♣ 43	♣ QJ4	♣ 95	♣ QJT86	♣ Q764

Hand 1: You do not have that much in high cards, but you have a good six-card suit and you have nice distribution. All you need from partner is a couple of Spades and a few cards in the right places. Given that you have the ingredients for a bid, you should take the optimistic view and bid.

Hand 2: You have more points, but you have a balanced hand with only a five-card suit. It is much wiser to pass with hands like this one. Remember this: If your partner has a few points, you may be able to set 1 No Trump. If your partner does not have a few points or if she has bad Spades, you could be in trouble in a 2 Spades contract.

Hand 3: This hand is different. If you are thinking that you would like to bid with this hand, you are right. You have only 10 points, but they are all in your two suits. Also you have good spot cards as well. But which suit should you bid? See the discussion in the section "Hamilton, Cappelletti Pottage."

Hand 4: This is the kind of hand that should double. You have 16 points, but equally as important, you have a fine opening lead. It is true that if your partner is broke, your opponents will make 1 No Trump doubled; if your partner has a few points, however, you will do well. Do not take the view that when they open 1 No Trump, you should automatically retire from the bidding.

Hand 5: This hand has 15 HCP, but it has no good suit to lead. No rule says you have to bid when you have 15 or 16 HCP. With poor-quality points and with no useful 10 spots, you should pass and wait for a different battle.

If you decide to bid a suit against a strong No Trump or if you decide to make one of the bids that shows two suits, high card points are not nearly as important as the quality of your suits. If you have two five-card suits with 8 HCP in your two suits and perhaps a 10 spot, too, bidding is fine. If you have, for instance, 11 HCP but only 5 of them in your two suits, it is more dangerous to bid. In like fashion, if you have only one suit to bid, you need at least QJ9854. Suits like Q87543 or K97432 should be avoided unless you have additional useful points elsewhere. This is not an area of bidding where you can specify such, and such points are required.

Let's go back to the third hand. It is the most frequent kind of hand you will have for bidding against a strong 1 No Trump opening bid:

♠ AJ984
♥ 3
♦ KQT64
♣ 95

If you guess to bid 2 Spades, you will be okay if your partner has Spades; if she has one Spade and three or four Diamonds, however, Diamonds will be your best suit by far. Likewise, if you bid 2 Diamonds, you might find your partner with bad Diamonds and good Spades. How can you ensure getting to the right suit?

I'm going to teach you the two most commonly used conventional defenses against No Trump, although there are others.

Landy

The oldest convention in use against an opening 1 No Trump bid is Landy. It works very simply. When your RHO bids 1 No Trump (or if your LHO bids 1 No Trump, which is passed to you), you bid as follows:

- **Double.** You have a penalty hand, usually with a nice 15 points or better.

- **2 Clubs.** You have both major suits, Spades and Hearts, usually five of each. This way you show both of your suits at once and because they are the majors, they are the two most important suits to show. This can be exciting because the 2 Clubs bidder may bid this way with no Clubs at all. Like all conventions, it is important that your partnership remember them. Remember that you need 8 or more good HCP in your suits if you are going to make this bid.

- **2 Diamonds.** You have a good Diamond suit, almost surely six or more, and the expectation that you can take six or more tricks. You must have a good suit. Keep in mind that your partner might have a singleton. Suits like KT7642 will not be good trump suits if your partner has no support.

The bids 2 Hearts and 2 Spades say essentially the same thing. You have a nice six-card suit and likely good shape, such as you have on Hand 1 in the previous example.

In all of these cases, your partner should pass unless she has something obvious to say. If she has support and unexpected distribution and some points, she can raise. Normally she passes.

Landy is a fine convention, but it has one drawback: It allows you to show both major suits, but it is not so good when you have two other suits. This is where the scientists of the world got busy and developed Hamilton, Cappelletti, and Pottage.

> **Bridgebit**
>
> Landy is named after its creator, Alvin Landy (1905–1967), who received his law degree from Western Reserve University in 1927 and served in World War II. He was Life Master #24 in the American Contract Bridge League.

Hamilton, Cappeletti, and Pottage

Here are the rules for Hamilton:

- ◆ **Double.** You have a 1 No Trump opening hand (15 to 18 HCP), and your opponents bid it before you could.

- ◆ **2 Clubs.** You have a one-suited hand. Your suit must be at least six cards in length. The suit is undefined. This says nothing about Clubs. IF your partner wants to know which suit you have, she bids 2 Diamonds. As always, if you are making a bid that shows one suit or two suits, you have good suits.

- ◆ **2 Diamonds.** You are 5–5 in the major suits (Hearts and Spades). This says nothing about Diamonds.

- ◆ **2 Hearts.** You have a five-card Heart suit and five cards in an undesignated minor.

- ◆ **2 Spades.** You have a five-card Spade suit and five cards in an undesignated minor.

> **Bridgebit**
>
> It has many names because, serendipitously, three different players invented it at the same time. In California, Fred Hamilton came up with the idea. On the East Coast, it was Michael Cappelletti. In Europe, it was Julian Pottage. For our purposes here, we'll refer it to it as Hamilton.

> **Bridgebit**
>
> Here is a Hamilton trick. If the bidding goes Pass (by you)–1 No Trump–Pass–Pass, because you are a passed hand you cannot have a big hand. If your LHO opens 1 No Trump and it is passed to you, you can use a variation of this convention by doubling to say that you have Clubs. Your partner can pass (if she wants to defend 1 No Trump doubled) or retreat to 2 Clubs. If you bid 2 Clubs instead of doubling, you are saying that you have an unknown one-suited hand but Clubs is not one of your suits.

Responding to Partner's Hamilton Bid

If your partner bid …

- ◆ **2 Clubs.** If your RHO player passes, you are expected to bid 2 Diamonds, asking your partner to show her suit. If she has Diamonds she passes 2 Diamonds. Otherwise, she bids her suit if it's passed to her. You can pass 2 Clubs if you have wonderful Clubs and you can bid 2 of a major if you have a very good suit of your own, but 2 Diamonds is bid almost all of the time. If your RHO bids over

2 Clubs, you do not have to do anything. If you have a clear bid, go ahead and bid, but do so only because you have a good hand, not because you feel you have to bid.

♦ **2 Diamonds.** You know that your partner is showing the major suits. Normally you bid 2 of your better major. Ideally you will have three or four cards, but now and then you have to bid a major with only two cards. You may jump in a major if you have 10 nice support points; and if you have 13 or so points with a good fit, you should bid a game.

♦ **2 Hearts.** Your partner has Hearts and one of the minors. If you have two or more Hearts, passing is usually best. If you have lesser Hearts, you can find out which minor your partner has by bidding 2 No Trump. This asks your partner to bid her minor suit. In the event that you have Hearts support and at least 10 support points, raise to 3. If you have 13 or more with a fit, go to game.

♦ **2 Spades.** Your partner has Spades and one of the minor suits. You respond to 2 Spades exactly as you would respond to 2 Hearts.

♦ **Double.** You usually pass and hope to set them, even if you have a poor hand. If you have a hand with distribution and you really are unhappy defending, you can bid as if your partner had opened 1 No Trump. A 2 Clubs bid by you would ask for a major suit, a 2 Diamonds or 2 Hearts bid by you would be a transfer to Hearts or Spades, assuming you are playing Jacoby Transfer.

Quiz

Here are four hands. They open 1 No Trump and your partner makes one of the following bids. What do you do?

2 Clubs
2 Diamonds
2 Hearts
2 Spades
Double

1. ♠ Q9875	2. ♠ 4	3. ♠ A87	4. ♠ AQT876
♥ J83	♥ 84	♥ JT87	♥ 74
♦ 8	♦ K87	♦ Q532	♦ 8
♣ A874	♣ QJ87653	♣ Q6	♣ Q832

If she bids 2 Clubs, showing an unknown long suit …

Hand 1: 2 Diamonds. If she has Diamonds she will pass and you will be declarer. Not lovely, but because your partner has six or more Diamonds, 2 Diamonds is likely to be an okay spot.

Hand 2: Pass. You know that Clubs is your best suit. Pass it out.

Hand 3: 2 Diamonds, asking for partner's suit. Whichever it is will be fine.

Hand 4: 2 Spades. You can, if you have a terrific suit, show it instead of bidding 2 Diamonds, which your partner might pass.

If she bids 2 Diamonds, showing both majors …

Hand 1: 3 Spades (or even 4 Spades if you feel optimistic). You have lovely Spades, nice points, and excellent distribution.

Hand 2: 2 Hearts and hope you are not doubled.

Hand 3: 2 Hearts. You almost have enough to bid 3 Hearts.

Hand 4: 4 Spades. Your partner has both majors and you have a terrific hand for Spades.

If she bids 2 Hearts, showing a Hearts suit and one of the minor suits …

Hand 1: Pass. Almost worth a raise.

Hand 2: Pass. Your partner has five Hearts. This will be an okay spot. If you are doubled, you can retreat to 3 Clubs.

Hand 3: Pass, but no real fault if you judged to bid 3.

Hand 4: 2 Spades. You know Spades is a fair spot. If you choose to pass 2 Hearts, that is not terrible.

If she bids 2 Spades, showing a Spades suit and one of the minor suits …

Hand 1: 4 Spades. What a nice partner you have.

Hand 2: 2 No Trump. Your partner will bid her minor, which you are sure is Diamonds.

Hand 3: Pass. If partner has Diamonds, you might prefer to play there, but with 3 Spades you know you are in a nice contract.

Hand 4: 4 Spades.

If she doubles, showing an opening 1 No Trump hand or better …

Hand 1: Pass. You should trounce 1 No Trump doubled. If you want to get to Spades, bid 2 Hearts, a transfer to Spades.

Hand 2: 3 Clubs. 2 Clubs is Stayman. 3 Clubs is natural.

Hand 3: Pass and expect to get rich. (If you have 2 points instead of 9, you should pass with this distribution. Setting 1 No Trump doubled is more likely than you finding a good place for your pair to play the hand as declarer.)

Hand 4: 2 Hearts, transferring to Spades, and then raise to game.

New Minor Forcing

Your partner opens with one of a suit and you bid a major. Your partner rebids 1 No Trump. What do you bid with this hand?

♠ KJ874
♥ 87
♦ AJ8
♣ QT4

2 Spades is too weak a bid. Opener will pass it most of the time, and that might cause you to miss a game.

3 Spades is too strong a bid. If your partner has a minimum with only two Spades, you could be too high.

A good solution is called *New Minor Forcing* (NMF). It works this way.

If your partner rebids 1 No Trump, and you have a five-card major with invitational values, you can bid 2 of the unbid minor suit. If the bidding started with 1 Heart–Pass–1 Spade, you have to use 2 Clubs as your asking bid.

Your bid promises at least invitational values (10 HCP and a five-card major), and it is possible that you have more. Your main intent with the NMF bid is to find out whether your partner has a fit for your major.

If your partner has three-card support, she bids 2 of your major with a minimum and 3 of your major with a maximum. If she does not have a fit, she shows 4 of the other major if she has it. If she cannot bid a major, she bids 2 No Trump with a minimum and 3 No Trump with a maximum.

Quiz

Now you're ready to take the following quiz.

West	North	East	South
1 Diamond	Pass	1 Spade	Pass
1 No Trump	Pass	?	

1. ♠ QJ874	2. ♠ AQ874	3. ♠ KT874	4. ♠ J9874
♥ 32	♥ Q73	♥ AK	♥ T9764
♦ QJ7	♦ 73	♦ K873	♦ A3
♣ KJ8	♣ K73	♣ 98	♣ 9

Hand 1: Pass. You have a balanced hand with too few points to worry about game. It is quite acceptable to forget about the Spades.

Hand 2: 2 Clubs, NMF. You have enough points to invite game. If your partner bids 2 Spades, you will know she has a minimum opening with three Spades; if she bids 3 Spades, you will know she has a maximum opening with three Spades. You will go to game if she shows a maximum. If she bids 2 Diamonds, denying a major holding, or 2 Hearts, showing four Hearts but denying three Spades, you will bid 2 No Trump. She can go on to 3 No Trump with a maximum.

Hand 3: 2 Clubs, NMF. You have game points but want to check whether 4 Spades is the right game or 3 No Trump.

Hand 4: 2 Hearts. This is a rare situation. This is just about the only auction where responder can bid a new suit, which does not force opener to bid again. This auction occurs when your partner rebids 1 No Trump and you are able to show Spades and then Hearts. You are allowed to bid 1 Spade and then 2 Hearts when you have five Spades and four or five Hearts and less than 10 HCP.

Tricks of the Trade

Often, players are tempted to use NMF with less-than invitational hands. Don't succumb to this temptation because by making a NMF bid you are promising your partner specific values. If you make it without them, you don't know what your partner is going to do. She might have a big hand and take you to a game or slam, relying on your bid, when you don't belong there. Bridge is a game of trusting your partner. If you unilaterally deviate from your agreements, you are just making it more difficult for your partner to trust you.

If your partner has opened 1 Club instead of 1 Diamond, the NMF bid would be Diamonds rather than Clubs. That's why it's called "new" minor. You bid the unbid minor suit to show your hand. However, if the bidding goes 1 Club–1 Diamond–1 No Trump, the NMF bid is 2 Clubs, even though you have bid it.

Two-over-One System

In Standard American, which is what this book teaches, if you have a five-card suit and 10 points and your partner has opened the bidding by bidding 1 of a suit, you may bid your suit at the 2 level. In such event, when responder bids a new suit, opener is required to bid again. It's "forcing for one round."

A very popular system that is used by almost all tournament players is one called the Two-over-One system. In this system, when a player makes a Two-over-One response such as 1 Diamond–Pass–2 Clubs, she promises enough points that the partnership can make a game. Because of this, all subsequent bidding is game forcing, even if it sounds weak.

Take this auction:

West	East
1 Spade	2 Clubs
2 Diamonds	2 Spades

East responds with 2 Clubs and then gives a preference to Spades. In standard bidding, this sequence shows at least 10 points with Spades support. It is invitational. In Two-over-One bidding, the rebid of 2 Spades shows that in addition to the values of an opening bid promised by the initial response of 2 Clubs; it also shows Spades support. Although in Standard American this could be passed by opener, in Two over One, all bids after the initial Two-over-One response are forcing to game, so the opener must bid again.

The advantage to this is that there is no need for jumping around in the bidding. Bidding space can be used to find the best fit and then determine whether to play in 3 No Trump or in a suit or in a slam. If someone does jump, it is not because that player has extra points but because that player has some important distributional feature to show.

If you play the Two-over-One system, however, if your partner opens the bidding at the 1 level and you make a nonjump response at the 2 level, such as 1 Diamond–Pass–2 Clubs, your partner (opener) must keep the bidding open until one of you has bid game. Because this is a game-forcing bid, this can obviously cause a lot of bidding problems. What if your partner opens 1 Spade and you hold the following:

♠ 53
♥ KQ97
♦ 94
♣ AJT53

That's not a bad hand. But you can't bid 2 Clubs because that would force your partner to bid to game and, if partner has a minimum opener, you probably can't make game. You can't pass and you can't bid 2 Clubs and you can't bid 2 Spades because (1) you're too strong for such a weak bid, and (2) you don't have three Spades, which this response promises. What to do?

The answer is a bid that was created for the Two-over-One system, Forcing No Trump.

The Forcing 1 No Trump Response

This system has a built-in problem just shown, but fortunately there is an answer, and that is to play that a 1 No Trump response to an opening bid of one of a Major is forcing for one round, and one round only. The idea is that because you can't go to the 2 level with 10 or 11 points, you have to have a waiting bid that allows you to show your points on the next round.

If you have 6 to 11 points and your partner opens with a bid that doesn't allow you to make a response at the 1 level, you bid 1 No Trump. This is *forcing* for one round. That is, your partner must make another bid. In an ordinary Standard American auction, a 1 No Trump response is generally an invitation to pass because it's describing the hand. If you've opened a minimum, your partner's response of 1 No Trump is telling you that you probably don't have game, and you may pass, and often do.

If you're playing Forcing No Trump, however, if you opened and your partner bid 1 No Trump, you must say "forcing" to tell opponents that you are required to bid again. Look at the following hands for examples of hands where you would bid 1 No Trump Forcing after your partner opens 1 Spade:

1. ♠ J4	2. ♠ 3	3. ♠ 8	4. ♠ 7	5. ♠ 2
♥ A984	♥ KQ984	♥ 873	♥ QJ74	♥ 7653
♦ K873	♦ 876	♦ AJ873	♦ 9	♦ 8732
♣ J84	♣ Q872	♣ K874	♣ KJ98763	♣ AQ84

A 1 No Trump response to a major usually shows a 6 to 9 point hand that you would have bid 1 No Trump with in standard bidding. In Two-over-One bidding, however, the 1 No Trump response can show invitational hands, too.

How Does Opener Bid After a Forcing 1 No Trump Response?

Opener follows a set of rules. If she has a strong or invitational hand, she makes the same rebid she would make in standard bidding. It is when she has minimum hands that her bidding has a couple of odd twists:

- If opener has a six-card major, she rebids it.

- If opener started with 1 Spade and happens to have four Hearts, she bids 2 Hearts.

- If opener has six Spades and four Hearts, she bids her stronger major.

- If opener has a four- or five-card minor, she bids it.

- If opener has a balanced hand without a six-card suit and without a four-card suit, she bids her lower three-card minor. Responder knows that opener may have to bid a three-card minor, so she will treat this suit gingerly.

Once a year, opener has four Spades and five Hearts and two in each minor. What you do is bid a brave 2 Clubs and hope that nothing bad happens.

If opener has a good balanced hand, she bids 2 No Trump with 18 to 19 HCP. If she has a little less, she bids according to the list above and later can bid 2 No Trump when she has 17 HCP.

Quiz

Find out if you can solve the following challenge:

South	West	North	East
1 Spade	Pass	1 No Trump	Pass
?			

	1.	♠ QT9874	2.	♠ AKQ84	3.	♠ KQJ84	4.	♠ AJ743	5.	♠ J8763
		♥ 3		♥ J874		♥ KQ		♥ K3		♥ AQ
		♦ KQ8		♦ K3		♦ AJ8		♦ AQ82		♦ AQ8
		♣ AJ4		♣ 73		♣ K84		♣ T8		♣ 873

Hand 1: 2 Spades, showing a six-card suit and a minimum hand.

Hand 2: 2 Hearts, showing four Hearts. Don't worry that your Spades are so good and your Hearts so bad.

Hand 3: 2 No Trump. You promise 18 to 19 HCP, so you do not have to worry that this is too conservative. You have exactly what you promise.

Hand 4: 2 Diamonds. You don't have a six-card suit or a four-card Hearts suit, so you bid your four-card minor.

Hand 5: 2 Clubs. Do not bid 2 Diamonds. Yes, the Clubs are bad and the Diamonds good, but bidding Clubs leaves the partnership more room to bid. If you bid 2 Clubs, you can always get to Diamonds if your partner wants to bid them. If you bid 2 Diamonds and your partner has good Clubs, she has to go to the 3 level.

After opener makes her rebid, responder continues with her second bid, which describes what she really has. Responder can pass opener's rebid, but most of the time she finds a second bid. Here is one example auction with some examples of how responder bids on the second round with the minimum hands shown above in which you responded with a forcing 1 No Trump.

South	West	North	East
1 Spade	Pass	1 No Trump	Pass
2 Diamonds	Pass	?	

	1.	♠ J4	2.	♠ 3	3.	♠ 8	4.	♠ 7	5.	♠ 2
		♥ A984		♥ KQ984		♥ 873		♥ QJ74		♥ 7653
		♦ K873		♦ 876		♦ AJ873		♦ 9		♦ 8732
		♣ J84		♣ Q872		♣ K874		♣ KJ98763		♣ AQ84

Hand 1: 2 Spades. Give a preference to Spades. You did not raise the first time, so your partner will expect only two.

Hand 2: 2 Hearts. You can show a good suit at the 2 level without implying extra points. Your 1 No Trump bid suggested you had a weak hand.

Hand 3: 3 Diamonds. With 8 to 10 points and five cards in your partner's minor suit, you can raise. Be aware that she may have only three Diamonds.

Hand 4: 3 Clubs. You hate partner's suits and you have a good one of your own. You do not promise a good hand, just a long suit.

Hand 5: Pass. You have nowhere to go, and you do have four Diamonds. Hopefully, partner has four, too.

Some Problem Hands

Here are some problem hands of a different sort. It is possible that the forcing 1 No Trump bidder has an invitational hand. It happens about one hand in five.

South	West	North	East
1 Heart	Pass	1 No Trump	Pass
2 Clubs	Pass	?	

1. ♠ 83
   ♥ AJ8
   ♦ 873
   ♣ KQ873

2. ♠ K84
   ♥ 3
   ♦ AQT976
   ♣ J87

3. ♠ K83
   ♥ 87
   ♦ AJ874
   ♣ QJ7

Hand 1: 3 Hearts. You have a hand worth a limit raise in Hearts, but you only have three-card support. Bidding 1 No Trump and jumping to 3 of your partner's major is how you show a three-card limit raise. It is important that you do not bid 3 Hearts with this on the first round. Partner would expect a fourth trump. Do not be distracted by your Clubs support.

Hand 2: 3 Diamonds. You are not strong enough to bid 2 Diamonds originally, so start with 1 No Trump, forcing. Partner bid 2 Clubs, and that leaves you room to bid 2 Diamonds or 3 Diamonds. With a maximum hand and with a six-card suit, you can jump to show this hand.

Hand 3: 2 No Trump. You promise around 11 HCP with stoppers. This is an invitational bid.

Reverse Drury and Semiforcing 1 No Trump

Players have known for a long time that it is wise to open very aggressively in third seat. It is not uncommon to open 1 Spade on a hand like this one:

♠ KQ875
♥ A74
♦ 984
♣ JT

Bidding 1 Spade makes life tougher for the opponents and it may help you on defense, but it comes with a downside. If your partner has a maximum-passed hand, she may start jumping around, getting you too high.

Here are two bidding tricks that are well worth knowing.

Reverse Drury

When your partner opens one of a major in third or fourth seat, you need a way to show your good hands. Often you will have a hand worth 10 or 11 points in support of partner's suit. You might like to jump to 3 of the major, but if she has a weak or subminimum opening bid you may go down.

The answer is this. If you have a limit raise for your partner's major, bid 2 Clubs. This is artificial, stating that you have a maximum-passed hand with at least three-card support. Take the following quiz.

West	North	East	South
		Pass	Pass
1 Spade	Pass	?	

1. ♠ KJ84	2. ♠ J72	3. ♠ JT754	4. ♠ 974
♥ Q83	♥ AK983	♥ 3	♥ 64
♦ Q983	♦ K6	♦ AJ84	♦ AJ43
♣ J3	♣ 732	♣ QT8	♣ KQ97

Hand 1: 2 Spades. Make your normal bid. You need 10 good support points for a Drury bid.

Hand 2: 2 Clubs. This is the Drury bid. It says nothing about Clubs. It says you have better than a normal raise, typically a good 10 points and up. Do not bid 2 Hearts. Your partner can pass a Two-over-One bid when you are a passed hand.

Hand 3: 3 Spades. The jump raise is still the limit, but it promises excellent trumps and a singleton. If you do not have a singleton, your hand is somewhat balanced and is better handled by using Drury.

Hand 4: 2 Clubs, Drury. You do have three trumps and you have 11 HCP along with a doubleton.

Opener Rebids After Your Partner's Drury Bid

When opener rebids after your partner's Drury bid:

- ◆ **2 Diamonds**. Opener says she has a full opening bid and is interested in game if responder has a good Drury hand. It is possible that opener has a very big hand and is waiting to see what responder does next. Opener may have real Diamonds, but she may just be wanting to see what responder thinks.

- ◆ **2 of the major.** In this case, 2 Spades. If opener rebids her major, it shows a weak hand and denies any possibility of game. Responder should pass.

Opener can bid other things besides 2 Diamonds or 2 of the major. Other bids confirm a full opening bid, too.

West	North	East	South
		Pass	Pass
1 Spade	Pass	2 Clubs	Pass
?			

1. ♠ AKJ87
   ♥ 87
   ♦ Q87
   ♣ 873

2. ♠ Q9874
   ♥ 3
   ♦ AKT8
   ♣ KT5

3. ♠ J9874
   ♥ AK
   ♦ 92
   ♣ AQ84

4. ♠ KJ98743
   ♥ 2
   ♦ AK7
   ♣ AQ

5. ♠ QJ874
   ♥ KQJ
   ♦ KQ9
   ♣ AJ

6. ♠ KJ763
   ♥ KQ
   ♦ Q98
   ♣ QT4

Hand 1: 2 Spades. You have less than an opening bid and want your partner to pass. When opener rebids the major, responder always passes no matter how good his passed hand happens to be.

Hand 2: 2 Diamonds. Counting distribution, you have better than a minimum. You are willing to go to game if your partner has a maximum hand. If your partner has a minimum Drury hand, she will bid 2 Spades and you will pass.

Hand 3: 4 Spades. Counting distribution, you have around 16 points and your partner has 10 or more with Spades support. Bid game. Do not bother bidding Clubs. Why tell the opponents something you prefer they do not know?

Hand 4: 4 No Trump. Ask for Aces and bid a slam if Partner has one or two Aces. You have about 22 HCP now that Spades have been supported.

Hand 5: 4 Spades. Just bid a game. You have a big hand, but East has a maximum of 11 points. When you know game is worth bidding and when you know there is no slam, do not waste time making bids that you do not have to make.

Hand 6: 2 Spades. This is a 13-HCP hand, but it is balanced and minimum and it has poor-quality points (Queens and Jacks).

If you have a hand with Clubs and no support for your partner's major, you cannot bid 2 Clubs because that would promise support for her major. Bid 1 No Trump and hope for a sane result. Conventions all come with benefits, but they all have the occasional drawbacks, too.

Bridgebit

Doug Drury invented this convention because his partner, Eric Murray, kept opening light in third seat and kept going down a lot. Drury designed this method to cater to Murray's excesses. Originally the opening bidder bid 2 Diamonds to show a weak hand and 2 of the major to show a full opening bid. Then, as always happens, players got their hands on the convention and they dabbled with it and eventually switched the bids so that opener's 2 of a major shows a weak hand and 2 Diamonds shows a good hand. This is sensible because it gives the partnership more bidding room. Reverse Drury is now the most common version.

If your partner uses Drury after you open 1 of a major in third or fourth seat and you have a full opening bid or more, it is usually best to bid 2 Diamonds because it tells the opponents very little about your hand. Bid another suit instead of 2 Diamonds if you see a reason to do so, but for the most part bidding 2 Diamonds is wise.

If your partner opens a major in third or fourth seat and the next player doubles or overcalls 1 Spade, you should continue to use Drury. The rule is that 2 Clubs is the *only* Drury bid. Note that if your RHO overcalls 1 No Trump, the Drury bid does not exist. It works only if your RHO passes, overcalls 1 Spade, or makes a takeout double.

Semiforcing 1 No Trump Response

This is an extension of Two-over-One bidding. If your partner opens in third or fourth seat with 1 of a major and you have a hand that is tempting you to bid 2 No Trump, just bid 1 No Trump. Play that a passed hand 1 No Trump response is semiforcing. Your partner will do one of two things.

- If she has too weak a hand to imagine a game, she passes 1 No Trump.

- If she has a nice 14 or more points or if he has good distribution, she makes her normal rebid.

If opener passes 1 No Trump, your partnership is high enough. If opener bids again, responder can now bid 2 No Trump to say he has a maximum-passed hand.

More Quizzes

Here is a quiz for responder; you are sitting East:

West	North	East	South
		Pass	Pass
1 Spade	Pass	?	

1. ♠ Q
   ♥ J983
   ♦ KT84
   ♣ Q985

2. ♠ J4
   ♥ T874
   ♦ AQT9
   ♣ KJ4

Hand 1: 1 No Trump. The 1 No Trump bid is forcing if you are not a passed hand. Here you have passed, so your 1 No Trump is semiforcing. What this means is that your partner will bid again only if she has a full opening bid. This hand is typical of most of the hands that responder will have for 1 No Trump; 6 to 9 HCP is the expected range.

Hand 2: 1 No Trump. Here you have 11 nice points, about as many as you c have for a passed hand. Still 1 No Trump is the correct bid. Opener will pass bid if she has a minimum hand. If she has 14 or more points, she will rebid wl ever her hand suggests, and then you will bid again to show your extra points.

Here is a quiz for opening bidder; you are sitting West:

West	North	East	South
		Pass	Pass
1 Spade	Pass	1 No Trump	Pass
?			

1. ♠ AJ874
   ♥ 83
   ♦ KQ8
   ♣ Q84

2. ♠ KQ983
   ♥ AJ84
   ♦ K3
   ♣ 73

Hand 1: Pass. The semiforcing 1 No Trump response asks you to bid again if you have 14 or more points. This hand is a minimum opening bid, and you know that because your partner is a passed hand you do not have a game. You also know that your partner does not have Spades support. If she did, she would have raised to 2 Spades or would have bid Drury.

Hand 2: 2 Hearts. You can pass 1 No Trump so when you make a rebid, you promise a good opening bid.

Evaluation of Semiforcing 1 No Trump Responses

If you have adopted a 1 No Trump forcing response to 1 of a major in first and second seat and are comfortable with using this treatment, it is a short step to using the semi-forcing 1 No Trump response after a third and fourth seat opener. It is a very good convention that will help keep your bidding at a safe level on hands where responder has a maximum pass but opener has a rock-bottom minimum or even worse.

Two-Suited Hands

You will definitely want to learn and use two very special conventions: the Unusual No Trump overcall and the Michaels Cue bid. These two conventions have a lot in common, but they also have enough differences that you will want to study them separately.

Unusual No Trump

In its basic form, the bid works like this. Your RHO opens with 1 Heart or 1 Spade and you have a hand with 5–5 in the minors. Something like this:

♠ 3
♥ 43
♦ AQ987
♣ KQJ63

Bridgebit
The Unusual No Trump was invented by Alvin Roth, a name that is synonymous with Bridge theory.

Tricks of the Trade

When your opponents open with 1 of a suit, there is almost no chance that you will have an opening 2 No Trump bid. It is wise to use 2 No Trump for something else, and the Unusual No Trump is ideal. If you ever do have 21 HCP and they open, you can make a takeout double and bid strong later.

If you have the Unusual No Trump bid available, you can bid 2 No Trump, which tells your partner that you have both minors. Because their side has an opening bid, it is unlikely that your side will be able to make many games; if your partner likes one of your suits, however, you may be able to raise the bidding fast enough that their bidding gets off track. It is also possible that you can bid 5 of a minor expecting to go down but not down so much that it is a disaster. If they can make 4 Spades, vulnerable, for example, it is profitable for you to go down only 300 in 5 Clubs doubled. This is known as sacrificing.

After many years of using this convention, players learned that it is useful to change the definition slightly. Instead of saying that 2 No Trump shows the minors, the best definition is to say that it shows the lower two unbid suits. If they open a major, 2 No Trump shows the minors; if they open, say 1 Diamond, however, the 2 No Trump bid would show the two lower unbid suits, which are Hearts and Clubs. Used this way, you will get many additional opportunities to use this convention.

What Do You Need for an Unusual No Trump Bid?

Use caution. Many players, armed with a new convention, go off to war with it and immediately abuse it to the point that it does not work. You can get other viewpoints, but this is the way to start:

♦ **Not vulnerable.** Not less than 9 HCP, and if at the bottom of your range, you must have good suits. You can have any upper range of points, but this is the minimum.

◆ **Vulnerable.** Generally, not less than 12 HCP; if both of your suits are good, however, you can do it with 11 HCP.

You *must* have five cards of the lower two unbid suits to use Unusual No Trump. Many players abuse the bid by using it when they're 5–4 in the two lower unbid suits. Don't succumb to this temptation. Do not do this with only four cards in one of the suits.

Do not use this convention more aggressively than this. Keep in mind that if you make an Unusual No Trump bid, you will be pushing

Tricks of the Trade

The Unusual No Trump bid is usually used after their side opens with 1 of a suit. You can use it after the opponents have bid two suits too. Say they have opened 1 Diamond and responded with 1 Spade. If you have a hand with five Hearts and five Clubs, the two unbid suits, you can bid 2 No Trump here, too.

your partnership to at least the 3 level. If your partner does not like your suits, the last word on this from the opponents may be "Double." Further, if you make an Unusual No Trump bid and the opponents play the hand, they will know of your distribution and will play the hand very well.

Look closely at the following example; no one is vulnerable:

RHO	You
1 Spade	?

1. ♠ 83	**2.** ♠ J	**3.** ♠ 8	**4.** ♠ A72
♥ 3	♥ K3	♥ 9	♥ --
♦ QJ984	♦ Q8763	♦ AKJ74	♦ AQJ87
♣ AQJ53	♣ AJ652	♣ KJT974	♣ KQJT6

Hand 1: 2 No Trump. You have a minimum hand but you have good minor suits. If vulnerable, this is a Pass. Having 5–5 in the minors is not, of itself, an excuse to be bidding.

Hand 2: Pass. You have poor-quality suits. Remember, if you bid with this hand, your partner will be declaring at least the 3 level. If she has a poor hand with no fit for you, someone will double and it will be costly.

Hand 3: 2 No Trump. 5–5 is necessary, but 6–5 is nicer.

Hand 4: 2 No Trump. Your hand is good enough that you intend to bid again.

How Does Responder Bid?

When your partner makes an unusual 2 No Trump bid, it is very important that responder bids what his hand is worth. Here are the basic rules.

Alert

Do not fall into the trap of making an Unusual No Trump bid and then bidding again when you do not have extra values. You need about 15 useful points to bid 2 No Trump and then to consider bidding again. Of course, if your partner shows enthusiasm, you can bid again with less.

◆ **Rule 1.** If you do not have a fit, make a minimum bid unless you have a huge hand.

◆ **Rule 2.** If you do have a good fit, you should be willing to do more than make a minimum bid in one of your partner's suits. If you have 10 or more points with a nice fit, you can jump to the 4 level or you can make a free bid if your RHO has bid something in the meantime. If you have a fit and 14 or so points, you can bid a game. Note that trying to count points is not a perfect solution here because most of the time you are not trying to make a contract. Often you are trying to frustrate your opponents.

All of these themes will come up in the following example, where no one is vulnerable:

LHO	Partner	RHO	You
1 Spade	2 No Trump	Pass	?

1. ♠ QT76	2. ♠ AJ874	3. ♠ T764	4. ♠ Q8763
♥ KJ7653	♥ 975	♥ AJ5	♥ 2
◆ 2	◆ Q87	◆ K986	◆ K4
♣ T5	♣ 84	♣ J7	♣ Q9874

Hand 1: 3 Clubs. Remember this awful hand. If you bid 2 No Trump and your partner bids 3 Clubs, she might have a stinker like this one. If you keep on bidding and she has this hand, there will be trouble. Note that you do not bid 3 Hearts. That would show a better suit and a better hand.

Hand 2: 3 Diamonds. This is not a bad hand. You would like a fourth trump, but this is, relatively speaking, an okay hand. It is not good enough to go to the 4 level, but it is good enough that if your partner goes to the 4 level you will be safe.

Hand 3: 4 Diamonds. This is a nice hand. Your bid of 4 Diamonds shows some honest values. Your partner can bid 5 if she wishes. If East had bid 3 of a major, you would have been happy to bid 4 Diamonds.

Hand 4: 5 Clubs. This is a super hand. You have excellent shape, you have the King of Diamonds, and you have five Clubs. It is not hard to imagine that five Clubs will make.

 Alert

The Unusual No Trump has many applications other than the basic one of showing the two lower unbid suits when bid over an opening bid. As you learn more about this important convention, you will discover that it can be used on far more hands than shown here.

The Michaels Cue Bid

This is a relative of the Unusual No Trump. The Michaels Cue bid is used when an opponent opens with 1 of a minor suit. If you have 5–5 in the majors, you can cue-bid 2 of opener's minor, which states that you have the major suits. The major suits are the powerhouses of Bridge, and when you have both of them you can often win the bidding. This can be done by reaching a makeable contract or by causing your opponents to misjudge what they can make. Because you have the major suits and therefore the important suits, the Michaels Cue bid is much more important than the Unusual No Trump.

The requirements for a Michaels Cue bid are about the same as for the Unusual No Trump:

- **Not vulnerable.** At least 5–5 in the majors and 8 HCP with the points in your suits

- **Vulnerable.** At least 5–5 in the majors and 10 useful HCP

Alert

It is important that the responder to a Michaels Cue bid knows to bid a lot when she has a good hand. If responder fails to bid when she should, the Michaels Cue bidder will not know when her side should be going higher or when it should get out of the auction. In a good partnership, the Michaels bidder knows that when her partner shows no interest, it is likely that she has a bad hand.

The big deal, if you are going to get good results from this convention, is that responder bids what her hand is worth. Many fine Michaels Cue bids go to waste because the partner does not bid enough. Many Michaels hands go down in flames because the Michaels bidder bid again when she should not have done so.

So what would you do with this bid in the following example? Again, no one is vulnerable.

LHO	Partner	RHO	You
1 Club	2 Clubs	Pass	?

1. ♠ 32	2. ♠ Q84	3. ♠ QJ93	4. ♠ AJ87	5. ♠ 43
♥ 94	♥ 82	♥ A4	♥ 2	♥ AQ7
♦ JT974	♦ AJ984	♦ Q9653	♦ AT874	♦ 983
♣ KQJ9	♣ 743	♣ 84	♣ JT4	♣ AJ764

Hand 1: 2 Hearts. Always, when you have equal length in your partner's majors, bid Hearts. There is no particular reason for this. The one thing you should not do is bid 2 No Trump. Forget about playing in No Trump and try to get to a low and undoubled contract when you have a dog like this.

Hand 2: 2 Spades. Remember that partner has 5–5 in the majors. If, by some chance, your opponents bid to 3 Clubs, you can bid 3 Spades with this hand.

Hand 3: 3 Spades. A jump is invitational. It says you are interested in game. Your bid just shows around 11 support points. If RHO bid 3 Clubs, you would also bid 3 Spades.

Hand 4: 4 Spades. Counting your distribution, you have an opening bid in support of Spades. You also have four Spades and you have Aces and shape. It would be sad to bid just 2 or 3 with this fine a hand.

Hand 5: 3 Hearts, even though you have only three of them. Your partner has five, so you know this is good enough support.

Alert

The hands in this section show how important it is that your bids are disciplined and that you don't "stretch" your bid and lie to your partner by either bidding without the promised shape of at least 5–5, or with the promised HCP. Your partner will be trusting you that you have your bid and will bid accordingly. If you bid Michaels with only 3 HCP and your partner jumps to game, as in Hand 4, you could be in a world of hurt. Moral: Be disciplined!

As mentioned earlier, it is important to bid Michaels when appropriate, but you won't get much benefit if your partner does not cooperate with you.

Western Cue Bid

Some time ago a pair of good players had a hand much like this one:

West	*East*
♠ K2	♠ 53
♥ AK974	♥ 32
♦ KJ98	♦ AQT742
♣ 96	♣ AJ4

West	North	East	South
1 Heart	1 Spade	2 Diamonds	2 Spades
3 Diamonds	Pass	4 Clubs	Pass
4 Diamonds	Pass	5 Diamonds	Pass
Pass	Pass		

East played in 5 Diamonds and went down one after a Spade lead. North took two Spades winners, and the defense later got a Club trick when the Heart suit did not divide well.

This is a disaster for East-West because West can make 3 No Trump. There is no defense to it. How do you think the bidding should have gone? Some players thought that West should bid No Trump instead of raising Diamonds, but that seems like a biased view. For all West knew, slam in Diamonds was available.

There is a convention that would have gotten West to 3 No Trump. It has many names, but the most popular is the Western Cue bid.

The way it works is simple. The opponents have bid a suit but your side is marked with most of the HCP. If your side has found a minor suit fit and if it is clear that your side does not have a major suit contract available, a cue-bid of the opponents' suit does not show a control, as do many cue-bids. It instead says, "I think we can make 3 No Trump if you have a stopper in their suit."

On this hand, East could have bid 3 Spades instead of 4 Clubs. West has a Spade stopper and bids 3 No Trump. West is not worried

Tricks of the Trade

A Western Cue bid is almost always made at the 3 level and almost always your side has found a minor suit fit or one of you is known to have a good minor suit.

about Clubs because no one has bid them and, East rates to have something in Clubs given he has shown a good hand.

You do have to be careful about the Western Cue bid. If your side is bidding a major suit, the cue-bid is not the Western Cue bid. It applies only when your side has no major suit fit that you can play in.

♠ AJ
♥ 74
♦ A3
♣ AKQT743

West	North	East	South
1 Club	1 Heart	1 Spade	Pass
?			

West has a super hand and wants to be in game somewhere. If East has a Hearts stopper, 3 No Trump is a likely contract. West might bid 3 Clubs, but that bid is only invitational showing about 17 points and good Clubs. West has much more than that.

Here is where confusion often sets in. If West bids 2 Hearts, that bid should be interpreted by East as a cue-bid for Spades. East will not understand what is wanted of him. What West can do on this hand is to bid 2 Diamonds. Reverses were discussed in Chapter 13. One thing you learned was that a reverse is a forcing bid. If East raises Diamonds, for instance, West can now bid 3 Hearts and that will be interpreted as a Western Cue bid looking for a Hearts stopper.

Here is a more normal example.

West	*East*
♠ AQ	♠ 874
♥ 87	♥ QJ92
♦ AKJ875	♦ Q942
♣ JT8	♣ A9

West	North	East	South
		1 Heart	
2 Diamonds	Pass	3 Diamonds	Pass
3 Hearts	Pass	3 No Trump	Pass
Pass	Pass		

South opens 1 Heart and West bids 2
Diamonds. West does not have enough to
double first and so is obliged to overcall. East
makes a good raise to 3 Diamonds. Do not
forget to raise your partner's overcalls when
you have support. A raise does a lot of good.
West can see six likely Diamond tricks, and
with South opening the bidding it is pretty sure
that if a Spades finesse is needed, it will work.
So West bids 3 Hearts, asking if East has a
Hearts stopper. He does and he bids 3 No
Trump as requested because 3 No Trump will
make almost all the time. It would take extreme
bad luck to go down.

Tricks of the Trade

One big advantage of the
Western Cue bid is that the
player with the stopper is
the declarer. If you have Kx
or AQ or QTx of your
opponents' suit, it is crucial that
the opening lead come up to
your hand. If you were dummy,
the opening lead would come
through your hand, and that
could cost you the contract.

Here is another example:

West	*East*
♠ A8	♠ K72
♥ KQ874	♥ AJ92
♦ AT3	♦ QJ962
♣ 932	♣ A

West	North	East	South
	1 Diamond	Pass	
1 Heart	1 Spade	3 Hearts	Pass
3 Spades	Pass	?	

East must not think in terms of the Western Cue bid in this auction. East and West
have found a certain Hearts fit and when you have done that, the Western Cue bid is
not in use. West is making a cue bid for a Hearts slam and East should make a cue bid
of his own with 4 Clubs. The partnership will end in 6 Hearts, which will make six or
seven depending on where the King of Diamonds is.

The Least You Need To Know

♦ Roman Key Card Blackwood asks for five key cards, the four Aces and the King of trump.

♦ Hamilton and Landy allow you to describe your hand with one bid at the 2 level when opponents open 1 No Trump.

♦ New Minor Forcing allows responder to tell opener she has a five-card major and invitational values with her second bid.

♦ In the Two-over-One system, your first nonjump response at the 2 level after your partner's 1-level opening bid is game forcing.

♦ When your partner opens 1 of a major in third or fourth seat, a Reverse Drury bid of 2 Clubs tells your partner you have a limit raise.

♦ The overcalls of Michaels Cue bid and the Unusual No Trump tell partner you have a two-suited hand.

♦ The Western Cue bid asks your partner whether she has a stopper in your opponents' suit.

Appendix A

Guide to Bids and Responses

Opening Bids

Opening Bid	Requirements
1 of a suit major	13–21 points; at least five cards in a major suit; at least three cards in a minor suit
1 No Trump	15–17 HCP; no singletons or voids, and not more than two doubletons
2 Diamonds, 2 Hearts, or 2 Spades	At least 22 points; at least five cards in the suit or a guarantee of at least nine tricks if opening a major and 10 tricks if opening a minor
2 Clubs	Same as above, or 22–24 points with no five–card suit, except Clubs
2 No Trump	20–21 HCP; no singletons or voids; and not more than two doubletons
3 of a suit	A seven-card suit; a suit headed by at least the Queen–Ten; 4–9 HCP; no outside Ace; not more than one outside King; when opening in a minor suit, no four-card major
3 No Trump	25–26 HCP; no singletons or voids, and not more than two doubletons
4 in a suit	At least eight cards in length; at least two of the top four honors in your long suit; 4–9 HCP; no outside Ace; only one outside King; if opening a minor suit, no four-card major

Opening Bids

Opening Bid	Requirements
5 in a suit	Must be Clubs or Diamonds; Eight- or nine-card suit; suit must be headed by at least two of the top four honors; 4–9 HCP; no outside Ace; not more than one outside King

Responses to Partner's Opening Bid

Opening Bid	Holding	Response
1 of a suit	0–5 points	Pass
	6–16 points	1 of a higher ranking four-card suit at the 1 level
	10–16 points plus a five-card major or four-card minor	2 of the long suit
1 of a major	6–9 points with at least three cards in opener's suit	2 of opener's suit
	6–9 points w/o a higher ranking four-card suit or at least three cards in opener's suit; no singletons or voids	1 No Trump
	10–12 points; and three or four cards in opener's suit	3 of opener's suit
	13–15 HCP; balanced hand; stoppers in the three unbid suits; no four-card higher ranking major	2 No Trump
	16–18 HCP; balanced hand; stoppers in the three unbid suits; no four-card higher ranking major	3 No Trump
	16 or more points; does not deny four cards in opener's suit; can be totally unbalanced	Jump shift
	6–10 points; five cards in opener's suit; at least one singleton or void	Jump to game
1 of a minor	6–9 points; no four-card major; five cards in opener's suit	2 of opener's suit
	10–12 points; no four-card major; five cards in opener's suit	3 of opener's suit

Opening Bid	Holding	Response
1 of a minor	12–15 HCP; no four-card major; stoppers in all suits unbid by opener	2 No Trump
	16–18 HCP; no four-card major; stoppers in all suits unbid by opener	3 No Trump
1 No Trump	0–7 HCP	Pass
	0–7 HCP; at least five cards in either Hearts or Spades, or six cards in Diamonds	2 of long suit
	8–9 points; no four-card major	2 No Trump
	8+ points; at least one four-card major	2 Clubs (Stayman)
	10+ points; five-card major	2 Clubs, then jump to 3 of your suit if partner doesn't bid your suit; jump to 4 in your suit if she bids your suit
	9+ points; a six-card major	Jump to game in your suit
	10–14 HCP; no four-card major	3 No Trump
	15–16 HCP; no four-card major	4 No Trump (quantitative, not forcing)
	17–19 HCP; no four-card major	6 No Trump
	20+ HCP; no four-card major	7 No Trump
	6–7 HCP; broken six-card minor with nothing outside	Jump to 3 of minor
2 No Trump	0–4 HCP	Pass
	5–10 HCP; no four-card major, no singletons or voids	3 No Trump
	11–13 HCP; No Trump distribution	4 No Trump
	14–15 HCP; No Trump distribution	6 No Trump
	16+ HCP; No Trump distribution	7 No Trump
	5+ HCP; four-card major	3 Clubs (Stayman)
	5+ points; six-card major	4 of your major
2 Diamonds, 2 Hearts, or 2 Spades (Strong)	Five-card suit headed by King-Jack	Bid the five-card suit
	3+ points; at least one King; three-card support for your partner's suit	Raise partner's suit one level
	0+ points; no five-card suit; less than three-card support for your partner's suit	2 No Trump

Responses to Partner's Opening Bid

Opening Bid	Holding	Response
2 Clubs	0+ points; no five-card suit; less than three-card support for your partner's suit	2 Diamonds
	4+ points; five-card suit headed by King-Jack level	Bid the five-card suit at the 2
3 of a suit	0–14 points; no support for your partner's suit	Pass, partner is weak
	7–14 points; support for your partner's suit	Raise partner's suit
	0–6 points	Pass
	15+ points; a good five-card suit; no support for your partner's suit	Bid your long suit (forcing)
4 in a minor	Less than extra values	Pass
	Extra values	Bid game or explore for slam
4 in a major	Less than extra values	Pass
	Extra values	Explore for slam if your hand justifies it; remember, your partner is weak, even though the opening bid is game

Opener's Rebid After Opening 1 of a Suit

Responder's Bid	Holding	Response
1 of a new suit at the 1 level	13–15 points; four cards in a suit higher ranking than the suit	1 of your higher-ranking suit bid by responder
	13–15 points; less than six cards in your suit; less than four cards	1 No Trump in responder's suit; balanced hand
	13–15 points; six cards in your suit	Rebid your suit at the 2 level
	13–15 points; less than six cards in your suit; a four-card suit lower ranking than your opening suit	Bid your lower-ranking four-card suit at the 2 level
	13–15 points; less than six cards in your suit, but four-card support for your partner's suit	Raise partner's suit at the 2 level
	18–19 points; all unbid suits stopped	2 No Trump
	20–21 points; all unbid suits stopped	3 No Trump
	16–18 points, six-card opening suit	Jump to 3 of opening suit

Responder's Bid	Holding	Response
	17+ points; five cards in opening suit; four cards in higher-ranking suit	Reverse to four-card suit
	19+ points; a second biddable suit	Jump shift to second suit
	16–19 points; four cards in your partner's major suit bid	Jump to 3 of partner's major suit
	20+ points, four-card support for your partner's major suit bid	Jump to game in partner's suit
New suit at 2 level without jumping	13–15 points; five-card opening suit; less than three cards in your partner's major suit bid or less than four cards in your partner's minor suit bid; unbid suits stopped; no singletons or voids	2 No Trump
	Same, but with support for your partner's suit	Raise partner's suit
	16–19 points; support for your partner's major suit	Jump raise partner's suit
	16–19 points; no support for your partner's suit; unbid suits stopped	3 No Trump
	17+ points; five cards in opening suit; four cards in higher ranking suit	Reverse to four-card suit
	19+ points; a second biddable suit	Jump shift to second suit
1 No Trump	13–15 points; balanced hand	Pass
	13–15 points; a singleton or void	2 of a lower ranking suit
	13–15 points; six-card suit or a good five-card suit if your hand is unbalanced	Rebid your opening suit at the 2 level
	16–18 points; no singleton or void	2 No Trump
	16–18 points; six-card suit	Jump rebid your suit at the 3 level
	17+ points; unbalanced	Reverse
	19+ points; unbalanced	Jump shift
	19+ points; no singleton or void	3 No Trump
2 No Trump after major suit opening	13–15 points; six-card suit	4 of your suit
	13–15 points; five-card suit	3 No Trump
	16+ points	Bid a new suit (forcing) for a slam invitation

continues

Opener's Rebid After Opening 1 of a Suit (continued)

Responder's Bid	Holding	Response
2 No Trump after a minor suit opening	13–17 points; balanced	3 No Trump or 4 in a suit
	18+ points; balanced	4 No Trump (quantitative) or 4 in a suit as a slam invitation
3 No Trump	13–15 points; balanced	Pass
	13–15 points; a singleton or void	4 in a suit
	16+ points; balanced	4 No Trump (quantitative)
	16+ points; a singleton or void	4 in a suit as a slam invitation
Jump shift	13–15 points; five-card opening suit	Lowest No Trump bid available
	13–15 points; six-card suit	Rebid opening suit
	16+ points	Jump to 3 No Trump
One level raise of your suit	13–15 points	Pass
	16–19 points	Raise to 3 level if a major suit; 2 No Trump if a minor
	20+ points	Jump to game in your suit if a major; bid 3 No Trump if a minor
Jump raise of your major suit	13–19 points	4 of your suit (game)
	20+ points	4 No Trump (Blackwood)
Jump raise of your minor suit	13–15 points unbid suits stopped	3 No Trump
	13–19 points unbalanced	4 of suit or new suit or Pass
	20+ points	Explore slam
3 No Trump after major suit opening	13–15 points	4 of your suit (game)
	16+ points	4 No Trump (Blackwood)
3 No Trump after minor suit opening	13–15 points	Pass
	16+ points; no singletons or voids	Bid slam or explore slam

B

Other Bridge Variations

This book has concentrated on playing rubber bridge, which is the game played by the vast majority of players. However, there are other forms of bridge that are just as much fun.

Duplicate Bridge

In Duplicate Bridge everybody plays the same hands. Duplicate is played by eight players or more. In tournaments, there are thousands of players. After bidding, the hands are played in the same way, but the cards aren't put in the middle of the table when playing to each trick, as is done in Rubber Bridge.

In Duplicate, each player plays his card on the table in front of him. When the trick is completed, each player keeps the card in front of him, placing it face down horizontally if he wins the trick, vertically if the opponents win the trick.

When the hand concludes, each player takes his cards and places them in a duplicate board, which has spaces for each of the four hands: North, East, West, and South. After a certain number of boards is played, usually between two and five, all boards are passed to the next lower-ranking table.

The players sitting North-South remain stationary. The players sitting East-West move to the next higher-ranking table after the set of boards is played. Players move up. Boards move down.

At the end of the evening all East-West pairs have played the same hands and all North-South pairs have played the same hands. Scoring is based on how your scores on each hand compare with the scores of the other players who played the hands. For example, if you bid and make a small slam but everyone else bids and makes a grand slam on that hand, you get the worst score on the hand—zero.

It's very competitive. One of the big advantages is that winning doesn't depend on the luck of the deal because everyone plays the same cards. If you have a Yarborough, every player sitting in your seat will have to play that Yarborough. Whoever does the best with it will have the highest score for that board.

Chicago

Chicago, also known as Four Deal Bridge, is a very popular type of Bridge that shortens the normal game of Rubber Bridge. Instead of playing until one pair wins two games, which can last a long time if one pair does a lot of defensive bidding, Chicago consists of one round of four hands, scored as follows:

1. For the first hand, neither pair is vulnerable.

2. For the second and third hands, dealer's pair is vulnerable.

3. For the fourth hand, both pairs are vulnerable.

Cards are dealt and played. The deal rotates to the left, as in Rubber Bridge. At the end of the fourth round, after each player has dealt once, the scores are added and a winner is determined.

You may play as many rounds as you like, and you may either change partners or not, as you like, after each round.

A nonvulnerable game gets a 300-point bonus above the line. A vulnerable game gets a 500-point bonus above the line. A partscore on the first three hands gets a 50-point bonus. If you get a partscore on the fourth hand, you get a 100-point bonus.

Resources

The American Contract Bridge League

Players who are interested in organized Bridge will find several sources of such games through the American Contract Bridge League (ACBL). Based in Memphis, Tennessee, the ACBL offers traditional Duplicate Bridge via tournaments and Bridge clubs.

Information on all activities offered by the ACBL is available by calling 1-800-264-2743 (8786 from Canada). You may write the ACBL at 2990 Airways Blvd., Memphis, TN 38116-3847. The ACBL's e-mail address is 74431.3434@CompuServe.com. The ACBL page on the World Wide Web is at www.acbl.org.

The ACBL is the sanctioning body for tournament Bridge in North America. Nearly every one of the 1,000 plus tournaments sanctioned annually has games for beginners. There are ACBL affiliated Bridge clubs in most major cities throughout North America. Most offer lessons and most have games for new players. Often they will find you a partner if you need one.

Bridge on the Internet

You can play Bridge with live people on the Internet without leaving your living room. The original bridge game on the Internet is called OKBridge.

You play with people all over the world, and games are available 24 hours a day, 7 days a week.

Players range from beginners to experts. You can join games on various levels: beginner, intermediate, advanced, or expert. You can also join any table you want and just watch, without playing.

You can contact OKBridge at the following:

OKBridge
4655 Cass Street, Suite 204
San Diego, CA 92109
619-490-6770

Toll free: 1-888-652-7434
Fax: 619-490-6771
e-mail: help@okbridge.com
Internet: www.okbridge.com

Microsoft also has an online bridge game at http://zone.msn.com/en/bridge/default. htm. This site enables you to play against live people or computers. If you choose computers, you can designate the skill level.

Here are three additional online bridge games:

- ◆ Swan Games (www.swangames.com/main/index.html)
- ◆ e-bridge (www.e-bridgemaster.com/base/vert_homepage_new.asp)
- ◆ Bridge Base (www.bridgebase.com)

Glossary

100 honors   Four of the top five cards in the trump suit in one hand. A player holding 100 honors receives a bonus of 100 points above the line.

150 honors   All five of the top honors in the trump suit in one hand. A player holding 150 honors receives a bonus of 150 points above the line.

150 Aces   All four Aces in one hand when the hand is played in No Trump. A player holding 150 Aces receives a bonus of 150 points above the line.

4–3–3–3   Description of a totally balanced hand, with four cards in one suit and three cards in the other three suits.

above the line   Points entered on the scoresheet above the horizontal line for overtricks, bonuses, and penalties. These points do not count toward making game.

attitude   A signal to your partner telling her whether you like the suit she led or not. A high card generally indicates you like the suit; a low card generally indicates you don't like the suit and discourages her from continuing it if she retains the lead.

auction   A series of bids between the partnerships to obtain the contract.

balancing   To make a bid or double at a low level to keep the auction from being passed out after opponents have stopped bidding and there have been two consecutive passes.

below the line   Points entered on the scoresheet below the horizontal line indicating the points scored for exactly the number of tricks bid and made.

bid   Any call made by a player that predicts the number of tricks the player's pair will take in a specified trump or in No Trump.

Blackwood   A conventional bid in which the bid of 4 No Trump asks partner to respond with the number of Aces in her hand. A response of 5 Clubs means zero Aces, 5 Diamonds means one Ace, 5 Hearts means two Aces, and 5 Spades means three Aces.

block   You block your partner's suit when your partner has several good cards remaining in a suit but you must take the trick because your only card in the suit is higher ranking than the remaining cards in your partner's suit, and there's no way back into your partner's hand to allow her to cash her tricks.

board   Another name for the exposed hand in dummy.

body cards   Eights, Nines, and Tens.

book   The first six tricks taken by the declaring side. Defenders' book is the number of tricks required to be taken, after which the next trick won by defenders will set the contract.

bypass   Failing to bid a lower-ranking suit or a suit at a lower level to, instead, bid a higher-ranking suit or a suit at a higher level when bidding the lower-ranking suit or the suit at a lower level would be the standard bid.

call   Any bid, double, redouble, or pass.

Cappelletti   A conventional overcall in defense against a No Trump opening by opponents. Double is penalty, 2 Clubs shows a one-suited hand, 2 Diamonds shows 5–5 in the majors, 2 Hearts shows 5 Hearts and an undesignated five-card minor, 2 Spades shows five Spades and an undesignated five-card minor (see Hamilton, Pottage). This name is used on the East Coast and in major portions of America.

cheaper minor   A bid of the lowest unbid minor suit available at the time of responder's second call. This is a standard method of making a weak response to a strong 2 Clubs opening bid.

Clubs   The lowest ranking of the four suits in a deck of cards.

cold   To be able to make a contract easily with no chance of failure.

competing   To make a bid to contest with opponents without implying to your partner that you're interested in contracting for game.

competition When both pairs are bidding to get the contract.

connecting honor A holding of two consecutive honor cards in the same suit, like King–Queen or Jack–Ten.

contract The commitment of the declaring side to win a specified number of tricks with a specified suit as trump or with No Trump.

conventional bid A bid with a defined meaning other than the standard meaning.

count An indication of an even or odd number of cards in your hand by discarding high to low to indicate an even number of cards in the suit led and low to high to indicate an odd number of cards in the suit led.

cover Play by second or third hand of a higher honor card over an honor played by opponent.

crossruff The ability to ruff losers in different suits in the hands of both partners.

cue-bid A bid of opponents' suit that conveys something to your partner other than a holding in that suit.

dealer The person who distributes the cards in clockwise order; the player with the first opportunity to make a call.

declarer The player who is playing the hand with her partner as dummy.

Deuce The two-spot card of each suit.

Diamonds The second lowest ranking of the four suits.

direct seat The player sitting as the LHO of opening bidder.

discard The play of a nontrump card not of the suit led.

distribution points Points in counting the hand for voids, singletons, and doubletons.

D0PI Double = Zero, Pass = One. A response to Blackwood over interference telling your partner how many Aces you have in your hand.

double A call by an opponent of declarer that increases the value of tricks or undertricks made by declarer.

doubleton Any total holding in a suit that is exactly two cards in length.

doubling into game A double of a partial score that, if unsuccessful, will result in opponents getting at least 100 points below the line when they wouldn't have gotten 100 points below the line without the double.

down   Undertricks. Any hand that does not make the contracted number of tricks is down; synonymous with set.

down the line   To bid the higher ranking of suits of equal length first.

drawing trump   For declarer to lead trump until the opponents no longer have any trump in either of their hands.

drop-dead bid   A bid that asks your partner to pass and allow the bidder to play the hand in the bid made by the drop-dead bidder.

duck   To not take a trick when you have a high card that would enable you to win that trick.

dummy   The hand that belongs to declarer's partner. Dummy is always played face up on the table.

Duplicate   The form of tournament Bridge where each player plays the same hand as the other players. This is accomplished by the hands being dealt into boards and the boards are passed from table to table.

empty   No support for an honor, as in "Jack empty," meaning a holding of a Jack with several low-ranking cards.

end play   To put the opponents in the lead in a situation in which anything led will gain you a trick.

entry   A card that allows a partner to get the lead into a specific hand by leading to it.

equal vulnerability   When both sides have the same vulnerability.

establish   To set up a suit in which a player may play the remaining cards as winners without any danger of losing them to a higher card or a trump.

extra values   Points in excess of a minimum opening bid.

favorable vulnerability   When your pair is not vulnerable and your opponents are vulnerable.

feature   A King– or Queen–Jack in a suit in response to an asking bid of 2 No Trump by responder when you have opened with a Weak Two bid.

finesse   Any play that depends on finding a specific card in a specific place.

first seat or position   The dealer, the first person to have an opportunity to make a bid on the hand.

first round control   When a card or absence of cards in your hand assures you of the ability to take the trick the first time a particular suit is led. An Ace or a void constitutes first round control in a nontrump suit in a trump contract.

fit   When a partnership has the majority of cards in a suit between the two hands.

five-card major   A system of bidding in which you cannot open the bidding with 1 of a suit in a major suit unless you hold at least five cards in the suit. Also describes a major suit in which you have five cards, as in "I did not have a five-card major."

follow suit   Playing a card of the same suit that is led.

forcing bid   A bid that forces a player's partner to bid again, regardless of the quality of the holding in her hand.

forcing No Trump   Because a 2-level overcall is game forcing in Two over One, if responder has enough points but no suit to bid, she bids 1 No Trump, which is "forcing" on opener to bid once more.

fourth from longest and strongest   The fourth highest card in your longest suit. A preferred opening lead when defending against a No Trump contract.

fourth seat or position   The player to dealer's right, the fourth player to have an opportunity to bid in the bidding rotation.

free bid   A bid made by a player with no obligation to bid.

game   Obtaining 100 points below the line in one hand or a succession of hands before the opposing pair obtains 100 points below the line in the same hands.

game forcing   A bid made by a player that requires her partner to keep bidding until the pair has bid a game.

get in   To get the lead.

grand slam   Bidding and making all 13 tricks.

Hamilton   A conventional overcall in defense against a No Trump opening by opponents. Double is penalty, 2 Clubs shows a one-suited hand, 2 Diamonds shows 5–5 in the majors, 2 Hearts shows five Hearts and an undesignated five-card minor, 2 Spades shows five Spades and an undesignated five-card minor (see Cappelletti, Pottage). This name is used in California.

HCP   High-card points. *See* entry below.

Hearts   The second-ranked suit in the deck of cards.

high-card points   Total points in a hand determined by adding up 4 points for each Ace, 3 points for each King, 2 points for each Queen, and 1 point for each Jack.

high-low   Discarding a higher card at your first opportunity, then a lower card of the same suit at your second opportunity, generally to indicate an even number of cards in the suit led.

hit   Another term for double. Sometimes called smash, bend, or hammer.

hold up   To refuse to take a trick you have the capability to take.

honors   Aces, Kings, Queens, Jacks, and Tens.

interference   A bid made by opponents of the opening bidder.

invitational bid   A bid asking your partner to bid again, but not requiring her to, generally to game or slam if she has a certain number of points in her hand or to pass if she does not have that number of points in her hand.

Jacoby Transfer   A response of 2 Diamonds or 2 Hearts to a No Trump opening bid requiring partner to bid the next higher suit.

jump   To skip a level of bidding and bid the same suit.

jump shift   To skip a level of bidding and change suits.

jump overcall   To skip a level of bidding and bid a new suit after an opening bid by opponents.

kibitz   To watch a game as a spectator without being a participant.

Landy   A conventional overcall in defense against a No Trump opening by opponents. Double is penalty, showing at least 15 HCPs. 2 Clubs shows two five-card majors. 2 Diamonds, Hearts, or Spades shows you have a good suit in the suit bid, almost surely six or more, and the expectation that you can take six or more tricks.

lead-directing double   A double, generally of a conventional bid, made not for penalty, but to tell your partner what suit to lead if she has the opening lead.

lead   The first card to be played to a trick.

lead up   To lead to a higher card.

leading through strength   An opening lead of a suit bid by dummy or any lead of a suit bid by leader's LHO, or a lead by dummy's RHO through a strong suit exposed by dummy.

LHO   Left-hand opponent.

limit raise   A jump raise in the suit first bid by partner at responder's first opportunity to bid, showing at least three cards in the suit and between 10 to 12 points.

loser   A card that will not take a trick if led.

major suits   Spades and Hearts.

making   Taking the number of tricks declarer contracted to take.

marked card   A card that is known to be in a certain hand because of previous play or bidding.

maximum   The highest level of a known bidding range.

Michael's Cue bid   A cue-bid of two of opener's minor suit opening bid, showing 5–5 in the majors.

minimum   The lower level of a known bidding range.

minor suits   Diamonds and Clubs.

Moysian fit   A 4–3 fit in the trump suit between you and partner.

natural bid   A bid that indicates a holding in the suit bid or in No Trump if No Trump is bid; a nonconventional bid.

New Minor Forcing   If your partner rebids 1 No Trump, and you have a five-card major with invitational values, you can bid 2 of the unbid minor suit, which shows that your 1-level major suit is a five-card suit with at least 10 HCPs.

No Trump   A contract where there is no trump suit.

off the top   To take all the tricks you need or can get without allowing the opponents to get the lead.

on   Continuing to play a system after an interfering bid by opponents or after your partner has made an overcall instead of an opening bid. *See also* Systems on.

onside   A card that is in a position that if you take a finesse, it will win.

open   The first bid made on a hand.

opening lead   The first lead in the play of the hand, made by declarer's LHO.

opening light   To open a hand with less than 13 points.

outside suit   A nontrump suit.

overcall   The first bid made by opponents of opening bidder.

overtrick   Tricks scored beyond the contracted bid.

partial   Bidding and making a contract less than game.

partial stopper   A card that, in combination with a holding in partner's hand, might stop opponents from running a suit, like Qx or Jxx.

partscore   The score received for bidding and making a contract less than game.

pass   Declining to make a bid, double, or redouble when it's your turn.

passed hand   A hand that doesn't have a bid and doesn't make a bid.

passout seat   After bidding has commenced, the position of the player sitting after two consecutive passes.

play for the drop   To lead high-ranking cards hoping that a missing high card, lower ranking than the cards you lead, will have to be played because holder is short in the suit, rather than finessing for it.

point count   The total of the points in your hand.

Pottage   A conventional overcall in defense against a No Trump opening by opponents. Double is penalty, 2 Clubs shows a one-suited hand, 2 Diamonds shows 5–5 in the majors, 2 Hearts shows five Hearts and an undesignated five-card minor, 2 Spades shows five Spades, and an undesignated five-card minor. This name is used in Europe. (*See* Cappelletti, Hamilton)

preempt   A weak bid showing a long suit and not many high-card points.

preemptive jump shift   A bid and system that promises that a jump shift by responder shows a long suit and a weak hand, generally a hand with at least six cards in the suit bid and less than 6 points in the hand.

pulling trump   *See* drawing trump.

quantitative bid   A bid, usually No Trump, that is not conventional and asks partner to bid slam if she's at the maximum but to pass if she isn't at the maximum.

quick tricks   A high-card holding that generally promises that it will win a trick, like an Ace, or a King–Queen of the same suit.

renege (revoke)   Failure to follow suit when you are able to follow suit.

reopening double   A part of the negative double system in which the opening bidder doubles at his first rebid opportunity if his LHO has overcalled, partner has passed, and opening bidder has shortness in the overcalled suit.

Reverse Drury   When your partner opens 1 of a major in third or fourth seat, you need a way to show your good hand. If you have a limit raise for partner's major, bid 2 Clubs. This is artificial, stating that you have a maximum passed hand with at least three-card support.

responder   Partner of the first person to bid on a hand.

response   The bid that opening bidder's partner makes.

restricted choice   A theory that states that in the play of the hand, if one of your opponents drops an honor, you should play his partner for the other honor.

return   A standard lead by the partner of the opening leader, to lead the suit led by opening leader at partner's first opportunity.

reverse   When opener rebids a suit at the 2 level that is higher ranking than the suit with which she opened at the 1 level. Responder may also reverse.

RHO   Right-hand opponent.

Roman Key Card Blackwood   In addition to the four aces, the King of trump becomes a key card to be used in responding to 4 No Trump Ace-asking Blackwood. 5 Clubs shows zero or three key cards. 5 Diamonds shows one or four key cards. 5 Hearts shows two key cards without the Queen of trump. 5 Spades shows two key cards with the Queen of trump.

RONF   *R*aise is the *o*nly *n*on*f*orcing bid. A response to a Weak Two opening bid in which a raise of partner's opening suit may be passed, but any other bid by responder is forcing on partner to bid again for one round.

rubber   The unit of measurement for home or "party" Bridge. The first pair to win two games ends the rubber, and the winner is the pair with the most points scored during play of the rubber.

ruff   To win a nontrump trick by playing a trump.

ruffing finesse   A finesse taken into a void, with the intention of ruffing if the card led is covered by leader's LHO, or discarding another suit if the card led is not covered.

rule of 2, 3, and 4   A system used to determine when to open a preemptive hand. With unfavorable vulnerability you may open by overbidding your hand by two tricks. With equal vulnerability you may open by overbidding your hand by three tricks. With favorable vulnerability, you may open by overbidding your hand by four tricks.

rule of 11   If partner leads fourth from longest and strongest you subtract the number of the card she leads from 11 and the result is the number of cards higher than the card led in the three hands other than opening leader's hand.

run   To set up a long suit and take all the remaining cards in the suit without fear of losing a trick by opponents playing a higher card or trumping.

sacrifice   A bid you make with no hope of making the contract to keep your opponents from making a game, generally to keep them from making a vulnerable game.

safety play To intentionally lose a trick in order to retain an entry.

second hand low A familiar rule in play of the hand, that the hand immediately to the left of the leader should play a low card.

second seat or position Dealer's LHO, the player with the second opportunity to make a call.

secondary suit A nontrump suit in which you hope to take tricks after pulling trump.

semiforcing No Trump This is an extension of Two-over-One bidding. If your partner opens in third or fourth seat with 1 of a major and you have a hand that is tempting you to bid 2 No Trump, just bid 1 No Trump. Play that a passed hand 1 No Trump response is semiforcing. Your partner will do one of two things. If she has too weak a hand to imagine a game, she passes 1 No Trump. If she has a nice 14 or more points or if he has good distribution, she makes her normal rebid.

sequence A consecutive series of cards three or more in a row.

set To fail to make a contract.

set up To establish a suit in which a player may play the remaining cards as winners without any danger of losing them to a higher card or a trump.

shortage points Points added to your HCP for short suits. Also called distribution points.

shuffling The process of mixing the cards after each hand.

signals Plays of certain cards to communicate a specific holding of cards in your hand.

sign-off bid A bid that indicates to the partner that the bidder does not want any more bidding.

simple raise To raise your partner's first bid suit one level at your first opportunity to bid.

singleton A suit that has only one card in it.

slam Contracting for 12 or 13 tricks.

slow shows A metaphor meaning that keeping the bidding low and bidding slowly shows a good hand.

small slam Bidding and making 12 tricks.

Spades The highest ranking of the four suits in a deck of cards.

splinter A double jump shift showing a singleton or void, an opening hand, and promising four cards in partner's suit.

Spot cards The cards from 2 to 10 are sometimes called "spot cards." For example, some bridge players will refer to a card as the "nine spot," instead of just the "nine."

Standard American A system of bidding and play taught in this book.

standard leads A list of leads that are considered normal and understood as conveying the same information to all players.

Stayman convention A conventional bid where a response of 2 or 3 Clubs to partner's opening bid of 1 or 2 No Trump asks partner to bid her lowest-ranking four-card major or to bid Diamonds at the lowest level available to deny holding a four-card major.

stiff A singleton.

stopper A card in a suit that will take a trick and protect against opponents running the suit.

strain Spades, Hearts, Diamonds, Clubs, or No Trump.

strip To take away the opponents' cards that they can safely lead without giving you a trick.

strip and end play A method of playing a hand to force opponents to lead into a tenace or give declarer a ruff and a sluff.

support Help in the suit bid by partner. If partner has shown a five-card suit, support should be three cards. If partner has shown a six-card suit, support should be at least two cards. If partner has bid a second suit, promising only four cards, support must be at least four cards.

system A method of bidding where certain bids mean certain things.

systems on An agreement between partners that a system they are playing will continue to be played even if opponents interfere or if a bid is made as an overcall or response and not as an opening bid.

takeout double A double of opponents' last bid suit asking partner to bid her longest suit.

tenace A holding of two cards, one of which is two levels below the other.

tenace position When there is only one card outstanding remaining between a holding of two cards.

third hand high   A familiar rule in play of the hand, that the partner of the player making the lead of a low card should play the highest card possible in the suit led.

third seat or position   The dealer's partner, the player with the third opportunity to make a call.

tight   A holding of only the specified cards. "King–Queen tight" means you hold only the King and the Queen in that suit and no other cards.

top connecting honors   A standard lead of the highest of two sequential honors.

transportation   The ability to get the lead back and forth between a pair's two hands.

trick   The play of four cards, one card by each player, in rotation.

trump   The suit in which the hand is played, which, for that hand, becomes the most powerful suit in the deck.

two demand   An opening bid at the 2 level that requires a partner to keep the bidding open until game has been bid or opening bidder has rebid his opening suit.

Two-over-One system   A very popular system which is used by almost all tournament players is one called the Two-over-One system. In this system, when a player makes a Two-over-One response such as 1 Diamond–Pass–2 Clubs, she promises enough points that the partnership can make a game. Because of this, all subsequent bidding is game forcing, even if it sounds weak.

unblock   To discard a higher card and retain a lower card to allow partner to remain in the lead and run a suit.

underlead   To lead a lower-ranking card.

unfavorable vulnerability   When you are vulnerable and your opponents are not vulnerable.

unilateral bid   A bid by a player without regard to what the player's partner has bid or not bid.

Unusual No Trump   When opponents open at the 1 level, an immediate jump overcall of 2 No Trump shows you have two five-card suits, either both minors, if opponents opened a major, or Hearts and the other minor if opponents opened a minor suit.

up the line   Bidding the lower-ranking of suits of equal length first.

void   A suit in which a player holds no cards.

vulnerable   A pair who has won a game and is subject to greater penalties for under-tricks and greater rewards for bidding and making games.

waiting bid   A bid that communicates nothing about the suit to the partner who has made a strong opening bid, but just keeps the bidding open so partner may make a rebid.

Weak Two   A modern bidding convention in which an opening bid in Diamonds, Hearts, or Spades at the 2 level shows a long suit and a weak hand.

Western Cue bid   The opponents have bid a suit, but your side is marked with most of the high-card points. If your side has found a minor suit fit and if it is clear that your side does not have a major suit contract available, a cue-bid of the opponents' suit does not show a control, as do many cue-bids. It instead says, "I think we can make 3 No Trump if you have a stopper in their suit." So a 3-level cue-bid of their suit asks partner to bid 3 No Trump with a stopper in opponents' suit.

winners   A card that will definitely win a trick, used in evaluating your hand after the contract has been made but before you start play as declarer in No Trump.

Yarborough   A balanced 4–3–3–3 hand containing no card higher than a Nine.

Index